THE ANTHROPOLOGY OF OBESITY IN THE UNITED STATES

D1606145

This volume examines the biocultural dimensions of obesity from an anthropological perspective in an effort to broaden understanding of a growing public health concern. The United States of America currently has the highest rates of obesity among developed countries, with an alarming rise in prevalence in recent decades which promises to affect the nation for years to come.

Anna Bellisari helps students to grasp the complex nature of this obesity epidemic, demonstrating that it is the consequence of many interacting forces which range from individual genetic and physiological predispositions to national policies and American cultural beliefs and practices. As much a social problem as an individual one, the development of obesity is in fact encouraged by the pattern of high consumption and physical inactivity that is promoted by American economic, political, and ideological systems.

With a range of up-to-date scientific and medical data, *The Anthropology of Obesity in the United States* provides students with a comprehensive picture of obesity, its multiple causes, and the need for society-wide action to address the issue.

Anna Bellisari is Professor Emerita of Anthropology at Wright State University, USA.

THE ANTHROPOLOGY OF OBESITY IN THE UNITED STATES

Anna Bellisari

Routledge
Taylor & Francis Group

LONDON AND NEW YORK

First published 2016
by Routledge
2 Park Square, Milton Park, Abingdon, Oxon OX14 4RN

and by Routledge
711 Third Avenue, New York, NY 10017

Routledge is an imprint of the Taylor & Francis Group, an informa business

British Library Cataloguing-in-Publication Data
A catalogue record for this book is available from the British Library

Library of Congress Cataloging-in-Publication Data
Names: Bellisari, Anna W., 1939– author.
Title: The anthropology of obesity in the United States / Anna Bellisari.
Description: Milton Park, Abingdon, Oxon ; New York, NY : Routledge, 2016. |
    Includes bibliographical references.
Identifiers: LCCN 2015035826 | ISBN 9781138927858 (hbk : alk. paper) |
    ISBN 9781138927865 (pbk. : alk. paper) | ISBN 9781315682211 (e-book)
Subjects: LCSH: Obesity—United States. | Obesity—United States—History. |
    Lifestyles—United States.
Classification: LCC RC628 .B358 2016 | DDC 362.1963/98—dc23
LC record available at http://lccn.loc.gov/2015035826

ISBN: 978-1-138-92785-8 (hbk)
ISBN: 978-1-138-92786-5 (pbk)
ISBN: 978-1-315-68221-1 (ebk)

Typeset in Bembo
by Swales & Willis Ltd, Exeter, Devon, UK

Printed and bound in the United States of America by Publishers Graphics,
LLC on sustainably sourced paper.

To Maria and the memory of Joyce

CONTENTS

ILLUSTRATIONS

Figures

Tables

ACKNOWLEDGMENTS

Many colleagues, friends, and family members inspired this book, and I thank them all for their many ideas, suggestions, and encouragements. Financial support, release time, and clerical assistance came from Sociology and Anthropology Department Chair Robert Riordan, College of Liberal Arts Deans Mary Ellen Mazey and Sharon Nelson, and Lifespan Health Research Center Directors Alex Roche, Roger Siervogel, Richard Sherman, and W. Cameron Chumlea. My colleagues in the Lifespan Health Research Center, in particular Ellen Demerath and Stefan Czerwinski, and the LHRC staff were especially helpful. To cultural anthropologists Erika Bourguignon and Mary Howard, I am especially grateful for pointing me to valuable sources. And to my teachers Professors Frank Poirier and Ojo Arewa of the Ohio State University Department of Anthropology, who taught me the biocultural approach, I owe immense gratitude.

To all, my heartfelt thanks and best wishes for a healthy future.

1

INTRODUCTION

Obesity in America

The problem of obesity

The United States faces an *epidemic* of *obesity*, an alarming rise that far exceeds levels for a healthy life. About 35 percent of American adults have obesity (Ogden et al. 2014b), the highest *prevalence* among high-income nations. The epidemic continues unchecked, despite continuing concern and advice from biomedical and public health experts. It is having a severe impact on the health and wellbeing of Americans, contributes to already disproportionate health care costs, and promises to affect the nation for years to come. In a constant stream of scientific and media messages Americans are alerted to the widespread impacts of the obesity epidemic.

- Military leaders report that more than 60 percent of all young Americans are ineligible to serve in armed forces because of criminal records, inadequate education, and overweight and obesity (MissionReadiness.org). In five states 75 percent or more are ineligible.
- The fashion industry has inflated clothing sizes so that a former size 12 dress is now labeled size 8 (Brody 2004).
- About one-third of incoming and current U.S. firefighters have obesity; heart attacks cause more firefighters' deaths while on the job than any other cause. In Oklahoma 15 percent of new police recruits in the state's five largest cities failed the physical agility test (Levi et al. 2011).
- A nine-year-old boy was removed from his mother's custody when his weight reached 200lbs, but he was returned to her after losing 50lbs (Sheeran and Franko 2012).
- Teenagers' trendy clothes, hotel beds, restaurant and theater chairs, and children's car safety seats have expanded in size, as have hospital beds, stretchers,

wheelchairs, and MRI and CT scanners (Fountain 2002; Haskell 2002; Perez-Pena and Glickson 2003; Trifiletti et al. 2006).

- Longer hypodermic needles for intramuscular injections are required to reach the gluteal muscle in patients with thick fat layers at the injection site (Nisbet 2006).
- Compared to 1994, 10 times as many stomach-reduction surgeries were performed in 2005 to promote weight loss in individuals with extreme obesity (Robinson 2009).
- The London Royal Opera House canceled the contract of a famous American opera star because she had become too large for the role of Ariadne of Naxos (Pogrebin 2004).
- A potential 2012 Republican primary election candidate for president was subjected to media evaluation of his weight and pronounced "too fat to be President." He did not enter the race (Bruni 2001).
- To avoid the embarrassment, individuals with obesity can now attend yoga classes for large persons only at Buddha Body Yoga or Mega Yoga in Manhattan and in many other establishments in the US (Eckel 2009).
- Ohio pet dogs and cats are growing fatter along with their owners and for the same reason – a glut of tasty foods and lack of opportunity to run around outdoors. Outcomes for the animals' health are similar to those for humans with obesity (Frolik 2012).
- Support organizations for persons with obesity are springing up all around the country to counter "fatism," prejudice, and discrimination against large people (Goldberg 2000).
- Movies like "Shallow Hal," "Shrek," and "Fat Girl" attempt to sensitize Americans to fat bias, while "Supersize Me" and "Food, Inc." warn of the dangers of American mass-produced food (Kuczynski 2001).
- The Goliath Casket Company of Lynn, Indiana specializes in the manufacture of triple-wide coffins for deceased persons with obesity, raising standard burial costs by as much as $3000 (St. John 2003).
- Some airlines require passengers with obesity to purchase two seats for a flight, or even refuse to carry them (Higgins 2010).
- A survey of male active duty Army personnel found that from 1988 to 2007 their average body weight had increased 6.7 kg (15 lb), with no increase in average body height. The changes in weight and other body dimensions necessitated development of a greater range of size categories for uniforms and equipment (Bradtmiller et al. 2009).
- Pittsburgh's Water Limo had to reduce the number of passengers carried to Pittsburgh Steelers games from 49 to 39 per boat since the U.S. Coast Guard issued new rules that reflect an increase in the average weight of boat passengers from 140 lbs to 185 lbs (Maher 2012).

The novelty of such news items has worn off because Americans have become accustomed to obesity in the US. Obesity rates have continued to climb for several decades and are now rapidly increasing in other parts of the world as well. Despite the plethora of scientific discoveries and their dissemination through numerous scientific journals dedicated to obesity research, such as *Obesity Reviews, Journal of Obesity, Obesity Research, International Journal of Obesity, International Journal of Obesity and Related Metabolic Disorders*, and many others, most Americans lack access to accurate information about obesity and are unaware of its associated health problems.

Most scientific investigations of obesity focus on intrinsic biology and individual unhealthy behaviors. The "upstream" environmental influences that interact with the "downstream" genetic and physiological factors involved in human energy acquisition and metabolism have until recently received little attention. For a full understanding of human obesity, and particularly the U.S. obesity epidemic, the *obesogenic environment* and its influence on human biology and behavior deserves more scientific attention (Hill et al. 2003). Although the prevailing perception is that individual Americans are responsible for their own personal health and weight control, it is abundantly clear that external factors beyond individual control may be even more important. The U.S. obesity epidemic is the consequence of many interacting forces, ranging from individual genetic and physiological predispositions to national policies and American cultural beliefs and practices. All of this information must be considered to develop effective ways of stemming the harmful and costly obesity epidemic.

Obesity development in America

There have always been at least a few "corpulent" individuals in every human society in history and prehistory (Figure 1.1).

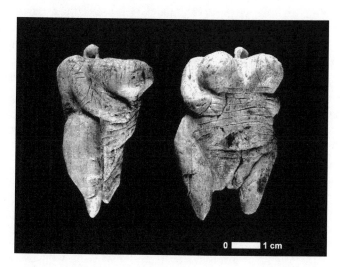

FIGURE 1.1   The Hohle Fels female figurine. The earliest-known human female
representation, 35,000 years old, from Aurignacian deposits in
southwestern Germany. A loop for hanging from a string replaces the head
of the figurine carved from mammoth ivory (Conard 2009).

Photo: H. Jenson. Copyright: University of Tübingen. Reprinted with permission.

As long ago as the 5th century BC, Hippocrates of Kos, the "father of medicine," had noticed unusually high numbers of sudden deaths among individuals with obesity, and had linked obesity with disease (Hu 2008). But only in the last four decades has obesity risen to worrying population levels in many parts of the world, particularly in the US and other developed countries. Why did this happen, and why are obesity rates higher in the US than in any other industrialized country?

In contrast to countries that joined the global marketplace relatively recently and saw a very sudden increase in obesity rates, the American obesity epidemic began gradually during the 19th-century Industrial Revolution when increasing wealth created a growing middle class and a consumer-based economy. Greater spending power and more inexpensive, mass-produced, commercially distributed foods allowed for steady replacement of meals prepared at home. Food industrialization is now strongly implicated in the current American obesity epidemic (AP 2006; Cutler et al. 2003). Key historical events in food industrialization include the establishment of the first grocery chain in 1859, the sale of Coca-Cola beginning in 1886 in Atlanta, marketing of the first Fritos Corn Chips in 1932, and openings of the first Dairy Queen in 1940 and McDonald's in 1955. In 1967 *high-fructose corn syrup (HFCS)* was developed for commercial purposes and became the primary sweetener for foods and beverages in the US. Between 1962 and 2000 caloric sweetener use increased by 83 calories per day (Popkin and Nielsen 2003). Each year Americans eat even more new commercially prepared and vigorously marketed ready-to-eat food products, known to contain more calories and fewer essential nutrients than home-cooked items prepared from scratch (Tillotson 2004).

In addition to cheaper, more easily available prepared foods, American corporations market labor-saving devices and gadgets to ease the exertions of work, travel, and not least, food preparation. Automated factories, household appliances, mechanized farming equipment and vehicles, electric tools, computers, and countless devices for leisure time use reduced the need for physical effort and energy expenditure in work and play. By the end of the 20th century, ease, convenience, and passive entertainment characterized the Good Life and constituted a large part of what is known around the world as the *American Dream*.

At first a gradual, barely noticeable increase in the number of overweight Americans paralleled these commercial developments (Komlos and Brabec 2010). During most of the 19th century the predominant health concern had been the lack of adequate nutrition for America's growing children and the health consequences of *malnutrition* and *underweight* (Dawes 2014). Stoutness was an admired trait, especially in men, in part because it was relatively rare and unachievable for most Americans. The word "diet" had only one meaning then – the nutritional regimen required for good health. But by the beginning of the 20th century young women began efforts to control their weight. "Diet" gained a new meaning – restricted food consumption and constrained eating to prevent overweight and obesity. Yet from 1900 to the 1980s Americans steadily gained weight, at first only an average of one pound, then two pounds per decade (Stearns 2002). By 1960, 10–15 percent of the U.S. population had obesity. Then in the 1980s health professionals noted with alarm a dramatic increase in obesity (Figure 1.2). By 2000, 25–30 percent of Americans had obesity (Hu 2008). Today more than two-thirds of American adults are *overweight* or have obesity (Flegal et al. 2012).

Significant ethnic disparities became apparent, especially among women. Today women in ethnic minority and low-income groups have the highest rates of obesity, and related disease burdens. They also suffer greater *stigma* related to over-weight and obesity (Muenning et al. 2006) and more employment limitations than men (Tunceli et al. 2006). Among all men obesity prevalence ranges from 31–7 percent, regardless of ethnicity and socioeconomic status. But 59 percent of black women and 44 percent of Hispanic women have obesity, compared with 33 per-cent of white women (Flegal et al. 2012).

Obesity has also increased among children, especially older children and adoles-cents. Since 1980, the prevalence of overweight among children aged 2–19 years has tripled to 17 percent (Ogden et al. 2012), with higher rates among black and Hispanic children than among non-Hispanic white children (Figure 1.3). Obesity rates are also very high among pre-school Native American boys and girls (Caballero et al. 2003; Zephier et al. 2006), double the rates of Asian and white children (Anderson and Whitaker 2009). Asian-American adolescent girls have the lowest prevalence of childhood obesity (4 percent) (Wang and Beydoun 2007). U.S. childhood obesity rates first began to climb among black girls born in the 1940s, and then also accelerated in black boys, white girls, and white boys born in the mid-1950s and early-1960s (Johnson et al. 2012; Komlos et al. 2009). The most recent statistics for American children indicate that obesity rates have remained stable since 2003 and even

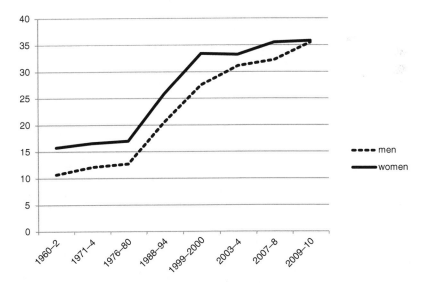

FIGURE 1.2   Shift in obesity among U.S. adults, 1960–2010. The percentage of U.S. adults (≥20 years) who are obese more than doubled between 1960 and 2010.

Adapted from Leonard (2014).

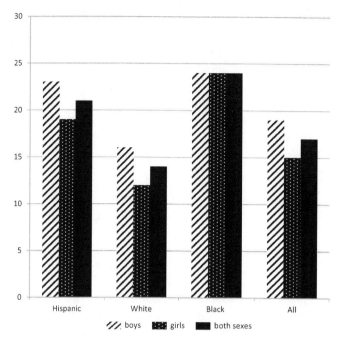

FIGURE 1.3 Obesity rates in U.S. children and adolescents aged 2 to 19 years.
Adapted from Ogden et al. (2012).

decreased significantly among the youngest, two- to five-year-old children (Ogden et al. 2014a). Possibly because of different methods of collecting information, some national surveys show that U.S. obesity rates continue to rise while others indicate that obesity prevalence among adults and children has remained stable in recent years (Flegal et al. 2012; Ogden et al. 2012; Yanovski and Yanovski 2011). Regardless, obesity prevalence remains very high in both children and adults, and obesity-related diseases continue to increase.

Children and adolescents with obesity tend to become adults with obesity (Cunningham et al. 2014; Deshmukh-Taskar et al. 2006; Guo et al. 2002; Singh et al. 2008; Taveras et al. 2011; The et al. 2010), and children who had obesity as five-year-old kindergartners are four times more likely to have obesity in adulthood. Children seem to be particularly vulnerable during the transition from childhood to adolescence, when obesity begins to develop in many and persists in others who already have the condition (Gordon-Larsen et al. 2004). Tracking of childhood obesity into adulthood is more common among blacks than whites and may be one of the reasons for higher obesity rates among black women (Freedman et al. 2005a). *Type 2 diabetes* and fatty liver disease, previously known only in adults, have recently emerged in children and adolescents and affect especially large numbers of black and Latino children (Al Khater 2015; Dabelea et al. 2014; Ludwig 2007). Although diabetes-related deaths decreased among U.S. youths between

1999 and 2008, the prevalence of pre-diabetes/diabetes increased from 9 percent to 23 percent, and an estimated 215,000 young people under age 20 had diabetes (CDC 2012; May et al. 2012). Some experts conclude that by the middle of the 21st century average U.S. life expectancy will have decreased by two to five years due to increasing cases of adult diseases related to obesity.

Globesity

Adult and child obesity rates have climbed very rapidly all around the world in response to global economic development and acculturation to western lifestyles, even in many low- and middle-income countries (Ng et al. 2014). The *World Health Organization* notes that worldwide obesity has more than doubled since 1980 and estimates that at least 600 million adults (13 percent of world population) had obesity in 2014 (who.int), a trend that has been called the "*globesity* epidemic." Figure 1.4 compares obesity rates for men and women in selected countries.

While still lower than U.S. rates, obesity has risen in countries from Morocco to China, from Sweden to South Africa, and from Canada to Chile (see various issues of the journal *Obesity Reviews*). For example, adult obesity rates in China have doubled since 1993 (Xi et al. 2011), while one-third of the Hong Kong adult population now has obesity (Ko and Chan 2008). In Taiwan 19 percent of men and 13 percent of women have obesity (Huang 2008). Concerned about increasing obesity, the Japanese government initiated an *anti-metabo* (anti-overweight) campaign mandating that Japanese people between the ages of 40 and 74 have their waistlines measured as part of their annual medical checkups and, if found to exceed government limits, be provided with dietary guidance and monitoring (Onishi 2008). *Waist circumference* measurements taken in 63 countries during the International Day for the Evaluation of Abdominal Obesity (IDEA) showed that obesity rates ranged from 4 percent of East Asian men to 40 percent of Middle Eastern women (Balkau et al. 2007). *Abdominal obesity* increased very rapidly in some countries; between 1993 and 2009 the prevalence of abdominal obesity in China tripled among men and nearly doubled among women (Xi et al. 2011). Only the very poorest Sub-Saharan and Asian countries continue to have low rates of obesity.

The highest rates of obesity in the world are actually in small Western Pacific island nations. More than 75 percent of urban adult Samoan women and 60 percent of urban adult Samoan men have obesity. In Nauru, 80 percent of the tiny island nation's population has obesity. Obesity rates climbed very rapidly in these countries in response to recent rapid economic and social changes which made western-style, high-calorie foods widely available, reduced the need for manual labor in farming and fishing occupations, and introduced automobile travel (Popkin and Gordon-Larsen 2004).

While wealthier individuals in lower- and middle-income countries became obese, the poorest individuals in these countries remained undernourished (Gordon-Larsen and Popkin 2005; Neuman et al. 2011; Olatunbosun et al. 2011). A *double burden* now exists in many developing nations, such as Indonesia where 11 percent of households include both underweight children and overweight

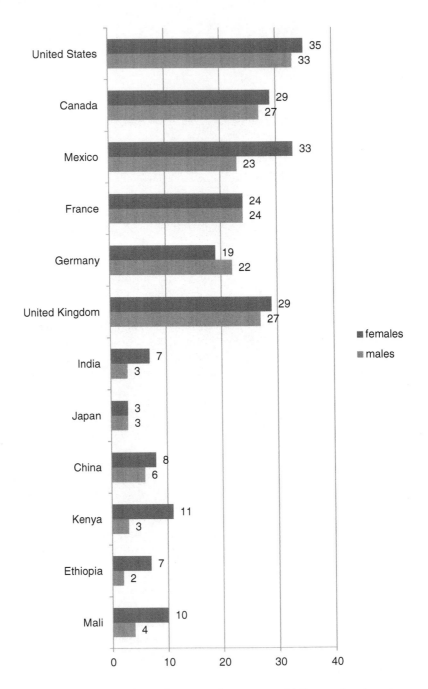

FIGURE 1.4 Obesity prevalence for men and women aged ≥18 years in selected countries, 2014.

Adapted from WHO (2015).

adults (Caballero 2005). This pattern is most likely due to the recent importation of cheap, high-calorie, nutrient-poor foods which contribute to adult obesity but also to childhood malnutrition. Urban Tanzanian women of reproductive age have experienced a doubling of obesity from 1995 to 2004, at the same time that women's rates of underweight and severe underweight have declined very little (Villamor et al. 2006). India is experiencing a sudden increase in obesity among wealthier urban residents, although malnutrition still predominates in rural areas (AP 2004). In the middle-income countries of Eastern Europe, Latin America, and Asia, the fourth most common cause of disease is malnutrition and underweight, and the fifth is obesity (Hossain et al. 2007). Under-nutrition lowers resistance to infectious disease, and nutrient deficiencies cause anemia, rickets, impaired vision, and a number of other serious health conditions. Under-nutrition and nutrient deficiencies also interfere with normal growth and development in children and with fertility in adult women (Pelletier et al. 1995; Wildman and Medeiros 2000).

Increasing childhood obesity is a general concern in virtually all countries in the Americas, Europe, South East Asia, the Western Pacific, the Eastern Mediterranean, and Africa (Wang and Lobstein 2006). The French, who made McDonald's more profitable than any other European country, are facing increasing obesity rates among their children for the first time (Sciolino 2006). European Union countries expect an increase of 300,000 children with obesity per year (Jackson-Leach and Lobstein 2006). Obesity among urban preschoolers in China increased from 1.5 percent to 12.6 percent in just eight years (Ogden et al. 2007), and childhood obesity in China now matches rates in the rest of the world (Cheng 2004).

The global diabetes burden related to obesity and labeled *diabesity* (Astrup and Finer 2000) is expected to increase from 171 million victims in 2000 to 366 million in 2030, most of them in developing countries and among U.S. ethnic minorities (Wild et al. 2004). India, for example, has experienced a sudden boom of Type 2 diabetes prevalence which is still growing. Nine percent of the Indian population (64 million people) now has diabetes (Shetty 2012). Nearly 12 percent of Chinese (114 million) have diabetes, and 50 percent of the population is estimated to have pre-diabetes (Xu et al. 2013). A conservative global estimate of obesity-related diseases among children is for 20,000 cases of childhood Type 2 diabetes, 400,000 cases of impaired glucose tolerance (which often leads to full-blown diabetes), and over 1 million children with the *metabolic syndrome*, precursor of heart disease (Lobstein and Jackson-Leach 2006). The World Health Organization fears that affected children may actually die before their parents (Alvarez 2003).

Defining obesity

Overweight and obesity are defined relative to a standard measure of normal weight. For persons concerned with physical appearance and weight goals, body weight is the critical measure of overweight or obesity. But for the purpose of scientific description of body weight and variations within and among social groups and populations, the *Body Mass Index (BMI)* is used. Body weight alone is not very informative; it must be standardized by height to be meaningful, since taller people are generally heavier. The BMI was developed by 18th-century Belgian statistician and scientist Lambert Adolphe Quetelet to hold height constant while comparing weights (Ulijaszek et al. 1998). BMI is an individual's weight divided by height squared. It is used in epidemiological studies and clinical settings as a proxy for *adiposity*, the level of body fatness.

$$BMI = weight\ (kg)/height^2\ (cm^2)$$
$$BMI = weight\ (pounds) \times 703/height^2\ (inches^2)$$

BMI values are categorized by their association with *risk* of illness and death. The thresholds for underweight, normal, overweight, and obesity are related to different *morbidity* and *mortality* rates. BMI = 18.5–24.9 (normal) is the optimal range for health, while both underweight and obesity are associated with higher risks of morbidity and mortality. Underweight is associated with increased mortality from chronic wasting diseases, smoking, and cancer (Ahima and Lazar 2013). Risks related to overweight and Class 1 obesity are equivocal; several studies have shown that, although often associated with biological indicators of disease such as elevated cholesterol levels, they may actually protect against some diseases and death (Flegal et al. 2005; Flegal et al. 2007; Flegal et al. 2013; Orpana et al. 2009; Prescott et al. 2014; Zajacova 2011). Several recent studies found that mortality risk in patients with obesity declines with age ≥70 years (Mehta et al. 2014; Patel et al. 2014; Rolland et al. 2014), but BMI in the Class 2 and Class 3 obesity range significantly increases the risk of death due to cardiovascular diseases, diabetes, cancer, and many other associated conditions, increasing in prevalence and severity with each class category (Figure 1.5). The US has seen a dramatic shift to higher BMI values in the last three decades, a strong indicator of changing health status.

The real threat to health is not BMI or body weight per se, which is actually a measure of total body mass composed of bone, muscle, and fat, but rather its fat component. The World Health Organization defines obesity as abnormal or excessive fat accumulation that may impair health (WHO 2009). BMI is a convenient screening tool for assessing public health, but it is only an indirect measure of fatness. Nevertheless BMI generally correlates with total adiposity and its health consequences (Wells 2014). It is still a useful indicator of obesity in population studies involving large numbers of participants (Flegal et al. 2008). The use of BMI has made it possible to

TABLE 1.1 Body Mass Index (BMI) categories (WHO 2009)

Classification	BMI Range
Underweight	<18.5
Normal weight	18.5–24.9
Overweight	25–29.9
Obesity	>30
Class 1	30–34.9
Class 2	35–39.9
Class 3	>40

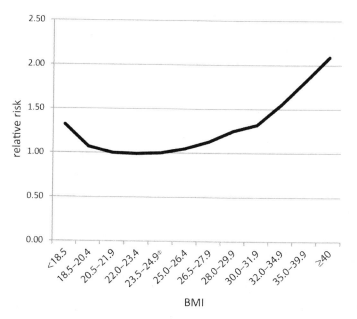

FIGURE 1.5 Relative risk of death among men and women according to Body Mass Index (BMI). Underweight lowers resistance to infectious disease and increases the risk of nutritional deficiencies; obesity is associated with chronic diseases.

Adapted from Calle et al. (2005).

★ represents the reference category made up of subjects with BMI = 23.5–24.9

observe trends in obesity prevalence, both in the US and globally, and to study the relationship between obesity and disease risk in many populations (Wells 2014).

Nevertheless, BMI values do not correspond to the same degree of adiposity in all populations. Asians have more and Pacific Islanders have less body fat than Europeans at the same BMI level, so BMI thresholds for Asians are three to four units lower, and Pacific Islanders' are one to two units higher (Hubbard 2000). In Asian populations, it is not uncommon for individuals with normal BMI and body weight to have higher than normal abdominal adiposity and a greater risk for diabetes (Chan et al. 2009). For children aged 2–19 years BMI percentiles are used as obesity cutoffs because the risk-related criteria for growing children are less clearcut than those for adults (Ogden et al. 2007), and BMI changes do not always reflect changes in adiposity (Demerath et al. 2006). The 85th percentile of childhood BMI distribution is considered overweight and the 95th percentile is obese.

BMI is used very carefully to assess individual body mass and health because in some people, such as certain athletes whose muscle bulk yields high BMI values, health risks would be overestimated, while in sedentary individuals with large abdominal fat deposits but low BMI values the risks of illness would be underestimated (Prentice and Jebb 2001). The interpretation of BMI also varies with age and ethnicity. Nevertheless, BMI cutoffs for men are the same as for women, in spite of women's greater proportion of body fat (about 20–30 percent in healthy women, 10–20 percent in healthy men) (Langin et al. 2009). One reason is that health risks for men develop at a lower level of fatness than for women.

The close relationship between excess body fat and chronic disease has been conclusively demonstrated over and over again (Wang and Beydoun 2007). Obesity is now considered to be the second leading preventable cause of disease and death in the US after tobacco use (USDHHS 2001), and the negative health effects of excess adiposity now outweigh all the benefits of the recent decline in Americans' smoking habits (Stewart et al. 2009).

More precisely, it is the distribution of body fat that is relevant for health. Humans have two major deposits of white fat, *subcutaneous adipose tissue (SAT)* of varying thicknesses located beneath the skin in a continuous layer over most of the trunk, arms, and legs, and *visceral adipose tissue (VAT)* surrounding internal organs in the abdomen (Figure 1.6).

Adipose tissue also accumulates between muscles as *intermuscular adipose tissue (IMAT)* (Gallagher et al. 2005). In addition, some humans possess varying smaller deposits of *brown adipose tissue (BAT)* along the sides of the neck and in the upper back. The unique color of this adipose tissue is due to its high concentration of mitochondria, energy-generating organelles which contain iron and give a reddish-brown color to the cells. Once thought to be present in and physiologically relevant only for newborn infants as a mechanism for regulating body temperature, BAT turns out to exist also in a number of healthy adults (Cypess et al. 2009). A drop in environmental temperature activates BAT, which generates heat (*adaptive thermogenesis*) to maintain normal body temperature by burning energy instead of storing it in fat cells (Virtanen et al. 2009). This metabolic property has inspired some researchers to seek ways to boost the amount of BAT or its activity to promote energy-release instead of storage (Moyer 2014; Ravussin and Kozak 2009).

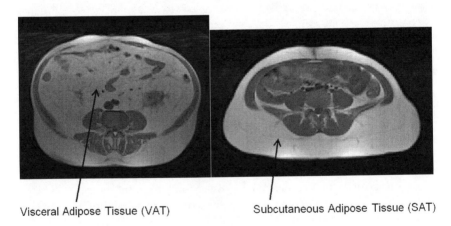

Visceral Adipose Tissue (VAT) Subcutaneous Adipose Tissue (SAT)

FIGURE 1.6 Visceral and subcutaneous adipose tissues in abdominal MRI cross-sections.

Source: Stefan Czerwinski, Ph.D., Lifespan Health Research Center, Wright State University School of Medicine.

Skinfold measurements at prescribed body sites are used to assess SAT on the trunk and limbs (Lohman et al. 1988). Although it contributes to overall adiposity, SAT seems to have little relation to health risks. VAT and IMAT are more directly responsible for the negative health consequences of obesity (Demerath et al. 2008). These fat deposits release *free fatty acids* and other chemicals into the bloodstream and play a major role in many chronic illnesses such as heart disease, diabetes, and some cancers.

Medical imaging is the only direct method for measuring deposits of VAT and IMAT. The most promising imaging method is *magnetic resonance imaging (MRI)*, which does not expose participants to ionizing radiation (Hu et al. 2011), but is expensive and not feasible for collecting data from the large numbers of individuals needed for population-wide research. An alternative estimate of abdominal adiposity is waist circumference (WC>40 in or 102 cm for men, WC>35 in or 88 cm for women), a more accurate predictor of obesity-related diseases such as heart disease than BMI and much more convenient for clinical assessment of individual obesity (Wang and Beydoun 2007). Persons with abdominal obesity (central fat distribution, large VAT deposits) are said to be apple-shaped, while those with greater fat deposits on the hips and thighs (peripheral fat distribution, greater SAT) are considered to be pear-shaped. Apple shape, more common in men than in women, is a strong indicator of cardiovascular disease risk and all-cause mortality in men (Arsenault et al. 2007; Kuk et al. 2006; Mitka 2005), while generally pear-shaped women actually seem to benefit from the protective metabolic activity of fat deposits on hips and thighs (Bos et al. 2005).

Since 1960 the average waist circumference of adult Americans has steadily increased (Ford et al. 2014; Li et al. 2007; Wang and Beydoun 2007). In 1999 the prevalence of abdominal obesity among American adults of all ethnic groups and both sexes was 46 percent; it had risen to 54 percent by 2012, despite BMI stability since 2003. Abdominal obesity has also increased among children and adolescents (Li et al. 2006; Xi et al. 2014), reaching a prevalence of 19 percent by 2012. Waist circumference cutoffs for health risks vary with ethnicity, with Asians having significantly higher risks for diabetes and cardiovascular disease at lower waist circumference measurements than Europeans (Hu 2008). Cutoffs for black men are also lower, while there is no difference in cutoffs for black and white women (Zhu et al. 2005). It is interesting to note that black female adolescents with large waist circumferences usually do not have the typical high blood pressure, cholesterol, or glucose indicators of cardiovascular disease that are associated with abdominal obesity in Latino and white adolescents (Johnson et al. 2009). This difference may be related to population variation in VAT and SAT mass – abdominal VAT is higher in white men and women than in blacks, while blacks tend to have more SAT at abdominal sites (Katzmarzy et al. 2010; Katzmarzyk et al. 2013).

The functions of fat

White *adipose tissue* is a complex organ composed of specialized cells called *adipocytes* embedded in connective tissue and surrounded by nerve cells and small blood

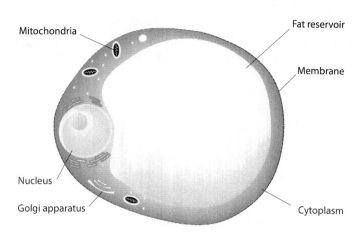

FIGURE 1.7 Adipocyte (fat storage cell). The lipid droplet occupies 90 percent of the cell volume. The cell's cytoplasm is stretched into a thin peripheral rim, and the cell nucleus is flattened against the cell wall. Adipocytes can increase their volume 1,000-fold (Langin et al. 2009). Courtesy of Designua via Shutterstock.com.

vessels (Figure 1.7). It forms layers of varying thicknesses beneath the surface of the skin (SAT) and internally around abdominal organs (VAT) (Langin et al. 2009). Excess energy that has been consumed but not used is converted to fat and stored as *lipid* droplets in adipocytes. Each mature adipocyte contains one large lipid droplet, the body's primary energy store. One pound of adipose tissue (0.45 kg) contains the equivalent of 3,500 calories of stored energy.

Both the number of adipocytes and their size influence the amount of energy that can be sequestered in a human body. Adipocyte number is determined by cell division. Individuals with obesity may have more than twice as many adipocytes as individuals with normal weight (Knittle et al. 1979; Pond 1998). Cell size is determined by insulin stimulation of adipocytes to accumulate and store lipids and to become enlarged. Obesity is the result of *sustained positive energy balance* over an extended period of time as more fat gradually accumulates in adipocytes. Adipose tissue stores fat for long-term energy needs; when energy is required by the body, blood insulin level drops, stimulating adipocytes to undergo *lipolysis*, the breakdown of stored lipids and their entry into the bloodstream as free fatty acids. Consequently adipocyte volume is reduced (Pond 1998). Compared to lean individuals, individuals with obesity have increased fat storage and decreased fat removal by lipolysis (Arner et al. 2011).

It is now abundantly clear that adipocytes have many important regulatory and survival functions. Adipose tissue is the body's largest energy reservoir (Norgan 1997), an internal portable supply of stockpiled energy, which allows normal-weight humans to survive up to 60 days without food (persons with obesity can survive up to 120 days) while preserving protein mass (muscle) and maintaining glucose levels necessary for brain functioning (Eckel 2003; Langin et al. 2009). As *New York Times* science writer Natalie Angier puts it, "our fat tissue, by efficiently absorbing the excess packets of energy we put in our mouths, has our best interest at heart" (Angier 2007). Because of their relatively greater fat mass, women often outlive men, and adults outlive children during periods of famine (Eckel 2003). Adipose tissue layers also insulate against heat loss and may also help to protect the body from physical trauma (Pond 1998).

Fat is a primary component of all cell membranes (Zechner and Madeo 2009). It is also an important component of immune cells and is involved in their functioning to protect the body against infection (Calder 2004). One class of fatty acid found in food and also produced by adipocytes regulates glucose uptake from the blood and reduces inflammation (Muoio and Newgard 2014). Individuals with obesity and insulin resistance are deficient in this type of fatty acid, in contrast to the high levels of other fats associated with obesity. Fat is essential for *fecundity*, *gestation*, and *lactation*, which have very high energy costs for females (Dey 2005; Ellison 2003). Beginning at puberty, increasing levels of estrogen suppress fat oxidation in human females, who therefore store fat more efficiently and thus accumulate a higher proportion of body fat than males in preparation for the energy demands of reproduction (O'Sullivan 2008). Fat is a major component of brain tissue, forming the insulating myelin sheaths of neurons (McKenzie et al. 2014), and influences the speed of electric impulses and thus learning. Biologists have pointed out that the exceptionally large brains of humans could not have evolved without substantial fat reserves. In older adults, a larger fat mass may actually be beneficial, helping to maintain greater bone density and thus preventing osteoporosis and bone fractures. It is also an energy reserve during chronic illness when appetite and energy intake are curtailed (Ogden et al. 2007).

But adipose tissue is not simply a passive fat storage organ. In recent years scientists have made many remarkable discoveries regarding its metabolic activity and its many essential functions. Adipocytes metabolize and store *androgens*, *estrogens*, and hormones regulating *glucose* levels, remove glucose and fatty acids from the blood, store lipid-soluble substances such as Vitamin D, and produce and release *adipokines*, chemicals that help to regulate appetite, *energy balance*, and *body composition* (Ahima and Flier 2000). The hormone *leptin*, for example, is an adipokine that signals the status of the body's energy reserves to the brain, which accordingly regulates fat accumulation and appetite. Leptin also has an important role in maturation of the female reproductive system and thus links nutritional status and reproductive function (Ellison 2001). Cells of the human lymph system depend upon certain fatty acids stored in nearby adipocytes for the precursors of inflammation-fighting prostaglandins and leukotrienes (Pond 2005). Adipocytes in skin infected by *Staphylococcus aureus* bacteria produce an antimicrobial peptide (Miller 2015; Zhang et al. 2015). Fatty acids produced by adipocytes also act as messenger molecules that control certain cellular processes, including gene expression (DiGirolamo et al. 2000). In addition, adipose tissue includes a variety of receptors for hormones, neuro-transmitters, cytokines, and growth factors (Langin et al. 2009).

Fat is essential, but an excessive amount of stored fat and its disproportionate secretion of messenger molecules and fatty acids is responsible for the disruption of energy balance and the development of a number of chronic diseases and other health problems. Adipocytes can expand to store lipids, but that ability has a limit beyond which they die, stimulating the immune system and contributing to the development of chronic, low-level systemic inflammation, which gives rise to obesity-related metabolic diseases, including cardiovascular disease, diabetes, and others (Bai and Sun 2015; Pecht et al. 2014; Pietilainen et al. 2011).

Obesity studies

Many scientific projects monitor obesity rates and attempt to understand the causes of the growing epidemic (Wang and Beydoun 2007). The Behavioral Risk Factor Surveillance System (BRFSS) is an ongoing national monitoring survey begun in 1984 and conducted by health departments in each of the 50 United States. Data are used to support health-related legislation, plan state health programs, and implement disease-prevention activities (Mokdad 2009). BRFSS obesity and diabetes surveys document the rising obesity and diabetes rates in the US, which are particularly prominent in southern states. In fact, 15 southern states constitute a "diabetes belt" where diabetes rates are above 11 percent (Barker et al. 2011).

Because the BRFSS telephone survey depends on self-reports of height, weight, and health status, and because there are always some respondents who under-report weight and over-report height (Chiolero et al. 2007; Gorber et al. 2007; Richmond et al. 2015; Wen and Kowaleski-Jones 2012), its BMI values are considered somewhat less accurate than those reported by the National Health and Nutrition Examination Survey (NHANES) study series, which depends on direct measurement of these variables from a representative sample of the general American population (faqs.org/nutrition/Met-Obe/National-Health-and-Nutrition). The first NHANES was conducted by the National Center for Health Statistics in the 1970s, and was followed by other surveys in the 1970s and 1980s which paid special attention to ethnic minorities. Beginning in 1999, NHANES became a continuous, annual survey.

In 1991 the Youth Risk Behavior Surveillance System was initiated to monitor behaviors that lead to social problems, disability, and death among Americans; in this survey height and weight are based on self-reports. The National Longitudinal Survey of Adolescent Health (Add Health) follows youths aged 12 to 17 years into adulthood, collecting both self-reported and directly measured height and weight. This survey oversamples minority youths including Asians and Native Americans to ensure their statistical representation. The Add Health study showed that the proportion of adolescents who became and remained obese in the transition to adulthood more than doubled to 22 percent during a five-year study period (Gordon-Larsen et al. 2004), and only a small proportion of adolescents with obesity (1.6 percent) became non-obese in adulthood.

In addition to these large-scale, national surveys, numerous other research programs focus on some particular issues of obesity and its relation to health in specific populations. Among these is the Gila River Indian Community Study of the Arizona Akimel O'Odham (River People, commonly called Pima) whose 7,500 members have the highest prevalence of obesity and diabetes in the US. This longitudinal study was initiated in 1965 and involves close collaboration between the Pima community and *National Institutes of Health (NIH)* scientists in Phoenix. All community members over age five are examined every two years for diabetes and obesity status, and the results are compared with a corresponding white population. Pima diabetes prevalence is 19 times higher than that of the Rochester, Minnesota population. Pima adolescents have more than 10 times the Type 2 diabetes rate of other Native American teens (Fagot-Campagna et al. 2000). Adult Pima men and women born after 1945 manifest higher BMI levels than those born before 1945, a rapid *secular* increase that coincided with more modest increases in other countries and other ethnic groups in the US (Price et al. 1993). The Pima living across the border in Mexico, who share a common ancestry and genetic heritage with the Arizona community, have an average BMI of 25, while the Arizona community average is 38 (Ravussin et al. 1994), clear evidence for environmental influences upon obesity development. Sadly, all the detailed information of Pima genetics and physiology that has accumulated and contributed so much to the knowledge of obesity has so far not helped to stem the obesity epidemic among the Pima or the general U.S. population.

The largest and longest continuous study of body composition and its relation to health and disease is the Fels Longitudinal Study, begun in 1929 in Yellow Springs, Ohio, among mostly white, middle-class Americans, and currently conducted by the Lifespan Health Research Center at Wright State University's Boonshoft School of Medicine (Roche 1992). Other regional scientific studies of obesity and related diseases include the Coronary Artery Risk Detection in Appalachian Communities (CARDIAC) school project in West Virginia, a state with very high obesity rates (Muratova et al. 2002); the Bogalusa Heart Study of cardiovascular disease risk factors among children in a multiethnic Louisiana community (Broyles et al. 2010); the Framingham Heart Study of a random sample in a Massachusetts community; the Nurses' Health Study, actually a series of investigations of women's health in selected states; and the National Weight Control Registry at the University of Colorado, which monitors individuals who have successfully maintained significant weight losses for many years. And that is only a very short list of American research projects; there are many others. Research efforts have grown to multicenter, multiethnic, and multinational projects to identify the causes of obesity and related chronic diseases and to develop prevention and treatment methods.

An important challenge in obesity research is measurement accuracy, not only of body mass, fat mass, and physiological indicators, but also of dietary intake, physical activity levels, TV watching time, nutritional knowledge, and many other behavioral factors that affect energy intake and expenditure (Hu 2008). Whether increasing obesity is primarily the result of excess energy intake or of low energy expenditure is still being debated today (Bleich et al. 2008), but obesity research tends to focus more on food consumption than physical inactivity, in part because energy intake is somewhat easier to conceptualize and measure than energy expenditure (Clark et al. 2009;

Tully et al. 2014). Although manual labor in the workplace has been largely replaced by mechanization (Leonard 2010; Tillotson 2004), little is actually known about the energy costs of occupational and domestic work. One regrettable consequence is the common belief that the primary cause of obesity is overeating, which supposedly can be readily controlled by conscious effort to reduce energy intake.

Research on obesity and its causes and consequences is a work in progress. As in all cases of ongoing research, new discoveries sometimes replace outdated ideas and at other times provide more comprehensive explanations. Readers of this volume should expect the information presented here to change with further scientific developments.

The obesity epidemic

The *Dictionary of Epidemiology* (2008, Oxford University Press) defines an epidemic as the "occurrence of health-related events clearly in excess of normal expectancy." Although some authors criticize the use of the term "epidemic" and reject the medical crisis model of obesity (Moffat 2010), arguably the United States is in the midst of an epidemic of obesity. There is no question that the prevalence of obesity increased dramatically in recent decades and now affects a large proportion of the U.S. population. As in infectious disease epidemics, there is some evidence that obesity spreads through social networks (Christakis and Fowler 2007), more often appearing in widening clusters of friends and relatives, even those who live at great distances from each other, than among neighbors who are outside the social circle of a person with obesity.

Recently the American Medical Association resolved to view obesity as a disease and to treat it as such (ama-assn.org), since it impairs normal physiological functioning and contributes to ill health. Obesity has a complex biological basis and is closely related to the most serious chronic diseases. This new medical approach to obesity aims to counter the excessive concern for physical appearance and the inordinate moralistic tone applied to individuals with obesity that are responsible for bias and outright discrimination, particularly against poor women, Latinos, and blacks who happen to manifest the highest obesity rates in the US (Campos 2004; Guthman 2011; Julier 2008; Lyons 2009; Ogden et al. 2007). Considering obesity a disease encourages physicians to be more attentive to this growing public health problem and minimizes the social stigma associated with obesity. However, critics contend that the new approach inappropriately medicalizes a normal human physical condition and promotes unnecessary and often ineffective clinical procedures and treatments. Indeed, expensive new prescription weight loss drugs regularly appear on the market, although most of their users lose little weight and many cannot tolerate the drugs and give up on the regimen.

Other critics view obesity as a normal biological response to an environment that has changed dramatically in the past century (Chaput et al. 2012), too quickly for biological adaptation. Some skeptics assert that physical fitness can counter the adverse health consequences of obesity. For instance, Medicare retirees who are physically active, including those with obesity, have much lower health care costs than their peers who report no physical activity, regardless of age (Wang et al. 2005). But the *fat-but-fit hypothesis*, that cardiorespiratory-fit individuals do not manifest the typical risk factors associated with obesity, is not conclusively supported by evidence (Fogelholm 2010; Hu 2008; Kramer et al. 2013). Physical fitness, although beneficial, does not entirely eliminate the negative effects of obesity.

There is a subclass of individuals with obesity categorized as *Metabolically Healthy Obese (MHO)* (Denis and Obin 2013). About 25–30 percent of U.S. adults with BMI in the obesity range manifest few of the usual blood pressure, blood sugar, cholesterol, inflammation, and other metabolic indicators of health risk associated with obesity, and also have lower fat mass and VAT (Camhi and Katzmarzyk 2014). Weight loss may not improve the health of such individuals, while weight loss does benefit individuals with obesity and metabolic dysfunctions (Brown and Kuk 2015). However, there is some evidence that MHO individuals are also not entirely protected from the negative consequences of obesity and are at some risk for the typical metabolic disturbances and diseases (Gomez-Ambrosi et al. 2014; Kramer et al. 2013). Another group of about 8 percent of U.S. adults with normal BMI manifest high risk factors for chronic diseases despite being slim (Ahima and Lazar 2013). They are at risk for Type 2 diabetes, insulin resistance, elevated cholesterol, and premature coronary heart disease even though they do not have excess body fat (Hu 2008). Clearly the variations in obesity and its consequences have not yet been unraveled and completely understood.

Doubters also refer to an American Paradox, the fact that despite increasing obesity rates, mortality related to heart disease, cancer, and stroke declined and life expectancy increased slightly in recent years (NCHS 2011). Improvements in medical treatments to lower blood pressure and blood lipid concentrations have prevented fatal strokes and heart attacks in many individuals with obesity (Basham and Luik 2008). Fewer persons die of obesity-related conditions, but many more Americans are living with chronic disability and disease brought on by obesity, accounting for nearly half of the U.S. illness burden. The US ranks low on population health in comparison to other wealthy nations of the world (Murray 2013).

Some point out that exaggerated attention to obesity is linked to the financial interests of medical professionals, pharmaceutical companies, and other commercial ventures developing and marketing various anti-obesity treatments and programs. They point out that conflicts of interest arise when obesity scientists and researchers whose work is government-funded consult for private pharmaceutical and diet product companies (Lyons 2009; Rothblum 2011). However, it must also be said that many critics themselves, most of them political scientists, lawyers, journalists, and academics outside the medical profession, have financial stakes in the American food production system which understandably aims to protect its customer and profit base (Krugman 2005), often at the expense of public health. For instance, the authors of an article in the *Journal of American Medical Association* questioning the evidence relating consumption of sweetened beverages to rising obesity rates (Allison and Mattes 2009) disclose that they receive grants, honoraria, donations, and consulting fees from numerous food, beverage, and pharmaceutical companies.

Many Americans think of obesity as a weighty, aesthetic issue rather than one of health and wellbeing. The popular view is that persons with obesity are unattractive, even repulsive in a society that values lean and fit bodies, or are moral failures who cannot or will not control their impulses and desires. Public health professionals, on the other hand, focus on the disease dimension and are deeply concerned about the health risks associated with high obesity rates in the US. Persons with obesity face a long list of potential medical conditions related to excess body fat. The average life expectancy of non-smoking men and women with obesity is reduced by six to seven years (Hu 2008). Their quality of life is compromised by chronic diseases, disability, life-long medical expenses, and mobility restrictions, as well as by discrimination and psychosocial stress. Former Surgeon General of the US David Satcher's personal commentary in a recent *F as in Fat* report (Levi et al. 2011) is appropriate here:

> The U.S. Centers for Disease Control and Prevention (CDC) estimate that obesity kills more than 110,000 Americans a year. Not only that: obesity plays a role in many millions of cases of chronic illness, including high blood pressure, high cholesterol, diabetes, heart disease, stroke, fatty liver disease, osteoarthritis, and cancer. Even when they don't result in death, these ailments can make life painful and difficult for patients and their families.

Obesity itself may not be a deadly disease, but it is currently incurable – there is no effective medical, surgical, pharmaceutical, or behavioral therapy known to reverse excessive body fat in all sufferers. As in the case of many epidemics of viral or bacterial origins, prevention is currently the most effective approach to stemming the obesity epidemic.

According to Dr. Satcher, "Obesity is also enormously expensive . . . America spends more than $150 billion annually on health care linked to obesity." The nation pays a hefty price for rising obesity rates, including the direct financial costs to individuals and governments for medical treatment of chronic conditions related to obesity, the social and personal losses associated with excessive body weight, and the costs of lost productivity due to increased absenteeism from work and premature death.

Health and wellness

Excess body fat is directly linked to the most common chronic illnesses and to a two to three times higher risk of death compared to normal adiposity (Adams et al. 2006; Calle et al. 2005; Pischon et al. 2008) (Figure 1.8). Not all individuals with obesity will contract chronic diseases, and not all patients with such conditions have obesity (Stefan et al. 2008). Nevertheless, even though it is not possible to predict whether a specific individual will suffer from a particular chronic disease, obesity does increase the probability of such an occurrence. For example, even in individuals with normal weight, the odds of developing impaired lung functioning are twice as high in those with abdominal obesity compared to those with normal waist circumference (Leone et al. 2009).

Nearly 35 percent of adult Americans and 50 percent of Americans over 60 years have the metabolic syndrome, a cluster of three or more risk factors that together culminate in heart disease, Type 2 diabetes, and certain cancers (Aguilar et al. 2015;

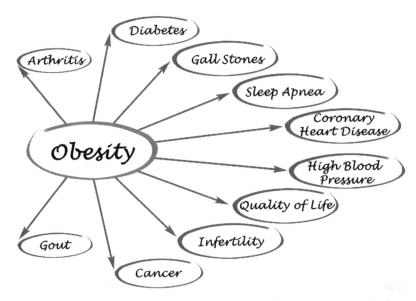

FIGURE 1.8 Obesity-related health risks. Courtesy of Arka38 via Shutterstock.com.

O'Neill and O'Driscoll 2015). Heart disease is the leading cause of death in America and in individuals with obesity. The risk factors making up the metabolic syndrome include abdominal obesity, insulin resistance, high blood pressure, and low high-density lipoprotein (HDL)-cholesterol. The World Health Organization has estimated that as much as 7 percent of total health care costs in developed countries are attributable to obesity-related conditions, particularly diabetes (WHO 2009).

Type 2 diabetes was once considered to be an adult-onset disease mainly related to obesity, but it now appears frequently in children and adolescents who may already develop debilitating symptoms in early adulthood (Hannon et al. 2005). In 2010 25 million adult Americans were afflicted with diabetes (CDC 2011). Pediatricians have serious concerns about children taking adult medications for the diabetes, high blood pressure, high cholesterol, and acid reflux exacerbated by obesity (Saul 2008). At least several hundred thousand American children are currently taking such drugs, which have not been tested in pediatric populations and are not formulated for children. They will have to take these medications for the rest of their lives at great cost in both finances and possible side effects.

Cancer death rates are more than 50 percent higher in persons with obesity compared with individuals of normal weight (PCP 2007). Other conditions associated with obesity are gallbladder disease, osteoarthritis, sleep disturbances, recurrent venous blood clots, pancreatitis, asthma, periodontitis, urinary incontinence, skin infections and ulcers, gastro-esophageal reflux disease (GERD), dementia, anxiety, and depression (Eichinger et al. 2008; Jacobson et al. 2006; Sise and Friedenberg 2008; Stecker and Sparks 2006; Suvan et al. 2011). Many of these conditions require surgical intervention. Appropriate dosing of anesthetics and administration of procedures such as cardiopulmonary bypass are more difficult, time in surgery is longer, respiratory and wound infections are more likely, and loss of organ transplants is more common in patients with obesity (Choban and Flancbaum 1997). Although the chance of dying during surgery is generally the same for all patients, obesity does complicate many surgical procedures, patients with obesity require extra care to prevent or mitigate these problems, and treatment outcomes are poorer.

Compared to individuals with normal weight, patients with obesity are hospitalized more frequently for injuries such as strains, sprains, and dislocations due to falls and overexertion (Matter et al. 2007). Factory workers with obesity have more than twice as many workplace injuries as their normal-weight co-workers (Pollack et al. 2007). Children with obesity sustain two and a half times more serious injuries to their arms and legs (Pollack et al. 2008). Clinical examinations such as blood pressure measurement, abdominal and pelvic exams, and mammography are more challenging in patients with obesity (Silk and McTigue 2010).

Individuals with obesity may fare much worse in auto accidents – they seem to have a five to eight times higher risk of dying due to blunt trauma suffered in car crashes (Zhu et al. 2006), but a recent study contradicts this finding – adults with obesity have a significantly lower chance of death due to injury from auto accidents and falls (Wang et al. 2015). Children with obesity have greater risks for head and chest injuries (Kim et al. 2015). They also experience more complications during recovery from accidental burns. Children with obesity suffer more joint and bone pain. Young girls with obesity are five times more likely to require hip replacement than their healthy peers. Walking and other forms of physical activity are more difficult, and a vicious cycle of weight gain and physical inactivity develops (Abbate et al. 2006; Ding et al. 2005; Shultz et al. 2009; Taylor et al. 2006; Wearing et al. 2006).

Fertility is compromised by obesity (Huss-Ashmore 1980; Stotland 2008). Women with obesity are subject to menstrual irregularity, have greater difficulty becoming pregnant, and are more likely to develop complications during pregnancy and delivery (Galtier-Dereure et al. 2000; Metwally et al. 2008; Raatikainen et al. 2006). Mothers with obesity are more likely to have prolonged labor and are two to three times more likely to require cesarean delivery than women with normal BMI (Chu et al. 2009; Mills et al. 2010; Poobalan et al. 2008). Miscarriages and stillbirths, as well as preterm births and low birth weight babies, occur more often in women with obesity than in those of healthy weight (McDonald et al. 2010; Aune et al. 2014; Lutsiv, et al. 2015). They are more likely to suffer from urinary tract infections, pregnancy-related high blood pressure, gestational diabetes, anesthesia-related complications, and a higher incidence of cesarean or episiotomy wound infection. Children of mothers with obesity may also suffer adverse effects, developing birth defects of the heart and spine (Ramsay and Greer 2006). Perinatal mortality rates of infants born to mothers with obesity are up to three times higher than for infants born to healthy mothers. Obesity also diminishes a mother's ability to produce milk to nurse her child (Rasmussen and Kjolhede 2004). For women with obesity, contraception doses have to be adjusted for greater body mass to be effective (Edelman et al. 2014).

Individuals who did not have obesity before reaching adulthood have lower risks of obesity-related diseases and premature mortality than those who became obese in childhood or adolescence (Hirko et al. 2015). And although women have higher rates of obesity than men, their obesity-related health risks are generally lower than men of all ages. Nevertheless, some weight loss is beneficial, even for elderly individuals with obesity, because it improves insulin sensitivity, helps control Type 2 diabetes, reduces arthritis of the joints, and improves cholesterol levels and blood pressure. Even minor weight loss improves the quality of life and substantially reduces health risks and medical costs, especially for patients with very high BMI (Cawley et al. 2014). Called the "10 percent solution," it is a more realistic approach to managing obesity than drastic weight reduction, which is virtually impossible to maintain over the long term (Poobalan et al. 2004; Wadden et al. 1999). Nevertheless, efforts to lose weight may have serious health consequences. A University of Minnesota study of dieting among 2,500 teenage girls found that nearly two-thirds used unhealthy weight control methods such as diet pills, laxatives, vomiting, or skipping meals (Ruth 2006). Teens who engage in unhealthy dieting are actually three times more likely to become overweight. Most dieters who do achieve significant weight loss later relapse and regain the amount lost and more. Weight cycling, the repeated loss and regain of body weight through restrictive dieting, tends to permanently lower metabolic rate and thus induce weight regain (Rosenbaum et al. 2008). The only effective weight loss procedure for extreme obesity – *bariatric surgery* – is not without some serious risks (Robinson 2009).

Obesity is actually a form of malnutrition. A regular diet of high-calorie foods is satisfying and provides plenty of quick energy but lacks adequate amounts of fiber and many essential *micronutrients*, such as the vitamins and minerals from fruits and vegetables. American children with obesity often avoid drinking milk and are deficient in Vitamin D, essential for normal bone growth (Kumar et al. 2009; Turer et al. 2013). Individuals with obesity have a 35 percent higher prevalence of Vitamin D deficiency than individuals with healthy weight (Pereira-Santos et al. 2015).

An important general indicator of a population's health and wellbeing is average adult stature. Populations that are well nourished, in generally good health, and not subject to famine and disease are more likely to reach their genetic potential for adult stature than chronically malnourished ones. In human prehistory, Paleolithic human ancestors were on average tall and healthy, most likely because of their excellent nutrition and physical fitness. But the start of the *Neolithic Agricultural Revolution* was accompanied by nutritional deficiencies and infectious diseases and marked by shorter stature in early farming populations, until they finally developed a variety of new crops to improve dietary balance. Since colonial times until the mid-20th century, white Americans were the tallest and healthiest people in the world (Komlos and Lauderdale 2007). But since the 1950s mean stature has leveled off among adult Americans, while the height of Europeans recovering from the stressful effects of World War II continued to increase rapidly until today when the Dutch are the tallest. Americans are now low on the list of average statures among developed nations. The reason for the relative decline of average American stature is not clear, but it happens to coincide with the U.S. obesity epidemic. Obesity may inhibit healthy growth due to a dietary imbalance between energy (fats, sugars) and essential micronutrients (vitamins, minerals).

Financial and economic costs

Rising obesity rates drive medical spending in the US (Thorpe and Philyaw 2012). Not only has the prevalence of obesity-related conditions risen in recent decades, the average patient cost has also increased substantially with new and better treatments; for patients with obesity total health care expenses rose by 25 percent since 1998 (An 2015). Compared to those of healthy weight, patients with obesity make one-third or more additional visits to primary care physicians. They also purchase nearly twice the number of prescribed drugs, including six times the number of diabetes medications and more than three times the number of cardiovascular medications (Finkelstein et al. 2005). Since 1998 the increase in prescription costs for patients with obesity rose by 62 percent (An 2015). Today adult per capita medical spending attributable to obesity may be as much as $2,826 more (in 2005 dollars) than for individuals of normal weight (Cawley and Meyerhoefer 2010). Individuals with severe obesity, the fastest-growing segment of the population with obesity, incur even greater costs – nearly four times the cost of health care compared to normal-weight individuals (Grieve et al. 2013; Li et al. 2015). The estimated combined cost of treating obesity-related diabetes, heart disease, and cancer among adult Americans is expected to increase by approximately $1 trillion by 2030 (Wang et al. 2011).

Americans with obesity take more sick leave than their healthy-weight co-workers (Neovius et al. 2008). Absenteeism due to obesity-related illnesses costs U.S. employers between $3 and $6 billion per year (Trogdon et al. 2008). Workers with obesity are less productive and more likely to be restricted by disability, costing businesses as much as an additional $9 billion per year. Students with obesity are more likely to be absent from school than their normal-weight peers (Geier et al. 2007).

There is also evidence that personal wealth is limited by obesity. Since 1979 the National Longitudinal Survey of Youth has followed the socioeconomic development of young people born between 1957 and 1964 (Zagorsky 2005). The survey found that among white Americans the net worth of men and women with obesity is $20,000 to $40,000 less than the net worth of those in the normal BMI category. Teenagers with obesity are less likely to acquire marketable skills and to gain employment and high earnings in adulthood than those who do not have obesity (Lundborg et al. 2014).

Individuals with obesity, particularly women, are more often excluded from high-paying professional and technical occupations than those of healthy weight (Finkelstein et al. 2005). They are also more than twice as likely to be subject to long-term unemployment and to earn less than their normal-weight counterparts in the same occupation. Women with obesity report more illness conditions that limit their work and their quality of life when compared with healthy working women (Muenning et al. 2006; Tunceli et al. 2006).

Individuals with diabetes are sometimes refused jobs because of disability dis-crimination or are fired because of their need for special accommodations at work, even though these are often trivial. Some companies refuse to hire a person with diabetes because of the increased cost of health care, which can be as much as five times more than for workers without diabetes. Federal law prohibits individuals with diabetes from serving in the armed forces and prevents patients taking insulin from becoming commercial pilots (Kleinfeld 2006).

Personal costs

Obesity compromises a person's daily quality of life. Individuals with obesity have more problems with physical pain, gum disease, mobility issues, urinary incontinence, discomfort, lack of vitality, anxiety, depression, and reduced social functioning than their healthy peers (Kim and Kawachi 2008; Subak et al. 2009; Suvan et al. 2011; Wolf et al. 2003). Children with obesity are also more likely to have lower self-esteem (Friedlander et al. 2003). Adults and children with obesity face intolerance, discrimination, and harassment in schools and workplaces, cruelties that can lead to depression and withdrawal from society. The majority of adolescents enrolled in weight loss camps reported that they were teased, cyber-bullied, and even physically attacked by peers, friends, teachers, coaches, and parents, even when they were no longer overweight (Faith et al. 2011; Puhl and Brownell 2006; Puhl and Heuer 2009; Puhl et al. 2013).

In the US individuals with obesity are especially subject to anti-fat bias and deprived of friendships, intimate relationships, and respect. Even highly educated adult Americans, including college professors and medical professionals, have shown prejudice toward persons with obesity, considering them to be solely responsible for their self-inflicted condition and lacking in willpower and moral strength to overcome their weight problems. Some primary care physicians view obesity as an individual problem and share society's negative stereotypes about their patients' personal attributes, which include ugliness, laziness, and presumed noncompliance with medical recommendations (Foster et al. 2003).

Anthropology and obesity

Most of the information and advice about obesity comes from various fields of *biomedicine*, and is relatively inaccessible and incomprehensible to the majority of Americans who wish to understand the obesity epidemic, both for the sake of their personal lives and for the nation's health. Most scientific research reports and clinical writings focus on one or another genetic, physiological, or behavioral aspect of obesity and present a rather simplified and individualized view of the obesity epidemic. Knowing that there is much more to the obesity epidemic than personal failure or any other single cause, anthropologists have questioned the limited, per-sonalized approach to studying obesity (Guthman 2011; Guthman 2013; Moffat 2010). Because researchers in various scientific disciplines investigating obesity work independently and understand the problem differently (Ulijaszek 2008), they are often unaware of the complex interactions between biological and environmental influences. The focus on individual and single biological factors overlooks the multiple, powerful external forces that actively promote excessive energy consumption and physical inactivity.

Anthropologists are keenly aware that humans exist within social and cultural systems and constantly face numerous and sometimes conflicting external influences upon their personal decisions and behaviors. To understand the American obesity epidemic, anthropologists examine not only internal factors, but also the broader context and external factors that enable or impede healthy choices (Ulijaszek and Lofink 2006). The American obesity epidemic is situated within a specific social-political-economic-ideological environment and a unique constellation of cultural characteristics. Anthropologists specialize in exploring this big picture and consider both the proximate and ultimate causes of obesity, the complex interactions between human biology and culture, the physical environment and human adaptive responses, and the individuals and the society involved. Rudolph Virchow, a 19th-century physician, pathologist, and anthropologist, linked a typhus outbreak in his native Upper Silesia to widespread poverty and declared that the epidemic could not be resolved by treating individuals with drugs alone, but required improvement in the living conditions of the entire population (Ackerknecht 1953). He is considered to be the "father of social medicine," a forerunner of modern medical anthropology, which in subsequent years identified many other environmental factors related to disease and recognized the roles of social class, economic status, gender, and ethnicity in its *holistic* approach to health and illness.

Anthropologists also view the world through the lens of evolution and species *adaptation* to environmental stresses (Frisancho 1993). To maintain *homeostasis* and to survive over millions of years, the evolving human species had to adapt to the powerful stressor of energy scarcity – persistent or periodic – related to an unreliable energy supply and the need for rigorous physical activity. Negative energy balance (energy intake < energy expenditure) ultimately led to the extinction of human ancestors unable to obtain adequate energy to support body maintenance, function, and reproduction, favoring those who were able to maximize energy intake with minimal energy expenditure.

Throughout evolutionary history humans responded to nutritional stress by becoming ever more efficient at obtaining, storing and using energy by means of an arsenal of adaptive mechanisms. Genes and physiology evolved to regulate metabolism more efficiently, and human technologies modified the nutritional environment both for lowering energy needs and obtaining energy more effectively. These adaptations may be incompatible with survival in today's world, in areas where the energy supply is constant, reliable, and excessive and the need for physical activity is low. The resulting positive energy balance (energy intake > energy expenditure) has led to high rates of obesity and its associated chronic diseases and other health risks. So far humans have not developed effective adaptations to positive energy balance; there has been too little time for that. Even though techno-cultural methods to reverse obesity could be developed relatively quickly, genetic and physiological adaptations are not easily reversed and will continue to affect metabolic rates.

Biological and cultural variations are essential for human survival in various environmental conditions and therefore of great importance to anthropologists. Sex differences in body composition and in tendencies to become obese are of special interest, as is the differential impact of obesity on the lives of men and women. Female reproduction requires a large, stable energy supply, an energy demand not shared by males. Women are able to store more energy than men and rely more on fat deposits as an energy source, while men rely more on stored glucose. In America today a woman with obesity is likely to suffer social and economic deprivations, but in the past, including the prehistoric past, she was probably greatly admired and desired for her relatively high fertility.

Compared to women, who have a greater tendency to become obese, a larger proportion of men's total body fat is VAT (Demerath et al. 2007), rendering them more vulnerable to metabolic disorders and chronic disease than women. For example, American boys of all ethnic groups have higher blood pressure than girls (Jago et al. 2006). While obesity is generally more common among women around the world, in some regions men predominate, as is the case in some Mediterranean countries (Papandreou et al. 2008). Such differences intrigue anthropologists.

Anthropologists trying to understand the dimensions of the obesity epidemic also take special note of variations in obesity rates among different socioeconomic and ethnic groups and observe differences in obesity prevalence among countries, major regions of the US, and local communities such as the boroughs of New York City. The southern states, which are also among the poorest in the nation, have the highest obesity (and diabetes) rates in the country (Barker et al. 2011). Populations living in New York City census tracts with a mix of residential and commercial buildings, high population density, and many subway and bus stops have the lowest average BMI values, possibly because of their pedestrian-friendly environment (Rundle et al. 2007). These variations offer clues to the causes of the obesity epidemic in the US.

One-third of Americans have obesity, but the rest do not, suggesting that there is variation in the genetic predisposition to obesity. How some individuals avoid overweight or obesity in the calorie-rich, obesogenic environment of the US may hold a key to solving the obesity epidemic (Field et al. 2013).

Anthropologists make global comparisons to better understand issues of health and disease in their own society. Many less developed nations that experienced very rapid and dramatic increases of obesity prevalence serve as a natural laboratory for tracing the economic, political, social, and cultural changes related to globalization and modernization and their linkage with excessive body weight. Discoveries in these societies may well shed light on environmental changes in the US related to the American obesity epidemic.

The American obesity epidemic

Why does the US have the highest obesity prevalence in the developed world? This book offers several answers to complement the dominant biomedical perspective by considering both the biological and environmental dimensions of obesity and their complex interactions, offering a broad overview of this multifaceted problem. This book is an effort to review, synthesize, and translate for a general audience information about obesity from a number of independent research disciplines and their distinctive perspectives, to highlight the inter- and intra-population variation in obesity prevalence and its possible causes, to strongly encourage further exploration of the issue using an integrated, biocultural approach, and to promote a demand for changes in social, economic, and political policies which function as barriers to healthy living in America.

Chapter 2 reviews the ultimate cause of the obesity epidemic. It takes a very deep look through time at the origin of the human species and its subsequent *evolution*, which was basically a process of meeting the need for energy to survive and procreate. In contrast to the constant quest to obtain and consume enough energy in the past, the issue today is too much energy intake and too little energy expenditure, a condition modern humans are not biologically designed or culturally prepared for, lacking the metabolic or behavioral controls on energy intake and storage to avoid overweight or obesity.

Subsequent chapters review several proximate causes of the American obesity epidemic to explain why it is difficult for Americans to raise energy expenditure and lower energy intake. Chapter 3 focuses on the intricate genetic-physiological system which maintains energy balance. This complex energy-regulating system, its components and functions not yet fully understood, is strongly biased toward energy acquisition and accumulation, but its ability to limit consumption and storage is weak. In the presence of constant abundance it can be overwhelmed by excessive fat accumulation and production of chemical signals, leading to chronic imbalances in endocrine and immune systems.

Chapter 4 explores the internal microbiotic and external physical and chemical environments interacting with obesity-susceptibility genes and physiology. U.S. obesity rates rose dramatically in the last decades, not because of genetic changes, but rather because of sweeping changes in the external environment (Brownell and Nestle 2004). In the modern obesogenic environment energy abundance is no longer balanced by periodic scarcity or high physical activity as in the past. An important aspect of the modern environment is exposure to industrial chemicals, some of which disrupt normal gene expression and hormonal pathways (Casals-Casas et al. 2008).

A relatively new trend in medical anthropology considers the relationship between socioeconomic status and health (Goodman and Leatherman 2001), and Chapter 5 of this book reviews these links with obesity in the US. Americans with low incomes have limited access to nutritious foods and safe physical activity. In the last decade the number of Americans living in poverty increased, while housing costs and food prices rose, forcing the poor – disproportionately represented by ethnic minorities and women – to reduce spending on healthy food (FRAC 2011). The recent global economic crisis raised food costs everywhere. Growing poverty continues and can be expected to worsen obesity in the future.

Chapter 6 notes that American obesity is the literal embodiment of a cultural ideology of hyper-consumerism driven by the capitalist, corporate-driven economy and government policies. Sophisticated marketing schemes encourage Americans to consume food and drink far above nutritional needs and to purchase numerous time- and labor-saving devices that reduce the need for healthy physical activity. Farm subsidies protect the prices of agricultural commodities and lower prices of some of the very products that contribute to obesity. Americans are constantly confronted by opposing cultural values that pit public health, good nutrition, and adequate physical activity against corporate profit, consumer practices, and government policies.

Body weight has great symbolic meaning in America, where external appearance has especially strong cultural value. Fashion models, movie stars, and other celebrities convey a physical image of slimness emblematic of beauty, self-sacrifice, industriousness, and morality. This ideal body image is virtually impossible for most Americans to achieve, yet there is little allowance for body size variation. Individuals with obesity are considered social deviants who have exceeded the limits of acceptable appearance and behavior, and they suffer persistent criticism and prejudice as a result (Crandall and Schiffhauer 1998).

Conclusion

Obesity is much more than a matter of individual failure to control consumption and to engage in regular exercise to maintain the balance between energy intake and energy expenditure. The mechanisms that predispose humans to become obese are inherent in genes and physiology as a result of millions of years of biological adaptation to energy scarcity. There is no apparent upper limit to the amount of energy that can be acquired and stored in the human body. All human populations everywhere share the same genetic and physiological heritage and have the capacity to become obese, but different environments, political structures, social arrangements, and cultural traditions account for the variations in obesity rates.

American culture and lifestyle promote development of obesity. Powerful external forces guide decisions and behaviors in direct opposition to public and individual efforts to limit intake and expend more energy. They encourage Americans to consume to excess, and to acquire and use technological devices that facilitate a sedentary lifestyle. Most Americans find it very difficult to resist the dominant cultural pattern of high consumption and physical inactivity that is promoted by American economic, political, and ideological systems.

Obesity is not simply a problem of physical attractiveness. It is not just the outcome of the two "deadly sins" of gluttony and sloth, or the result of ignorance and poor lifestyle choices. It is the natural consequence of interaction between the finely tuned human metabolic system designed to acquire, store, and defend energy and the social and cultural pressures of the unique American environment which drive consumption and inactivity. The American obesity epidemic is both an individual and a social issue.

References

Abbate, L. M. et al. (2006). Anthropometric measures, body composition, body fat distribution, and knee osteoarthritis in women. *Obesity* **14**: 1274–1281.

Ackerknecht, E. H. (1953). Rudolf Virchow: Doctor, Statesman, Anthropologist. Madison, WI: University of Wisconsin Press.

Adams, K. F. et al. (2006). Overweight, obesity, and mortality in a large prospective cohort of persons 50 to 71 years old. *New England Journal of Medicine* **355**: 763–778.

Aguilar, M. et al. (2015). Prevalence of the metabolic syndrome in the United States, 2003–2012. *JAMA* **313**(19): 1973–1974.

Ahima, R. S. and J. S. Flier (2000). Adipose tissue as an endocrine organ. *Trends in Endocrinology and Metabolism* **11**(8): 327–332.

Ahima, R. S. and M. A. Lazar (2013). The health risk of obesity – better metrics imperative. *Science* **341**: 856–858.

Al Khater, S. A. (2015). Pediatric non-alcoholic fatty liver disease: an overview. *Obesity Reviews* **16**: 393–405.

Allison, D. B. and R. D. Mattes (2009). Nutritively sweetened beverage consumption and obesity: the need for solid evidence on a fluid issue. *JAMA* **301**(3): 318–320.

Alvarez, L. (2003). U.S. eating habits, and Europeans, are spreading visibly. New York Times, 10/31/03.

An, R. (2015). Health care expenses in relation to obesity and smoking among U.S. adults by gender, race/ethnicity, and age group: 1998–2011. *Public Health* **129**: 29–36.

Anderson, S. E. and R. C. Whitaker (2009). Prevalence of obesity among US preschool children in different racial and ethnic groups. *Archives of Pediatrics & Adolescent Medicine* **163**(4): 344–348.

Angier, N. (2007). Its poor reputation aside, our fat is doing us a favor. New York Times, 8/7/07.

AP (2004). Urban Indians growing fatter. New York Times, 11/15/04.

AP (2006). Key events in food industrialization. New York Times, 3/18/06.

Arner, P. et al. (2011). Dynamics of human adipose lipid turnover in health and metabolic disease. *Nature* **478**: 110–113.

Arsenault, B. J. et al. (2007). Visceral adipose tissue accumulation, cardiorespiratory fitness, and features of the metabolic syndrome. *Archives of Internal Medicine* **167**(14): 1518–1525.

Astrup, A. and N. Finer (2000). Redefining type 2 diabetes: 'diabesity' or 'obesity dependent diabetes mellitus'? *Obesity Reviews* **1**(2): 57–59.

Aune, D. et al. (2014). Maternal body mass index and the risk of fetal death, stillbirth, and infant death. *JAMA* **311**(15): 1536–1546.

Bai, Y. and Q. Sun (2015). Macrophage recruitment in obese adipose tissue. *Obesity Reviews* **16**(2): 127–136.

Balkau, B. et al. (2007). International Day for the Evaluation of Abdominal Obesity (IDEA): a study of waist circumference, cardiovascular disease, and diabetes mellitus in 168,000 primary care patients in 63 countries. *Circulation* **116**: 1942–1951.

Barker, L. D. et al. (2011). Geographic distribution of diagnosed diabetes in the U.S.: a diabetes belt. *American Journal of Preventive Medicine* **40**(4): 434–439.

Basham, P. and J. Luik (2008). Head to Head: Is the obesity epidemic exaggerated? Yes. *British Medical Journal* **336**: 244.

Bleich, S. N. et al. (2008). Why is the developed world obese? *Annual Review of Public Health* **29**: 273–295.

Bos, G. et al. (2005). Opposite contributions of trunk and leg fat mass with plasma lipase activities: the Hoorn Study. *Obesity Research* **13**: 1817–1823.

Bradtmiller, B., C. Gordon, and S. Paquette (2009). Anthropometric change in the U.S. Army: implications for design. International Congress of Physiological Anthropology, Delft, The Netherlands, 2009. Vol. Proceedings of the 9th International Congress of Physiological Anthropology, pp. 53–56. ICPA.

Brody, J. E. (2004). The widening of America, or how size 4 became size 0. New York Times, 1/20/04.

Brownell, K. D. and M. Nestle (2004). The sweet and lowdown on sugar. New York Times, 1/23/04.

Broyles, S. et al. (2010). The pediatric obesity epidemic continues unabated in Bogalusa, Louisiana. *Pediatrics* **125**: 900–905.

Bruni, F. (2001). The round and the oval. New York Times, October 1, 2011.

Caballero, B. (2005). A nutrition paradox – underweight and obesity in developing countries. *New England Journal of Medicine* **352**: 1514–1516.

Caballero, B. et al. (2003). Body composition and overweight prevalence in 1,704 school-children from 7 American Indian communities. *American Journal of Clinical Nutrition* **78**: 308–312.

Calder, P. C. (2004). Dietary lipids and immune function. *In* Functional Foods, Ageing and Degenerative Disease. C. Remacle and B. Reusens, eds. pp. 349–393. Boca Raton: CRC Press.

Calle, E. E., L. R. Teras, and M. J. Thun (2005). Letter to the Editor: Obesity and mortality. *New England Journal of Medicine* **353**(20): 2197–2199.

Camhi, S. M. and P. T. Katzmarzyk (2014). Differences in body composition between metabolically healthy obese and metabolically abnormal obese adults. *International Journal of Obesity* **38**: 1142–1145.

Campos, P. (2004). The Obesity Myth: Why America's Obsession With Weight Is Hazardous to Your Health. New York: Gotham Books.

Casals-Casas, C., J. N. Feige, and B. Desvergne (2008). Interference of pollutants with PPARs: endocrine disruption meets metabolism. *International Journal of Obesity* **32**: S53–S61.

Cawley, J. and C. Meyerhoefer (2010). The medical care costs of obesity: an instrumental variables approach. NBER Working Paper #16467. Cambridge, MA: National Bureau of Economic Research.

Cawley, J. et al. (2014). Savings in medical expenditures associated with reductions in body mass index among US adults with obesity, by diabetes status. *PharmacoEconomics* **33**(7): 707–722.

CDC (2012). MMWR: Diabetes death rates among youths aged < 19 years – United States 1968–2009. *JAMA* **308**(24): 2558–2559.

Chan, J. C. N. et al. (2009). Diabetes in Asia: epidemiology, risk factors, and pathophysiology. *JAMA* **301**(20): 2129–2140.

Chaput, J.-P., E. Doucet, and A. Tremblay (2012). Obesity: a disease or a biological adaptation? An update. *Obesity Reviews* **13**(8): 681–691.

Cheng, T. O. (2004). Letter to the Editor. *New England Journal of Medicine* **350**(23): 2415.

Chiolero, A., I. Peytremann-Bridevaux, and F. Paccaud (2007). Associations between obesity and health conditions may be overestimated if self-reported body mass index is used. *Obesity Reviews* **8**(4): 373–374.

Choban, P. S. and L. Flancbaum (1997). The impact of obesity on surgical outcomes: a review. *Journal of American College of Surgery* **185**: 593–603.

Christakis, N. A. and J. H. Fowler (2007). The spread of obesity in a large social network over 32 years. *New England Journal of Medicine* **357**(4): 370–379.

Chu, S. Y., S. Y. Kim, and J. Lau (2009). Letter to the Editor. *Obesity Reviews* **10**(4): 487–488.

Clark, B. K. et al. (2009). Validity and reliability of measures of television viewing time and other non-occupational sedentary behaviour of adults: a review. *Obesity Reviews* **10**(1): 7–16.

Conard, N. (2009). A female figurine from the basal Aurignacian of Hohle Fels Cave in southwestern Germany. *Nature* **459**: 248–252.

Crandall, C. S. and K. L. Schiffhauer (1998). Anti-fat prejudice: beliefs, values, and American culture. *Obesity Research* **6**(6): 458–460.

Cunningham, S. A., M. R. Kramer, and K. M. V. Narayan (2014). Incidence of childhood obesity in the United States. *New England Journal of Medicine* **370**: 403–411.

Cutler, D. M., E. L. Glaeser, and J. M. Shapiro (2003). Why have Americans become more obese? *Journal of Economic Perspectives* **17**(3): 93–118.

Cypess, A. M. et al. (2009). Identification and importance of brown adipose tissue in humans. *New England Journal of Medicine* **360**(15): 1509–1517.

Dabelea, D. et al. (2014). Prevalence of type 1 and type 2 diabetes among children and adolescents from 2001–2009. *JAMA* **311**(17): 1778–1786.

Dawes, L. (2014). Childhood Obesity in America: Biography of an Epidemic. Cambridge: Harvard University Press.

Demerath, E. W. et al. (2008). Visceral adiposity and its anatomical distribution as predictors of the metabolic syndrome and cardiometabolic risk factor levels. *American Journal of Clinical Nutrition* **88**(5): 1263–1271.

Demerath, E. W. et al. (2006). Do changes in body mass index percentile reflect changes in body composition in children? Data from the Fels Longitudinal Study. *Pediatrics* **117**(3): e487–e495.

Demerath, E. W. et al. (2007). Anatomical patterning of visceral adipose tissue: race, sex, and age variation. *Obesity* **15**(12): 2984–2993.

Denis, G. V. and M. S. Obin (2013). 'Metabolically healthy obesity': origins and implications. *Molecular Aspects of Medicine* **34**: 59–70.

Deshmukh-Taskar, P. et al. (2006). Tracking of overweight status from childhood to young adulthood: the Bogalusa Heart Study. *European Journal of Clinical Nutrition* **60**: 48–57.

Dey, S. K. (2005). Fatty link to fertility. *Nature* **435**: 34–35.

DiGirolamo, M., J. Harp, and J. Stevens (2000). Obesity: definition and epidemiology. *In* Obesity: Pathology and Therapy. D. H. Lockwood and T. H. Heffner, eds. pp. 3–28. New York: Springer.

Ding, C. et al. (2005). Knee structural alteration and BMI: a cross-sectional study. *Obesity Research* **13**: 350–361.

Eckel, R. H. (2003). Obesity: Mechanisms and Clinical Management. Philadelphia: Lippincott, Williams & Wilkins.

Eckel, S. (2009). Striking a pose for girth. New York Times, 5/14/09.

Edelman, A. B. et al. (2014). Correcting oral contraceptive pharmacokinetic alterations due to obesity: a randomized controlled trial. *Contraception* **90**: 550–556.

Eichinger, S. et al. (2008). Overweight, obesity, and the risk of recurrent venous thrombo-embolism. *Arch Intern Med* **168**(15): 1678–1683.

Ellison, P. T. (2003). Energetics and reproductive effort. *American Journal of Human Biology* **15**: 342–51.

Ellison, P. T. (2001). On Fertile Ground: A Natural History of Human Reproduction. Cambridge: Harvard University Press.

Fagot-Campagna, A. et al. (2000). Type 2 diabetes among North American children and adolescents; an epidemiological review and a public health perspective. *Journal of Pediatrics* **136**: 664–672.

Faith, M. S. et al. (2011). Evidence for prospective associations among depression and obesity in population-based studies. *Obesity Reviews* **12**: e438–e453.

Field, A. E., C. A. Camargo Jr., and S. Ogino (2013). The merits of subtyping obesity: one size does not fit all. *JAMA* **310**(20): 2147–2148.

Finkelstein, E. A., C. J. Ruhm, and K. M. Kosa (2005). Economic causes and consequences of obesity. *Annual Review of Public Health* **26**: 239–257.

Flegal, K. M. et al. (2012). Prevalence of obesity and trends in the distribution of body mass index among US adults, 1999–2010. *JAMA* **307**(5): 491–497.

Flegal, K. M. et al. (2005). Excess deaths associated with underweight, overweight, and obesity. *JAMA* **293**(15): 1861–1867.

Flegal, K. M. et al. (2007). Cause-specific excess deaths associated with underweight, overweight, and obesity. *JAMA* **298**(17): 2028–2037.

Flegal, K. M. et al. (2013). Association of all-cause mortality with overweight and obesity using standard Body Mass Index categories. *JAMA* **309**(1): 71–82.

Flegal, K. M. et al. (2008). Comparisons of percentage body fat, body mass index, waist circumference, and waist-stature ratio in adults. *American Journal of Clinical Nutrition* **89**: 500–508.

Fogelholm, M. (2010). Physical activity, fitness and fatness: relations to mortality, morbidity and disease risk factors. A systematic review. *Obesity Reviews* **11**: 202–221.

Ford, E. S., L. M. Maynard, and C. Li (2014). Trends in mean waist circumference and abdominal obesity among US adults, 1999–2012. *JAMA* **312**(11): 1151–1153.

Foster, G. D. et al. (2003). Primary care physicians' attitudes about obesity and its treatment. *Obesity Reviews* **11**(10): 1168–1177.

Fountain, H. (2002). Our just (burp!) desserts. New York Times, 11/13/02.

FRAC (2011). A Tightening Squeeze: The Declining Expenditures on Food by American Households. Food Research and Action Center, U.S. Department of Agriculture.

Freedman, D. S. et al. (2005a). Racial differences in the tracking of childhood BMI to adulthood. *Obesity Research* **13**: 928–935.

Friedlander, S. L. et al. (2003). Decreased quality of life associated with obesity in school-aged children. *Archives of Pediatrics & Adolescent Medicine* **157**: 1206–1211.

Frisancho, A. R. (1993). Human Adaptation and Accommodation. Ann Arbor: University of Michigan Press.

Frolik, C. (2012). Overfed, sedentary pets packing on the pounds. Dayton Daily News, 05/21/12.

Gallagher, D. et al. (2005). Adipose tissue in muscle: a novel depot similar in size to visceral adipose tissue. *American Journal of Clinical Nutrition* **81**: 903–910.

Galtier-Dereure, F., C. Boegner, and J. Bringer (2000). Obesity and pregnancy: complications and cost. *American Journal of Clinical Nutrition* **71**(5): 1242S-1248S.

Geier, A. et al. (2007). The relationship between relative weight and school attendance among elementary schoolchildren. *Obesity* **15**(8): 2157–2161.

Goldberg, C. (2000). Citing intolerance, obese people take steps to press cause. New York Times, 11/5/00.

Gomez-Ambrosi, J. et al. (2014). Increased cardiometabolic risk factors and inflammation in adipose tissue in obesity subjects classified as metabolically healthy. *Diabetes Care* **37**: 2813–2821.

Goodman, A. H. and T. L. Leatherman (2001). Traversing the chasm between biology and culture: an introduction. *In* Building a New Biocultural Synthesis: Political-Economic Perspectives on Human Biology. A. H. Goodman and T. L. Leatherman, eds. pp. 3–41. Linking Levels of Analysis. Ann Arbor: University of Michigan Press.

Gorber, S. C. et al. (2007). A comparison of direct vs. self-report measures for assessing height, weight and body mass index: a systematic review. *Obesity Reviews* **8**: 307–326.

Gordon-Larsen, P. et al. (2004). Five-year obesity incidence in the transition period between adolescence and adulthood: the National Longitudinal Study of Adolescent Health. *American Journal of Clinical Nutrition* **80**(3): 569–575.

Gordon-Larsen, P. and B. M. Popkin (2005). Global perspectives on adolescent obesity. *In* Childhood Obesity: Contemporary Issues. N. Cameron, N. G. Norgan, and G. T. H. Ellison, eds. pp. 13–23. Boca Raton: CRC - Taylor & Francis.

Grieve, E. et al. (2013). The disproportionate economic burden associated with severe and complicated obesity: a systematic review. *Obesity Reviews* **14**(11): 883–894.

Guo, S. et al. (2002). Predicting overweight and obesity in adulthood from body mass index values in childhood and adolescence. *American Journal of Clinical Nutrition* **76**: 653–658.

Guthman, J. (2011). Weighing In: Obesity, Food Justice, and the Limits of Capitalism. Berkeley: University of California Press.

Guthman, J. (2013). Fatuous measures: the artifactual construction of the obesity epidemic. *Critical Public Health* **23**(3): 263–273.

Hannon, T. S., G. Rao, and S. A. Arslanian (2005). Childhood obesity and type 2 diabetes mellitus. *Pediatrics* **116**(2): 473–480.

Haskell, K. (2002). Sizing up teenagers. New York Times, 10/13/02.

Higgins, M. (2010). Practical traveler: excuse me, is this seat taken? New York Times, 2/28/10.

Hill, J. O. et al. (2003). Obesity and the environment: where do we go from here? *Science* **299**: 853–855.

Hirko, K. A. et al. (2015). Body mass index in young adulthood, obesity trajectory, and premature mortality.

Hossain, P., B. Kawar, and M. El Nahas (2007). Obesity and diabetes in the developing world – a growing challenge. *NEJM* **356**(3): 213–215.

Hu, F. B. (2008). Obesity Epidemiology. New York: Oxford University Press.

Hu, H. H., K. S. Nayak, and M. I. Goran (2011). Assessment of abdominal adipose tissue and organ fat content by magnetic resonance imaging. *Obesity Reviews* **12**(5): e504–e515.

Huang, K.-C. (2008). Obesity and its related diseases in Taiwan. *Obesity Reviews* **9**(s1): 32–34.

Hubbard, V. S. (2000). Defining overweight and obesity: what are the issues? *American Journal of Clinical Nutrition* **72**(5): 1067–1068.

Huss-Ashmore, R. (1980). Fat and fertility; demographic implications of differential fat storage. *Yearbook of Physical Anthropology* **23**: 65–91.

Jackson-Leach, R. and T. Lobstein (2006). Estimated burden of paediatric obesity and co-morbidities in Europe. Part 1. The increase in the prevalence of child obesity in Europe is itself increasing. *International Journal of Pediatric Obesity* **1**: 26–32.

Jacobson, B. C. et al. (2006). Body-mass index and symptoms of gastroesophageal reflux in women. *New England Journal of Medicine* **354**: 2340–2348.

Jago, R. et al. (2006). Prevalence of abnormal lipid and blood pressure values among an ethnically diverse population of eighth-grade adolescents and screening implications. *Pediatrics* **117**(6): 2065–2073.

Johnson, W. et al. (2012). A changing pattern of childhood BMI growth during the 20th century: 70 y of data from the Fels Longitudinal Study. *American Journal of Clinical Nutrition* **95**: 1136–1143.

Johnson, W. D. et al. (2009). Prevalence of risk factors for metabolic syndrome in adolescents: National Health and Nutrition Examination Survey (NHANES), 2001–2006. *Archives of Pediatrics & Adolescent Medicine* **163**(4): 371–377.

Julier, A. (2008). The political economy of obesity: the fat pay all. *In* Food and Culture: A Reader. C. Counihan and P. Van Esterik, eds. pp. 482–499. New York: Routledge.

Katzmarzyk, P. T. et al. (2010). Racial differences in abdominal depot-specific adiposity in white and African American adults. *American Journal of Clinical Nutrition* **91**: 7–15.

Katzmarzyk, P. T., S. B. Heymsfield, and C. Bourchard (2013). Clinical utility of visceral adipose tissue for the identification of cardiometabolic risk in white and African American adults. *American Journal of Clinical Nutrition* **97**(3): 480–486.

Kim, D. and I. Kawachi (2008). Obesity and health-related quality of life. *In* Obesity Epidemiology. F. B. Hu, ed. pp. 234–260. New York: Oxford University Press.

Kim, J-E. et al. (2015). Risk and injury severity of obese child passengers in motor vehicle crashes. *Obesity* **23**: 644–652.

Kleinfeld, N. R. (2006). Diabetics in the workplace confront a tangle of laws. New York Times, 12/26/06.

Knittle, J. L. et al. (1979). The growth of adipose tissue in children and adolescents. Cross sectional and longitudinal studies of adipose cell number and size. *Journal of Clinical Investigation* **63**: 239–246.

Ko, G. T. C. and J. C. N. Chan (2008). Burden of obesity – lessons learnt from Hong Kong Chinese. *Obesity Reviews* **9**(s1): 35–40.

Komlos, J. and M. Brabec (2010). The trend of mean BMI values of US adults, birth cohorts 1882–1986 indicates that the obesity epidemic began earlier than hitherto thought. *American Journal of Human Biology* **22**: 631–638.

Komlos, J., A. Breitfelder, and M. Sunder (2009). The transition to post-industrial BMI values among US children. *American Journal of Human Biology* **21**: 151–160.

Komlos, J. and B. E. Lauderdale (2007). Underperformance in affluence: the remarkable relative decline in US heights in the second half of the 20th century. *Social Science Quarterly* **88**(2): 283–305.

Kramer, C. K., B. Zinman, and R. Retnakaran (2013). Are metabolically healthy overweight and obesity benign conditions? A systematic review and meta-analysis. *Annals of Internal Medicine* **159**: 758–769.

Krugman, P. (2005). Girth of a nation. New York Times, 7/4/05.

Kuczynski, A. (2001). Charting the outer limits of inner beauty. New York Times, 11/11/01.

Kuk, J. L. et al. (2006). Visceral fat is an independent predictor of all-cause mortality in men. *Obesity* **14**(2): 336–341.

Kumar, J. et al. (2009). Prevalence and associations of 25-hydroxyvitamin D deficiencies in US children. *Pediatrics* **124**: e362–e370.

Langin, D. et al. (2009). Adipose tissue development, anatomy and functions. *In* Obesity: Science to Practice. G. Williams and G. Fruehbeck, eds. pp. 78–108. West Sussex, UK: John Wiley & Sons.

Leonard, W. R. (2010). Size counts: evolutionary perspectives on physical activity and body size from early hominids to modern humans. *Journal of Physical Activity and Health* **7**(Suppl 3): S284–S298.

Leonard, W. R. (2014). The global diversity of eating patterns: human nutritional health in comparative perspective. *Physiology & Behavior* **134**: 5–14.

Leone, N. et al. (2009). Lung function impairment and metabolic syndrome: the critical role of abdominal obesity. *American Journal of Respiratory Critical Care Medicine* **179**: 509–516.

Levi, J. et al. (2011). F as in Fat: How Obesity Threatens America's Future 2011. Trust for America's Health, Robert Wood Johnson Foundation.

Li, C. et al. (2007). Increasing trends in waist circumference and abdominal obesity among U.S. adults. *Obesity* **15**: 216–224.

Li, C. et al. (2006). Recent trends in waist circumference and waist-height ratio among US children and adolescents. *Pediatrics* **118**: 1390–1398.

Li, Q. et al. (2015). The economic burden of obesity by glycemic state in the United States. *PharmacoEconomics* doi 10.1007/s40273-014-0248-5.

Lobstein, T. and R. Jackson-Leach (2006). Estimated burden of paediatric obesity and co-morbidities in Europe. Part 2. Numbers of children with indicators of obesity-related disease. *International Journal of Pediatric Obesity* **1**: 33–41.

Lohman, T. G., A. F. Roche, and R. Martorell (1988). Anthropometric Standardization Reference Manual, abridged edition. Champaign, IL: Human Kinetics.

Ludwig, D. S. (2007). Childhood obesity – the shape of things to come. *New England Journal of Medicine* **357**(23): 2325–2327.

Lundborg, P., P. Nystedt, and D-O. Rooth (2014). Body size, skills, and income: evidence from 150,000 teenage siblings. *Demography* **51**(5): 1573–1596.

Lutsiv, O. et al. (2015). The effects of morbid obesity on maternal and neonatal health outcomes: a systematic review and meta-analysis. *Obesity Reviews* **16**(7): 531–546.

Lyons, P. (2009). Prescription for harm: diet industry influence, public health policy, and the "obesity epidemic". In The Fat Studies Reader. E. Rothblum and S. Solovay, eds. pp. 75–87. New York: New York University Press.

Maher, K. (2012). Boat operators struggle with heavier load. Wall Street Journal, 05/08/12.

Matter, K. C. et al. (2007). A comparison of the characteristics of injuries between obese and non-obese inpatients. *Obesity* **15**: 2384–2390.

May, A. L., E. V. Kuklina, and P. W. Yoon (2012). Prevalence of cardiovascular disease risk factors among US adolescents, 1999–2008. *Pediatrics* **129**(6): 1035–1041.

McDonald, S. et al. (2010). Overweight and obesity in mothers and risk of preterm birth and low birth weight infants: systematic review and meta-analysis. *British Medical Journal* **341**: c3428.

McKenzie, I. A. et al. (2014). Motor skill learning requires active central myelination. *Science* **346**(6207): 318.

Mehta, T. et al. (2014). Obesity and mortality: are the risks declining? Evidence from multiple prospective studies in the United States. *Obesity Reviews* **15**(8): 619–629.

Metwally, M., W. L. Ledger, and T. C. Li (2008). Reproductive endocrinology and clinical aspects of obesity in women. *Ann NY Acad Sci* **1127**: 140–146.

Miller, L. S. (2015). Adipocytes armed against *Staphylococcus aureus*. *New England Journal of Medicine* **372**(14): 1368–1370.

Mills, J. L. et al. (2010). Maternal obesity and congenital heart defects: a population-based study. *American Journal of Clinical Nutrition* **91**(6): 1543–1549.

Mitka, M. (2005). Obesity's role in heart disease requires apples and pears comparison. *JAMA* **294**(24): 3071–3072.

Moffat, T. (2010). The "childhood obesity epidemic": health crisis or social construction? *Medical Anthropology Quarterly* **24**(1): 1–21.

Mokdad, A. H. (2009). The Behavioral Risk Factors Surveillance System: past, present, and future. *Annual Review of Public Health* **30**: 43–54.

Moyer, M. W. (2014). Why turning down the thermostat could help win the battle of the bulge. *Scientific American* **311**(2): 30–32.

Muenning, P. et al. (2006). Gender and the burden of disease attributable to obesity. *American Journal of Public Health* **96**(9): 1662–1668.

Muoio, D. and C. B. Newgard (2014). The good in fat. *Nature* **516**: 49–50.

Muratova, V. N. et al. (2002). The relation of obesity to cardiovascular risk factors among children: the CARDIAC project. *West Virginia Medical Journal* **98**(6): 263–267.

Murray, C. J. L. (2013). The State of US Health, 1990–2010. *JAMA* 310(6): 591–606.

NCHS (2011). Health, United States, 2010: In Brief. National Center for Health Statistics, Centers for Disease Control and Prevention, U.S. Department of Health and Human Services.

Neovius, K. et al. (2008). Obesity status and sick leave: a systematic review. *Obesity Reviews* **10**(1): 17–27.

Neuman, M. et al. (2011). The poor stay thinner: stable socioeconomic gradients in BMI among women in lower- and middle-income countries. *American Journal of Clinical Nutrition* **94**(5): 1348–1357.

Ng, M. et al. (2014). Global, regional, and national prevalence of overweight and obesity in children and adults during 1980–2013: a systematic analysis for the Global Burden of Disease Study 2013. *The Lancet* **384**(9945): 766–781.

Nisbet, A. C. (2006). Intramuscular gluteal injections in the increasingly obese population: retrospective study. *British Medical Journal* **332**: 637–638.

Norgan, N. G. (1997). The beneficial effects of body fat and adipose tissue in humans. *International Journal of Obesity* **21**: 738–746.

O'Neill, S. and L. O'Driscoll (2015). Metabolic syndrome: a closer look at the growing epidemic and its associated pathologies. *Obesity Reviews* **16**: 1–12.

O'Sullivan, A. J. (2008). Does oestrogen allow women to store fat more efficiently? A biological advantage for fertility and gestation. *Obesity Reviews* **10**: 168–177.

Ogden, C. L. et al. (2007). The epidemiology of obesity. *Gastroenterology* **132**: 2087–2102.

Ogden, C.L. et al. (2012). Prevalence of obesity and trends in body mass index among US children and adolescents. *JAMA* **307**(5): 483–490.

Ogden, C. L. et al. (2014a). Prevalence of childhood and adult obesity in the United States, 2011–2012. *JAMA* **311**(8): 806–814.

Ogden, C. L. et al. (2014b). Prevalence of childhood and adult obesity in the United States, 2011–2012. *JAMA* **311**(8): 806–814.

Olatunbosun, S. T., J. S. Kaufman, and A. F. Bella (2011). Prevalence of obesity and overweight in urban adult Nigerians. *Obesity Reviews* **12**: 233–241.

Onishi, N. (2008). Japan, seeking trim waists, measures millions. New York Times, 6/13/08.

Orpana, H. M. et al. (2009). BMI and mortality: results from a national longitudinal study of Canadian adults.

Papandreou, C. et al. (2008). Obesity in Mediterranean region (1997–2007): a systematic review. *Obesity Reviews* **9**: 389–399.

Patel, A. V., J. S. Hildebrand, and S. M. Gapstur (2014). Body mass index and all-cause mortality in a large prospective cohort of white and black U.S. adults. *In* PLOS One. pp. e109153, Vol. 9.

PCP (2007). 2006–2007 Annual Report. President's Cancer Panel.

Pecht, T. et al. (2014). Peripheral blood leucocyte subclasses as potential biomarkers of adipose tissue inflammation and obesity subphenotypes in humans. *Obesity Reviews* **15**(4): 322–337.

Pelletier, D. L. et al. (1995). The effects of malnutrition on child mortality in developing countries. *Bulletin of the World Health Organization* **73**(4): 443–448.

Pereira-Santos, M. et al. (2015). Obesity and vitamin D deficiency: a systematic review and meta-analysis. *Obesity Reviews* **16**(4): 341–349.

Perez-Pena, R. (2006). Dialysis in N.Y. lags as diabetes ruins kidneys. New York Times, 12/28/06.

Perez-Pena, R. and G. Glickson (2003). As obesity rises, health care indignities multiply. New York Times, 11/29/03.

Pietilainen, K. H. et al. (2011). Association of lipidome remodeling in the adipocyte membrane with acquired obesity in humans. *PLoS Biology* **9**(6): e1000623–e1001077.

Pischon, T. et al. (2008). General and abdominal adiposity and risk of death in Europe. *New England Journal of Medicine* **359**(20): 2105–2120.

Pogrebin, R. (2004). Soprano says her weight cost her role in London. New York Times, 3/9/04.

Pollack, K. M. et al. (2007). Association between Body Mass Index and acute traumatic workplace injury in hourly manufacturing employees. *American Journal of Epidemiology* **166**(2): 204–211.

Pollack, K. M. et al. (2008). Body mass index and injury risk among US children 9–15 years old in motor vehicle crashes. *Injury Prevention* **14**(6): 366–371.

Pond, C. M. (1998). The Fats of Life. Cambridge: Cambridge University Press.

Pond, C. M. (2005). Adipose tissue and the immune system. *Prostaglandins, Leukotrienes, and Essential Fatty Acids* **73**: 17–30.

Poobalan, A. et al. (2004). Effects of weight loss in overweight/obese individuals and long-term lipid outcomes – a systematic review. *Obesity Reviews* **5**: 43–50.

Poobalan, A. S. et al. (2008). Obesity as an independent risk factor for elective and emergency caesarean delivery in nulliparous women – systematic review and meta-analysis of cohort studies. *Obesity Reviews* **10**(1): 28–35.

Popkin, B. M. and P. Gordon-Larsen (2004). The nutrition transition: worldwide obesity dynamics and their determinants. *International Journal of Obesity* **28**: S2–S9.

Popkin, B. M. and S. J. Nielsen (2003). The sweetening of the world's diet. *Obesity Research* **11**(11): 1325–1332.

Prentice, A. M., and S. A. Jebb (2001). Beyond body mass index. *Obesity Reviews* **2**: 141–147.

Prescott, H. C. et al. (2014). Obesity and 1-year outcomes in older Americans with severe sepsis. *Critical Care Medicine* **42**(8): 1766–1774.

Price, R. A. et al. (1993). Obesity in Pima Indians: large increases among post-World War II birth cohorts. *American Journal of Physical Anthropology* **92**: 473–479.

Puhl, R. and K. D. Brownell (2006). Confronting and coping with weight stigma: an investigation of overweight and obese adults. *Obesity* **14**(10): 1802–1815.

Puhl, R. M. and C. A. Heuer (2009). The stigma of obesity: a review and update. *Obesity* **17**(5): 941–964.

Puhl, R. M., J. L. Peterson, and J. Luedicke (2013). Weight-based victimization: bullying experiences of weight loss treatment-seeking youth. *Pediatrics* **131**(1): e1–e9.

Raatikainen, K., N. Heiskanen, and S. Heinonen (2006). Transition from overweight to obesity worsens pregnancy outcome in a BMI-dependent manner. *Obesity Research* **14**: 165–171.

Ramsay, J. E. and I. Sattar Greer, N. (2006). ABC of obesity: obesity and reproduction. *British Medical Journal* **333**: 1159–1162.

Rasmussen, K. M. and C. L. Kjolhede (2004). Prepregnant overweight and obesity diminish the prolactin response to suckling in the first week postpartum. *Pediatrics* **113**(5): e465–e471.

Ravussin, E., and L. P. Kozak (2009). Have we entered the brown adipose tissue renaissance? *Obesity Reviews* **10**: 265–268.

Ravussin, E. et al. (1994). Effects of a traditional lifestyle on obesity in Pima Indians. *Diabetes Care* **17**(9): 1067–1074.

Richmond, T. K. et al. (2015). Racial/ethnic differences in accuracy of body mass index reporting in a diverse cohort of young adults. *International Journal of Obesity* **39**: 546–548.

Robinson, M. K. (2009). Surgical treatment of obesity – weighing the facts. *New England Journal of Medicine* **361**: 520–521.

Roche, A. F. (1992). Growth, Maturation, and Body Composition: The Fels Longitudinal Study 1929–1991. Cambridge: Cambridge University Press.

Rolland, Y. et al. (2014). Body-composition predictors of mortality in women aged >75 y: data from a large population-based cohort study with a 17-y follow-up. *American Journal of Clinical Nutrition* **100**(5): 1352–1360.

Rosenbaum, M. et al. (2008). Long-term persistence of adaptive thermogenesis in subjects who have maintained a reduced body weight. *American Journal of Clinical Nutrition* **88**(4): 906–912.

Rothblum, E. D. (2011). Fat studies. *In* The Oxford Handbook of the Social Science of Obesity. J. Cawley, ed. pp. 173–183. New York: Oxford University Press.

Rundle, A. et al. (2007). The urban built environment and obesity in New York City: a multilevel analysis. *American Journal of Health Promotion* **21**(4s): 326–334.

Ruth, D. (2006). New study shows teenage girls' use of diet pills doubles over five-year span.

Saul, S. (2008). Priced out of weight loss camp. New York Times, 8/16/08.

Sciolino, E. (2006). France battles a problem that grows and grows: fat. New York Times, 1/25/06.

Sheeran, T. and K. Franko (2012). Obese 9-year-old boy removed from Ohio home sheds 50 lbs, is allowed to return to mom's care. The Washington Post, 05/11/12.

Shetty, P. (2012). India's diabetic time bomb. *Nature* **485**: s14–s16.

Shultz, S. P., J. Anner, and A. P. Hills (2009). Paediatric obesity, physical activity and the musculoskeletal system. *Obesity Reviews* **10**(5): 576–582.

Silk, A. W. and K. M. McTigue (2010). Reexamining the physical examination for obese patients. *New England Journal of Medicine* **305**(2): 193–194.

Singh, A. S. et al. (2008). Tracking of childhood overweight into adulthood: a systematic review of the literature. *Obesity Reviews* **9**(5): 474–488.

Sise, A. and F. K. Friedenberg (2008). A comprehensive review of gastroesophageal reflux disease and obesity. *Obesity Reviews* **9**(3): 194–203.

St. John, W. (2003). On the final journey, one size doesn't fit all. New York Times, 9/28/03.

Stearns, P. N. (2002). Fat History: Bodies and Beauty in the Modern West. New York: New York University Press.

Stecker, T. and S. Sparks (2006). Prevalence of obese patients in a primary care setting. *Obesity Research* **14**: 373–376.

Stefan, N. et al. (2008). Identification and characterization of metabolically benign obesity in humans. *Archives of Internal Medicine* **168**(15): 1609–1616.

Stewart, S. T., D. M. Cutler, and A. B. Rosen (2009). Forecasting the effects of obesity and smoking on U.S. life expectancy. *New England Journal of Medicine* **361**: 2252–2260.

Stotland, N. E. (2008). Pregnancy plus: obesity and pregnancy. *British Medical Journal* **337**: a2450.

Subak, L. L. et al. (2009). Weight loss to treat urinary incontinence in overweight and obese women. *New England Journal of Medicine* **360**(5): 633–640.

Suvan, J. et al. (2011). Association between overweight, obesity and periodontitis in adults: a systematic review. *Obesity Reviews* **12**(5): e381–e404.

Taveras, E. M. et al. (2011). Crossing growth percentiles in infancy and risk of obesity in childhood. *Archives of Pediatrics & Adolescent Medicine* **165**(11): 993–998.

Taylor, E. D. et al. (2006). Orthopedic complications of overweight in children and adolescents. *Pediatrics* **117**(6): 2167–2174.

The, N. S. et al. (2010). Association of adolescent obesity with risk of severe obesity in adulthood. *JAMA* **304**(18): 2042–2047.

Thorpe, K. E. and M. Philyaw (2012). The medicalization of chronic disease and costs. *Annual Review of Public Health* **33**: 409–423.

Tillotson, J. E. (2004). America's obesity: conflicting public policies, industrial economic development, and unintended human consequences. *Annual Review of Nutrition* **24**: 617–643.

Trifiletti, L. B. et al. (2006). Tipping the scales: obese children and child safety seats. *Pediatrics* **117**(4): 1197–1202.

Trogdon, J. G. et al. (2008). Indirect costs of obesity: a review of the current literature. *Obesity Reviews* **9**: 489–500.

Tully, M. A., J. Panter, and D. Ogilvie (2014). Individual characteristics associated with mismatches between self-reported and accelerometer-measured physical activity. *PLoS One* **9**(6): e99636.

Tunceli, K., K. Li, and L. K. Williams (2006). Long-term effects of obesity on employment and work limitations among U.S. adults, 1986 to 1999. *Obesity* **14**(9): 1637–1646.

Turer, C. B., H. Lin, and G. Flores (2013). Prevalence of vitamin D deficiency among overweight and obese US children. *Pediatrics* **131**(1): e152–e161.

Ulijaszek, S. J. (2008). Seven models of population obesity. *Angiology* **59**(Suppl 2): 34S–38S.

Ulijaszek, S. J., F. E. Johnston, and Preece M. A., eds. (1998). The Cambridge Encyclopedia of Human Growth and Development. Cambridge: Cambridge University Press.

Ulijaszek, S. J. and H. Lofink (2006). Obesity in biocultural perspective. *Annual Review of Anthropology* **35**: 337–360.

USDHHS (2001). The Surgeon General's Call to Action to Prevent and Decrease Overweight and Obesity 2001. U.S. Department of Health and Human Services.

Villamor, E. et al. (2006). Trends in obesity, underweight, and wasting among women attending prenatal clinics in urban Tanzania, 1995–2004. *American Journal of Clinical Nutrition* **83**(6): 1387–1394.

Virtanen, K. A. et al. (2009). Functional brown adipose tissue in healthy adults. *New England Journal of Medicine* **360**(15): 1518–1525.

Wadden, T. A., D. A. Anderson, and G. D. Foster (1999). Two-year changes in lipids and lipoproteins associated with maintenance of 5% to 10% reduction in initial weight: some findings and some questions. *Obesity Research* **7**(2): 170–178.

Wang, F. et al. (2005). BMI, physical activity, and health care utilization/costs among medicare retirees. *Obesity Research* **13**: 1450–1457.

Wang, W. et al. (2015). The relationship between excess body weight and the risk of death from unnatural causes. *Accident Analysis & Prevention* **80**: 229–235.

Wang, Y. and M. A. Beydoun (2007). The obesity epidemic in the United States – gender, age, socioeconomic, racial/ethnic, and geographic characteristics: a systematic review and meta-regression analysis. *Epidemiological Reviews* **29**: 6–28.

Wang, Y. and T. Lobstein (2006). Worldwide trends in childhood overweight and obesity. *International Journal of Pediatric Obesity* **1**: 11–25.

Wang, Y. C. et al. (2011). Health and economic burden of the projected obesity trends in the USA and the UK. *The Lancet* **378**: 815–825.

Wearing, S. C. et al. (2006). Musculoskeletal disorders associated with obesity: a biomechanical perspective. *Obesity Reviews* **7**(3): 239–250.

Wells, J. C. K. (2014). Commentary: the paradox of body mass index in obesity assessment: not a good index of adiposity, but not a bad index of cardio-metabolic risk. *International Journal of Epidemiology* **43**(3): 672–674.

Wen, M. and L. Kowaleski-Jones (2012). Sex and ethnic differences in validity of self-reported adult height, weight and Body Mass Index. *Ethnicity & Disease* **22**: 72.

WHO (2009). Obesity and Overweight. New York.

WHO (2015). WHO Global Infobase: Data for Saving Lives. *In* www.who.int/infobase/comparisons.aspx.

Wild, S. et al. (2004). Global prevalence of diabetes: estimates for the year 2000 and projections for 2030. *Diabetes Care* **27**(5): 1047–1053.

Wildman, R. E. C. and D. M. Medeiros (2000). Advanced Human Nutrition. Boca Raton: CRC Press.

Wolf, A. M., J. E. Manson, and G. A. Colditz (2003). The economic impact of overweight, obesity, and weight loss. *In* Obesity: Mechanisms and Clinical Management. R. H. Eckel, ed. pp. 523–549. Philadelphia: Lippincott, Williams & Wilkins.

Xi, B. et al. (2011). Secular trends in the prevalence of general and abdominal obesity among Chinese adults, 1993–2009. *Obesity Reviews* **13**(3): 287–296.

Xi, B., J. Mi, and M. Zhao (2014). Trends in abdominal obesity among US children and adolescents. *Pediatrics* **134**(2): e334–e339.

Xu, Y. et al. (2013). Prevalence and control of diabetes in Chinese adults. *JAMA* **310**(9): 948–955.

Yanovski, S. Z. and J. A. Yanovski (2011). Obesity prevalence in the United States – up, down, or sideways? *New England Journal of Medicine* **364**(11): 987–989.

Zagorsky, J. L. (2005). Health and wealth: the late-20th century obesity epidemic in the U.S. *Economics and Human Biology* **3**: 296–313.

Zajacova, A. (2011). Overweight adults may have the lowest mortality – do they have the best health? *American Journal of Epidemiology* **173**(4): 430–437.

Zechner, R. and F. Madeo (2009). Another way to get rid of fat. *Nature* **4458**: 1118–1119.

Zephier, E. et al. (2006). Increasing prevalences of overweight and obesity in Northern Plains American Indian children. *Archives of Pediatrics & Adolescent Medicine* **160**: 34–39.

Zhang, L. et al. (2015). Dermal adipocytes protect against *Staphylococcus aureus* skin infection. *Science* **347**(6217): 67–71.

Zhu, S. et al. (2005). Race-ethnicity-specific waist circumference cutoffs for identifying cardiovascular disease risk factors. *American Journal of Clinical Nutrition* **81**(2): 409–415.

Zhu, S. et al. (2006). Obesity and risk for death due to motor vehicle crashes. *Am J Public Health* **96**(4): 734–739.

2

ORIGINS OF OBESITY IN HUMAN EVOLUTION

Introduction

The question "Why do so many Americans have obesity?" has several answers. Both the bountiful food supply and labor-saving technology of modern life and the ancient evolutionary heritage of the human species are responsible for the high prevalence of obesity in the US. All humans today have inherited a highly efficient metabolic system perfected during millions of years of human evolution. It was designed for storing a great deal of energy within the human body to be readily available at all times. During periods of food scarcity and nutritional stress, conditions faced by some populations even today, this energy store functioned as a special adaptation to prevent death by starvation and to ensure the survival of *Homo sapiens*. A look deep into the human past at its evolutionary origins helps to explain this powerful ability to store energy.

Paleoanthropologists usually assess skeletal changes to trace the course of human evolution – modification of the primate postcranial skeleton to accommodate human bipedal walking, changes in dentition and bony features of the skull, and increases in the size of the cranium that houses the brain. Human *energetics*, the gradually increasing efficiency in obtaining and using higher-quality foods to meet increasing human energy needs, can also be tracked in the fossil and archaeological records and even in the human genome. Some ancient *hominin* relatives became extinct because they could not acquire and maintain an adequate energy supply for both body maintenance and reproduction. However, the direct ancestors of modern humans succeeded by diversifying their food supply, increasing nutrient and energy extraction from foods through technology, developing new food sources, and improving metabolic efficiency. The capacity to store great amounts of energy as body fat is one part of this constellation of behavioral and biological adaptations to nutritional stress and is deeply embedded in human genes and metabolic systems. It enabled human ancestors to survive the rigors of the past, but today it is a major contributor to the obesity epidemic.

Adaptation, or adjustment to environmental conditions to survive, has several forms (Frisancho 1993), and humans have used all of them. This chapter will describe the unique constellation of inherited (genetic) adaptations, developmental adjustments, functional and physiological accommodations, and cultural techniques that evolved from early prehistory to the present day to optimize human energy acquisition and storage and maintain metabolic homeostasis.

Humans are primates

Along with prosimians, monkeys and apes, the species *Homo sapiens* belongs to the *Order Primates*, a taxonomic group noted for its unique physical and behavioral traits and eclectic diets. Similarities in adiposity, metabolism, and genetics of obesity (Bousquet-Mélou et al. 1995; Comuzzie et al. 2003; Schwartz and Kemnitz 1992; Woods et al. 1988) reflect the common evolutionary ancestry of humans and other primates. Compared to other mammals, primates expend only about half the expected daily energy for physical activities and body maintenance, a metabolic adaptation that allows for greater allocation of energy to the development and functioning of their relatively large brains, while also slowing daily growth rates and extending lifespans (Pontzer et al. 2014). All primates seek out a variety of nutrient-dense, high-quality foods to support their active lives, relatively large brains, and long gestation and lactation periods; humans have simply carried this to extremes (Milton 1993; Schoeninger 2014). Because of the shared primate history and biology, it is worth taking a closer look at the dietary and activity habits of great apes, humans' nearest primate relatives, for clues to the nutritional past and evolutionary origins of modern human obesity.

The largest non-human primates, the great apes of Africa and Asia — bonobos, chimpanzees, gorillas, orangutans — are remnants of a once very large and diverse group of grassland and forest dwellers that lived from 23 to 5 million years ago (Hartwig 2007). After that time, global climate changes reduced the once uninterrupted forest cover extending over much of Africa, Asia, and Europe to patches interspersed with woodlands, grassy savannas and deserts. Tropical forests disappeared altogether in Europe and most of Asia. The loss of their natural habitat and stiff competition from the growing number of monkey species that thrived in this novel habitat brought the great Age of Apes to an end. The few survivors, including the common African ancestor of humans, chimpanzees, and gorillas, took refuge in the remaining forest patches and survived on sweet fruits and diverse vegetation there.

Living apes and humans share a genetic trait that evolved during this time of dramatic environmental change (Johnson and Andrews 2010). This mutation silences the uricase gene coding for an enzyme that degrades uric acid. A diet of meats and fruits typical of both humans and apes therefore elevates uric acid due to the absence of uricase. Fructose (the sugar in fruits) in the presence of uric acid stimulates fat storage in the abdomen and liver (*lipogenesis*), an adaptive advantage during periods of nutritional stress.

About seven million years ago hominins diverged from their ape relatives, stood up on their hind legs, and walked about in the forest on two feet instead of four while still retaining some skeletal features to enable them to climb trees. Dietary and activity patterns of these earliest human ancestors were probably very similar to those of today's living great apes in the African rainforests. For several million years they continued to share the forest habitat with the apes, but eventually they moved to the more open woodlands and savanna to establish a new lifestyle.

The first primates had appeared about 65 million years ago as descendants of tiny insect-eating mammals that scurried about on the forest floor. These ancient ancestors adopted an arboreal lifestyle and a diet of fruits, gum, flowers, nectar, seeds, and foliage to supplement the protein-rich insects they preyed upon in the treetops (Cartmill 1972; Milton 1993). Extant prosimians, the direct descendants of these early primates, still retain some of these food habits, and the smallest of them are nearly exclusive insect-eaters, getting most of their food energy from protein (Gursky 2007).

Monkeys and apes, also descended from those early primates, consume a variety of plant resources, even including tree bark, but prefer a diet of young leaves and fruits (Robinson and Janson 1987). These high-quality foods provide protein and simple carbohydrates and contain little indigestible fiber and plant toxin. Small amounts of animal foods – insects, grubs, eggs, birds, small mammals – add a little more protein and fat (Utami and Van Hooff 1997). On the whole, monkeys and apes are primarily herbivores, deriving most of their nutrients from many types of plants, diversifying their diet to minimize fiber and plant toxin content, but also consuming some animal protein.

Some monkeys have specialized digestive systems to accommodate high-fiber, low-energy mature leaves, which are very difficult to digest but are always readily available. Leaf-eating monkeys have sacculated stomachs with special fermentation chambers for bacterial breakdown of cellulose to produce energy-rich carbohydrates (Milton 1987). Their long colons allow food to pass through slowly for maximum nutrient absorption. Gorillas, the largest of the great apes dependent on leafy diets, lack the sacculated stomach but also possess an extremely large colon, which makes up almost half the volume of the digestive tract (Remis 2003; Schmidt et al. 2005). They slowly digest and ferment fibrous leaves, bark, pith, stems, and shoots of various plants, which they eat in huge quantities throughout the day. To aid digestion and conserve energy, gorillas move slowly through the landscape and lounge around a great deal, gently playing, grooming each other, and napping.

Chimpanzees and bonobos are the great apes most genetically similar to humans. Although their gut proportions are comparable to those of gorillas, they consume much richer foods that are more easily digested, especially high-carbohydrate fruits. Their diet allows for faster digestion and intestinal transport, which helps to prevent poisoning by plant toxins (Strier 1993). They avoid extremely fibrous fruits and other plants, or stash them as wedges in their cheeks until every bit of juice and pulp has been sucked out. Rather than swallowing the remaining fibrous masses, they spit them out (Goodall 1986).

Chimpanzees are smaller than gorillas and more active in their food search because of the uneven distribution of their much preferred fruits, and they more often include animal protein in their diets. Although plants are their primary source of protein (Malenky et al. 1994; Milton 1993), adult males hunt singly or in excited groups to aggressively pursue and capture small mammals such as bushpigs, bushbucks, and even monkeys (Boesch and Boesch-Achermann 2000; Goodall 1986). Isotope analysis has confirmed that some adult males regularly consume the meat of captured animals, while female chimpanzees are less likely to do so (Fahy et al. 2013). Jane Goodall and her colleagues have reported that about 5 percent of the diet of the common chimpanzees in Tanzania's Gombe Park consists of meat from red colobus monkeys and small African antelopes (Stanford 2001). From one such small animal a chimpanzee can derive as much protein and fat as from 3,000 of the figs that are its main food source (Wrangham et al. 1993). Meat is a highly prized food item, densely packed with essential nutrients and fats, but eaten much less frequently than vegetable matter. Meat also seems to have an important social function. It is the only food that is regularly shared with others or bartered for future cooperation and support (Stanford 2001). The successful hunter, even if he is the dominant male, reluctantly gives scraps and pieces of meat to begging friends and allies or to females with whom he may want to mate in the future. These lucky females may allow their clinging infants to get a taste by taking tiny pieces of flesh directly from their mouths.

Bonobos, the very rare chimpanzees of central Africa, have not been observed to hunt, but they are opportunistic meat eaters (De Waal and Lanting 1997; White 1996). They share the common chimpanzees' taste for meat and occasionally eat it, but seem to lack the aggressive drive to pursue prey. In contrast to the sometimes brutal chimpanzees, bonobos are well known for their avoidance of violence and aggression. Perhaps because their rainforest environment provides more fruit and tender terrestrial vegetation as well as grubs and other small protein sources than Gombe Park, they have no need to hunt.

Insects and nuts also provide protein, but require special skills to exploit. Female chimpanzees are especially expert tool users in their avid quest for termites and ants that provide significant amounts of fat and protein (Goodall 1986; McGrew 2001). They carefully prepare fishing wands by removing leaves from a twig or by breaking a strong grass stem to the appropriate length. Dipping their tools into a termite mound or anthill into which they have poked holes with their fingers, they quickly strip off the clinging insects with hands and lips and pop them into their mouths. Fire ants can give nasty bites, but the chimpanzees are willing to pay this price for the precious fat, protein, calcium, and vitamins the ants contain, and they eat them in substantial quantities. Tools also aid in cracking nuts that are too hard to be opened with teeth and jaws. With a large rock, log, or branch, wild chimpanzees in the Taï Forest of western Africa prepare an anvil, find an appropriate stone or chunk of wood to use as a hammer, collect a supply of nuts, and crack them open one after another (Boesch and Boesch-Achermann 2000). The resulting meal of protein and fat is well worth all the patience and effort, not to mention the many months and years of practice needed to develop nutcracking skills.

Some Taï Forest chimpanzees have also been observed spearing sleeping bushbabies, small primitive primates, with sharpened tools they fashioned of sturdy sticks chewed at one end (Pruetz and Bertolani 2007). After withdrawing the speared animals from their sleeping nests in tree hollows, they eat them with relish.

Goodall has noted that chimpanzees seem to crave variety, eating a large number of different plant foods – 184 vegetable foods from 141 species of trees and other plants at Gombe (Goodall 1986). Of these foods, about half are fruits and another quarter are leaves. On any given day an individual chimpanzee eats an average of 13 different food types, supplying them with healthy nutrient diversity.

Monkeys and apes must expend a great deal of energy to obtain food (Oates 1987; Strier 2003; Suarez 2006). Since food sharing is rare and food storage is totally unknown, they must forage individually every day. Even recently weaned youngsters can count on their mothers to do no more than lead them to appropriate food sources. Gorillas virtually live within their larder and can easily find plenty of edible vegetation in the trees and on the ground, but they have to travel each day to new food sources after exhausting the supply in one area (Tutin 1996; Watts 1996). Lowland gorillas travel more than 1 km per day, and venture even farther when they know that fruit is available. The fruits preferred by chimpanzees, while higher in nutrient quality than leafy vegetation, mature intermittently and are also more widely dispersed (Strier 2003; Wrangham et al. 1993). Not only must chimpanzees know when and where to find ripe fruit, they must also travel considerable distances to feeding sites; up to one-third of a chimpanzee's day is spent just traveling to find food. The Gombe chimpanzees trek 1 to 5 km per day in search of food, and spend 35 percent to 65 percent of their day feeding (Goodall 1986). Energy expenditure is an especially important consideration for large male chimpanzees and for mothers carrying and nursing young infants. Chimpanzee travel involves climbing trees and other strenuous activities such as leaping, suspensory movement from branch to branch and tree to tree, and walking on the ground. And sometimes vigorous displays and attacks are necessary to defend food sources from intruders and competitors (Wilson and Wrangham 2003).

Even though they eat almost continuously, wild chimpanzees and gorillas do not become obese. Caloric return for their physical efforts is rather low. Their predominantly vegetarian diet, although diverse and nutritious, provides virtually no excess energy to be stored for future use. The calories they do consume are used up in the daily effort of finding food. *Linear enamel hypoplasia* of the teeth, horizontal disruptions of enamel deposition due to periods of nutritional stress during dental development, are not infrequent in chimpanzees and other primates (Guatelli-Steinberg and Benderlioglu 2006; Hannibal and Guatelli-Steinberg 2005; Lukacs 2001).

That is not to say, however, that apes entirely lack the potential to gain weight. Apes confined in zoos or reserves, which do not have to forage and whose activity is constrained, may become obese. Most likely because of richer diets and lower activity levels, captive gorilla females are heavier than wild females, for instance (Leigh 1994). And captive primates can develop obesity-related metabolic abnormalities and comorbidities like cardiovascular disease and diabetes mellitus just as humans do (Howard and Yasuda 1990; Rosenblum et al. 1981; Shively and Clarkson 1988).

Under very special conditions, even wild primates become fat, but only tempo-rarily. After an annual fattening period when the main food is sugar-laden fruit, the nocturnal fat-tailed dwarf lemur of Madagascar enters a torpor phase lasting up to eight months (Mueller and Thalmann 2002). During fattening, these tiny primates nearly double their normal weight before entering torpor. They gradually decrease their activity and become very lethargic. The torpor phase coincides with a season of food shortage, so the cycle of fattening and inactivity seems to have the same function as hibernation in bears and other mammals.

Male squirrel monkeys of Central and South America become fattened in their shoulders and upper arms during the breeding season (Suarez 2006). Their testicles enlarge and sperm production increases. By the end of the six-month breeding season they have lost their extra layer of fat and are thin again. Their *dominance displays*, aggressive assaults, and sexual interactions end. From being the center of female attention they become semi-outcasts again, excluded from the tight-knit female society and forced to live on the group's periphery.

On the other side of the world live mandrills, the largest African forest-dwelling monkeys. Males have spectacular red, white, blue, and yellow faces and rumps. They come in graduated sizes, and the fattest, largest-rumped males dominate non-fatted males that have smaller testicles, lower testosterone levels, and only minimal development of the colorful sexual skin at the base of the tail (Setchell and Dixson 2001; Wickings and Dixson 1992). Fat males are more attractive to females and have more mating opportunities than their skinny friends. The extra fat that has accumulated in their rumps during reproductive development is lost during the mating season while they focus on breeding and also compete with females for food. Non-fatted males living on the group's edge eat freely without much com-petition and do not lose weight during the mating season. They are not entirely shut out of the mating game, but paternity definitely correlates with male fattening and dominance rank in these monkeys.

In at least one case, the ability to become fat threatened the health of a primate group. Studying the effect of stress on cardiac health, psychologist Robert Sapolsky (Sapolsky 2000) spent many years following a troop of olive baboons in the Maasai Mara National Reserve, Kenya, a popular tourist destination. The baboons con-sumed a highly untypical diet from a hotel garbage dump located in the middle of their range. Not only was their diet considerably enriched, but the new foods were perpetually available. The baboons moved their sleeping quarters into the trees surrounding the dump and had little need to rise early or to travel far to forage for the usual grasses, tubers, and leaves. Subsisting on left-over chicken drumsticks, slabs of beef, custard pudding, rotting fruit salad, and other atypical foods, these baboons easily survived drought and famine, and their young grew faster, matured earlier, and produced more infants. But like extremely well-fed humans, their insulin and cholesterol, especially *low-density lipoprotein (LDL)*-cholesterol, rose to levels far above those of wild baboons eating their standard diet. Unfortunately, bovine tuberculosis-contaminated meat eventually infected the garbage dump baboons and decimated the troop.

Temporary fattening also has a survival function for orangutans. Orangutans are mainly fruit-eaters and travel widely through their territories in search of this scarce, high-energy food. On the rare occasions of mast fruiting, when large amounts of fruit ripen simultaneously and contain more calories and less fiber than usual, orangutans gorge on fruit instead of eating their usual variety of leaves, bark, and some fruit (Knott 2001). Calorie consumption more than doubles during this time, and they develop noticeable fat deposits. Urine analysis during subsequent fruit-scarce times indicates the presence of ketones, the chemical byproducts of fat breakdown and thus the utilization of this temporary energy reserve. Fat accumulation in orangutans seems to be an adaptation to relatively low food availability and is linked to the very slow development of orangutan infants who depend on their mothers' milk for five to six years. Fat storage enables the orangutan mother to meet the high energetic demands of this long period of lactation and infant dependency. Reproductive success, absolutely necessary for survival of the species, depends on the capacity to acquire and maintain adequate energy stores.

The much greater human capacity to store enormous amounts of fat clearly has its origin in the primate and mammalian past. Primates are generally fatter than all other mammals and accumulate fat selectively in the abdomen (Pond and Mattacks 1987). Reproducing female primates tend to have greater fat deposits than males and non-reproducing females (Zihlman and Bolter 2015). The optimal proportion of mammalian body fat is only 5 percent, but in humans it ranges from 15 percent (in males) to 25 percent (in females), the highest level of adiposity among the primates. As in other mammals, layers of subcutaneous adipose tissue are located along the flanks and on the outer surface of the abdomen, but human fat deposits are more extensive because of erect posture and corresponding rearrangement of skeletal and muscular components. Human legs are longer, the pelvis wider, and the thorax more flattened than in four-legged animals, and the fat deposits over those body segments are greatly extended in comparison to similar sites in other mammals. Most mammals have little or no fat in the legs, but human fat depots cover much of the arms, thighs, buttocks, and calves and completely surround the thorax. Both the internal and superficial fat depots of humans can become excessively large and persistent (Pond 1997; Pond 1998).

All primate infants have well-developed fat reserves at birth and rapidly gain even more "baby fat" through infancy. Newborn humans have the largest fat stores of all primates and gain even greater amounts after birth. Fat accounts for 15 percent of human body mass at birth (Kuzawa 1998) and is probably one reason that human neonates, weighing on average 3.5 kg (about 7.5 lb), are much heavier than newborn gorillas at 2 to 2.5 kg (about 4.5 to 5.5 lb), even though gorilla mothers are at least as large as adult human females. In healthy human children the proportion of body fat and the body growth rate slowly decline from infancy to childhood.

At around age five, body growth rate is lowest, just as brain metabolism and growth are greatest (Kuzawa et al. 2014). As adults, humans are the fattest of all primates and, compared to other mammals, have 10 times as many adipocytes as expected for their body size (Pond 1998).

During puberty, humans gain in adiposity and develop sexually dimorphic patterns of adipose tissue deposits (Pond 1998; Power and Schulkin 2008) (see Figure 2.1). Under the influence of increasing estrogen levels that suppress fat oxidation (O'Sullivan 2008), females become proportionally fatter than males, with especially large adipose tissue deposits accumulating on breasts, hips, and thighs that give human females their distinctive hour-glass figures. Males gain a smaller proportion of body fat, which is primarily deposited in the abdominal region, both as visceral and subcutaneous adipose tissue, and accounts for the typical paunch of human males. Female hip and thigh fat is slow to decrease during weight reduction efforts and is less metabolically active than abdominal fat. It is mobilized during pregnancy and lactation and is clearly designed to support human reproduction (McFarland 1997). This difference between human males and females in amount and distribution of adipose tissue does not appear in other mammals, but some other primates (monkeys, apes) do temporarily develop sexually dimorphic fat patterns, which are relatively smaller than humans'.

Also unique is the anatomy of the human digestive tract. In contrast to gorillas and chimpanzees, the human small intestine makes up the greatest proportion of the gut, more than half of its entire volume (Milton 1987). The total human gut is relatively small compared to other animals of the same size, and food passes through it more slowly (Figure 2.2). Humans consume a great variety of very high-quality foods composed of nutrient-dense, high-calorie items that can be easily digested in the small intestine. They regularly consume relatively large amounts of meat and other sources of protein and fat and partially "pre-digest" food by processing

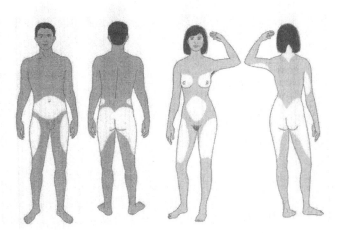

FIGURE 2.1   Fat patterning in men and women.

Source: Saladin, K. (2005) *Human Anatomy*. New York: McGraw Hill.

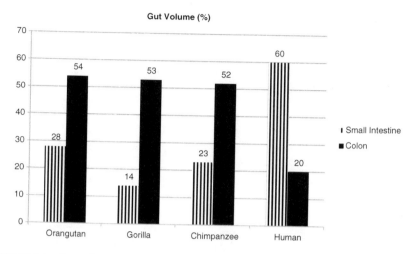

FIGURE 2.2 Gut volumes in apes and humans.

Adapted from Milton (1987).

it with tools and cooking before consumption. In contrast to other animals, the human diet is much richer in essential nutrients and energy content.

For humans, the primate legacy is a preference for sweet, carbohydrate–rich fruits and highly prized but rare, nutrient-dense animal flesh, and a herbivore digestive system modified to accommodate much high-quality, fat- and protein-rich food. Like other animals, humans store body fat, but have the unique ability to do so beginning in fetal life and to accumulate virtually unlimited amounts of adipose tissue after birth. Human fat depots are unique in their size and distribution, especially among females whose breast, hip, and thigh adipose tissue deposits are greater than the abdominal fat predominant in males. Thus humans in general and females in particular have evolved a selective advantage over other primates – the superior ability to store, retain, and use energy reserves for body maintenance, activity, and especially reproduction. The highly endangered status of wild ape populations today is in part due to low fertility related to limited energy resources, while human fertility is enhanced by greater energy storage to support reproduction and extended child care.

Humans are hominins

Living in Ethiopia 4.4 million years ago, the oldest undisputed human ancestor *Ardipithecus* (White et al. 2009) was probably preceded by earlier bipedal hominins as much as 7 million years ago (Brunet et al. 2002). These early hominins established the two-legged primate lineage that eventually evolved into modern humans. Like the apes sharing their African forest environment, these early human ancestors were highly frugivorous and relied on leafy vegetation and other forest foods when ripe fruits could not be found.

Early hominins resembled apes in many ways, including the relatively small size of their brains that were not much larger than those of chimpanzees. What clearly distinguishes them from apes, however, is their habitual bipedality. The two-legged gait of *Ardipithecus* was rather slow and deliberate because it also allowed for climbing and clambering about in trees by grasping branches with opposable great toes and curved finger bones. Later hominins, collectively known as *Australopithecines*, were still slow walkers in comparison with quadrupedal apes, but their feet were more stable and their bipedality was more efficient, reducing energy needed for locomotion by as much as 35 percent (Alexander 2002; Rodman and McHenry 1980; Sockol et al. 2007). Bipedality, marked by skeletal features such as a short, broad pelvis, fully extendable knees, and arched feet with convergent great toes (Lovejoy 1988), may have been the first stage in human energetic evolution, conserving locomotor energy and thus increasing energy available for other functions such as essential body maintenance and reproduction (Leonard and Robertson 2003). Among other advantages, walking on two legs instead of four left the hands free for carrying food. Food provisioning and sharing must have been enormously advantageous for hominins seeking adequate energy for survival (Anton et al. 2014). They subsisted on a variety of foods, including hard items such as nuts and seeds rich in vegetable fats (Eaton et al. 2002).

Africa was the exclusive home of the earliest hominins (Aiello and Andrews 2000). During their long existence they abandoned the tropical rainforests and embarked on life in the mixed environment of woodland and grassy *savanna*, where they were forced to adopt a very different diet from the soft fruits, flowers, and leaves of the forest, depending more on grasses, sedges, and succulents not consumed by forest apes (Sponheimer et al. 2013). Despite greater locomotor efficiency, they used more energy than apes in their search for widely dispersed food sources. Pronounced sexual dimorphism may have been one strategy to conserve energy for reproduction. Large males used their bulk and strength for defense against predators and to compete with other males for mates. Female size, however, was constrained by energetic demands of gestation, lactation, and infant transport, much as in highly dimorphic gorillas and orangutans (Fedigan 1982). But unlike infant apes that cling to their mothers' body hair with prehensile hands and feet, Australopithecine infants had to be supported and carried by their mothers. The tiny skeleton of a three-year-old child (Alemseged et al. 2006) suggests another Australopithecine energy-conserving strategy – delayed brain growth to lower daily caloric requirements of this very energy-expensive tissue by lengthening the development period (Dufour and Sauther 2002; Ulijaszek 2002). An ape infant is born with a relatively well-developed brain that grows to adult size in half the time it takes a human infant's brain to mature. But in humans, and apparently also in their hominin ancestors, brains took longer to grow and develop to adult size because of increased energy needs.

Two very different hominin groups descended from the Australopithecines. The genus *Paranthropus* (Figure 2.3) included three exclusively African species, all of which were stocky and robust. Their dentition was unique, with tiny anterior teeth suggesting that cutting and slicing foods and peeling fruits were not important

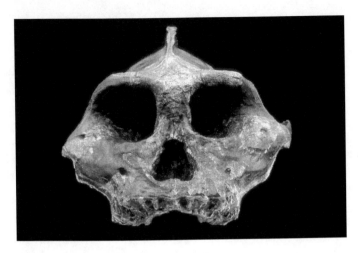

FIGURE 2.3 *Paranthropus aethiopicus.*

Source: David L. Brill (humanoriginsphotos.com).

functions (Ungar and Grine 1991). Instead, they used their massive premolar and molar teeth with large flat chewing surfaces and thick coats of hard enamel to crush and grind tough, gritty vegetation, hard seeds and nuts, fibrous stems and roots, and sedges and grasses (Robinson 1956; Schoeninger 2014). Large jaw bones and thick chewing muscles provided a powerful bite. With this specialized chewing machine these ancient hominins expanded their savanna diets to include a greater variety of foods than the soft fruits and leaves their ancestors had exploited in the forest. The rib cage of *Paranthropus* formed an inverted cone, hinting at a large, gorilla-like gut for digesting great amounts of bulky, low-quality vegetation to extract as much nutritional value as possible (Foley 2002; Milton 1999).

The archaeological evidence is sparse, but it is virtually certain that, much as the Taï Forest chimpanzees crack hard nuts with hammers and anvils (Boesch and Boesch-Achermann 2000), *Paranthropus* used simple tools to open nuts that were too hard to be cracked with their teeth. Seeds and nuts were precious food items, for they contained vegetable oils and protein and provided essential energy for active hominins. Perhaps they also used digging sticks to uncover deeply buried roots and tubers (Conklin-Brittain et al. 2002). These underground food sources are rich in carbohydrates and micronutrients and contain only small amounts of indigestible fiber.

Dental wear patterns and bone chemistry indicate that *Paranthropus* consumed at least some animal foods, possibly insects, grubs, eggs, and the flesh of birds and small animals (Lee-Thorp and Sponheimer 2006). *Paranthropus* had achieved a level of dietary diversity unknown to their forest-dwelling ancestors, but at the cost of travel over greater distances in their quest for food. As bipeds, they had several advantages over other woodland and savanna animals. Erect posture increased visibility over great distances and freed the hands for carrying food and other items. On the open savanna, upright posture minimized exposure to ultraviolet radiation since the tropical sun's rays fell mostly on the head and shoulders instead of the entire length of the body (Wheeler 1992a). The stout bodies of *Paranthropus* prevented excessive loss of body water, a real danger in the tropics (Wheeler 1992b). Nevertheless, locating sources of water must have been very important, and these hominins were probably on the go most of the day, foraging for food and drink. Besides hunger and heat, they faced the danger of large predatory cats that favored a meal of antelope or gazelle, but included a hominin on the menu when the opportunity arose. Long walks and hard work to collect food and water with their babies on their backs and occasional confrontations with fierce predators shaped a physically demanding lifestyle. It is unlikely that members of the *Paranthropus* species had the opportunity to accumulate fat stores under these conditions. After more than 1 million years of successful adaptation to the African savanna, *Paranthropus* was no longer able to muster adequate energy on a largely plant-based, low-energy diet for both body maintenance and reproduction. Paleoanthropologists have identified linear enamel hypoplasia, a sign of nutritional stress, in *Paranthropus* and also in other contemporary hominins (Guatelli-Steinberg 2003). *Paranthropus* became extinct without leaving any descendants about 1 million years ago.

Ancestral humans

Resource competition with another hominin species may well have contributed to the extinction of long-lived *Paranthropus*. Two and a half million years ago, the first humans (genus *Homo*) also descended from an Australopithecine lineage appeared in East Africa, and for some time coexisted with *Paranthropus* (Leakey et al. 1964).

Compared to forest apes, Australopithecines had increased their dietary diversity, but had done little to modify foods to improve their nutritional value. That was the primary achievement of this new and different type of hominin. Although no taller than their ancestors, the first humans had significantly larger brains, smaller teeth and faces and more delicately constructed skeletons (Anton et al. 2014). *Homo* collected appropriate stones and cobbles and deliberately struck them with another stone to create sharp- or rough-edged tools. The resulting flakes and choppers were used for slicing and pounding, mostly tough vegetation but also animal parts. Ancient animal bones with cut-marks and fractures indicate that meat was sliced from bones and limb bones were smashed to expose the fatty marrow inside (Ambrose 2001; Fernandez-Jalvo et al. 1999). The *Paleolithic* (Old Stone Age) period had begun.

Early humans were socially and technologically better equipped than Australopithecines for the savanna foraging life and became more efficient food procurers, initiating a trend that has continued to the present time. Their small molar teeth with sharp cusps and thin enamel were not meant for a diet of tough vegetation and hard seeds and nuts. Theirs were the teeth of true omnivores who intentionally and routinely consumed more animal foods than Australopithecines and processed vegetable matter to soften and detoxify it before consumption. They used stone tools for extracting food items that were otherwise not accessible and for softening hard foods, thus reducing the energetic stress of large teeth, jaws, and chewing muscles and improving overall diet quality.

The stone tools were used to butcher animal carcasses abandoned by predators or obtained by scavenging (Bunn 2001; Rose 2001; Shipman 1986). It is no coincidence that expansion of human brain capacity began with *Homo*, ultimately reaching a size three times larger than the brains of the earliest hominin ancestors. The meat that was cut from limb bones and the fatty marrow and brain tissue extracted from smashed bones and skulls were rich sources of the polyunsaturated fatty acids essential for human brain development (Cordain 2001). It is doubtful that the earliest humans actively hunted game, however. Their innovative tools were not designed to be used as weapons, and with their bare hands these small people could not have killed large animals. It is more likely that they took meat from abandoned carcasses, and possibly even confiscated prey from saber-toothed cats and other powerful and dangerous predators gathered around a kill. A lone human scavenger would have found this difficult, if not impossible. But a group of scheming, collaborating humans, using their wits rather than weapons or strength, would have succeeded where a single individual could not (van Valkenburgh 2001). Larger brains allowed for greater complexity of thought and behavior than was possible for Australopithecines with their ape-sized brains. As among living chimpanzees, the collaboration required to obtain substantial amounts of meat and animal fat was sustained by sharing the prized food among family members and allies, not only to enhance their nutrition and survival but also to maintain strong social bonds and the expectation of future cooperation (Stanford 2001).

Chimpanzees are essentially individualistic eaters, rarely sharing food and then only tiny amounts of meat distributed to others with whom they cultivate cooperative relationships. Consistent food sharing is a hallmark of humanity and sets *Homo* apart from other primates (Isaac 1978; Ulijaszek 2002). Human ancestors more regularly shared food in an intensely sociable setting. Discovery of an ancient "home base" in Olduvai Gorge, although open to alternative interpretations, suggests that early humans habitually lived, worked, and ate in social groups (Plummer 2004). Stone tools and the bony remains of meals are scattered about the site showing continuous or at least repeated occupation. A ring of large stones surrounding the site may have supported branches stuck into the ground to form a windbreak for the little camp. Social dining is well known to stimulate eating (Lieberman 2008), as is the novelty of food variety provided by different members of a foraging group. In a series of feeding experiments, for example, monkeys provided with a luxury, high-fat, high-cholesterol diet were more sociable and initiated less contact aggression than those fed a prudent, low-fat diet (Kaplan et al. 1991). Cholesterol influences brain activity related to social behavior. Early human sociability and food sharing may have formed a positive feedback loop with meat and animal fat consumption at the very beginning of human evolution.

The first members of *Homo* had crossed an adaptive threshold. With the aid of technology and social collaboration, the earliest humans were able to tap the richest source of food energy and supplement their intake of plant carbohydrates and fiber with substantial animal protein and fat (Milton 1999). Meat supplies all the amino acids that humans need, and in the proper proportions. Even a small amount of meat packs a large supply of nutrients and provides many essential vitamins and minerals. Animal protein gave human savanna dwellers a tremendous energetic advantage over the hominins focusing on plant foods in the forests and woodlands that first preceded and then coexisted with them (Fish and Lockwood 2003; Lieberman 1987; Ungar et al. 2006). The remains of smashed and cut animal bones testify to their skills in obtaining meat and marrow (Figure 2.4). In the search for animal prey, early humans undoubtedly came across natural salt licks, which provided them, as other savanna animals, with an important nutrient not available in their foods that helped to conserve body water in a hot, dry climate.

The evolutionary success of the first humans with their larger brains, more modern body proportions, and more sophisticated stone tools for food procurement and processing began to dominate the savanna 2 to 3 million years ago and witnessed the final extinction of *Paranthropus*. Climatic and tectonic events around the time of the first appearance of *Homo* favored dietary and mental flexibility and enabled them to adapt successfully to newly diverse habitats (Anton et al. 2014). Some tool makers chipped flakes from both sides of a stone core to form an extremely sharp, straight-edged tool that could easily cut through the thick hide of an elephant (Ambrose 2001). The *handaxe*, a multipurpose tool with two sharp edges and a pointed tip for cutting, scraping, smashing, and digging, was the hallmark of advanced technology, designed for efficiently processing meat and other animal products, some of them possibly obtained by actual cooperative hunting of dangerous but high-yield large game (see Figure 2.5).

Advanced stone tool technology enabled humans to increase their meat consumption. Stone tools for dissecting and processing carcasses and the bony remains of many butchered animals are direct evidence for an increased animal-based diet

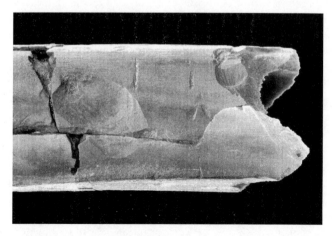

FIGURE 2.4 Fossil antelope tibia shaft which has been shattered, smashed, and cut-marked by stone tools; Bouri, Ethiopia, 2.5 million years old.

Source: David L. Brill (humanoriginsphotos.com).

FIGURE 2.5 Handaxe, a multipurpose stone tool created and used by *Homo*.

Photo by Werner Forman/Universal Images Group/Getty Images.

(Foley 2002). Now-extinct giant baboons and elephants as well as more familiar game such as wild pigs, buffalo, deer, and other hoofed herbivores were processed and eaten. Carnivorous predators leave few remains of young prey for human scavengers, so the presence of the tiny bones of very young animals in campsites is also testimony to the hunting strategy. Based on known consumption rates among contemporary foraging populations (Kaplan et al. 2000), early human hunters ate up to 10 times more meat than chimpanzees and earlier hominins who lacked the human level of collaborative hunting skills and sophisticated tools for capturing and butchering animals.

Another human technological innovation was the controlled use of fire for cooking and warmth and presumably also for lighting dark caves (Campbell et al. 2006). Remains of hearths, fireplaces, and burned bones appear in the archaeological record and also suggest that meats and probably also tubers and tough vegetables were cooked (Wrangham 2001). Heat destroys cell walls, making the tough more tender, the indigestible more accessible, and the toxic more tolerable. Cooked foods are more tasty and digestible and therefore higher in nutritional quality than raw items.

Cooking may also have intensified social behavior. There may have been a division of labor in which some individuals traveled far to find foods, which they carried back to others. Perhaps elderly individuals who could no longer travel great distances became responsible for preparing the foods brought home by hunters and collectors. They may have seen to it that cooked food was shared equitably among members of a family, including very young children who were unable to feed themselves. Much more than a simple cooking facility and source of warmth, the hearth may have been the place to rest and socialize, share food and stories, and plan future activities by the light of the flickering flames (Pfeiffer 1969).

More fully committed to bipedalism than their predecessors, humans had longer and more muscular legs than their shorter ancestors. Their powerful Achilles tendons and arched feet functioned like springs to absorb and release energy with each step. They had a long, energy-saving stride for very efficient walking and endurance running over the long distances they had to travel in their pursuit of prey (Bramble and Lieberman 2004; Steudel-Numbers and Tilkens 2004). Their foraging territories were many times larger than the ranges of their ancestors (Kaplan et al. 2000), and they were more physically active (Leonard and Robertson 1992). But their improved locomotor anatomy and the high nutritional quality of meat from great herds of herbivores that filled the expanding savanna grasslands offset the energetic cost of hunting and scavenging. Anatomical changes in the shoulder joint that allowed for accurate, high-speed throwing of projectiles constituted another biological adaptation contributing to their defense against predators, hunting skills, and evolutionary success (Roach et al. 2013).

Homo individuals were taller and heavier than their predecessors. Female body size increased by fully 50 percent, effectively reducing extreme sex differences in height and weight that characterized earlier hominins (Aiello and Key 2002). One advantage of a larger female body was the ability to give birth to larger infants with bigger brains, although they were quite helpless at birth and completely dependent on adult care for years (Leigh 2004). Maternal energetic requirements were much higher for these humans than for their predecessors because of the greater metabolic demands of a bigger developing fetus and a large-brained growing infant that nursed for several years. Mothers met the demand by consuming significant amounts of animal protein and storing on their bodies considerable amounts of fat. By birthing infants at a much earlier stage in their development than other hominins (Alemseged et al. 2006), and by lengthening the infancy, childhood, and juvenile stages and thus lowering the rate of growth and development, daily energy requirements of both mother and child could be met even in the harshest of environments (Aiello and Key 2002; Foley and Lee 1992). Increased fat storage buffered energy needs during periods of low food availability and thus supported body and brain growth (Kuzawa 1998).

It is likely that the sexually dimorphic pattern of human body composition originated with *Homo* when females began to accumulate greatly enlarged fat stores at puberty and developed distinctive adipose tissue deposits on breasts, hips, and thighs (Ellison 2001). This may also have been the evolutionary stage when a comparatively high level of human fetal adiposity originated and continued throughout infancy (Kuzawa 1998). During periods of famine, the body fat acquired by neonates and infants provides the energy to support brain development and functioning and to protect against muscle protein loss.

The human lifespan was extended during this evolutionary stage as well, altering social lives by the addition of a third generation to the family (Aiello and Key

2002; O'Connell et al. 1999). Grandparents, no longer capable of reproduction themselves, provided care, food, and protection for growing grandchildren, helping to boost infant survival and relieving mothers of the sole responsibility for child care. This new behavioral adaptation allowed mothers to maintain energy stores and conceive and produce another infant in a relatively short time. It is likely that fathers became more involved in child care as well. Like hunting and scavenging, successful child rearing required collaboration and cooperation by adult members of the group, and was rewarded with higher fertility rates and species survival (Emery Thompson 2013; Kramer and Ellison 2010).

The large, muscular human body was energetically expensive, but had a greater capacity for work, consumed less energy per unit body mass than the smaller bodies of earlier hominins, and could store larger fat deposits. *Homo* could therefore better accommodate fluctuations in food supplies and could tolerate longer starvation times (Ellison 2003). A large body has a correspondingly larger brain, and both approached modern human size in *Homo* about 2 million years ago. The brain of modern *Homo* requires five times more energy than that of other mammals of equivalent body mass; fully one-quarter of human basal metabolic energy is committed to brain function (Kaplan et al. 2000; Leonard and Robertson 1992). The largely vegetarian diet of apes and early hominins could not have sustained such large-brained, physically active humans. But the high-quality, meat-based diet of *Homo* provided adequate energy for both muscular activity and brain functioning and also lowered the energetic demands of digestion by allowing for reduction of the digestive tract, as suggested by the "Expensive Tissue Hypothesis" (Aiello and Wheeler 1995; Zihlman and McFarland 2000). This dietary shift changed the configuration of the rib cage from the funnel-shape of earlier hominins to the barrel-shaped rib cage associated with a shorter colon and a longer small intestine in modern humans. It also provided the energy resources required for increasing brain size, initiated with the evolution of *Homo* (see Table 2.1).

A meat-based diet and the use of fire for warmth enabled groups of early humans to migrate out of their tropical African homeland to Europe and Asia nearly 2 million years ago (Anton and Swisher 2004). Here they faced a more variable climate and annual seasons of cold when wild food plants were unavailable. As the modern Arctic Inuit and Inupiat did until very recently, they subsisted almost exclusively on meat and fat from wild game during at least part of the year, supplemented by the few nuts and roots that could be collected during the coldest

TABLE 2.1 Human brain size evolution. Adapted from Fuentes (2011).

Time (million years ago)	Hominin	Brain Size
7–1	Australopithecines	320–500 cc
2.5–1.5	Early *Homo*	500–800 cc
2–0.2	*Homo erectus*	650–1250 cc
0.2–0	*Homo sapiens*	1100–1750 cc

months. Because their main food supply was constantly on the move, they were nomads and could not put food in storage or carry heavy supplies and equipment. Daily life in cold climates, carrying tools and children on long annual treks, and the hunting, butchering, and transporting of meat all must have had a high energetic cost (Cordain et al. 1997).

Foragers need a large territory to find enough to eat and must journey long distances to obtain food. Taller bodies, longer legs, and smaller guts allowed early humans to conserve energy during their movements through woods and grasslands in search of meat and other foods. Their enriched diets and stored body fat ensured survival, even in cold northern regions. *Homo* had established an effective energetic system to maintain large bodies and brains, sustain high physical activity even in colder climates, and increase fertility rates and population sizes. Their foraging strategy both required and supported greater cognitive complexity and the ability to learn new skills (Kaplan et al. 2000; Ulijaszek 1992). It should come as no surprise then that a comparison of recently mapped chimpanzee and human *genomes* (Uddin et al. 2004) shows that the human genes related to cognition and energy metabolism had undergone the most dramatic evolutionary changes since the divergence of the two primate species about 6 to 8 million years ago. For *Homo* cognition and energy regulation co-evolved and are linked in increasing brain size, neuronal activity, and cultural development.

After more than 1 million years these early humans, represented finally only by one species, *Homo erectus*, evolved into two more recent forms. Neandertals (*Homo neandertalensis*) appeared in Eurasia, while modern humans (*Homo sapiens*) arose somewhat later in Africa and subsequently emigrated to Europe and Asia. The lifestyle established by early humans, gathering wild plants but relying mainly on large game for protein, continued to support the archaic Neandertals, who perfected their stone tool kits for even greater efficiency in processing foods and other items. Although the long, low skulls, thick eyebrow ridges, large faces, and stocky bodies of Neandertals gave them a decidedly primitive appearance, their brains had reached fully modern proportions. Since body size had not increased further, their brains were absolutely and relatively larger, and, of course, required even greater energetic support (Campbell et al. 2006).

Isolated from other human populations in Ice Age Europe, Neandertals were the first humans to adapt successfully to extreme arctic conditions. Although they have sometimes been portrayed as primitive brutes, they must have been intelligent, active, and successful foragers and hunters of large game (Sorensen and Leonard 2001) to survive so long in such extreme conditions. They produced a variety of sophisticated stone tools, using a new method of tool manufacture. It involved the preparation of a stone core before knocking off flakes to be used as cutting tools for working with wood and animal hides as well as for cutting up carcasses (Ambrose 2001). Bone chemistry indicates that, like carnivorous predators of the highest level, Neandertals ate mainly meat, fat, and marrow from reindeer, bear, mammoth, bison, and wild cattle and horses, which allowed them to meet the energetic challenges of their cold environment, high activity levels, and very bulky physiques (Schoeninger 2014). In Kebara Cave, Israel, large piles of accu-mulated bone refuse from butchered prey were found along the sides of the shelter inhabited by Neandertals (Tchernov 2001). Undoubtedly they also ate plant foods, at least during the seasons when these were available. Remains of berries, nuts, and other plant foods have been found in association with Neandertal skeletal remains.

Neandertals, like today's arctic populations, had powerful, stocky bodies with short limbs for conserving body heat in the cold. Large and thick bones, bulging muscles, and brains that were on average even larger than ours allowed Neandertals to meet the physical and intellectual challenges of their arctic environment. But the need to maintain an adequate body temperature in a persistently cold habitat, to support a large musculature and a very large brain, and to mobilize energy for pursuit and capture of large animal prey created an extreme energy demand (Carbone et al. 2007), estimated to be as high as 4,000 calories per day, about twice the daily energy requirement of modern humans (Leonard and Robertson 2003; Sorensen and Leonard 2001). Nutritional stress among Neandertals is indicated by a high prevalence of linear enamel hypoplasia (Guatelli-Steinberg et al. 2004) and archaeological evidence for survival cannibalism. Deposits at Moula-Guercy Cave in France, dated to 100,000 years ago, contain bones of red deer and humans with identical cut-marks and percussion scars created by defleshing carcasses and fractur-ing long bones and skulls to obtain the marrow and brain tissue within (Defleur, et al. 1999). Unlike Neandertal remains elsewhere, which were deliberately buried in graves, these human remains received the same treatment as food animals and were left unburied. Some Neandertals may have eaten each other in their desperate quest for nourishment.

Despite extremely stressful conditions, Neandertals thrived in Europe and west-ern Asia from 350,000 to 28,000 years ago, but when the climate became even colder during the Last Glacial Maximum, their time ran out. Metabolic require-ments outstripped even their best efforts to supply adequate energy (Churchill 2008). Although they finally abandoned northern and central Europe and settled along the Mediterranean seacoast where the climate was somewhat milder, their numbers gradually declined (Finlayson et al. 2006). Their primary food source, large game, became more difficult to find. Even so, they might have survived for quite some time, perhaps even until the return of a warmer climate, but for a new challenge – the arrival in Europe of *Homo sapiens*, known as Cro-Magnon, which had migrated from its African homeland. For some 10,000 years Neandertals coex-isted and competed with these immigrants for the increasingly scarce resources so essential to their survival. The newcomers possessed tall and slim physiques that betrayed their tropical African origin and scaled down their daily energy needs, as did the extremely extended childhood and adolescent periods of their offspring (Bogin 1999; Thompson and Nelson 2011).

In the presence of increased cold and this new competitor, Neandertals could not meet the energetic needs for individual survival and also maintain fertility, not unlike the robust *Paranthropus* species in competition with early humans in Africa thousands of years earlier. Demographic modeling of modern human and

Neandertal populations has shown that a very small disadvantage in mortality, less than 2 percent, would have led to total extinction of Neandertals within 1,000 years after the arrival of *Homo sapiens* (Zubrow 1989). Without a trace of inter-group violence, Neandertal populations dwindled and disappeared, leaving the entire Earth to *Homo sapiens*.

Homo sapiens (anatomically modern humans) originated in Africa 200,000 years ago (McDougall et al. 2005). About 100,000 years later they began to make their way into Asia and Europe and finally into previously uninhabited Australia and the American continents. They reached southeastern Europe about 40,000 years ago, during the Last Glacial Maximum, and made their way north and west along sea-coast and river routes. Before leaving Africa they had already modified their stone tool kits and developed sturdy, heated shelters. They designed elaborate ovens for heating and cooking, sewed warm, tailored clothing with bone needles, and created traps and snares, spear throwers, and bows and arrows for killing prey from a safe distance. Birds, marine mammals, and fish were caught with bone hooks and barbed harpoons. Beautifully depicted animals, humans, and mysterious markings were painted and carved on cave walls in some of the earliest forms of artistic expression (Campbell et al. 2006).

They left behind numerous small ivory, bone, and stone sculptures of female figures. The 35,000-year-old female representation from Germany (see Figure 1.1) has the enlarged breasts, belly, and buttocks of a woman with abundant fat deposits (Conard 2009). She may have symbolized a well-nourished woman, a model of feminine beauty of her day, or even an ideal of female fertility, since adiposity supports the energetic demands of gestation and lactation (Nelson 1993). This little mammoth ivory carving and many others like it signify that at least some individuals had the opportunity to develop sizeable adipose tissue deposits.

The diet of Paleolithic hunters was probably the most nutritious and healthy in all of human history. By combining archaeological data from ancient populations with ethnographic descriptions of the few remaining peoples who still live by foraging today, scientists have reconstructed their rich and highly varied diet (Eaton et al. 1999; Eaton and Konner 1985). Daily calorie consumption was very high, an average of 3,000 calories per person, and meat from both large and small animals constituted an enormous 35–50 percent of the diet, with a great variety of wild plant foods making up the remainder. The high protein content of Paleolithic meals is entirely contradictory to modern recommendations for red meat intake, but wild game contains much less *saturated fat* and up to five times more healthful *polyunsaturated fat* than meat from today's farm animals (Cordain et al. 2002). Supermarket beef from grain-fed cattle, for example, contains more than double the fat of wild game, two to three times more saturated fat, and only about half as much polyunsaturated fat. Pasture-fed beef is somewhat lower in saturated fat, but also contains less polyunsaturated fat, particularly the desirable Ω-3 fatty acids that help prevent cardiovascular disease. The combination of meat, wild nuts, fruits, and vegetables was lower in carbohydrates and higher in protein and micronutrients than the modern industrial diet. It contained less sodium, more fiber, and more of virtually every vitamin and mineral – potassium, calcium, Vitamin B, Vitamin C, iron, folate. Skeletal remains of these foraging populations testify to their tall stature and generally good skeletal and dental health (Giesen and Sciulli 1988). Paleolithic foraging enabled humans to adapt their diets to a variety of environmental conditions and establish permanent populations all over the world.

Some scientists (Cordain 2002; Eaton et al. 1989) proposed the modern weight-loss Paleolithic Diet based on this high-protein, low-carbohydrate prehistoric nutrition – large amounts of meat, fish, poultry, eggs, nuts, and seeds, as well as vegetables and fruits. To be avoided in this diet are grains, dairy foods, peas, and beans, as well as processed and highly sweetened foods, items that were not available to ancient foragers. However, modern meats, eggs, and other foods differ greatly in nutrient content from the corresponding wild foods eaten by human ancestors, and it is even likely that they did include some wild grains and legumes in their diets. It seems virtually impossible to emulate the authentic Paleolithic diet today.

Although healthy, foragers' food sources were unreliable and irregular. Even though wild food was relatively easy to obtain – one large animal could feed a small group for several days – periodic food shortages were not uncommon. Even though they could usually find some less-preferred and lower-quality "famine foods," there is evidence in the skeletons of some European Paleolithic foragers that they experienced periodic nutritional stress (Holt and Formicola 2008), during the very time that Neandertals became extinct. The ability to store fat on their bodies during periods of plenty helped them to survive these times of scarcity and stress. Invariably, however, fat stores were depleted and even muscle tissue may have been sacrificed for energy to tide them over until food again became available. Foragers' subsistence-related physical exertions involved three times the energy expenditure of typical modern human workers who have access to labor-saving technology and a more sedentary work environment (Ulijaszek 2000). Only rarely could fat stores be accumulated and maintained to the degree depicted by the Paleolithic figurine. She may have represented an ideal, well-fed body image, but one rarely achieved by foraging women.

The few remaining modern foragers who maintain a traditional diet today avoid the high cholesterol levels associated with heart disease, the primary cause of death in industrial countries. But they do not always enjoy good nutritional health. Even though foragers have strong food-sharing traditions, nutrient deficiencies are common and contribute to high infant and child mortality and to delays in child growth and development. These conditions were much rarer in Paleolithic populations, because they had complete access to their foraging territories and could move to a new location whenever food resources were depleted. Today's foragers are severely limited in their access to traditional foods. They are no longer able to move freely through their original hunting grounds and have been forced to live in marginal areas where wild foods are less abundant.

A group of westernized, middle-aged, overweight, diabetic Australian aborigines who still remembered their food gathering traditions participated in an experiment to demonstrate the importance of a high-quality Paleolithic diet (O'Dea 1992).

Returning to the outback and resuming the subsistence practices of earlier generations for only seven weeks reduced their weight, blood pressure, fasting blood glucose levels, and blood lipids to healthy or nearly healthy levels. The traditional Australian forager diet had been diverse and abundant in wild meat, animal organs, plant fiber, and vitamins. Minimal food preparation prevented the loss of nutrients due to overcooking and required slow digestion for maximum absorption of nutrients. At frequent feasts, large quantities of meat were shared with others, ensuring that all group members had access to adequate food and fat to sustain them in lean times. Favorite foods, such as energy-dense honey and fats, were only rarely available and consumed in small amounts.

Only a tiny number of foraging societies survive in the modern world. Although certainly not equivalent because of the passage of time and very different environmental conditions, their lifestyles are considered to be more representative of ancient foraging humans than agricultural or industrial populations. The diets of these contemporary foragers living in diverse habitats vary greatly, but provide adequate energy and nutrients. For example, the traditional Inuit diet shows that humans can thrive on high-protein foods, remarkably unbalanced by modern standards, and yet avoid the cardiovascular diseases of western industrialized populations (Draper 1977). The Inuit secret was the nutrient content of their predominantly meat and fat meals that provided plenty of energy but also contained high levels of polyunsaturated fatty acids and all the essential vitamins. Fish bones consumed along with the flesh provided Vitamin C and calcium. Drinking plenty of water with meals prevented the uremic poisoning usually associated with excessive protein intake. Even though they consumed virtually no plant fiber and very little other plant food, Inuit nutritional health was excellent as long as they avoided western-style foods. General undernutrition, not specific dietary deficiencies, was the greatest challenge to their health and survival.

The traditional !Kung of the southern African Kalahari semi-desert are also considered foraging exemplars (Lee 1968). Until recently they subsisted exclusively on wild foods that varied greatly by season. !Kung bands were constantly on the move to collect animal and plant products and to find water. Their staple food was the mongongo nut, full of protein and fat, storable, and available during most of the year. But the favorite, most highly prized, and rarest food was meat from large animals, which were hunted with considerable effort and risk by men armed only with spears and bows and arrows. The overall diet was evenly divided among meat, nuts, and wild vegetables including bulbs, roots, berries, and fruits, the latter being supplied for the most part by women. An average of only two and one-half days' work of collecting could provide enough food to supply each member of a band with 3,000 kcal per day for an entire week. Although the !Kung were hungry during the annual dry season and invariably lost significant amounts of body weight, mongongo nuts and less favored foods usually provided enough nourishment until the next collecting season.

The Hadza are a modern foraging people who live in the dry African savanna and eat a primarily plant-based diet (Bunn 2001). Their staple food is the fruit of the boabab tree. Its seeds, which have a high protein and fat content, are processed into flour to make the nutrients more accessible. The fruit pulp contains calcium and Vitamin C in addition to providing carbohydrate energy. Roots and tubers are also important sources of carbohydrates, but are too fibrous to be readily digested and require processing before being consumed. In their cheeks, the Hadza carry wadges of fibrous foods from which they suck all the nutrients they can before spitting out the remainder.

It should be evident that, like modern foragers, Paleolithic ancestors must have been extremely active in their daily quest for food and water. Hunters expended much energy in walking great distances to find their prey, running in pursuit, hurling spears, cutting up carcasses, and carrying home their heavy burdens of butchered meat and bone. They probably did not hunt every day, but rested or did light work between hunting trips. Women carried digging implements and containers, and finally also several days' worth of wild foods collected on their long trips. They also brought their infants on these foraging ventures, conserving energy by using slings to carry infants still too young to cling to their mothers (Wall-Scheffler et al. 2007). They climbed trees for fruits and honey, dug deeply into the hard earth for roots and tubers, and sometimes fought off competitors. With their stone axes they chopped wood to be carried home, and they collected and carried water as well. Shelters were built and rebuilt when families moved to new locations. Everything was accomplished with simple but effective hand implements and containers plus a great deal of manual labor and effort. As a result of these extreme levels of physical activity, even the elderly in today's few remaining foraging societies do not manifest the cardiovascular and metabolic symptoms considered virtually a fact of life for older people in industrial societies. Foraging subsistence, now almost completely gone, is a stark contrast to the modern, convenient, labor-saving sedentary way of life in which only a few actually engage in food production and labor-intensive work.

Taken together, these ethnographic accounts of modern foraging societies testify to great regional diversity in the food resources exploited by foragers and to the nutritional adaptability of human populations. Pre-agricultural peoples had perfected their abilities to identify, collect, process, and digest a great variety of foods from which they extracted maximum nutrients and energy with basic technology and a digestive tract adapted for rapid extraction of nutrients from high-quality foods. Meat and other animal-based foods like fat, blood, organs, fish, shellfish, eggs, and insects provided plenty of protein and essential fatty acids for the development and maintenance of muscle and brain tissue. Plants were major sources of carbohydrate energy and important micronutrients. Pound for pound, wild fruits and vegetables contain more protein, fructose, fiber, vitamins, minerals, and micronutrients than domesticated ones, and wild protein sources, including meats, are less fatty and more easily digested than those available in supermarkets today (Cordain et al. 2000). Sugar, alcohol, and tobacco were unknown. Diets were nutrient-dense but energy-poor, and food supplies were not always stable and predictable. The work of obtaining food required much effort that could be sustained during lean times only by energy stored as excess body fat. In short, from the beginning, humans and their ancestors were much better adapted to an environment of a highly nutritious but limited food supply, high activity levels, and a more or less regular cycle of accumulation and depletion of fat reserves than to perpetual bounty, ease, and high adiposity.

Paleolithic foragers optimized energy intake by diversifying their diets to include nutrient-rich meats and fats and minimized the energy expenditure of foraging by developing increasingly sophisticated tools for collecting and processing animal and plant foods before consumption. Throughout human prehistory bodies and brains evolved to increase energy efficiency through improved bipedality and intellectual capabilities. Both supported development of a complex, culturally based subsistence strategy involving division of labor and food sharing that ultimately evolved into a new way to maximize the energy supply with minimal energy expenditure beginning with the origin of agriculture.

The agricultural revolution

Foraging for wild plant and animal foods was the primary subsistence strategy during most of human life on Earth. Paleolithic ancestors adapted not only behaviorally, but also genetically and physiologically to a nutritious and varied diet, but one that was not consistently reliable. Their food acquisition and preparation skills were highly developed, but because they were nomads, they could not accumulate surplus food for times of scarcity. Internal energy storage was the primary mechanism for surviving periodic food shortages, and this energy reservoir was regularly depleted and needed frequent replenishing.

Agriculture began in 10 widely separated centers of origin in the Fertile Crescent of Mesopotamia, China, Mesoamerica, the Andes/Amazonia region of South America, the eastern United States, the African Sahel, tropical West Africa, Ethiopia, southern India, and New Guinea (Balter 2007; Riehl et al. 2013). Foragers in these regions independently made similar decisions to settle down and produce food rather than collecting wild plants and hunting wild animals for food. These centers were home to the most domesticable of the indigenous wild plants and animals that had previously been exploited by Paleolithic foragers, and from them the ideas of animal husbandry and plant cultivation spread to the rest of the world. Domesticated forms of wheat, barley, sheep and goats appeared in southwest Asia, dogs, squash, maize, and beans in the Americas, rice in eastern Asia, cattle in Africa, and bananas in New Guinea.

No one really knows why the great global shift from Paleolithic foraging and food collection to food production, known as the Neolithic Revolution, came about. The name reflects the use of novel, smoothly ground stone implements by early farmers and the enormous impact of subsistence change on the course of human history. In providing food for large populations, agriculture became the foundation for early civilization and ultimately for modern industrial life. Perhaps it began because of a general warming of the Earth's climate after the Last Glacial Maximum, when many large game animals disappeared. Bison, reindeer, mammoth, elephants, and rhinoceros migrated north or became extinct, and people were forced to rely on small mammals, birds, and fish and on an increasing abundance of wild cereals for food. Perhaps because these items could be found and collected without traveling great distances, people adopted sedentary lifestyles (Ruff et al. 2015) and learned to appreciate the taste of these formerly less favored food sources. Perhaps increasing population pressure made foraging for wild foods impractical and impossible, necessitating planting and cultivation. Whatever the reason or reasons, gradually the Paleolithic subsistence pattern underwent a universal change from foraging and food collection to domestication and food production. The impact on the human diet was dramatic.

Farming actually grew quite naturally out of foraging almost simultaneously all over the world. During the Paleolithic period, humans had unknowingly passed undigested seeds from fruits and berries through their intestines, thereby enhancing germination and distributing seeds over the landscape. Foragers replaced heads of wild yam, sowed a few wild seeds for later harvesting, and attempted to control the migrations of wild herds (Harlan 1995). They began to increase their use of small-grained grasses, preliminary to the use of wild cereals and finally, domesticated grains (Weiss et al. 2004). Analyses of human coprolites (paleofeces) from a 3,000-year-old site in Kentucky document the value of stored grains, which in this case were eaten out of season, possibly during a time when preferred wild foods were unavailable (Gremillion 1996; Gremillion and Sobolik 1996). Without realizing it, foragers were becoming domesticators of plants and animals.

Events that led to agriculture and its diffusion throughout the world have been extensively documented by archaeologists. While the exact timing and the particular animals and plants involved were unique to each region of the world, the processes and results were similar everywhere (Balter 2007; de Wet 1992; Diamond 2002; Harlan 1995; Harris 1996; Heiser 1973; MacNeish 1991; Rindos 1984; Smith 1994; Wymer 1993). Instead of pursuing and killing large animals some distance from home, then butchering the carcasses and carrying the usable and edible portions back home, people kept, fed, and protected young animals and directed their reproduction as they matured. Instead of gathering whatever nature provided, people invested much time and labor in preparing fields, sowing seeds, cultivating the growing plants, and harvesting and storing their crops. Food processing to unlock full nutritional benefits and remove toxins was also a laborious process (Ragir 2000). Domesticated plants and animals eventually became genetically distinct from their wild ancestors, having been selected specifically for their high yields and pleasing flavors, and, in the case of animals, for their docility. They actually became dependent on humans for their survival; for instance, seeds required broad dispersal on prepared ground to germinate and produce healthy plants, which had to be cultivated to eliminate weeds competing for their space and nourishment. Although most agricultural products were consumed and otherwise exploited by humans, some were saved for future production and thus their survival as species was assured. In turn, humans came to rely completely on domestic plants and animals for their subsistence. Between 10,000 and 3,000 years ago farmers replaced foragers almost everywhere on Earth and began to establish a more dependable, high-calorie subsistence base that spurred the development of villages, towns, cities, and finally nations with their large populations and complex societies.

In some regions foragers adopted these novel ideas willingly because they immediately recognized their benefits, but elsewhere hunters simply withdrew to more distant territories in the face of farmers' permanent destruction of their hunting grounds. Small, nomadic foraging bands eventually found themselves demographically overwhelmed by farming societies. As a result of the sedentary lifestyle and constant access to food, women in farming communities could bear many more children in their lifetime.

But like progress everywhere, agricultural subsistence was not without its costs, which farmers were forced to accept because there was no longer any alternative to meet the growing demand for food for increasing populations. Plant cultivation and animal husbandry turned out to be hard work that left little time for rest and leisure. Crops sometimes failed and animals died prematurely or did not reproduce as expected. Pests and natural disasters destroyed hard-earned grain surpluses stored for future consumption. Even though stored food surpluses usually reduced seasonal food shortages, the nutritional value of agricultural products declined and chronic shortages and starvation were not uncommon. Domestic animals transmitted bacteria and parasites to humans, who passed them to other humans in densely populated farming settlements, causing epidemics of infectious diseases not experienced by nomadic foragers (Jackson 2000). To avoid succumbing to such infections, victims required extra energy to mobilize immune responses and compensate for lost body fluids and nutrients. The shift from foraging to farming involved trade-offs. Instead of pure progress, it was simply a new way to provide food, with its own set of advantages and disadvantages. Because farming had permanently altered the environment, however, the good old days of foraging were gone forever. Two well-known prehistoric examples suffice to demonstrate the problems associated with the transition to food production.

The Fertile Crescent

The oldest city in the world with the longest continuous record of human habitation is Jericho in the Levant, the western end of the ancient Fertile Crescent. The most complete record of the foraging-to-farming transition was uncovered here by archaeologists (Bar-Yosef 1998; Harris 1998; Hillman 1996; Twiss 2007). More than 13,000 years ago this was a cold, wet region of coastal plains and hills, dominated by oak woodlands with grassy undergrowth and plenty of wild foods for human foragers. In addition to seeds, pistachio nuts and fruits, there was much game – gazelle, deer, ibex and wild cattle, boar, sheep, and goats. The region's bounty attracted immigrants from the Nile Valley, the Syro-Arabian desert, and the Mediterranean steppe who together became the Natufians, the world's first farmers. The Natufians lived in small permanent settlements of stone houses, underground storage pits, and permanent graveyards. They harvested the game, water fowl, and fish with their barbed spears and bone arrows, and used bone tools for working hides and making baskets. Sickles, created by setting tiny, sharp stone flakes into wooden handles, were used to cut cereal grasses that left a glossy sheen on the bladelets. Whetstones of rough sandstone kept the sickles sharp, and wild wheat and barley seeds were ground with stone pestles in large stone mortars.

Drier conditions about 11,000 years ago forced the Natufians to travel farther afield in search of food, but they always returned to their hamlets to bury their dead. With the return of a wetter climate 1,000 years later, the Natufians began their experiments in cultivation. At first they simply planted near their homes some of the wild wheat and barley seeds they had collected. But soon, to obtain higher yields, they planted seeds they had deliberately selected for their large size. They also chose seeds that did not shatter easily from their stems and become lost on the ground. The sheep and goats they had previously hunted were domesticated by raising wild young in their settlements and selecting for breeding those with the most desirable characteristics.

By 9000 years ago, Jericho with 300–500 inhabitants had become one of the largest of many villages that dotted the region. Its inhabitants built permanent pit houses with stone foundations and mudbrick walls and stored their harvests in silos built of stone or brick. The rich, mixed environment near Jericho and other Natufian villages provided for a wide range of farming activities, including plant cultivation in the wet lowlands and pastoralism in the drier hills. In addition to cereal grains like wheat and barley, farmers cultivated peas, lentils, chickpeas, bitter vetch, and flax, and the dog became "man's best friend" (and dinner, for dogs were also eaten), serving as beast of burden, hunting companion, sheep and goat herder, and garbage scavenger (Harlan 1995; Morey 1994). Production of pottery vessels became an essential part of agricultural life, as external storage for food energy. The importance of pottery is signified by containers of many shapes and sizes that were elaborately decorated. A combination of foods could be cooked in a single pot into a tender and tasty mixture. Lidded ceramic pots held surplus grain for future use and kept it safe from insects and rodents. Precious drinking water was carried and stored in ceramic vessels.

By the end of the Natufian transition 8,000 years ago, full-fledged Neolithic agricultural food production had become the norm in the region. Where Paleolithic campsites had accommodated 5–15 persons and transitional hamlets had held 30–50 Natufians, Neolithic villages housed 300–2,000 persons. But the signs of trouble were already apparent. Compared to Paleolithic foragers, who were very tall and had healthy teeth, sturdy bones, and few endemic diseases, the Natufians were shorter and many of them had anemia. Lack of meat in the diet can cause iron deficiency, which appears as skeletal lesions. Many Neolithic villagers had growth disturbances related to severe malnutrition, high rates of dental disease due to the high-carbohydrate diet, dental attrition, and inflammatory diseases that left their marks on their bones (Eshed et al. 2010).

Eastern North America

The transition from foraging to farming is also well documented archaeologically in eastern North America, and its impact on human health is known in greater detail here than anywhere else (Cohen and Armelagos 1984). Here too a general warming of the climate due to the retreat of the Ice Age glaciers began 10,000 years ago. Herds of mastodon, mammoth, wild horse, and camel entirely disappeared, causing hunters to concentrate on bison and smaller game such as deer, beaver, muskrat, fowl, mussels, and fish. Wild plant foods included hickory and hazelnuts and the oily and starchy seeds of numerous wild plants. A few of these native plants (squash, goosefoot, marsh elder, and sunflower) were more intensively collected during the latter part of the archaic foraging period and actively cultivated during the transitional Woodland period, while hunting continued to supply the majority of protein. More cultivated plants were gradually added until farming became the dominant subsistence strategy. New cultigens (beans, peppers, *maize*) were imported from Mesoamerica where they had been domesticated thousands of years earlier. Maize is a tropical grass, entirely foreign to eastern North America, and its carbon isotopes are so different from those of native food plants that its chemical signature can be readily identified in the bone collagen of humans who have eaten maize. Analyses of temporal series of skeletons indicate when the adoption of maize agriculture occurred in eastern North America.

The original native cultigens were abandoned as they were less productive than maize with its large, flavorful seeds and high-carbohydrate energy load. Maize rapidly became the primary crop and hallmark of the fully agricultural Mississippian cultural tradition. Other than dogs and turkeys, no domesticated animals complemented this abundant source of carbohydrates with protein, so collection of fish and shellfish and hunting of small mammals continued. Nuts rich in protein and oil also continued to be an important resource.

As in other areas of the world, agriculture was the basis for urban development. The great mound city of Cahokia on the eastern bank of the Mississippi River, a major center of religion and trade, held political sway over an extensive region. Food producers brought their harvests to Cahokia for trade and possibly also as payment of tribute. Meat, a relatively rare commodity, became precious currency that may have been diverted to Cahokia's urban population at the expense of the nutritional health of the less politically powerful food producers in the hinterland.

Because many wild plants and most wild animals of eastern North America could not be domesticated, either because they could not survive in captivity, could not be tamed, or became less productive than the wild progenitor, agriculture had the unfortunate effect of reducing dietary diversity and permanently altering food preferences. All the important seed crops of today were derived from once low-priority food plants. But these particular plants could be readily domesticated, and their seeds safely stored for long periods. They were easily converted into delicious meals via newly developed food-processing techniques such as grinding and baking. Selective breeding for larger seeds greatly increased their yield, in contrast to cultivated native plants that produced small seeds even after generations of domestication. Maize had been converted in Mesoamerica from a plant with inch-long ears and tiny seeds to one with large cobs and huge starchy seeds. Worldwide, of the more than 200,000 seed-bearing plant species known, 3,000 had been used for food by Paleolithic foragers, 200 were domesticated, and 13 became important food plants, but only four dominate today in plant agriculture (Cordain 1999; Rindos 1984). These are all grasses – maize, wheat, rice, and sugar cane. Of the wide variety of animal species collected and eaten by Paleolithic foragers, about 50 were domesticated, and only a few of these were used for food in each region (llama, alpaca, pig, turkey, chicken, horse, buffalo, cattle, goat, sheep, dog). Domestic animals still have multiple functions, further limiting their use as food. In addition to meat, blood, milk, and eggs, animals provide wool and hides for clothing and shelter, dung for fertilizer and fuel, and labor for plowing and transportation. While seeds increased in size through domestication, animals became smaller, further reducing their absolute food yield, and they were relatively costly to feed and care for. To compensate for the shortage of animals, early farmers developed a variety of legumes to provide plant proteins (pea, lentil, bean, peanut, soybean) and root crops such as potato, sweet potato, taro, and yam for additional carbohydrate sources.

Not only was the long list of natural foods drastically pared down on the farmers' menu, but the dietary focus had shifted from animal protein and fat to plant carbohydrates. Chemical analysis of human bone showing a relative increase in carbon and depletion of nitrogen indicates clearly that plant foods became dominant and meat consumption was severely reduced. Even the skeletons of North American domestic dogs attest to increased maize consumption. Plant proteins and carbohydrates are less digestible and less nutritionally balanced than protein and fats from animals, and therefore needed in relatively larger quantities to satisfy nutrient and energy demands.

A detailed archaeological study of the transition from foraging to farming in the lower Illinois Valley traces dietary changes from nearly 10,000 years ago to the historical period. At the end of the archaic, the use of deer and other terrestrial mammals declined, and people turned to fish and smaller mammals like beaver and muskrat instead. Red meat and fat, vitamins (especially Vitamin A from animal organs), iron, and niacin became scarce as cultivation of local wild seeds and squash intensified. Fish did provide protein, energy, and calcium, and semi-aquatic animals did offer essential proteins and fats, but these were available only to people living near lakes and streams. Nuts and cultivated oily and starchy seeds therefore became the primary sources of protein, energy, and some vitamins and minerals. The starchy seeds such as knotweed, maygrass, goosefoot, and little barley were favored over the oily sunflower and marsh elder seeds, and the stage was set for the introduction of maize, the starchiest grain of all. By 1,000–800 years ago, the native grain cultigens had been abandoned and entirely replaced by the maize monocrop.

The global environment was irreversibly changed by agriculture. Plowing and cultivation disturbed the soil, encouraged the growth of weeds, and allowed open soils to erode. High-density, sedentary agricultural populations dispersed in villages and towns over the landscape and their conversion of forested lands into great expanses of fields and gardens severely reduced the natural habitat of wild animals and plants. Game animals declined in number and became more difficult to find. In many places they disappeared altogether, leaving those who had few or no domesticated animals without adequate sources of important nutrients. The commitment to farming became total and irreversible because the former habitats of food animals and plants were permanently changed and, with just a very few exceptions, ancient foraging knowledge and skills were eventually forgotten.

All the evidence points to a general decline in human health wherever agriculture replaced foraging subsistence systems, from North America to Egypt and Japan (Buikstra and Cook 1980; Cohen and Armelagos 1984; Goodman and Armelagos 2000; Sciulli 1978; Smith 1972; Sobolik 1994; Starling and Stock 2007; Steckel et al. 2002; Temple and Larsen 2007). Unequivocal signs of nutritional deficiencies, growth disturbances, and increasing disease burdens are evident in the skeletal remains of early farmers. Some of these conditions are still present today, especially in less developed countries where poor populations do not have access to adequate food for various ecological, economic, or political reasons. Seen from an evolutionary perspective, farming must have been a less desirable fallback strategy to supply food to growing human populations living in unstable environments. Later agricultural populations seem to have recovered their health by improving the nutritional content of their foods and developing agricultural technologies to reduce physical activity energy needs.

A journey back through time to two communities, both of them in Kentucky but separated by thousands of years of prehistory, illustrates the dramatic differences in nutritional health between foragers and farmers (Cassidy 1980). Without contact with European settlers, "Hardin Village" was occupied by native farmers from AD 1500 to 1675. During that time the population of the village grew to three times its original size before it was finally abandoned. Hardin Villagers had bows and arrows, pottery, and permanent houses, and ate corn, beans, and squash, supplemented with some meat from small mammals, deer, and elk, as well as wild turkey and box turtle. The Hardin Village diet leaned heavily toward carbohydrates, although the combination of corn and beans also supplied some protein.

There were no houses at "Indian Knoll," occupied from 5,300–4,000 years ago, but the amount of food refuse found there suggests that this was at least a semi-sedentary habitation site during archaic times. The site is marked by a huge shell midden eight feet high and composed mostly of mussel and snail remains. The midden also contained bones of small mammals, wild turkey, box turtle, fish, a few deer, and some wild food plant remains. Indications are that animal protein dominated the Indian Knoll diet, supplemented by a variety of wild plant foods.

Hardin Villagers suffered health problems that were not apparent in Indian Knollers. Iron-deficiency anemia and chronic protein-energy malnutrition left lesions in their skulls, and their limb bones show signs of chronic, severe food shortages. Such signs were absent in skeletons from Indian Knoll, although regular, mild food shortages did occur there. Tooth decay and abscesses were rampant among the farmers due to their starchy diet; Hardin Villagers averaged seven to nine caries, while residents of Indian Knoll had less than one per person, and young children had no tooth decay at all. The only dental abscesses appeared in elderly Indian Knollers whose teeth were heavily worn because of their very gritty diet. Hardin Villagers had 13 times as many bone infections as residents of Indian Knoll. Most infant deaths at Indian Knoll occurred during the first year of life, but at Hardin Village children died between ages one and three years when they were weaned and given adult foods. Hardin Village farmers had shorter lives than Indian Knollers, and more than half of Hardin Village children died before the age of 17.

At the archaeological site of Dickson Mounds in Illinois, where the transition from foraging to agriculture is extensively documented in artifacts and human remains, 80 percent of permanent teeth and 64 percent of deciduous teeth from skeletal remains of the farming population have linear enamel hypoplasia, severe enamel defects related to maternal and child malnutrition (Blakey and Armelagos 1985; Goodman and Armelagos 2000). These enamel defects themselves are benign, but all of the infants with dental lesions had died before the age of three, indicating that the stress must have been severe enough to have a permanent effect (Figure 2.6).

Skull lesions such as *porotic hyperostosis* in the frontal, parietal, and occipital bones and *cribra orbitalia* in the bony margins around the eye were the result of iron-deficiency anemia or infection. Outer skull bone layers became thin and perforated

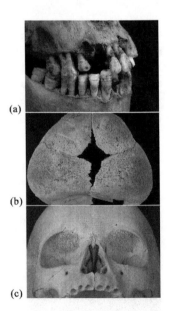

(a)

(b)

(c)

FIGURE 2.6 Lesions related to nutritional stress: (a) Linear enamel hypoplasia; (b) Porotic hyperostosis (catalogue #327074); (c) Cribra orbitalia (catalogue #256571). Courtesy of David R. Hunt/Smithsonian Institution, Physical Anthropology Division.

like sieves, while the inner layer of spongy bone expanded as bone marrow produced more red blood cells. Half of all infants and children in the farming settlements at Dickson Mounds had porotic lesions, double the rate found in the pre-agricultural population. During the transition from foraging to farming at Dickson Mounds, average life expectancy decreased from 26 to 19 years.

The poor health of early farmers contrasts sharply with the relatively good health of preceding foragers. Foragers lived longer than farmers, had lower infant and child mortality rates, and generally exhibited only the bone and enamel defects associated with temporary food shortages, such as mild linear enamel hypoplasia in teeth and catchup growth lines in long bones (Larsen 2002; Sobolik 1994; Williams 1994). Even though dental wear and tooth loss (some due to compression fractures from cracking hickory nuts) had occurred among foragers because of their coarser and more abrasive diet, they developed dental caries only late in life. Farmers had less dental wear but more occlusal abnormalities because they ate softer foods that did not stress jaw muscles, bones, and teeth. They also had greatly increased tooth loss and more dental caries and abscesses at all ages. Their lives were shorter, their growth and development was delayed, and their stature was stunted relative to foragers who preceded them.

Osteoporosis, the weakening of bone tissue at least in part due to calcium deficiency but also the result of physical inactivity, is completely absent in skeletons of foragers. *Periostosis*, a thickening of the fibrous outer layer of long bones caused by acute and chronic infections, occurs three times more frequently in farmers than in foragers. Tubercular bony lesions that are common in the spine and limb bones of farmers suggest that pulmonary tuberculosis infections may also have been a persistent problem. Osteoarthritis is more common among farmers than foragers. It is particularly prevalent in skeletons of women in early farming communities who performed many difficult food-processing chores. While grinding grains, they knelt before the grindstone and subjected their elbows and toes to frequent extreme bending. These joints were particularly affected.

The development of agriculture was also accompanied by the first signs of social stratification that became more pronounced in post-agricultural, urban, and industrial societies (Cohen 1998; Danforth 1999). Graves document the growing complexity of societies. While the common folks had simple burials, the most important members of society were laid to rest in elaborate tombs covered with large earthen mounds and were often accompanied by rare and precious grave goods. Elites were not only the wealthier and more powerful members of society, but also the better nourished, healthier, and longer-lived. Their skeletons show far fewer signs of nutritional stress than those of their lower-class contemporaries, indicating that their diets provided a more appropriate protein-carbohydrate balance. Differential wealth and corresponding nutritional health status characterized entire communities, such as the Dickson Mounds farmers in comparison to the urban citizens of Cahokia, the great prehistoric urban center on the Mississippi River.

The life of foragers had a "Paleolithic rhythm." Among the few modern foragers remaining today, men hunt and women gather for several days each week and stay at home between long collecting trips. However, "rest days" are filled with many chores – caring for children and elders, making and repairing tools, butchering and food preparation, carrying firewood and water, and moving to a new campsite. Even the entertainment is physically taxing, usually consisting of dances lasting long into the night. In spite of their settled life, farmers have no less work than foragers. Daily energy expenditures of modern-day maize cultivators in Guatemala and rice growers in the Philippines, who do most of their work by hand, are at least as great as those of hunter-gatherers in Paraguay (Ulijaszek 2000). Both face seasonal food scarcities and fluctuations in energy expenditure depending on work needed for obtaining food.

Although agriculture provided food for non-producers and surpluses for future needs, it reduced dietary diversity and created dependence on cereal grains that replaced minimally processed lean meat and fresh fruits and vegetables as primary sources of energy. Most of the dietary protein now came from cereals, but these fell far short of the nutrient quality of wild game. Today food allergies and deficiencies related to consumption of animal milk and cereals reflect the still incomplete human adaptation to these relatively new foods (Cordain 1999). The ability to digest the milk sugar lactose is a relatively recent human genetic adaptation to an agricultural diet, but only a few of the world's peoples have acquired it because selective pressures related to pastoralism and animal milk consumption were faced by a relatively small number of human groups. Another recent adaptation to an agricultural diet is copy multiplication of the human *AMY1* gene that promotes the production of salivary amylase, an enzyme required for digestion of starch (Perry et al. 2007).

Excessive, low-quality fat in meat from domesticated animals has replaced the healthful, long-chain polyunsaturated fatty acids of wild game and fish. Sugar, salt, oils, fats, and alcohol add satisfying taste to foods today but are often consumed in excessive amounts and contribute to insulin resistance, diabetes, and cardiovascular disease (Cordain et al. 2005). Many modern processed foods contain inadequate amounts of vitamins, minerals, and fiber that help to prevent cardiovascular disease and stroke. Agriculture provided a constant supply of low-cost, low-quality food energy, allowed for a relatively sedentary lifestyle, increased human fertility, and stimulated the development of civilization. But these benefits were gained at the cost of social disparities and overall declining nutritional health in poorer, less developed countries due to insufficient food supplies and calories and in wealthier developed countries because of overabundance.

Conclusion

Using the various modes of adaptation available to them, over the great span of evolutionary time humans exploited energy in ever more efficient ways in efforts to survive in energy-scarce environments. The unique human erect body, bipedal locomotion, and special digestive system inherited by all hominins, slow and flexible timing of growth and development from infancy to adulthood, complex adjustable and redundant neuroendocrine systems for regulating energy (described in Chapter 3), shared food and child care, tool manufacture and use, big game hunting and other special foraging techniques, cooking, domesticating plants and animals, and mass production of food are all human ways to procure an adequate energy supply. These biological and cultural adaptations vary in populations across the globe to meet the challenges of specific unique environments, but all are geared to ensure survival.

Industrialization tipped the balance in favor of excess energy and obesity in the US and other developed nations. Mass-produced agricultural products have made starvation (but not hunger) virtually impossible in the US, yet industrial foods have serious nutritional disadvantages. They are inexpensive, energy-rich, and attractive in taste and appearance, but low in many important nutrients and fiber. Food variety and ubiquity, large serving portions, aggressive marketing methods, and other influences encourage consumption far beyond what is needed for survival and for the minimal physical effort needed for work and play. Consequently most Americans continually store energy without ever having to use it. Even though a recent study (Pontzer et al. 2012) highlights similar physical activity levels and daily total energy expenditure in a modern foraging society (the Hadza) and populations in industrialized societies such as the US, it is the modern diet, providing much more saturated fat and simple carbohydrates, that accounts for energy imbalance and obesity in the US (Leonard 2014).

Chapter 3 examines more closely the human genetic and physiological legacy for survival in an energy-scarce environment. These biological adaptations to scarcity are a poor fit for the energy-rich modern world. Success in maximizing energy intake while minimizing physical effort to a degree previously unimaginable is not a healthy match with the powerful and ancient human biological system for storage and defense of body fat.

References

Aiello, L. C. and P. Andrews (2000). The Australopithecines in review. *Human Evolution* **15**(1–2): 17–38.

Aiello, L. C. and C. Key (2002). Energetic consequences of being a *Homo erectus* female. *American Journal of Human Biology* **14**: 551–565.

Aiello, L. C. and P. Wheeler (1995). The expensive-tissue hypothesis: the brain and the digestive system in human and primate evolution. *Current Anthropology* **36**: 199–221.

Alemseged, Z. et al. (2006). A juvenile early hominin skeleton from Dikika, Ethiopia. *Nature* **443**: 296–301.

Alexander, R. M. (2002). Energetics and optimization of human walking and running: the 2000 Raymond Pearl Memorial Lecture. *American Journal of Human Biology* **14**: 641–648.

Ambrose, S. H. (2001). Paleolithic technology and human evolution. *Science* **291**: 1748–1753.

Anton, S. C. and C. C. III Swisher (2004). Early dispersal of *Homo* from Africa. *Annual Review of Anthropology* **33**: 271–296.

Anton, S. C., R. Potts, and L. C. Aiello (2014). Evolution of early *Homo*: an integrated biological perspective. *Science* **345**(6192): 1236828–1–13.

Balter, M. (2007). Seeking agriculture's ancient roots. *Science* **316**: 1830–1835.

Bar-Yosef, O. (1998). The Natufian culture in the Levant, threshold to the origins of agriculture. *Evolutionary Anthropology* **6**(5): 159–177.

Blakey, M. and G. J. Armelagos (1985). Deciduous enamel defects in prehistoric Americans from Dickson Mounds: prenatal and postnatal stress. *American Journal of Physical Anthropology* **66**: 371–380.

Boesch, C. and H. Boesch-Achermann (2000). The Chimpanzees of the Tai Forest: Behavioral Ecology and Evolution. Oxford: Oxford University Press.

Bogin, B. (1999). Patterns of Human Growth. Cambridge: Cambridge University Press.

Bousquet-Mélou, A. et al. (1995). Control of lypolysis in intra-abdominal fat cells of nonhuman primates: comparison with humans. *Journal of Lipid Research* **36**: 451–461.

Bramble, D. M. and D. E. Lieberman (2004). Endurance running and the evolution of *Homo. Nature* **432**: 345–352.

Brunet, M. et al. (2002). A new hominid from the upper Miocene of Chad, Central Africa. *Nature Genetics* **418**: 145–151.

Buikstra, J. E. and D. C. Cook (1980). Palaeopathology: an American account. *Annual Review of Anthropology* **9**: 433–470.

Bunn, H. T. (2001). Hunting, power scavenging, and butchering by Hadza foragers and by Plio-Pleistocene *Homo. In* Meat-Eating & Human Evolution. C. B. Stanford and H. T. Bunn, eds. pp. 199–218. Oxford University Press.

Campbell, B. G., J. D. Loy, and K. Cruz-Uribe (2006). Humankind Emerging (9th ed). Boston: Pearson Education, Inc.

Carbone, C., A. Teacher, and J. M. Rowcliffe (2007). The costs of carnivory. *PLoS Biology* **5**(2): 0363–0368.

Cartmill, M. (1972). Arboreal adaptations and the origin of the Order Primates. *In* Functional and Evolutionary Biology of Primates. R. Tuttle, ed. pp. 97–122. Chicago: Aldine-Atherton.

Cassidy, C. M. (1980). Nutrition and health in agriculturalists and hunter-gatherers: a case study of two prehistoric populations. *In* Nutritional Anthropology: Contemporary Approaches to Diet & Culture. N. W. Jerome, R. F. Kandel, and G. H. Pelto, eds. pp. 117–145. Pleasantville, NY: Redgrave Publishing Company.

Churchill, S. E. (2008). Bioenergetic perspectives on Neanderthal thermoregulatory and activity budgets. *In* Neanderthals Revisited: New Approaches and Perspectives. K. Harvati and T. Harrison, eds. pp. 113–133. New York: Springer.

Cohen, M. N. (1998). The emergence of health and social inequalities in the archaeological record. *In* Human Biology and Social Inequality. S. S. Strickland and P. S. Shetty, eds. pp. 249–271. London: Cambridge University Press.

Cohen, M. N., and G. J. Armelagos, eds. (1984). Paleopathology at the Origins of Agriculture. New York: Academic Press.

Comuzzie, A. G. et al. (2003). The baboon as a nonhuman primate model for the study of the genetics of obesity. *Obesity Research* **11**: 75–80.

Conard, N. (2009). A female figurine from the basal Aurignacian of Hohle Fels Cave in southwestern Germany. *Nature* **459**: 248–252.

Conklin-Brittain, N. L., R. W. Wrangham, and C. C. Smith (2002). A two-stage model of increased dietary quality in early hominid evolution: the role of fiber. *In* Human Diet: Its Origin and Evolution. P. S. Ungar and M. F. Teaford, eds. pp. 61–76. Westport, CN: Bergin & Garvey.

Cordain, L. (1999). Cereal grains: humanity's double-edged sword. *In* Evolutionary Aspects of Nutrition and Health. Diet, Exercise, Genetics and Chronic Disease. World Rev Nutr Diet. A. P. Simopoulos, ed. pp. 19–73. Basel: Karger.

Cordain, L. (2001). Fatty acid composition and energy density of foods available to African hominids. *In* Nutrition and Fitness: Metabolic Studies in Health and Disease. World Review of Nutrition and Diet. A. P. Simopolous, ed. pp. 144–161. Basel: Karger.

Cordain, L. (2002). The Paleo Diet: Lose Weight and Get Healthy by Eating the Food You Were Designed to Eat. New York: John Wiley & Sons, Inc.

Cordain, L. et al. (2000). Plant-animal subsistence ratios and macronutrient energy estimations in worldwide hunter-gatherer diets. *American Journal of Clinical Nutrition* **71**: 682–692.

Cordain, L. et al. (2002). Fatty acid analysis of wild ruminant tissues: evolutionary implications for reducing diet-related chronic disease. *European Journal of Clinical Nutrition* **56**: 181–191.

Cordain, L. et al. (2005). Origins and evolution of the western diet: health implications for the 21st century. *American Journal of Clinical Nutrition* **81**: 341–354.

Cordain, L., R. W. Gotshall, and S. B. Eaton (1997). Evolutionary aspects of exercise. *World Review of Nutrition and Diet* **81**: 49–60.

Danforth, M. E. (1999). Nutrition and politics in prehistory. *Ann Rev Anthropol* **28**: 1–25.

De Waal, F. and F. Lanting (1997). Bonobo: The Forgotten Ape. Berkeley: University of California Press.

de Wet, J. M. J. (1992). The three phases of cereal domestication. *In* Grass Evolution and Domestication. G. P. Chapman, ed. pp. 176–198. Cambridge: Cambridge University Press.

Defleur, A. et al. (1999). Neanderthal cannibalism at Moula-Guercy, Ardeche, France. *Science* **286**: 128–131.

Diamond, J. (2002). Evolution, consequences and future of plant and animal domestication. *Nature* **418**: 700–707.

Draper, H. H. (1977). The aboriginal Eskimo diet in modern perspective. *American Anthropologist* **79**: 309–316.

Dufour, D. L. and M. L. Sauther (2002). Comparative and evolutionary dimensions of the energetics of human pregnancy and lactation. *American Journal of Human Biology* **14**: 584–602.

Eaton, S. B., S. B. III Eaton, and L. Cordain (2002). Evolution, diet, and health. *In* Human Diet: Its Origin and Evolution. P. S. Ungar and M. F. Teaford, eds. pp. 7–18. Westport, CN: Bergin & Garvey.

Eaton, S. B., S. B. Eaton, III, and M. J. Konner (1999). Paleolithic nutrition revisited. *In* Evolutionary Medicine. W. R. Trevathan, E. O. Smith, and J. J. McKenna, eds. pp. 313–332. New York: Oxford University Press.

Eaton, S. B. and M. J. Konner (1985). Paleolithic nutrition: a consideration of its nature and current implications. *New England Journal of Medicine* **312**(5): 283–289.

Eaton, S. B., M. Shostak, and M. Konner (1989). The Paleolithic Prescription: A Program of Diet & Exercise and a Design for Living. New York: Harper & Row.

Ellison, P. T. (2001). On Fertile Ground: A Natural History of Human Reproduction. Cambridge: Harvard University Press.

Ellison, P. T. (2003). Energetics and reproductive effort. *American Journal of Human Biology* **15**: 342–51.

Emery Thompson, M. (2013). Comparative reproductive energetics of human and nonhuman primates. *Annual Review of Anthropology* **42**: 287–304.

Eshed, V. et al. (2010). Paleopathology and the origin of agriculture in the Levant. *American Journal of Physical Anthropology* **143**: 121–133.

Fahy, G. E. et al. (2013). Stable isotope evidence of meat eating and hunting specialization in adult male chimpanzees. *Proceedings of the National Academy of Sciences* **110**(15): 5829–5832.

Fedigan, L. M. (1982). Primate Paradigms: Sex Roles and Social Bonding. Montreal: Eden.

Fernandez-Jalvo, Y., P. Andrews, and C. Denys (1999). Cut marks on small mammals at Olduvai Gorge Bed-I. *Journal of Human Evolution* **36**: 587–589.

Finlayson, C. et al. (2006). Late survival of Neanderthals at the southernmost extreme of Europe. *Nature* **443**: 850–853.

Fish, J. L. and C. A. Lockwood (2003). Dietary constraints on encephalization in primates. *American Journal of Physical Anthropology* **120**: 171–181.

Foley, R. (2002). The evolutionary consequences of increased carnivory in hominids. *In* Meat Eating & Human Evolution. C. B. Stanford and H. T. Bunn, eds. pp. 305–331. Oxford: Oxford University Press.

Foley, R. A. and P. C. Lee (1992). Ecology and energetics of encephalization in hominid evolution. *In* Foraging Strategies and Natural Diet of Monkeys, Apes, and Humans. A. Whiten and E. M. Widdowson, eds. pp. 63–72. Oxford: Clarendon.

Frisancho, A. R. (1993). Human Adaptation and Accommodation. Ann Arbor: University of Michigan Press.

Fuentes, A. (2011). Biological Anthropology: Concepts and Connections. New York: McGraw Hill.

Giesen, M. and P. W. Sciulli (1988). Long bone growth in a Late Archaic skeletal sample. *American Journal of Physical Anthropology* Suppl **75**: 213.

Goodall, J. (1986). The Chimpanzees of Gombe: Patterns of Behavior. Cambridge: Belknap Press of Harvard University Press.

Goodman, A. H. and J. Armelagos (2000). Disease and death at Dr. Dickson's mounds. *In* Nutritional Anthropology. D. Goodman, Pelto, ed. pp. 58–62. Mountain View, CA: Mayfield.

Gremillion, K. J. (1996). Early agricultural diet in eastern North America; evidence from two Kentucky rockshelters. *American Antiquity* **61**: 520–536.

Gremillion, K. J. and K. D. Sobolik (1996). Dietary variability among prehistoric forager-farmers of eastern North America. *Current Anthropology* **37**: 529–539.

Guatelli-Steinberg, D. (2003). Macroscopic and microscopic analyses of linear enamel hypoplasia in Plio-Pleistocene South African hominins with respect to aspects of enamel development and morphology. *American Journal of Physical Anthropology* **120**: 309–322.

Guatelli-Steinberg, D. and Z. Benderlioglu (2006). Brief communication: linear enamel hypoplasia and the shift from irregular to regular provisioning in Cayo Santiago rhesus monkeys (*Macaca mulatta*). *American Journal of Physical Anthropology* **131**: 416–419.

Guatelli-Steinberg, D., C. S. Larsen, and D. L. Hutchinson (2004). Prevalence and the duration of linear enamel hypoplasia: a comparative study of Neandertals and Inuit foragers. *Journal of Human Evolution* **47**: 65–84.

Gursky, S. (2007). Tarsiiformes. *In* Primates in Perspective. C. J. Campbell, A. Fuentes et al., eds. pp. 73–85. New York: Oxford University Press.

Hannibal, D. L. and D. Guatelli-Steinberg (2005). Linear enamel hypoplasia in the great apes: analysis by genus and locality. *American Journal of Physical Anthropology* **127**: 13–25.

Harlan, J. R. (1995). The Living Fields: Our Agricultural Heritage. Cambridge: Cambridge University Press.

Harris, D. R. (1998). The origins of agriculture in southwest Asia. *Review of Archaeology* **19**(2): 5–11.

Harris, D. R. ed. (1996). The Origins and Spread of Agriculture and Pastoralism in Eurasia. Washington, DC: Smithsonian Institution Press.

Hartwig, W. (2007). Primate evolution. *In* Primates in Perspective. C. J. Campbell, A. Fuentes, K. C. MacKinnon, M. Panger, and S. K. Bearder, eds. pp. 11–22. Oxford: Oxford University Press.

Heiser, C. B. Jr. (1973). Seed to Civilization: The Story of Man's Food. San Francisco: Freeman.

Hillman, G. (1996). Late Pleistocene changes in wild plant-foods available to hunter-gatherers of the northern Fertile Crescent: possible preludes to cereal cultivation. *In* The Origins and Spread of Agriculture and Pastoralism in Eurasia. D. R. Harris, ed. pp. 159–203. Washington DC: Smithsonian Institution Press.

Holt, B. M. and V. Formicola (2008). Hunters of the Ice Age: the biology of Upper Paleolithic people. *Yearbook of Physical Anthropology* **51**: 70–99.

Howard, C. F. and M. Yasuda (1990). Diabetes mellitus in nonhuman primates: recent research advances and current husbandry practices. *Journal of Medical Primatology* **19**: 609–625.

Isaac, G. (1978). The food-sharing behavior of proto-hominids. *Scientific American* **238**: 90–108.

Jackson, F. L. C. (2000). Human adaptation to infectious disease. *In* Human Biology: An Evolutionary and Biocultural Perspective. S. Stinson, B. Bogin, R. Huss-Ashmore, and D. O'Rourke, eds. pp. 273–293. New York: Wiley-Liss.

Johnson, R. J. and P. Andrews (2010). Fructose, uricase, and the back-to-Africa hypothesis. *Evolutionary Anthropology* **19**: 250–257.

Kaplan, H. et al. (2000). A theory of human life history evolution: diet, intelligence, and longevity. *Evolutionary Anthropology* **9**(4): 156–185.

Kaplan, H., S. B. Manuck, and C. Shively (1991). The effects of fat and cholesterol on social behavior in monkeys. *Psychosomatic Medicine* **53**: 634–642.

Knott, C. (2001). Female reproductive ecology of the apes: implications for human evolution. *In* Reproductive Ecology and Human Evolution. P. T. Ellison, ed. pp. 429–463. Hawthorne, NY: Aldine de Gruyter.

Kramer, K. L. and P. T. Ellison (2010). Pooled energy budgets: resituating human energy allocation trade-offs. *Evolutionary Anthropology* **19**: 136–147.

Kuzawa, C. W. (1998). Adipose tissue in human infancy and childhood: an evolutionary perspective. *Yearbook of Physical Anthropology* **41**: 177–209.

Kuzawa, C. W. et al. (2014). Metabolic costs and evolutionary implications of human brain development. *Proceedings of the National Academy of Sciences* **111**(36): 13010–13015.

Larsen, C. S. (2002). Post-Pleistocene human evolution: bioarcheology of the agricultural transition. *In* Human Diet: Its Origin and Evolution. P. S. Ungar and M. F. Teaford, eds. pp. 19–36. Westport, CN: Bergin & Garvey.

Leakey, L. B., P. V. Tobias, and J. R. Napier (1964). A new species of the genus *Homo* from Olduvai Gorge. *Nature* **202**: 7–9.

Lee-Thorp, J. and M. Sponheimer (2006). Contributions of biogeochemistry to understanding hominin dietary ecology. *Yearbook of Physical Anthropology* **49**: 131–148.

Lee, R. B. (1968). What hunters do for a living, or, how to make out on scarce resources. *In* Man the Hunter. R. B. Lee and I. DeVore, eds. pp. 30–48. Chicago: Aldine.

Leigh, S. R. (1994). Relations between captive and non-captive weights in anthropoid primates. *Zoo Biology* **13**(1): 21–43.

Leigh, S. R. (2004). Brain growth, life history, and cognition in primate and human evolution. *American Journal of Primatology* **62**(3): 139–164.

Leonard, W. R. (2014). The global diversity of eating patterns: human nutritional health in comparative perspective. *Physiology & Behavior* **134**: 5–14.

Leonard, W. R. and M. L. Robertson (1992). Nutritional requirements and human evolution: a bioenergetics model. *American Journal of Human Biology* **4**: 179–195.

Leonard, W. R. and M. L. Robertson (2003). Comparative energetics of human and primate locomotion. *American Journal of Physical Anthropology* Suppl **36**: 139.

Lieberman, L. S. (1987). Biocultural consequences of animals versus plants as sources of fats, proteins, and other nutrients. *In* Food and Evolution: Toward a Theory of Human Food Habits. M. Harris and E. B. Ross, eds. pp. 225–260. Philadelphia: Temple University Press.

Lieberman, L. S. (2008). Diabesity and Darwinian medicine. *In* Evolutionary Medicine and Health. W. R. Trevathan, E. O. Smith, and J. J. McKenna, eds. pp. 72–95. New York: Oxford University Press.

Lovejoy, C. O. (1988). Evolution of human walking. *Scientific American* **259**: 118–125.

Lukacs, J. R. (2001). Enamel hypoplasia in the deciduous teeth of great apes: variation in prevalence and timing of defects. *American Journal of Physical Anthropology* **116**: 199–208.

MacNeish, R. S. (1991). The Origins of Agriculture and Settled Life. Norman, OK: University of Oklahoma Press.

Malenky, R. K. et al. (1994). The significance of terrestrial herbaceous foods for bonobos, chimpanzees, and gorillas. *In* Chimpanzee Cultures. R. W. Wrangham, W. C. McGrew, F. B. M. deWaal, P. G. Heltne, and L. A. Marquardt, eds. pp. 59–76. Cambridge, MA: Harvard University Press & The Chicago Academy of Sciences.

McDougall, I., F. H. Brown, and J. G. Fleagle (2005). Stratigraphic placement and age of modern humans from Kibish, Ethiopia. *Nature* **433**: 733–736.

McFarland, R. (1997). Female primates: fat or fit? *In* The Evolving Female: A Life-History Perspective. M. E. Morbeck, A. Galloway, and A. L. Zihlman, eds. pp. 163–309. Princeton: Princeton University Press.

McGrew, W. C. (2001). The other faunivory: primate insectivory and early human diet. *In* Meat-Eating & Human Evolution. C. B. Stanford and H. T. Bunn, eds. pp. 160–178. The Human Evolution Series. Oxford: Oxford University Press.

Milton, K. (1993). Diet and primate evolution. *Scientific American* **269**: 86–93.

Milton, K. (1999). A hypothesis to explain the role of meat-eating in human evolution. *Evolutionary Anthropology* **8**(1): 11–21.

Milton, K. M. (1987). Primate diets and gut morphology: implications for human evolution. *In* Food and Evolution: Toward a Theory of Human Food Habits. M. Harris and E. B. Ross, eds. pp. 93–116. Philadelphia: Temple University Press.

Morey, D. F. (1994). The early evolution of the domestic dog. *In* Exploring Evolutionary Biology: Readings from American Scientist. pp. 140–151. Sunderland, MA: Sinauer.

Mueller, A. E. and U. Thalmann (2002). Biology of the fat-tailed dwarf lemur (*Cheirogleus medius* E. Geoffroy 1812): new results from the field. *Evolutionary Anthropology* Suppl **1**: 79–82.

Nelson, S. M. (1993). Diversity of the Upper Paleolithic "Venus" figurines and archeological mythology. *In* Gender in Cross-Cultural Perspective. C. B. Brettell and C. F. Sargent, eds. pp. 51–58. Englewood Cliffs, NJ: Prentice Hall.

O'Connell, J. F., K. Hawkes, and N. G. Blurton Jones (1999). Grandmothering and the evolution of *Homo erectus*. *Journal of Human Evolution* **36**: 461–485.

O'Dea, K. (1992). Traditional diet and food preferences of Australian aboriginal hunter-gatherers. *In* Foraging Strategies and Natural Diet of Monkeys, Apes and Humans. A. Whiten and E. M. Widdowson, eds. pp. 73–80. Oxford: Clarendon Press.

O'Sullivan, A. J. (2008). Does oestrogen allow women to store fat more efficiently? A biological advantage for fertility and gestation. *Obesity Reviews* **10**: 168–177.

Oates, J. F. (1987). Food distribution and foraging behavior. *In* Primate Societies. B. B. Smuts, D. L. Cheney, R. M. Seyfarth, R. W. Wrangham, and T. T. Struhsaker, eds. pp. 197–209. Chicago: University of Chicago Press.

Perry, G. H. et al. (2007). Diet and the evolution of human amylase gene copy number variation. *Nature Genetics* **39**(10): 1256–1260.

Pfeiffer, J. (1969). The Emergence of Man. New York: Harper & Row.

Plummer, T. (2004). Flaked stones and old bones: biological and cultural evolution at the dawn of technology. *Yearbook of Physical Anthropology* **47**: 118–164.

Pond, C. M. (1997). The biological origins of adipose tissue in humans. *In* The Evolving Female: A Life-History Perspective. M. E. Morbeck, A. Galloway, and A. L. Zihlman, eds. Princeton: Princeton University Press.

Pond, C. M. (1998). The Fats of Life. Cambridge: Cambridge University Press.

Pond, C. M. and C. A. Mattacks (1987). The anatomy of adipose tissue in captive macaca monkeys and its implications for human biology. *Folia primatologica* **48**: 164–185.

Pontzer, H. et al. (2012). Hunter-gatherer energetics and human obesity. *PLoS One* **7**(7): e40503.

Pontzer, H. et al. (2014). Primate energy expenditure and life history. *Proceedings of the National Academy of Sciences* **111**(4): 1433–1437.

Power, M. L. and J. Schulkin (2008). Sex differences in fat storage, fat metabolism, and the health risks from obesity: possible evolutionary origins. *British Journal of Nutrition* **99**: 931–940.

Pruetz, J. D. and P. Bertolani (2007). Savanna chimpanzees, *Pan troglodytes verus*, hunt with tools. *Current Biology* **17**: 412–417.

Ragir, S. (2000). Diet and food preparation; rethinking early hominid behavior. *Evolutionary Anthropology* **9**(4): 153–155.

Remis, M. J. (2003). Are gorillas vacuum cleaners of the forest floor? The roles of body size, habitat, and food preferences on dietary flexibility and nutrition. *In* Gorilla Biology: A Multidisciplinary Perspective. A. B. Taylor and M. L. Goldsmith, eds. pp. 385–404. Cambridge: Cambridge University Press.

Riehl, S., M. Zeidi, and N. J. Conard (2013). Emergence of agriculture in the foothills of the Zagros Mountains of Iran. *Science* **341**: 65–67.

Rindos, D. (1984). The Origins of Agriculture: An Evolutionary Perspective. New York: Academic Press, Inc.

Roach, N. T. et al. (2013). Elastic energy storage in the shoulder and the evolution of high-speed throwing in *Homo. Nature* **498**: 483–487.

Robinson, J. G. and C. H. Janson (1987). Capuchins, squirrel monkeys, and atelines: socio-ecological convergence with Old World primates. *In* Primate Societies. B. B. Smuts, D. L. Cheney, R. M. Seyfarth, R. W. Wrangham, and T. T. Struhsaker, eds. Chicago: University of Chicago Press.

Robinson, J. T. (1956). The dentition of the Australopithecinae. *Transvaal Museum Mem* **9**: 1–179.

Rodman, P. S. and H. M. McHenry (1980). Bioenergetics and the origin of hominid bipedalism. *American Journal of Physical Anthropology* **52**: 103–106.

Rose, L. M. (2001). Meat and the early human diet: insights from neotropical primate studies. *In* Meat-Eating and Human Evolution. C. B. Stanford and H. T. Bunn, eds. pp. 141–159. London: Oxford University Press.

Rosenblum, I. Y., T. A. Barbolt, and C. F. Howard (1981). Diabetes mellitus in the chimpanzee (*Pan troglodytes*). *Journal of Medical Primatology* **10**: 93–101.

Ruff, C. B. et al. (2015). Gradual decline in mobility with the adoption of food production in Europe. *Proceedings of the National Academy of Science* **112**(23): 7147–7152.

Sapolsky, R. M. (2000). Junk food monkeys. *In* Nutritional Anthropology: Biocultural Perspectives on Food and Nutrition. A. H. Goodman, D. L. Dufour, and G. H. Pelto, eds. pp. 71–73. Mountain View, CA: Mayfield.

Schmidt, D. A. et al. (2005). Fiber digestibility by the orangutan (*Pongo abeli*): in vitro and in vivo. *Journal of Zoo and Wildlife Medicine* **36**(4): 571–580.

Schoeninger, M. J. (2014). Stable isotope analysis and the evolution of human diets. *Annual Review of Anthropology* **43**: 413–430.

Schwartz, S. M. and J. W. Kemnitz (1992). Age- and gender-related changes in body size, adiposity, and endocrine and metabolic parameters in free-ranging rhesus macaques. *American Journal of Physical Anthropology* **89**: 109–121.

Sciulli, P. W. (1978). Developmental abnormalities of the permanent dentition in prehistoric Ohio Valley Amerindians. *American Journal of Physical Anthropology* **48**: 193–198.

Setchell, J. M. and A. F. Dixson (2001). Arrested development of secondary sexual adornments in subordinate adult male mandrills (*Mandrillus sphinx*). *American Journal of Physical Anthropology* **115**: 245–252.

Shipman, P. (1986). Scavenging or hunting in early hominids: theoretical framework and tests. *American Anthropologist* **88**: 27–43.

Shively, C. A. and T. B. Clarkson (1988). Body fat distribution and atherosclerosis. *In* Nonhuman Primate Studies on Diabetes, Carbohydrate Intolerance, and Obesity. C. F. Howard Jr., ed. pp. 43–63. New York: Alan R. Liss, Inc.

Smith, B. D. (1994). The origins of agriculture in the Americas. *Evolutionary Anthropology* **3**: 174–184.

Smith, P. (1972). Diet and attrition in the Natufians. *American Journal of Physical Anthropology* **37**: 233–238.

Sobolik, K. D. (1994). Paleonutrition: The Diet and Health of Prehistoric Americans. Carbondale, IL: Center for Archaeological Investigations, Southern Illinois University at Carbondale.

Sockol, M. D., D. A. Raichlen, and H. Pontzer (2007). Chimpanzee locomotor energetics and the origin of human bipedalism. *Proceedings of the National Academy of Sciences* **104** (30): 12265–12269.

Sorensen, M. V. and W. R. Leonard (2001). Neandertal energetics and foraging efficiency. *Journal of Human Evolution* **40**(6): 483–495.

Sponheimer, M. et al. (2013). Isotopic evidence of early hominin diets. *Proceedings of the National Academy of Sciences* **110**(26): 10513–10518.

Stanford, C. B. (2001). The ape's gift: meat-eating, meat-sharing, and human evolution. *In* Tree of Origin: What Primate Behavior Can Tell Us about Human Social Evolution. F. De Waal, ed. pp. 95–118. Cambridge: Harvard University Press.

Starling, A. P. and J. T. Stock (2007). Dental indicators of health and stress in early Egyptian and Nubian agriculturalists: a difficult transition and gradual recovery. *American Journal of Physical Anthropology* **134**: 520–528.

Steckel, R. H. et al. (2002). Skeletal health in the western hemisphere from 4000 B.C. to the present. *Evolutionary Anthropology* **11**: 142–155.

Steudel-Numbers, K. L. and M. J. Tilkens (2004). The effect of lower limb length on the energetic cost of locomotion: implications for fossil hominins. *Journal of Human Evolution* **47**: 95–109.

Strier, K. (1993). Menu for a monkey. *Natural History* **102**(3): 34–45.

Strier, K. (2003). Primate Behavioral Ecology. Boston: Allyn and Bacon.

Suarez, S. A. (2006). Diet and travel costs for spider monkeys in a nonseasonal, hyperdiverse environment. *International Journal of Primatology* **27**(2): 411–436.

Tchernov, J. D. S. (2001). Neandertal hunting and meat processing in the Near East: evidence from Kebara Cave (Israel). *In* Meat Eating and Human Evolution. C. B. Stanford and H. T. Bunn, eds. pp. 52–72. Oxford: Oxford University Press.

Temple, D. H. and C. S. Larsen (2007). Dental caries prevalence as evidence for agriculture and subsistence variation during the Yayoi Period in prehistoric Japan: biocultural interpretations of an economy in transition. *American Journal of Physical Anthropology* **134**: 501–512.

Thompson, J. L. and A. J. Nelson (2011). Middle childhood and modern human origins. *Human Nature* **22**: 249–280.

Tutin, C. E. G. (1996). Ranging and social structure of lowland gorillas in the Lope Reserve, Gabon. *In* Great Ape Societies. W. C. McGrew, L. F. Marchant, and T. Nishida, eds. pp. 58–70. London: Cambridge University Press.

Twiss, K. C. (2007). The Neolithic of the southern Levant. *Evolutionary Anthropology* **16**: 24–35.

Uddin, M. et al. (2004). Sister grouping of chimpanzees and humans as revealed by genome-wide phylogenetic analysis of brain gene expression profiles. *Proceedings of the National Academy of Sciences* **101**(9): 2957–2962.

Ulijaszek, S. J. (1992). Human dietary change. *In* Foraging Strategies and Natural Diet of Monkeys, Apes and Humans. A. Whiten and E. M. Widdowson, eds. pp. 111–121. Oxford: Clarendon Press.

Ulijaszek, S. J. (2000). Work and energetics. *In* Human Biology: An Evolutionary and Biocultural Perspective. S. Stinson, B. Bogin, R. Huss-Ashmore, and D. O'Rourke, eds. pp. 345–376. New York: Wiley-Liss.

Ulijaszek, S. J. (2002). Human eating behaviour in an evolutionary ecological context. *Proceedings of the Nutrition Society* **61**: 517–526.

Ungar, P. S. and F. E. Grine (1991). Incisor size and wear in *Australopithecus africanus* and *Paranthropus robustus*. *Journal of Human Evolution* **20**: 313–340.

Ungar, P. S., F. E. Grine, and M. F. Teaford (2006). Diet in early Homo: a review of the evidence and a new model of adaptive versatility. *Annual Review of Anthropology* **35**: 209–228.

Utami, S. S. and J. A. R. A. M. Van Hooff (1997). Meat-eating by adult female Sumatran orangutans (*Pongo pygmaeus abelii*). *American Journal of Primatology* **43**: 159–165.

van Valkenburgh, B. (2001). The dog-eat-dog world of carnivores: a review of past and present carnivore community dynamics. *In* Meat-Eating & Human Evolution. C. B. Stanford and H. T. Bunn, eds. pp. 101–121. New York: Oxford University Press.

Wall-Scheffler, C. M., K. Geiger, and K. L. Steudel-Numbers (2007). Infant carrying: the role of increased locomotory costs in early tool development. *American Journal of Physical Anthropology* **133**: 841–846.

Watts, D. B. (1996). Comparative socio-ecology of gorillas. *In* Great Ape Societies. W. B. McGrew, M. L. F., and T. Nishida, eds. pp. 16–28. London: Cambridge University Press.

Weiss, E. et al. (2004). The broad spectrum revisited: evidence from plant remains. *Proceedings of the National Academy of Sciences* **101**(26): 9551–9555.

Wheeler, P. (1992a). The thermoregulatory advantages of large body size for hominids foraging in savannah environments. *Journal of Human Evolution* **23**: 351–362.

Wheeler, P. (1992b). The influence of the loss of functional body hair on the water budgets of early hominids. *Journal of Human Evolution* **23**: 379–388.

White, F. J. (1996). Comparative socio-ecology of Pan paniscus. *In* Great Ape Societies. W. C. McGrew, L. F. Marchant, and T. Nishida, eds. pp. 29–44. London: Cambridge University Press.

White, T. D. et al. (2009). *Ardipithecus ramidus* and the paleobiology of early hominids. *Science* **326**: 64–86.

Wickings, E. J. and A. F. Dixson (1992). Testicular function, secondary sexual development, and social status in male mandrills (Mandrillus sphinx). *Physiology & Behavior* **52**: 909–916.

Williams, J. A. (1994). Disease profiles of archaic and woodland populations in the northern plains. *In* Skeletal Biology in the Great Plains: Migration, Warfare, Health, and Subsistence. D. W. Owsley and R. L. Jantz, eds. pp. 91–108. Washington: Smithsonian Institution Press.

Wilson, M. L. and R. W. Wrangham (2003). Intergroup relations in chimpanzees. *Annual Review of Anthropology* **32**: 363–392.

Woods, S. C. et al. (1988). Baboons as a model for research on metabolism, feeding and the regulation of body weight. *In* Nonhuman Primate Studies on Diabetes, Carbohydrate Intolerance, and Obesity. pp. 133–144.

Wrangham, R. W. (2001). Out of the pan, into the fire: how our ancestors' evolution depended on what they ate. *In* Tree of Origin: What Primate Behavior Can Tell Us about Human Social Evolution. F. De Waal, ed. pp. 121–143. Cambridge, MA: Harvard University Press.

Wrangham, R. W. et al. (1993). The value of figs to chimpanzees. *International Journal of Primatology* **14**: 243–256.

Wymer, D. A. (1993). Cultural change and subsistence: the Middle and Late Woodland transition in the Mid-Ohio Valley. *In* Foraging and Farming in the Eastern Woodlands. C. M. Scarry, ed. Gainesville: Florida University Press.

Zihlman, A. L. and D. R. Bolter (2015). Body composition in *Pan paniscus* compared with *Homo sapiens* has implications for changes during human evolution. *Proceedings of the National Academy of Science* **112**(24): 7466–7471.

Zihlman, A. L. and R. K. McFarland (2000). Body mass in lowland gorillas: a quantitative analysis. *American Journal of Physical Anthropology* **113**(1): 61–78.

Zubrow, E. (1989). The demographic modelling of Neanderthal extinction. *In* The Human Revolution: Behavioural and Biological Perspectives on the Origins of Modern Humans. P. Mellars and C. Stringer, eds. pp. 212–231. Princeton, NJ: Princeton University Press.

3
THE METABOLIC BASIS OF OBESITY

Introduction

Why do so many Americans have obesity? Couldn't they simply eat less and exercise more to lose excess weight or to avoid becoming fat in the first place? Isn't it a simple matter of matching energy output to energy intake?

$$ENERGY\ IN = ENERGY\ OUT$$

Unfortunately not! Obesity is not simply a problem of over-indulgence, laziness, and lack of willpower. In fact, the human body regulates energy input and output in a very complex process, with a multitude of genes and a profusion of at least 60 *hormones, neurotransmitters*, and other chemicals powerfully influencing and modifying every step from consuming food to using its energy (Trivedi 2014; Ulijaszek and Lofink 2006).

$$ENERGY\ IN \rightarrow ENERGY\text{-}REGULATING\ SYSTEM \rightarrow ENERGY\ OUT$$

The unique human evolutionary heritage consists of powerful adaptations that ensure the development of sufficient energy reserves. These adaptations include genetic predispositions, metabolic physiology, developmental adjustments, and cultural behaviors, all designed to support the function of the large human brain and to sustain life through famines, long, cold winters, multiple pregnancies, and rigorous physical labor. Some adaptations are designed to preserve and defend stored body fat after it has been accumulated and constitute a major and often insurmountable challenge to individuals with obesity who attempt to lose weight (Ochner et al. 2015). Human biology – genetic predisposition and energy-regulating physiology (energy *metabolism*) – is strongly skewed toward maximizing energy input and minimizing energy output. This chapter will examine some of the complex biological mechanisms underlying human obesity and related health consequences. It is important to keep in mind that these mechanisms evolved to preserve human life in challenging environments where energy availability was sporadic and unpredictable and energy expenditure was consistently high. Even though in modern America food energy is readily and constantly available and the work load is light, these mechanisms continue to function today.

Except in very rare cases, obesity is not due to malfunctioning of the metabolic system. Instead, it is an adaptation to an energy-rich environment which combines continuous access to excessive calories with few opportunities to use them through physical activity. "Weight cycling," which was the norm during the annual rounds of food abundance and food scarcity in the not-so-recent past, has largely disappeared in wealthier, developed countries where food is plentiful, inexpensive, and easy to obtain. The problem now is not where to find enough food to sustain life, but where to put the excess energy consumed and not spent.

A great deal of what is known today about the physiological and genetic basis of obesity comes from long-term studies of an indigenous American population, the Akimel O'Odham (Pima) of Arizona (Knowler et al. 1982; Lee et al. 2005; Ma et al. 2004; Muller et al. 2003; Norman et al. 1998; Pratley et al. 1997; Price et al. 1993; Ravussin and Gautier 2002; Ravussin et al. 1997). The entire Pima community of 7,500 individuals agreed many years ago to participate in numerous scientific investigations which have revealed much about the biological basis of obesity and its impact on health. The Pima have the highest rates of obesity and diabetes in the US, and nearly the highest in the world. For more than 40 years and spanning several generations, National Institutes of Health scientists have studied virtually every aspect of their biology and cultural history. As an extreme example of the development of obesity in a relatively small human community, they have contributed much to the understanding of obesity in the general American population. More details about the Pima follow in Chapter 4.

Life history of obesity development

The extended human lifespan offers many opportunities to accumulate fat. During periods of rapid growth humans are particularly prone to developing obesity. When a specific dietary component interacts with certain obesity-susceptibility genes during these sensitive periods, metabolic physiology is permanently altered to favor accumulation and storage of excess energy instead of expending it through elevated metabolism, heat generation, and energy dissipation.

No time is more important than the prenatal and early postnatal stages in the development of human physiology. The fetus is, of course, dependent on its mother for nourishment, so both maternal under-nutrition and over-nutrition leave their mark on an infant's developing metabolic system, and both may predispose to obesity throughout the rest of life. Metabolic imprinting during early development permanently fixes neural circuits and functions, and also establishes the expression of genes associated with appetite and energy metabolism for a lifetime. As noted in examples below, the remarkable human capacity to adjust to nutritional restriction during pre- and postnatal life stages helps to ensure the survival of the individual and the species, but at the price of potential obesity and associated health problems (such as diabetes) in later life. This trade-off in early development – sacrificing health for survival – is irreversible (Wells 2013).

A well-documented example of human metabolic adaptability occurred during the Dutch Winter Famine of 1944–5 in the German-occupied Netherlands (Lummaa 2003). Infants born to mothers who were pregnant during the famine weighed about 300 grams less than the average birth weight during pre-World War II times. Unexpectedly, children of mothers who experienced the famine in the first and second trimester of pregnancy were almost twice as likely to become obese in later life as other children of the same mothers. Maternal nutritional deprivation, especially of protein, permanently set fetal metabolism in preparation for a lifetime of nutritional stress. But post-war recovery and abundance promoted rapid weight gain after birth and the development of obesity, diabetes, and heart disease in adult-hood. This physiological response to maternal malnutrition established a *thrifty phenotype* in response to nutritional stress (Gluckman and Hanson 2006).

Food deprivation results in compromised organ development and fetal growth retardation, as well as maternal malnutrition. Brain development has the high-est priority in the growing fetus and neonate, so nutrients are diverted from other organs to the brain to guarantee it an adequate energy supply (Wells 2013). Consequently liver, kidneys, and pancreas are reduced in size and their metabolic functions are disrupted. The capacity of the pancreas to produce *insulin*, the energy storage hormone, is diminished and *glucose intolerance, hypertension,* and *hyperlipidemia* follow. The short-term fetal survival mechanism ultimately becomes a long-term disadvantage for adult health (Barker 2002; Gluckman and Hanson 2006).

Healthy babies of appropriate birth weight have an adequate supply of body fat, usually about 15 percent of their body mass, to tide them over postnatal nutritional disruptions (Kuzawa 1998). Small newborns with less stored energy grow very rapidly if adequately fed after birth, when they are free of maternal nutritional limi-tations. Although that rapid catch-up growth brings them quickly into the normal range of body mass, it is accompanied by as much as a five times greater risk of becoming obese in adulthood. Unfortunately poverty, wars, and famines are not rare events in today's modern world. At least one-third of the world's population is extremely poor and chronically undernourished. Maternal malnutrition is also quite common in the US, especially among poor women whose babies are there-fore at risk for adult obesity.

The children of mothers with obesity, mothers with excessive weight gain, and mothers with gestational diabetes also tend to become obese in adulthood. High concentrations of glucose and amino acids stimulate insulin production and adipose tissue development in the fetus, resulting in a larger infant, potential deliv-ery complications, birth defects, and increased infant mortality. Folic acid loses its protective benefit in mothers with obesity, which puts their infants at increased risk for neural tube defects such as spina bifida. Diabetic Pima mothers gave birth to fatter babies whose excess fatness tended to persist through childhood and who developed Type 2 diabetes in childhood and adulthood. Pima mothers whose own birth weight was below 2.5 kilograms (5.5 pounds) had the highest rates of diabetes during pregnancy (Dabelea et al. 2000; Pettitt and Knowler 1998). Among the Pima, overweight and obesity develop very early, in one- to six-month-old infants as well as in children between two and 11 years of age (Lindsay et al. 2002). Thus both maternal obesity and underweight create the potential for obesity which persists into adulthood and even into subsequent generations.

In healthy children body fatness increases during the first year of life, then decreases from the age of one to about six years of age (mid-childhood), and finally begins to increase again until adolescence. The time of the *adiposity rebound* is another sensitive period for the development of obesity. Girls who are early rebounders (before age five and a half years) tend to become larger and heavier as adults than those who rebound at age six or later. Genetic control of the rate of maturation combined with dietary factors such as high protein intake may underlie early adiposity rebound and later obesity (Cameron and Demerath 2002). Childhood obesity tracks into adulthood; that is, obesity at age seven reliably predicts obesity and associated health problems later in life (Guo et al. 2002). That is why the dramatic rise in overweight and obesity among U.S. children since 1980 is of such concern. Not only has Type 2 diabetes begun to appear in significant numbers among children and adolescents with obesity, but their chances of developing other chronic diseases related to obesity have skyrocketed.

Adolescence, the final stage on the path to adulthood, is marked by rapid growth. Sexual maturity is influenced by increasing levels of the reproductive hormones testosterone and estrogen. In addition to developing distinctive secondary sexual traits (external genitalia, body hair patterns, skin textures, voice pitch), boys and girls diverge in body shape and fatness at this stage (Ulijaszek et al. 1998). On average, healthy boys become taller and more muscular, with relatively broad shoulders and narrow hips. Healthy girls, on the other hand, cease height growth earlier and remain relatively shorter, their hips widen more than their shoulders, and they develop greater adiposity which persists through adulthood. Actually boys and girls carry nearly the same amount of body fat from childhood into adolescence, but because boys develop more muscle mass, their relative adiposity is lower, and they appear to lose fatness. Percent body fat in healthy adult females ranges from 25–30 percent, but only 15–20 percent in adult males. Boys' body fat shifts to the abdominal region and is concentrated in visceral adipose tissue. The body fat of girls is more widely distributed subcutaneously over breasts, hips, and thighs with less abdominal concentration. At this stage, girls have a greater risk of developing obesity than boys, especially if they mature earlier than the average age of 12 years. For many girls in the US, overweight and obesity also trigger early onset of puberty (Thompson et al. 2002).

Both boys and girls who have obesity in adolescence are more likely to develop obesity-related diseases later in life, even if they lose weight in adulthood. But although women are more likely to become obese at adolescence, men are more severely affected by obesity-related diseases because of their relatively greater visceral adipose tissue (VAT) deposits. According to the third National Health and Nutrition Examination Survey (NHANES), approximately 910,000 U.S. adolescents aged 12–19 years manifest a constellation of obesity-related conditions which lead to diabetes and heart disease. Thirty percent of all youngsters with obesity in the US are affected, and three times as many boys as girls (Bibbins-Domingo et al. 2007; Burniat et al. 2002; Cook et al. 2003; Lee 2008; Muntner et al. 2004; Thompson et al. 2002). All ethnic groups manifest the same fluctuating pattern of fatness from infancy to adulthood, but the timing of adiposity rebound and adolescent changes may vary. For example, male adiposity rebound occurs later in whites than in Mexican-Americans and indigenous Peruvian Nunoa, while the stabilization of subcutaneous adipose tissue (SAT) in adolescent girls occurs earlier in whites, blacks, and Mexican-Americans than in Yucatan Maya (Wolanski 1998).

Obesity prevention becomes especially crucial during the childhood and teenage years. This is just the time when youngsters gain greater autonomy over food choices, which are heavily influenced by advertising, peer pressure, and the availability of fatty foods and sweet drinks in schools and many other places away from home. There is some evidence that young boys' and girls' childhood food preferences for protein and carbohydrates change to fatty foods during adolescence (Bauer et al. 2009).

For many women pregnancy initiates the onset of persistent obesity, especially for those who are genetically predisposed (Linne et al. 2002; Roessner and Oehlin 1995). They gain more weight during pregnancy and tend to retain more weight after giving birth. The excess weight triples their risk for gestational diabetes and Type 2 diabetes. Obesity-susceptibility genes enable them to increase their own energy stores while nourishing a fetus, a highly advantageous trait in an environment of food scarcity but leading to overweight, obesity, and diabetes in the context of food abundance. Adolescent girls who become pregnant before reaching skeletal maturity are especially at risk for overweight, obesity, and development of excessive abdominal SAT (Hediger et al. 1997; Lenders et al. 2000). Since many adolescent girls know little about appropriate nutrition and consume poor diets during their pregnancies, both they and their offspring are at additional risk.

Pregnancy may alter metabolic processes and cause weight retention after birth, but the effects of smoking cessation, changes in eating habits, lactation patterns, and physical activity associated with motherhood cannot be ruled out. Weight gain during pregnancy varies greatly in American women; the highest gains have been observed in unemployed and unmarried women, those having fewer children, and those with lower income and education. Weight gain is generally greater in black women with lower pre-pregnancy weight and in white women with higher pre-pregnancy weight (Linne et al. 2002; Luke et al. 1996; Roessner and Oehlin 1995).

In adulthood healthy, well-nourished men and women slowly gain weight and reach maximum adiposity in middle age. Many individuals then begin to lose muscle and fat until the end of life. American women gain an average of two to five pounds during the menopausal transition, and some considerably more. Women's primarily peripheral fat reserves shift to a more abdominal distribution during menopause, and central body fatness increases. Increased obesity at this age is no doubt partly related to declining estrogen levels and reduction in physical activity, but possibly also to an age-related decline in sensitivity to *satiety* and energy-regulating hormones such as leptin. The same can be said for men whose testosterone levels and physical activity decline with age. Estrogen and testosterone, along with growth hormones, are the fat-mobilizing hormones, and their decline relative to insulin and *cortisol*, which enhance fat accumulation, promotes age-related weight gain (Bjorntorp and Rosmond 2000; Broglio et al. 2003; Marin and Bjorntorp 1993; Yen et al. 1999). Late adulthood-onset obesity is much less likely than childhood or adolescent obesity to lead to early death, but elderly persons with obesity have more quality-of-life issues such as reduced mobility and joint pain than older individuals who do not have obesity.

The neurobiology of energy metabolism

Dietary fat is digested and carried by transporter molecules via the bloodstream to adipose tissue. *Lipoprotein lipase*, an enzyme expressed by adipocytes, is up-regulated by insulin and clears fatty acids from the circulation. The fatty acids are taken up by adipocytes, where they are converted to *triglycerides* in a process known as *adipogenesis*. Triglycerides are then stored in large spaces in the adipocytes, which expand in size to accommodate the stored fat (Langin et al. 2009). Triglycerides are packages of highly concentrated, pure energy. One kilogram (2.2 pounds) of adipose tissue contains 100 grams of water, 800 grams of triglyceride, and 7000 calories of energy. A healthy human body includes approximately 15 kilograms of fat, enough to survive about 50–60 days of total starvation.

When energy is needed by muscles and other tissues, chemical messengers stimulate adipocytes to break up the stored triglycerides into free fatty acids and *glycerol* in a step-wise process known as lipolysis. The fatty acids are released into the circulation and transported to tissues requiring energy, where they are oxidized as fuel. While the stress hormone cortisol promotes free fatty acid entry into the portal circulation for delivery to the liver, insulin and other chemical messengers inhibit lipolysis to maintain fat stores (Bjorntorp and Rosmond 2000). Storage of excess fat, including re-storage of surplus fatty acids that are not oxidized, results in weight gain (positive energy balance).

Weight loss (negative energy balance) occurs when physical activity, elevated energy metabolism, or reduced energy intake create energy deficits. Normally energy intake and output are regulated by physiological adjustments to appetite, metabolic rate, energy storage, or energy release (Wisse et al. 2007). Most healthy individuals in a stable food environment maintain a relatively constant body weight within a narrow range of variation due to the body's ability to adjust its energy intake and output (Jequier and Tappy 1999; Morton et al. 2006; Ravussin and Gautier 2002; Rosenbaum et al. 1997; Webber 2003; Williams and Fruehbeck 2009). However, this equilibrium can be disrupted in the direction of chronic positive energy balance and weight gain when energy intake is unrelieved by energy expenditure. Once stabilized, the system actively defends the higher level of stored energy and returns to a lower level only with great effort. Attempts to lose fat are contrary to the functional design of the system, making permanent weight loss very difficult to achieve.

Between energy intake and energy expenditure is an intricate network of biochemical relationships and interactions which modulate the amount of energy entering the system, influence its fate as fuel, dissipated heat, or stored fat, and mobilize stored energy when it is needed. These biochemical processes, which are beyond voluntary human control, involve genes, neural pathways, and hormones, most of which are not dedicated to energy metabolism alone but are also active in many other physiological processes (Ahima and Flier 2000a; Ahima and Flier 2000b; Bjorntorp 1996; Marin and Bjorntorp 1993; Salbe and Ravussin 2000; Woods and Seeley 2002; Woods et al. 1998).

The brain is the executive director of the metabolic system, coordinating incoming cognitive, sensory, and biochemical signals about the body's energy state and organizing appropriate responses in the effort to maintain the balance between energy intake and expenditure (Woods et al. 1998). It has a built-in *lipostat* which constantly monitors the amount of energy stored in the body and responds with dual functions – short-term satiety control and longer-term adiposity adjustment. The first accounts for feelings of hunger or satiation and influences appetite; the second guides energy usage, dissipation, or storage and influences adiposity levels.

Much of what is known about energy metabolism comes from experiments conducted with rats and other animals but is nevertheless relevant to the understanding of human energy balance. Like rats, humans are warm-blooded, hair-covered, milk-producing mammals that also possess the fundamental mammalian ability to accumulate body fat when food is abundant and to use this energy reservoir in times of scarcity. Understanding the entire complex human energy system is like assembling a huge puzzle; only recently have scientists identified some of its many components and discovered how they function.

Satiety signals

The satiety system is one of the best-known components so far. Located deep within the brain is the *hypothalamus* (Figure 3.1), a one-cubic-centimeter (about the size of a fingertip) collection of nerve cells and fibers which regulate appetite and energy balance, along with many other vital functions (Morton et al. 2006; Schwartz and Porte 2005). Specialized nerve centers within the hypothalamus receive afferent neural messages from taste receptors and digestive organs, visual and olfactory cues from the external environment, and hormonal signals from various body tissues (Rolls 2007). They integrate these different messages and exchange information with other hypothalamic nerve centers, which send efferent signals via the lower brainstem to peripheral organs and tissues. The hypothalamus links sensory and cognitive messages with internal physiological ones, not only for energy regulation

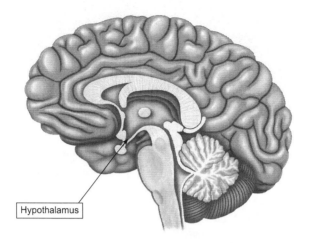

Hypothalamus

FIGURE 3.1 The hypothalamus. Courtesy of Alexilus via Shutterstock.com.

but also for the functions of the autonomic nervous system, the endocrine system, and the neural mechanisms underlying moods and motivations.

This message network conducts internal conversations about energy intake, utilization, and storage between brain and body tissues. Messages entering and leaving the hypothalamus are actually chemical signals which target receptors in specific brain and body tissues. These information relays are exquisitely coordinated. Some messages are duplicated in backup systems using different chemicals and neural pathways. The messages in these separate pathways involving hormones, neurotransmitters, and genes do not simply run in parallel, but reinforce and interact with each other.

Several powerful satiety signals control the amount of food consumed at each meal. The gut responds to food by secreting not only digestive enzymes but also hormones which signal the hypothalamus when enough has been consumed. The hypothalamus, highly sensitive to satiety signals, then responds by sending messages to end food intake. But if an individual has recently eaten little or no food, the hypothalamus is de-sensitized to meal-suppressing messages and does not signal to end food intake.

The *arcuate nucleus*, one of the hypothalamic nerve centers, contains two sets of neurons with opposing functions for controlling food intake, one as stimulator and the other as inhibitor (Ulijaszek and Lofink 2006; Woods et al. 1998). Generally, a signal that activates one set simultaneously inhibits the opposite set. For example, the neurons that stimulate food intake also turn down the rate of energy expenditure and heat dissipation to conserve energy. To resist eating, a dieter must consciously override this potent appetite-promoting, energy-conserving system. On the other hand, finishing a full meal sends satiety signals to turn off the appetite-stimulating neurons and suppresses further energy intake via efferent signals to the brainstem. The neurons that inhibit food intake simultaneously turn up the metabolic rate and energy dissipation. This system also monitors energy required for reproduction and in severely malnourished women shuts down ovulation.

Some satiety signals are mechanical in origin. Certain branches of the *vagus nerve* sense distension in a food-filled stomach, intestine, and duodenum and transmit stretch signals to the brainstem (Schwartz and Morton 2002; Woods et al. 2000). Another branch of the vagus nerve transmits signals from the tongue. Other gut satiety signals are chemical in nature. *Cholecystokinin (CCK)* is one of a number of gut proteins secreted by the intestine when it is full. CCK stimulates the vagus nerve to carry a satiety message to the brainstem, where it is combined with other signals which are transmitted to the hypothalamus. Other proteins are secreted along with CCK in combinations which vary according to each meal's nutrient content – proteins, carbohydrates, or fats. Foods with a high fat content are more satisfying than low-fat items because they evoke a relatively rapid response to the meal-cessation message, while more of the low-fat, high-carbohydrate foods must be consumed to get the same effect. This highly flexible signaling system is particularly important for appetite control in omnivores like humans, who eat a great variety of foods containing different types of nutrients (Murphy and Bloom 2006). At least 19 proteins activate neural messages to end food intake. They multiply messages about food consumption which converge upon the hypothalamus where meal size is evaluated and controlled (Delzenne et al. 2010; Murphy and Bloom 2006).

The hormone *ghrelin* is the primary human appetite-stimulating protein (Adams et al. 2011; Cummings and Shannon 2003; Kojima et al. 1999; Murphy and Bloom 2006; Zhang et al. 1994). Ghrelin is secreted by the stomach and circulates via the bloodstream to the hypothalamus, where it activates neurons to increase appetite, while simultaneously opposing the appetite-suppressing action of leptin. Individuals who are in a state of negative energy balance, such as low-calorie dieters, chronic exercisers, and anorexia nervosa patients, experience sharp increases in ghrelin levels. Thus ghrelin is a powerful component of the body's response to starvation, compensating for weight loss by increasing hunger and decreasing energy expenditure. Ghrelin is also involved in stimulating growth, and therefore ghrelin levels tend to be higher in young people than in the elderly. In addition to its roles in stimulating appetite and body growth, ghrelin influences pancreatic function, glucose metabolism, cardiovascular actions, cancer cell proliferation, immune responses, and sleep. Ghrelin may also play a role in regulating ovarian function.

Although the body of evidence is still slim, it appears that individuals with obesity are more sensitive to food cues and more highly motivated to consume energy than individuals of healthy weight (Hendrikse et al. 2015; Kenny 2011). A reward system similar to one involved in drug addiction is activated in hedonic brain circuits that predispose to overconsumption of energy, overriding the homeostatic circuits even when appetite is satisfied. In a recent study, for instance, individuals with obesity were more sensitive than participants who did not have obesity to the odor of chocolate and rated it more pleasant (Stafford and Whittle 2015). Sugar also appears to have addictive properties, the reason it is added to a great variety of mass-produced foods (Moss 2013).

Adiposity signals

The liver monitors and communicates information about daily glucose levels to the brain, which depends on glucose to fill its extremely high energy needs. When glucose levels are low, the liver converts other nutrients to glucose to insure the brain's energy supply (Wolfrum et al. 2004). Much like the liver's glucostatic mechanism, the lipostatic mechanism of the hypothalamus monitors fat stores, which are the primary energy source for muscles. Leptin circulates via the bloodstream to the brain in amounts proportional to fat stores. Thus adipose tissue itself signals the brain regarding its energy status (Ahima and Flier 2000b; Harris 2000; Margetic et al. 2002; Ravussin et al. 1997; Woods et al. 2000). Leptin-sensitive neurons in several hypothalamic regions respond to the strength of the leptin signal by secreting an array of neurotransmitters that stimulate certain regions in the lower brainstem to modify eating behavior and maintain energy balance. A weak leptin signal indicates low fat stores and evokes messages to increase food intake and simultaneously reduce energy expenditure. Large fat stores emit a strong leptin signal having the opposite effect. The leptin signal also counteracts the lipogenic effects of insulin to regulate body weight (Borer 2014).

Leptin interacts with other circulating hormones that affect its signaling power (Farooqi and O'Rahilly 2009; Klok et al. 2006). Insulin amplifies the leptin signal, while the stress hormone cortisol and the male reproductive hormone testosterone inhibit it. Regardless of adiposity state, acute infection raises leptin levels and reduces appetite, while cold exposure inhibits leptin production and increases appetite. Hypothalamic regions integrate leptin signals with other internal adiposity signals and with information from the external environment, such as the sight and smell of food, the memory of tastes, and the social situations that stimulate or inhibit eating. This highly integrated, individualized message is then forwarded to the brainstem which translates it into action – to increase or decrease appetite and to simultaneously decrease or increase body temperature and energy expenditure.

Several rare cases of total leptin deficiency in extremely obese, insatiable mice and humans first led researchers to assume that leptin could be used to treat obesity in the general population, especially after both mice and humans responded to leptin injections by losing weight (Ahima and Flier 2000b; Chicurel 2000). But it soon became apparent that most individuals with obesity are not leptin deficient but resistant to the leptin signal (Chicurel 2000). Genetic mutations desensitize hypothalamic leptin receptors so that rising levels of the circulating hormone are not detected and the appetite-suppressing response is not evoked. Leptin is now considered to be mainly a weight-conserving hormone which functions primarily to prevent the negative effects of starvation (or fasting or dieting). In humans faced with periodic famines, leptin effectively increases appetite, lowers energy metabolism, and enhances fat storage. During times of nutritional stress leptin signaling is usually futile if food is unavailable, and increased appetite cannot be satisfied.

Since leptin activates other regulatory mechanisms, leptin therapy for obesity has potentially serious side effects (Ahima and Flier 2000b; Goumenou et al. 2003;

Harris 2000; Mantzoros 2000; Moschos et al. 2002; Paz-Filho et al. 2011; Sabogal and Munoz 2001; Velloso et al. 2009). For example, leptin plays a role in controlling blood pressure through activation of the sympathetic nervous system and is involved in the formation of blood cells and growth of blood vessels, but high levels of leptin in excessive adipose tissues increase blood pressure (Simonds et al. 2014). Leptin is still considered to be a potential treatment for obesity, but the most effective dosage and timing of its therapeutic use have not yet been identified (Friedman and Mantzoros 2015; Rosenbaum and Leibel 2014).

Leptin in the placenta and in human milk plays a role in fetal and infant growth and development. Leptin inhibits secretion of cortisol from the adrenal glands and thereby mitigates the body's stress response. Leptin enhances the immune response and also helps to reduce the inflammatory damage to blood vessel walls which leads to atherosclerosis. Leptin along with insulin plays a role in regulating osteocalcin secretion by bones of the skeleton. Osteocalcin is a hormone that also regulates glucose and energy metabolism (Ferron and Lacombe 2014).

Leptin also appears to be essential for human reproduction. It has long been known that women, who bear the energetic burden of pregnancy and lactation, must develop a critical amount of body fat to sustain reproduction (Frisch 2002). The capacity to store large amounts of energy is one reason for the remarkably high human fertility rates compared to other primates. Leptin is essential for the regulation of fat to provide energy for the mother and developing fetus, but it also has a more direct role in human fertility (Goumenou et al. 2003; Harris 2000; Mantzoros 2000; Moschos et al. 2002; Sabogal and Munoz 2001). It is necessary for maturation of the reproductive system and stimulates the release of the pituitary hormone which activates sperm and ovum development. In maturing boys, a surge of leptin precedes a rise in testosterone production and the onset of puberty, but the increased testosterone then inhibits leptin expression. Maturing girls, on the other hand, continue to produce leptin and achieve leptin levels which are three times as high as those of boys. It is probably women's high leptin levels that inform the hypothalamus when adequate fat stores are available to support reproduction. The hypothalamus relays that message to the pituitary gland, which initiates the recurring pattern of hormone secretion involved in the menstrual cycle. Leptin produced in the ovary helps to induce ovulation, and leptin produced in SAT helps to ensure that an adequate energy supply is available to maintain a pregnancy and support lactation.

Energy expenditure and fat storage

Satiety and adiposity signals interact to maintain energy balance. A healthy individual who has overeaten to the point of gaining weight usually has a depressed appetite for some time afterwards and voluntarily reduces meal sizes, while a person who has lost weight tends to eat larger meals to make up for the deficiency. One of the reasons that maintaining weight loss after a diet is so difficult is that both short-term hunger and long-term adiposity signals indicate negative energy balance, which is vigorously opposed by the metabolic system. Physiological indicators of individuals who have lost a large amount of weight indicate that they are in a starving state, not that they have achieved a "normal" energy state at their reduced weight (Rosenbaum et al. 2008). The brain's chemical control system is so powerful that only 5–10 percent of people who attempt significant weight loss can successfully overcome it for an extended period of time.

The metabolic system determines how energy is used, and whether the calories consumed will be stored in adipose tissue (adipogenesis) or oxidized as fuel or heat (*thermogenesis*). *Adiponectin* secreted by adipocytes stimulates fatty acid *oxidation* in muscle tissue (Badman and Flier 2007; Matsuzawa et al. 2004), in addition to preventing inflammatory damage to blood vessels. Circulating adiponectin levels are much lower and oxidation is less efficient in individuals who have obesity than in those who are lean. Fat oxidation increases slowly in response to increased dietary fat intake, and some individuals (for example, the Pima) have low fat oxidation rates, contributing to obesity. Others respond to high-calorie meals with thermogenesis, producing heat to "waste" excess energy instead of storing it as fat (Blaak 2009; Wijers et al. 2009).

As in the case of energy intake, the hypothalamus plays the role of coordinator of adiposity signals from several sources and transmits messages to the appropriate target tissues to adjust energy utilization. When fat stores and food are plentiful, the messages are to inhibit further energy intake and glucose production by the liver, and simultaneously to release fatty acids from storage and turn up oxidation rates (Schwartz and Porte 2005). When the hypothalamus is informed of energy shortage, it activates messages to increase food intake and glucose production, while also decreasing energy expenditure (Nogueiras et al. 2010). Defects in the signaling system, either in signal strength or signal reception, cause imbalances in glucose production by the liver and in levels of stored body fat.

In all but the most active individuals such as athletes, the largest component of *total daily energy expenditure (TDEE)* is for body maintenance. It is measured as *resting metabolic rate (RMR)*, which refers to energy utilization in bodily functions while at rest, including the pumping action of the heart, neural activity of the brain, and movement of the diaphragm during breathing (Ulijaszek 2000). RMR varies greatly in individuals, partly as a function of sex and age; for example, RMR in women is on average lower than in men throughout the adult years, and loss of muscle mass with age reduces energy requirements and RMR in most elderly persons. RMR is also partly hereditary, as was noted in studies of twins whose metabolic rates were more similar than those of ordinary siblings and parent-offspring pairs. One of the factors known to contribute to weight gain in Pima Indians and black women is a low RMR (Albu et al. 1998; Ravussin et al. 1988). Individuals who formerly had obesity and whose weight had stabilized after dieting have a lower RMR than individuals of the same age, sex, and weight who never had obesity, a difference of about 3–5 percent. In the well-known Minnesota starvation experiments involving extreme calorie reduction over 24 weeks, participants' average weight decreased by 25 percent, total energy expenditure declined by more than half, and RMR dropped by 40 percent (Keys 1950).

Another significant component of energy expenditure is the *thermic effect of food (TEF)*, the energetic cost of digestion, absorption, metabolism, and storage of nutrients. TEF is reduced in individuals with obesity compared to lean individuals, and thus energy related to nutrient intake is spared.

In addition to TDEE and TEF, energy is also used to maintain body temperature and to support physical activity, growth, and reproduction. As much as one-third of total energy expenditure is devoted to growth in early infancy, declining to 1 percent by age two years. Common childhood infections also increase energy requirements, and in marginally nourished populations often cause negative energy balance and growth faltering of infants and children.

Pregnancy and lactation have a high energy cost (Ellison 2001). Beginning in puberty, healthy women develop a relatively large fat mass and store even more fat during the first half of a pregnancy. It is thought that women's higher level of estrogen lowers fat oxidation and promotes fat storage in gluteal and femoral deposits to prepare for pregnancy and lactation (Lovejoy et al. 2009; O'Sullivan 2008). Women in developed countries are usually well nourished and have a large supply of stored fat to support these reproductive processes. In less developed countries many women have no excess energy to store and cannot increase energy intake during pregnancy and lactation. Energy-conserving physiological mechanisms may then down-regulate metabolic rates and reduce the usual cost of physical activity. Whenever possible, women curtail workloads and physical activity to save energy as well. In less developed countries seasonal variation in food availability is not unusual, and food shortages and weight loss before the next harvest are a common experience. Conception and birth may therefore be limited to the more bountiful seasons. Under extreme conditions bearing and nursing a number of children in rapid succession depletes energy stores in adult women and results in gradual weight loss until menopause, quite contrary to the experience of well-nourished women in developed countries who gradually gain weight with multiple pregnancies and increasing age.

Physical work and exercise involve skeletal muscle contractions which are fueled by the oxidation of fatty acids. Physical activity accounts for about 70 percent of TDEE in trained athletes, but only 30 percent in most individuals who are typically not so active (Blaak 2009). Endurance training increases lipolytic action and shifts energy expenditure up. Even apparently negligible physical activity such as *non-exercise activity thermogenesis (NEAT)*, better known as fidgeting, significantly increases energy expenditure in some individuals (Levine et al. 1999). Among Pima men but not women, low spontaneous physical activity is a familial trait, possibly a hereditary contributor to energy conservation and obesity (Kriska et al. 1993; Ravussin et al. 1994).

One aspect of energy metabolism not under tight control is the timing of meals. Flexibility regarding meal times is adaptive since it allows humans to eat whenever it is convenient or whenever food is available, without damage to health. The hypothalamus is sensitive to messages from the external environment such as the gathering of friends and family around the table, the sound of a dinner bell, the sight of the bowl of candy on the coffee table, the smell of a pot of chili cooking on the stove. All of these are at least partly learned signals which stimulate appetite, and may encourage eating even when one is not hungry. And higher cognitive ability can override the hypothalamus, so that regardless of satiety state, one can decide to continue eating more food for any number of reasons – the memory of a pleasant taste, social pressure to eat more, the promise of a cash prize for winning an eating contest (Berthoud 2006; Lieberman 2008; Rolls 2007).

Biological consequences of excess adiposity

The most important and compelling concern related to obesity, particularly among children and adolescents, is its association with serious chronic diseases (see Chapter 1). Obesity itself may not be directly life-threatening, but excess body fat sets off a cascade of damaging changes and physiological disturbances. It is no coincidence that morbidity and mortality related to chronic disease increased as obesity rates rose in the US (Hu 2008; Kopelman 2000; Pi-Sunyer 2002; Roessner 2002). There is no longer any doubt about the link between excess body fat and the leading causes of illness and death in developed countries, regardless of age, sex, class, or ethnicity. By definition obesity is a condition of excess body fat accumulation to the point of adverse effects on health; an individual with obesity has a much greater chance of becoming ill or dying of one or more chronic conditions. Physiological indicators such as cholesterol level and blood pressure, which link obesity with disease, help to predict which specific individuals are most likely to develop diabetes, heart disease, cancer, or any of the other diseases related to obesity.

Again, the Pima community deserves recognition for its valuable contributions to the science of obesity and its health consequences (de Courten et al. 1996; Lee et al. 2005; Ravussin et al. 1997; Young 1993). The participation of its members in many scientific studies has shown conclusively that obesity induces metabolic disorders such as Type 2 diabetes, cardiovascular diseases, and cancers (the three most common chronic diseases and biggest killers in the developed world), as well as numerous other conditions. Considering that fat is one of the largest components of the body and that adipose tissue is the body's biggest endocrine organ, it should come as no surprise that obesity has such wide-ranging effects. The multitude of hormones and other chemicals secreted by large masses of adipose tissue in dangerously excessive amounts confound not only energy metabolism but also many other bodily functions. For example, excessive circulating leptin stimulates cell growth and activates the development of cancerous tumors of the gastrointestinal tract (Howard et al. 2010).

Obesity is associated with chronic, low-level, systemic inflammation, the result of pro-inflammatory secretions by adipocytes and *macrophages*, cells embedded in the enlarged adipose tissue mass in excessive numbers (Coppack 2001; Lee et al. 2005; Medzhitov 2008; Odegaard and Chawla 2013; van de Woestijne et al. 2011). Fatty acids activate inflammation-related genes (Bensinger and Tontonoz 2008; Lee et al. 2005). Certain "western" foods such as meats of domestic animals, soft drinks, and fructose also induce inflammation (Egger and Dixon 2010). Inflammation in turn damages various tissues and contributes to insulin resistance, increased circulation of fatty acids, and atherosclerosis, the accumulation of fatty plaques in arterial walls that reduce blood flow and block the arteries (Dorresteijn et al. 2012; Faber et al. 2009; Fain 2006; Hotamisligil 2006). These changes eventually produce hypertension, heart attacks, strokes, and cancers of the breast, uterus, colon, kidney, esophagus, pancreas, and gallbladder (Dorresteijn et al. 2012; Hu 2008; Hursting and Dunlap 2012; Kahn et al. 2006; Van Gaal et al. 2006; Yehuda-Shnaidman and Schwartz 2012). Inflammation and mechanical stress on the major weight-bearing joints contribute to osteoarthritis of the hips and knees (Cicuttini and Spector 1998; Ding et al. 2005; Hart et al. 1999; Wearing et al. 2006).

Inflammation is part of the metabolic syndrome, a cluster of inter-related risk factors for cardiovascular disease and diabetes more often present in individuals with obesity – especially those with large VAT deposits and other *ectopic fat* deposits in muscle, heart, liver, and other internal organs – than in individuals with normal adiposity (Demerath et al. 2008; Depres and Lemieux 2006; Zhu et al. 2003). Ectopic fat spills out of SAT and VAT adipocytes which are saturated with triglycerides and cannot expand further (Virtue and Vidal-Puig 2008). In non-adipose tissues, ectopic fat is toxic, severely impairing insulin action. The metabolic syndrome also includes *insulin resistance*, hypertension, and high levels of low-density lipoprotein (LDL)-cholesterol (Alberti and Zimmet 2008; Eckel et al. 2005; Hu 2008; Lee et al. 2005; Medzhitov 2008; Moller and Kaufman 2005). Much remains to be explained about the link between inflammation and obesity, but it is already obvious that there is considerable individual variation in the distribution and function of inflammatory agents. For instance, pre-menopausal women have higher concentrations of the major inflammatory marker, C-reactive protein, while men have higher concentrations of interleukin-6 and tumor necrosis factor-α (Cartier et al. 2009). Weight gain after smoking cessation is greater in individuals who have higher levels of inflammatory markers (Duncan et al. 2003). Physical activity seems to reduce the effects of pro-inflammatory secretions (Schmidt et al. 2015). Some individuals with obesity lack typical inflammatory markers and also do not manifest obesity-related health risks such as cardiovascular disease (Pecht et al. 2014).

Although all adipocytes secrete chemicals which act on muscle, liver, and other tissue, VAT is more metabolically active, has a higher rate of lipolysis, and dumps large amounts of cellular products directly into the *portal vein* that drains into the liver. There fatty acid overabundance interferes with insulin-mediated glucose uptake and stimulates increased liver glucose production. Insulin, which regulates glucose uptake by liver and muscle tissues, is produced by the pancreas. Diabetes is characterized by high blood sugar levels due to insufficient insulin production or action and thus the inability to use sugar as energy. Excess glucose damages nerves and blood vessels throughout the body, causing hearing loss and constant pain or loss of feeling in hands and feet. It is the leading cause of blindness, limb amputations, and kidney failure and greatly increases the risk of heart attack and stroke. Diabetes is a devastating, chronic threat to health and quality of life. It requires constant monitoring of blood sugar levels, life-long medical care, and major lifestyle changes. Early onset of Type 2 diabetes in children and adolescents sentences them to a lifetime of complications and in many cases early death. Weight loss is recommended for diabetes patients, but the medications used to control their glucose levels and blood pressure induce weight gain.

Insulin resistance is accompanied by fatty liver disease, obstructive sleep apnea (disturbed breathing), and gout, polycystic ovary syndrome, gallstone formation, and chronic kidney disease. But the number one health risk of obesity is adult-onset Type 2 diabetes (Type 1 is an autoimmune disease unrelated to obesity, usually with onset in childhood). In the last 10 to 15 years the prevalence of Type 2 diabetes increased by 33 percent in the younger U.S. population, mostly among 30- to 39-year-olds. For the first time it has also appeared in significant numbers in adolescents and children (Lee 2008). The link with overweight and obesity is undeniable – 90 percent of individuals diagnosed with Type 2 diabetes have obesity or excess weight, and even modest weight gain during adulthood increases the risk for diabetes. Weight loss, on the other hand, dramatically reduces the symptoms of the disease.

Blood pressure is higher in persons with obesity because of the increased blood flow and greater blood volume and viscosity associated with greater body mass. The continuously elevated pressure overloads the heart muscle, and stimulates thickening of cardiac walls, enlargement of the left ventricle, irregular heartbeat, and the possibility of congestive heart failure. The burden of hypertension is further increased by elevated cholesterol deposition on vascular walls. A relative lack of *high-density lipoproteins (HDL)*, which remove cholesterol, allows deposits to completely block some blood vessels and cause heart attacks and strokes. Coronary heart disease is one of the most common causes of morbidity and mortality in persons with obesity, who have a five times greater risk than lean individuals. Even moderately overweight women have almost twice the risk of developing coronary heart disease than lean women. And sudden cardiac death is becoming more common, especially in young men with extreme obesity. In 2006, more than 31 percent of the adult U.S. population had hypertension, which was the primary or contributing cause of death for 319,000 Americans the previous year (cdc.gov). Hypertension prevalence is highest among American blacks and poor populations, almost perfectly paralleling obesity prevalence in the US.

Hypertension is on the rise in adolescents and children with obesity as young as nine years of age (Thompson et al. 2002). Along with increasing BMI levels (Muntner et al. 2004), this change constitutes a serious threat to the future health of today's young Americans, who are at greater risk for cardiovascular disease in adulthood than earlier cohorts. They will have to live more years with disease and with a lower life expectancy (Silva et al. 2006). According to the most conservative estimates, more than 100,000 excess cases of heart disease and more than 1,000 related excess deaths will occur by 2035, unless treatment can be initiated early in adulthood for hypertension and high cholesterol to counter the cardiovascular effects (Bibbins-Domingo et al. 2007).

Different populations with obesity exhibit variations in rates of cardiovascular disease. The Pima of the Gila River Community have lower rates than the

Oklahoma and South Dakota Indian communities participating in the Strong Heart Study, even though they have the highest rate of obesity among the three groups (Howard et al. 1996; North et al. 2003). It is thought that their (unexplained) relatively low sympathetic nervous system activity contributes to their obesity but also reduces their risk of hypertension. Blacks have the highest overall mortality from heart disease of any American ethnic group, especially at younger ages. They are particularly susceptible to a combination of hypertension and diabetes.

Although many Americans are aware of the diabetes and cardiac disease risks of obesity, few realize that individuals with obesity also have a greater possibility of developing certain forms of cancer (Calle 2008; Calle et al. 2003; Nieman et al. 2011). Non-smoking men and women with obesity have significantly increased risks for colorectal, kidney, esophageal, liver, and pancreatic cancer. In men with obesity prostate cancer is more aggressive, and women with extreme obesity have a three times greater mortality risk of breast cancer due to larger, more aggressive tumors than those of lean women. Overweight and obesity together account for 90,000 cancer deaths annually in the US, for 14 percent of cancer deaths in men over 50 years of age, and for 20 percent of cancer deaths of women of the same age (AICR 2007; Blair et al. 2005; Li et al. 2009; Ning et al. 2009; Rapp et al. 2005). The pathophysiology of cancer in obesity is not yet well understood. It may involve obesity-related elevated levels of circulating hormones, especially insulin and leptin (Calle 2008; Howard et al. 2010; Huang 2008; McTiernan et al. 2006; Sutherly 2007; Taubes 2012). Elevated insulin levels appear to increase glucose metabolism which activates DNA-damaging mutagens and supports the growth of cancer cells. Unfortunately, high adiposity interferes with diagnosis and treatment of tumors; the diagnosis of breast cancer is more difficult in women with obesity and is often made at advanced stages of tumor development when treatment is less successful.

Health consequences of obesity vary in U.S. ethnic groups (Folsom et al. 1998; Hu 2008; Okosun et al. 2003). Although they have higher obesity rates than whites, blacks have more HDL-cholesterol, lower triglycerides, and less VAT (lower-risk factors) but greater insulin resistance and higher blood pressure (higher-risk factors) (Hoffman et al. 2005). Mexican-Americans with obesity exhibit high-risk factors, yet their cardiovascular disease rates are lower than expected. In blacks excess weight is primarily associated with hypertension, and in whites with elevated levels of low-density lipoprotein (LDL)-cholesterol. The risk of developing diabetes is higher among Native Americans, Asians, Hispanics, and blacks than among whites. In general, Native American adults of every age group have higher rates of obesity than other U.S. ethnic groups, and also higher mortality rates associated with diabetes, but there is considerable regional variation (Young 1993). For example, the Navajo of Arizona and New Mexico and their close relatives, the Inuit and Athapaskans of Alaska, have the lowest diabetes-related mortality rates among all Indian groups (although they are increasing), while the Pima and other southwestern Indians have the highest.

The genetic component of obesity

The functioning of human energy metabolism is relatively easily disrupted by internal and external factors which tend to skew the system toward fat accumulation and weight gain. During the long course of human evolution, nutritional challenges selected for genes which promote super-efficient energy utilization and storage. Individuals who possessed these genes in the past had significant survival advantages; they were able to endure periods of energy scarcity and produce offspring who would carry these adaptive traits into succeeding generations. Modern humans are their descendants, but they live in a radically different environment of ease and abundance; those survival genes now sequester and defend the excessive energy consumed today.

The Pima of Arizona provide a striking example of the mismatch between genes and environment (Knowler et al. 1982; Price et al. 1993). For thousands of years, the ancestral Pima lived by desert subsistence farming, and, using ancient irrigation techniques, survived in a harsh environment. Their close relatives who share their genes, the Mexican Pima, continued to live more or less as their ancestors had done. But the Arizona population, deprived of access to water sources with the arrival of Anglo settlers in the late 19th century, became destitute and vulnerable to drought and famine. They survived because their ancestors had been subjected to severe selection for energy-conserving genes for thousands of years.

Today the Arizona Pima, in contrast to their Mexican relatives, have the highest rates of obesity and diabetes in the US, outranked in the world only by the Nauru Islanders of the South Pacific. In every decade since World War II, they have experienced dramatic increases in average BMI levels, paralleling similar but more modest increases in other American groups. Among the Pima, 70 percent of women aged 45–54 years have diabetes, while the rate among adult men is 40 percent. The difference between the two Pima groups is not genetic, but rather environmental. Yet all Mexican and all Arizona Pima do not respond the same way to their very different environmental settings. Despite low-energy diets, intense physical activity, and occasional food shortages, a few Mexican Pima have obesity, and despite an energy-rich environment and reduced activity, some Arizona Pima are lean and do not have diabetes. These differences are due to genetic variations within each population (Ravussin et al. 1994).

More than 40 years ago, anthropologist James Neel proposed that a "thrifty gene" had been an asset to human survival in the past, but has now become a liability (Neel 1962; Neel 1982; Neel 1999). According to Neel's hypothesis, the gene prompted quick release of insulin and efficient conversion of dietary sugar and its storage as body fat during times of food abundance. The stored fat then served as the primary energy source during food scarcity. But in the modern world of uninterrupted food abundance and lower physical exertion, the same gene promotes constant fat storage, overproduction of insulin, insulin resistance, and diabetes.

Neel's hypothesis of a thrifty gene for diabetes has not been supported by modern genetics, but did stimulate the search for the hereditary component in human metabolism. Research confirmed the existence of a powerful genetic predisposition for energy accumulation and conservation, which became an equally powerful liability in the modern environment by contributing to obesity. Albert Stunkard and his research team confirmed the heritability of obesity more than 20 years ago in a study of 540 Danish adoptees by showing that their range of adiposity levels, from very thin to very obese, more closely matched those of their biological than their adoptive parents (Stunkard et al. 1986). Further evidence for a genetic basis of obesity came from studies of identical twins, who have identical genes and greater similarity in obesity levels than other siblings, even when raised separately (Bouchard and Rankinen 2008; Stunkard et al. 1990).

In the decades since the concept of the *thrifty genotype* was proposed, new technologies such as human genome mapping and genome-wide association studies (GWAS) have identified 75 obesity-susceptibility genetic variants (Loos and Yeo 2014). Only about 5 percent of all cases of obesity are single-gene disorders, influenced by mutations in a few major-effect genes such as *LEP* and *LEPR*. Many more moderate-effect gene variants (for example, *FAIM2, BDNF, ETV5, FTO, GNPDA2, KCTD15, MC4R, MTCH2, NEGR1, SEC16B, SH2B1, TMEM18*) are associated with most cases of obesity (Li et al. 2010). Their effects are additive – individuals who carry more of the known risk *alleles* have higher BMI levels than those who have inherited fewer of them. Recently new genetic techniques have been used to identify more than 100 obesity-related genetic loci linked to hypothalamic regulation of adiposity, appetite control, development and differentiation of adipocytes, and other biological processes involved in metabolism and fat distribution (Locke et al. 2015; Shungin et al. 2015).

Many of the alleles that play a role in human obesity are also found in mice and other mammals, and even yeasts (Kadereit et al. 2008), a sign that the efficient use and storage of energy is a fundamental adaptive strategy shared by all animals. Humans are not mice but share a surprisingly large number of genes with the little rodents. Mutations in the *LEP* and *LEPR* genes associated with a form of early onset, extreme obesity in humans were first identified in very obese mice. The *LEP* mutation blocks normal leptin production by adipocytes. An individual with two copies of the mutant allele produces no leptin, and the hypothalamus receives no lipostatic signals. From early childhood the affected individual is constantly hungry and eats continuously in a vain effort to become satisfied. Insulin resistance and cold sensitivity due to reduced heat production are additional effects of the *LEP* gene mutation. The *LEPR* gene mutation has similar effects, but codes for a defective hypothalamic leptin receptor. In this case, leptin production is adequate but its lipostatic message is not being received (Farooqi and O'Rahilly 2009). Both *LEP* and *LEPR* mutations also prevent normal pubertal development.

Of the many moderate-effect genes, the most common is *FTO*, discovered in 2007 (Loos and Yeo 2014). The *FTO* (fat mass and obesity-associated) gene is found in all vertebrates and codes for a metabolic sensor regulating both food intake and energy expenditure. The gene influences energy metabolism in both the hypothalamus and adipose tissue (Loos and Bouchard 2008). In its normal form it increases adipocyte lipolytic activity and helps to protect against obesity. *FTO* gene mutations are very common in adults and children of European and Hispanic ancestry (Frayling et al. 2007; Li et al. 2008; Li et al. 2010; Scuteri et al. 2007). *FTO* variants have also been found in African, African-American, and Asian populations but at lower frequencies. These genetic variants are located on chromosome 16 and are the most widely distributed of all obesity risk alleles discovered so far. They not only predispose individuals to prefer and consume high-calorie foods, but also boost development of fat mass and diabetes (Beales and Farooqi 2009; Cecil et al. 2008). Individuals with metabolic syndrome carry numerous obesity risk alleles, including the *FTO* variant rs9939609, which are involved in regulating lipid metabolism (Povel et al. 2011). This gene and its variants exemplify the complexity of obesity inheritance.

An individual's level of adiposity depends on the cumulative effects of multiple obesity risk alleles and their interactions. External and internal environmental factors such as diet, physical activity, gut bacterial profiles, and the presence of other genetic mutations modify gene expression and the potential for developing obesity. Because so many thousands of gene combinations and gene-environment interactions are possible, there is great variation in obesity among individual humans and human populations (Casazza et al. 2011).

Gene expression may be altered by components of the diet. For instance, a gene that regulates formation of new adipocytes and their fatty acid uptake (*PPARγ*) is strongly activated by polyunsaturated fats but only weakly by saturated fatty acids (Ryan and Seeley 2013). A variant of a gene which is related to Type 2 diabetes (*TCF7L2*) sensitizes individuals with obesity to high-fat, low-carbohydrate diets so that they lose less weight than other individuals with obesity on the same weight loss diet (Grau et al. 2010). Interaction between saturated fatty acids in blood plasma and variants of yet other genes increases insulin resistance (Ferguson et al. 2010). Large amounts of high-fructose corn syrup in foods alter the expression of certain genes in the skeletal muscle of individuals with obesity, leading to increased fat deposition (Le et al. 2008), and the genetic risk for obesity is more pronounced in high consumers of sugar-sweetened beverages (Qi et al. 2012).

High levels of physical activity reduce the risk of obesity associated with *FTO* mutations by 30 percent in adults, while physical inactivity nearly doubles the risk of obesity in carriers of any one of the variants (Loos and Yeo 2014). A very large multiethnic study of North Americans, Europeans, and Asians showed that the effect of the rs9939609 *FTO* risk allele was reduced by an average of 30 percent in physically active compared to sedentary individuals, with the most pronounced interaction among North Americans (Kilpelainen et al. 2011).

Obesity risk alleles also interact with each other to enhance adiposity (Fisler and Warden 2007; Loos et al. 2007; Stone et al. 2006; Stutzmann et al. 2009;

Yang et al. 2007). For example, a region of the *FTO* gene interacts with the *IRX3* gene to regulate body mass and composition (Smemo et al. 2014). Individuals carrying specific alleles for adiponectin and a particular adiponectin receptor have lower fat oxidation and higher adiposity levels than persons with other allele combinations; BMI, insulin, and leptin levels are higher in individuals who carry several specific alleles involved in adipocyte differentiation and in lipolysis than in those who have just one of these variants; the combined effect of specific risk alleles of the *FTO* and *MC4R* genes on obesity is greater than the independent effects of each allele.

Individuals with obesity have a different combination of chemical signals or are less responsive to chemical messages than lean individuals. Their metabolic system is controlled by a complex genetic predisposition which alters energy regulation, raises stable weight range to a high level, and vigorously prevents weight loss (Wisse et al. 2007). In the energy-rich modern American context, high adiposity levels are actually the norm for much of the population. In fact, rather than asking "Why is the majority of the American population overweight or obese?" the question should be, "What keeps the minority of Americans lean? How do they avoid obesity in such an energy-rich environment?" Until the biochemical products and specific functions of obesity genes are identified and the exact genetic variants and combinations that respond to the obesogenic environment are known, that question remains unanswered.

A few genes seem to protect against obesity and promote leanness. Genes coding for *uncoupling proteins (UCPs)* promote heat production in muscle and fat to dissipate excess energy (Jia et al. 2009). The protein UCP-1 is important for maintaining body temperature and increasing metabolic activity and energy expenditure. Unfortunately for individuals who formerly had obesity, production of UCPs is reduced and daily energy expenditure decreased subsequent to weight loss. A rare variant of a gene that is absent in adults and children with obesity encodes the production of visfatin by visceral adipocytes and protects against obesity (Blakemore et al. 2009). Variants of another gene involved in the transmission of satiety signals are also associated with lower energy consumption (Loos et al. 2005).

Physical activity, once considered to be entirely under volitional control, has a genetic component as well. The Quebec and HERITAGE Family studies identified several genetic variants influencing physical activity levels (Loos et al. 2005; Rankinen and Bouchard 2008; Simonen et al. 2003). The Southwest Ohio Family Study also concluded that a common gene both predisposes to higher activity levels and reduces adiposity (Choh et al. 2009).

Current estimates of the *heritability* of obesity and BMI in the energy-rich environment of developed countries vary widely, ranging from 16 percent to 90 percent, with most clustering around 50 percent (Yang et al. 2007). That is to say, 50 percent of the population's total variation in body mass is due to variations in genetic inheritance. That contradicts popular thinking which assumes that obesity is simply a behavioral issue, a deficiency of willpower and self-control. Obesity genes are widespread among the populations of the world, but cannot be expressed in those that are not exposed to an obesity-promoting environment (Andreasen and Andersen 2009); they are revealed only when the environmental opportunity for excessive energy accumulation exists. For example, although *FTO* obesity risk alleles are present in a large Gambian population, most Gambians are lean because of their traditional low-energy, high-activity lifestyle (Hennig et al. 2009). So genes alone are not sufficient causes of obesity; their expression depends on an energy-rich environment as in highly developed societies. The recent increase in obesity prevalence in the US coincided with several environmental shifts during the last 100 years, shifts associated with industrialization, new methods of food production and marketing, and changes in physical activity, which combined to produce constant positive energy balance. Although it is "in the genes," obesity is actually the outcome of their complex interaction with the obesogenic environment.

Conclusion

Obesity is the result of a complex biological adaptive system designed to adjust metabolic rates to energy availability, but that has become overwhelmed and can no longer achieve metabolic homeostasis. Most humans are biologically programmed to acquire and store a large amount of fat and to release it very grudgingly. The modern obesity epidemic is simply an outcome of this unique survival strategy, a special human evolutionary legacy. Nature favored humans with multiple mechanisms for efficient accumulation, storage, and conservation of fat, but until recently there was precious little opportunity to build permanent sizeable energy stores.

Genetic variations influencing metabolic physiology help to account for adiposity variations in human populations. In populations lacking access to adequate energy, obesity genes are silent, but where energy is abundant the diversity in genetic inheritance and physiological functioning becomes evident. Only in an obesogenic environment that promotes fat accumulation is a high-risk genetic profile expressed. Under such conditions, obesity is a normal physiological response, and the body's defense of stored energy usually overrides individual efforts to control body weight. Under current energy-abundant conditions, weight is easy to gain and hard to lose. The next step in understanding the American obesity epidemic is to take a closer look at the many ways the obesogenic environment influences obesity.

References

Adams, C. E., F. L. Greenway, and P. J. Brantley (2011). Lifestyle factors and ghrelin: critical review and implications for weight loss maintenance. *Obesity Reviews* **12**(5): e211–e218.

Ahima, R. S. and J. S. Flier (2000a). Adipose tissue as an endocrine organ. *Trends in Endocrinology and Metabolism* **11**(8): 327–332.

Ahima, R. S. and J. S. Flier (2000b). Leptin. *Annual Review of Physiology* **62**: 413–437.

AICR (2007). Food, Nutrition, Physical Activity, and the Prevention of Cancer: a Global Perspective. World Cancer Research Fund/American Institute for Cancer Research.

Alberti, K. G. M. M. and P. Z. Zimmet (2008). Should we dump the metabolic syndrome? No. *British Medical Journal* **336**: 641.

Albu, J. et al. (1998). Resting metabolic rate in obese, premenopausal black women. *American Journal of Clinical Nutrition* **66**(3): 531–538.

Andreasen, C. H. and G. Andersen (2009). Gene-environment interaction and obesity – further aspects of genomewide association studies. *Nutrition* **25**: 998–1033.

Badman, M. K. and J. S. Flier (2007). The adipocyte as an active participant in energy balance and metabolism. *Gastroenterology* **132**: 2103–2115.

Barker, D. J. P. (2002). Fetal origins of adult disease: strength of effects and biological basis. *Int J Epidemiol* **31**: 1235–1239.

Bauer, F. et al. (2009). Obesity genes identified in genome-wide association studies are associated with adiposity measures and potentially with nutrient-specific food preferences. *American Journal of Clinical Nutrition* **90**: 951–959.

Beales, P. L. and I. S. Farooqi (2009). Introduction. *In* Genetics of Obesity Syndromes. P. L. Beales, I. S. Farooqi, and S. O'Rahilly, eds. pp. 3–23. Oxford: Oxford University Press.

Bensinger, S. J. and P. Tontonoz (2008). Integration of metabolism and inflammation by lipid-activated nuclear receptors. *Nature* **454**(24): 470–477.

Berthoud, H-R. (2006). Homeostatic and non-homeostatic pathways involved in the control of food intake and energy balance. *Obesity* **14**(Suppl): 197S–200S.

Bibbins-Domingo, K. et al. (2007). Adolescent overweight and future adult coronary heart disease. *New England Journal of Medicine* **357**: 2371–2379.

Bjorntorp, P. (1996). The regulation of adipose tissue distribution in humans. *International Journal of Obesity* **20**: 291–302.

Bjorntorp, P. and R. Rosmond (2000). Obesity and cortisol. *Nutrition* **16**: 924–936.

Blaak, E. E. (2009). Energy balance in humans. *In* Obesity: Science to Practice. G. Williams and G. Fruehbeck, eds. pp. 166–183. West Sussex, UK: John Wiley & Sons.

Blair, C. K. et al. (2005). Anthropometric characteristics and risk of multiple myeloma. *Epidemiology* **16**(5): 691–694.

Blakemore, A. I. F. et al. (2009). A rare variant in the visfatin gene (*NAMPT/PBEF1*) is associated with protection from obesity. *Obesity* **17**(8): 1549–1553.

Borer, K. T. (2014). Counterregulation of insulin by leptin as key component of autonomic regulation of body weight. *World Journal of Diabetes* **5**(5): 606–629.

Bouchard, C. and T. Rankinen (2008). Experimental twin studies. *In* Obesity: Genomics and Postgenomics. K. Clement and T. I. Sorensen, eds. pp. 49–58. New York: Informa Healthcare.

Broglio, F. et al. (2003). The endocrine response to ghrelin as a function of gender in humans in young and elderly subjects. *Journal of Clinical Endocrinology and Metabolism* **88**(4): 1537–1542.

Burniat, W. et al. (2002). Child and Adolescent Obesity: Causes and Consequences, Prevention and Management. London: Cambridge University Press.

Calle, E. E. (2008). Obesity and cancer. *In* Obesity Epidemiology. F. B. Hu, ed. pp. 196–215. New York: Oxford University Press.

Calle, E. E. et al. (2003). Overweight, obesity and mortality from cancer in a prospectively studied cohort of U.S. adults. *New England Journal of Medicine* **348**: 1625–1638.

Cameron, N. and E. W. Demerath (2002). Critical periods in human growth and their relationship to diseases of aging. *Yearbook of Physical Anthropology* **45**: 159–184.

Cartier, A. et al. (2009). Sex differences in inflammatory markers: what is the contribution of visceral adiposity? *American Journal of Clinical Nutrition* **89**: 1307–1314.

Casazza, K. et al. (2011). Beyond thriftiness: independent and interactive effects of genetic and dietary factors on variations in fat deposition and distribution across populations. *American Journal of Physical Anthropology* **145**: 181–191.

Cecil, J. E. et al. (2008). An obesity-associated *FTO* gene variant and increased energy intake in children. *New England Journal of Medicine* **359**: 2558–2566.

Chicurel, M. (2000). Whatever happened to leptin? *Nature* **404**(6): 538–540.

Choh, A. C. et al. (2009). Genetic analysis of self-reported physical activity and adiposity: the Southwest Ohio Family Study. *Public Health Nutr* **12**(8): 1052–1060.

Cicuttini, F. and T. D. Spector (1998). Obesity, arthritis, and gout. *In* Handbook of Obesity. G. A. Bray, C. Bouchard, and W. P. T. James, eds. pp. 741–753. New York: Dekker.

Cook, S. et al. (2003). Prevalence of a metabolic syndrome phenotype in adolescents. *Archives of Pediatric & Adolescent Medicine* **157**: 821–827.

Coppack, S. W. (2001). Pro-inflammatory cytokines and adipose tissue. *Proceedings of the Nutrition Society* **60**(3): 349–356.

Cummings, D. E. and M. H. Shannon (2003). Roles for ghrelin in the regulation of appetite and body weight. *Archives of Surgery* **138**: 389.

Dabelea, D., W. C. Knowler, and D. J. Pettitt (2000). Effect of diabetes in pregnancy on offspring: follow-up research in the Pima Indians. *Journal of Maternal-Fetal Medicine* **9**(1): 83–88.

de Courten, M. P., D. J. Pettitt, and W. C. Knowler (1996). Hypertension in Pima Indians: prevalence and predictors. *Public Health Report* **111**(Suppl 2): 40–43.

Delzenne, N. et al. (2010). Gastrointestinal targets of appetite regulation in humans. *Obesity Reviews* **11**: 234–250.

Demerath, E. W., D. Reed, and N. Rogers (2008). Visceral adiposity and its anatomical distribution as predictors of the metabolic syndrome and cardiometabolic risk factor levels. *Am J Clin Nutr* **88**: 1263–1271.

Depres, J-P. and I. Lemieux (2006). Abdominal obesity and metabolic syndrome. *Nature* **444**: 881–887.

Ding, C. et al. (2005). Knee structural alteration and BMI: a cross-sectional study. *Obesity Research* **13**: 350–361.

Dorresteijn, J. A. N., F. L. J. Visseren, and W. Spiering (2012). Mechanisms linking obesity to hypertension. *Obesity Reviews* **13**: 17–26.

Duncan, B. B. et al. (2003). Inflammation markers predict increased weight gain in smoking quitters. *Obesity Research* **11**: 1339–1344.

Eckel, R. H., S. M. Grundy, and P. Z. Zimmet (2005). The metabolic syndrome. *The Lancet* **365**: 1415–1428.

Egger, G. and J. Dixon (2010). Inflammatory effects of nutritional stimuli: further support for the need for a big picture approach to tackling obesity and chronic disease. *Obesity Reviews* **11**: 137–149.

Ellison, P. T. (2001). On Fertile Ground. Cambridge, MA: Harvard University Press.

Faber, D. R., P. G. de Groot, and F. L. J. Visseren (2009). Role of adipose tissue in haemostasis, coagulation and fibrinolysis. *Obesity Reviews* **10**(5): 554–563.

Fain, J. N. (2006). Release of interleukins and other inflammatory cytokines by human adipose tissue is enhanced in obesity and primarily due to the nonfat cells. *Vitamins and Hormones* **74**: 443–477.

Farooqi, I. S. and S. O'Rahilly (2009). Human leptin and leptin receptor deficiency. *In* Genetics of Obesity Syndromes. P. L. Beales, I. S. Farooqi, and S. O'Rahilly, eds. pp. 37–47. Oxford: Oxford University Press.

Ferguson, J. F. et al. (2010). Gene-nutrient interactions in the metabolic syndrome: single nucleotide polymorphisms in *ADIPQ* and *ADIPOR1* interact with plasma saturated fatty acids to modulate insulin resistance. *American Journal of Clinical Nutrition* **91**: 794–801.

Ferron, M. and J. Lacombe (2014). Regulation of energy metabolism by the skeleton: osteocalcin and beyond. *Archives of Biochemistry & Biophysics* **561**: 137–146.

Fisler, J. S. and C. H. Warden (2007). The current and future search for obesity genes. *American Journal of Clinical Nutrition* **85**: 1–2.

Folsom, A. R. et al. (1998). Body mass index, waist/hip ratio, and coronary heart disease incidence in African Americans and Whites. *American Journal of Epidemiology* **148**(12): 1187–1194.

Frayling, T. M. et al. (2007). A common variant in the FTO gene is associated with body mass index and predisposes to childhood and adult obesity. *Science* **316**: 889–894.

Friedman, J. M. and C. S. Mantzoros (2015). 20 years of leptin: from the discovery of the leptin gene to leptin in our therapeutic armamentarium. *Metabolism Clinical and Experimental* **64**: 1–4.

Frisch, R. E. (2002). Female Fertility and the Body Fat Connection. Chicago: University of Chicago Press.

Gluckman, P. D. and M. A. Hanson (2006). Developmental Origins of Health and Disease. New York: Cambridge University Press.

Goumenou, A. G. et al. (2003). The role of leptin in fertility. *European Journal of Obstetrics Gynecology and Reproductive Biology* **106**(2): 118–124.

Grau, K. et al. (2010). *TCF7L2* rs7903146-macronutrient interaction in obese individuals' responses to a 10-wk randomized hypoenergetic diet. *American Journal of Clinical Nutrition* **91**: 472–479.

Guo, S. et al. (2002). Predicting overweight and obesity in adulthood from body mass index values in childhood and adolescence. *American Journal of Clinical Nutrition* **76**: 653–658.

Harris, R. B. S. (2000). Leptin – much more than a satiety signal. *Annual Review of Nutrition* **20**: 45–75.

Hart, D. J., D. V. Doyle, and T. D. Spector (1999). Incidence and risk factors for radiographic knee osteoarthritis in middle-aged women: the Chingford Study. *Arthritis and Rheumatism* **41**(1): 17–24.

Hediger, M. L., T. O. Scholl, and J. I. Schall (1997). Implications of the Camden Study of adolescent pregnancy: interactions among maternal growth, nutritional status, and body composition. *Ann NY Acad Sci* **817**: 281–291.

Hendrikse, J. J. et al. (2015). Attentional biases for food cues in overweight and individuals with obesity: a systematic review of the literature. *Obesity Reviews* **16**: 424–432.

Hennig, B. J. et al. (2009). FTO gene variation and measures of body mass in an African population. *Biomed Central Medical Genetics* **10**: 21–29.

Hoffman, D. J. et al. (2005). Comparison of visceral adipose tissue mass in adult African Americans and whites. *Obesity Research* **13**(1): 66–74.

Hotamisligil, G. S. (2006). Inflammation and metabolic disorders. *Nature* **444**: 860–867.

Howard, B. V. et al. (1996). Diabetes and coronary heart disease in American Indians. *Diabetes* **45**: s6–s13.

Howard, J. M., G. P. Pidgeon, and J. V. Reynolds (2010). Leptin and gastro-intestinal malignancies. *Obesity Reviews* **11**: 863–874.

Hu, F. B. (2008). Obesity Epidemiology. New York: Oxford University Press.

Huang, K.-C. (2008). Obesity and its related diseases in Taiwan. *Obesity Reviews* **9**(s1): 32–34.

Hursting, S. D. and S. M. Dunlap (2012). Obesity, metabolic dysregulation, and cancer: a growing concern and an inflammatory (and microenvironmental) issue. *Annals of the New York Academy of Sciences* **1271**(1): 82–87.

Jequier, E. and L. Tappy (1999). Regulation of body weight in humans. *Physiological Reviews* **79**(2): 451–480.

Jia, J-J. et al. (2009). The polymorphisms of UCP2 and UCP3 genes associated with fat metabolism, obesity and diabetes. *Obesity Reviews* **10**(5): 519–526.

Kadereit, B. et al. (2008). Evolutionarily conserved gene family important for fat storage. *Proceedings of the National Academy of Science* **105**(1): 94–99.

Kahn, S. E., R. L. Hull, and K. M. Utzschneider (2006). Mechanisms linking obesity to insulin resistance and type 2 diabetes. *Nature* **444**: 840–846.

Kenny, P. J. (2011). Reward mechanisms in obesity: new insights and future directions. *Neuron* **69**: 664–679.

Keys, A. (1950). The Biology of Starvation. Minneapolis: University of Minnesota Press.

Kilpelainen, T. O. et al. (2011). Physical activity attenuates the influence of *FTO* variants on obesity risk: a meta-analysis of 218,166 adults and 19,268 children. *PLoS Medicine* **8**(11): e1001116.

Klok, M. D., S. Jakobsdottir, and M. L. Drent (2006). The role of leptin and ghrelin in the regulation of food intake and body weight in humans: a review. *Obesity Reviews* **8**: 21–34.

Knowler, W. C. et al. (1982). Obesity, insulin resistance and diabetes mellitus in the Pima Indians. *In* The Genetics of Diabetes Mellitus: Serono Symposium No. 47. J. Koebberling and R. Tattersal, eds. pp. 243–250. New York: Academic.

Kojima, M. et al. (1999). Ghrelin is a growth-hormone-releasing acylated peptide from stomach. *Nature* **402**: 656–660.

Kopelman, P. G. (2000). Obesity as a medical problem. *Nature* **404**: 635–643.

Kriska, A. M. et al. (1993). The association of physical activity with obesity, fat distribution and glucose intolerance in Pima Indians. *Diabetologia* **36**: 863–869.

Kuzawa, C. W. (1998). Adipose tissue in human infancy and childhood: an evolutionary perspective. *Yearbook of Physical Anthropology* **41**: 177–209.

Langin, D. et al. (2009). Adipose tissue development, anatomy and functions. *In* Obesity: Science to Practice. G. Williams and G. Fruehbeck, eds. pp. 78–108. West Sussex, UK: John Wiley & Sons.

Le, K-A. et al. (2008). Effects of four-week high-fructose diet on gene expression in skeletal muscle of healthy men. *Diabetes & Metabolism* **34**: 82–85.

Lee, J. M. (2008). Why young adults hold the key to assessing the obesity epidemic in children. *Arch Pediatr Adolesc Med* **162**(7): 682–687.

Lee, Y. H. et al. (2005). Microarray profiling of isolated abdominal subcutaneous adipocytes from obese vs. non-obese Pima Indians: increased expression of inflammation-related genes. *Diabetologia* **48**: 1776–1783.

Lenders, C. M., T. F. McElrath, and T. O. Scholl (2000). Nutrition in adolescent pregnancy. *Current Opinions in Pediatrics* **12**(3): 291–296.

Levine, J. A., N. L. Eberhardt, and M. D. Jensen (1999). Role of nonexercise activity thermogenesis in resistance to fat gain in human. *Science* **283**: 212–214.

Li, D. et al. (2009). Body mass index and the risk, age of onset, and survival in patients with pancreatic cancer. *JAMA* **301**(24): 2553–2562.

Li, H. et al. (2008). Variants in the fat mass- and obesity-associated (FTO) gene are not associated with obesity in a Chinese Han population. *Diabetes* **57**: 264–268.

Li, S. et al. (2010). Cumulative effects and predictive value of common obesity-susceptibility variants identified by genome-wide association studies. *Am J Clin Nutr* **91**: 184–190.

Lieberman, L. S. (2008). Diabesity and Darwinian medicine. *In* Evolutionary Medicine and Health: New Perspectives. W. R. Trevathan, E. O. Smith, and J. J. McKenna, eds. pp. 72–95. New York: Oxford University Press.

Lindsay, R. S. et al. (2002). Early excess weight gain of children in the Pima Indian population. *Pediatrics* **109**(2): E33.

Linne, Y., B. Barkeling, and S. Roessner (2002). Long-term weight development after pregnancy. *Obesity Reviews* **3**(2): 75–83.

Locke, A. E. et al. (2015). Genetic studies of body mass index yield new insights for obesity biology. *Nature* **518**: 197–206.

Loos, R. J. F., and C. Bouchard (2008). *FTO*: the first gene contributing to common forms of human obesity. *Obesity Reviews* **9**: 246–250.

Loos, R. J. F. et al. (2005). Melanocortin-4 receptor gene and physical activity in the Quebec Family Study. *Int J Obesity* **29**: 420–428.

Loos, R. J. F. et al. (2007). Adiponectin and adiponectin receptor gene variants in relation to resting metabolic rate, respiratory quotient, and adiposity-related phenotypes in the Quebec Family Study. *American Journal of Clinical Nutrition* **85**: 26–34.

Loos, R. J. F. and G. S. H. Yeo (2014). The bigger picture of *FTO* – the first GWAS-identified obesity gene. *Nature Review Endocrinology* **10**(1): 51–61.

Lovejoy, J. C., A. Sainsbury, and Stock Conference 2008 Working Group (2009). Sex differences in obesity and the regulation of energy homeostasis. *Obesity Reviews* **10**: 154–167.

Luke, B., M. L. Hediger, and T. O. Scholl (1996). Point of diminishing returns: when does gestational weight gain cease benefiting birthweight and begin adding to maternal obesity? *J Matern Fetal Med* **5**(4): 168–173.

Lummaa, V. (2003). Early developmental conditions and reproductive success in humans: downstream effects of prenatal famine, birthweight, and timing of birth. *Am J Hum Biol* **15**(3): 370–379.

Ma, L. et al. (2004). Melanocortin 4 receptor gene variation is associated with severe obesity in Pima Indians. *Diabetes* **53**: 2696–2699.

Mantzoros, C. S. (2000). Role of leptin in reproduction. *Annals of the New York Academy of Sciences* **900**: 174–183.

Margetic, S. et al. (2002). Leptin: a review of its peripheral actions and interactions. *International Journal of Obesity* **26**: 1407–1433.

Marin, P. and P. Bjorntorp (1993). Endocrine-metabolic pattern and adipose tissue distribution. *Horm Res* **39**(Suppl 3): 81–85.

Matsuzawa, Y. et al. (2004). Adiponectin and metabolic syndrome. *Arteriosclerosis, Thrombosis, and Vascular Biology* **24**: 29–33.

McTiernan, A. et al. (2006). Relation of BMI and physical activity to sex hormones in postmenopausal women. *Obesity* **14**: 1662–1677.

Medzhitov, R. (2008). Origin and physiological roles of inflammation. *Nature* **454**(24): 428–435.

Moller, D. E. and K. D. Kaufman (2005). Metabolic syndrome: a clinical and molecular perspective. *Annual Review of Medicine* **56**: 45–62.

Morton, G. J. et al. (2006). Central nervous system control of food intake and body weight. *Nature* **443**: 289–295.

Moschos, S., J. L. Chan, and C. S. Mantzoros (2002). Leptin and reproduction: a review. *Fertility and Sterility* **77**(3): 433–444.

Moss, M. (2013). Salt Sugar Fat: How the Food Giants Hooked Us. New York: Random House.

Muller, Y. L. et al. (2003). A functional variant in the peroxisome proliferator-activated receptor gamma 2 promoter is associated with predictors of obesity and type 2 diabetes in Pima Indians. *Diabetes* **52**(7): 1864–1871.

Muntner, P. et al. (2004). Trends in blood pressure among children and adolescents. *JAMA* **291**: 2107–2113.

Murphy, K. G. and S. R. Bloom (2006). Gut hormones and the regulation of energy homeostasis. *Nature* **444**: 854–859.

Neel, J. V. (1962). Diabetes mellitus: a "thrifty" genotype rendered detrimental by "progress"? *Am J Hum Genet* **14**: 353–362.

Neel, J. V. (1982). The thrifty genotype revisited. *In* The Genetics of Diabetes Mellitus: Proceedings of the Serono Symposia, Volume 47. J. Koebberling and R. Tattersal, eds. pp. 283–293. London: Academic Press.

Neel, J. V. (1999). The "thrifty genotype" in 1998. *Nutrition Reviews* **57**: S2–S9.

Nieman, K. M. et al. (2011). Adipocytes promote ovarian cancer metastasis and provide energy for rapid tumor growth. *Nature Medicine* **17**(11): 1498–1504.

Ning, Y., L. Wang, and E. L. Giovannucci (2009). A quantitative analysis of body mass index and colorectal cancer: findings from 56 observational studies. *Obesity Reviews* **11**(1): 19–30.

Nogueiras, R., M. Lopez, and C. Dieguez (2010). Regulation of lipid metabolism by energy availability: a role for the central nervous system. *Obesity Reviews* **11**: 185–201.

Norman, R. A., P. A. Tataranni, and R. Pratley (1998). Autosomal genomic scan for loci linked to obesity and energy metabolism in Pima Indians. *American Journal of Human Genetics* **62**(3): 659–668.

North, K. E. et al. (2003). Evidence for distinct genetic effects on obesity and lipid-related CVD risk factors in diabetic compared to nondiabetic American Indians: the Strong Heart Family Study. *Diabetes-Metabolism Research and Reviews* **19**(2): 140–147.

O'Sullivan, A. J. (2008). Does oestrogen allow women to store fat more efficiently? A biological advantage for fertility and gestation. *Obesity Reviews* **10**: 168–177.

Ochner, C. N. et al. (2015). Treating obesity seriously: when recommendations for lifestyle changes confront biological adaptations. *Lancet Diabetes & Endocrinology* doi 10.1016/s2213–8587(15)00009–1.

Odegaard, J. I. and A. Chawla (2013). Pleiotropic actions of insulin resistance and inflammation in metabolic homeostasis. *Science* **339**: 172–177.

Okosun, I. S. et al. (2003). Trends of abdominal adiposity in white, black and Mexican-American adults, 1988 to 2000. *Obesity Research* **11**(8): 1010–1017.

Paz-Filho, G., M-L. Wong, and J. Licinio (2011). Ten years of leptin replacement therapy. *Obesity Reviews* **12**(5): e315–e323.

Pecht, T. et al. (2014). Peripheral blood leucocyte subclasses as potential biomarkers of adipose tissue inflammation and obesity subphenotypes in humans. *Obesity Reviews* **15**(4): 322–337.

Pettitt, D. J. and W. C. Knowler (1998). Long-term effects of the intrauterine environment, birth weight, and breast-feeding in Pima Indians. *Diabetes Care* **21**(Suppl 2): B138–141.

Pi-Sunyer, F. X. (2002). The obesity epidemic: pathophysiology and consequences of obesity. *Obesity Research* **10**(Suppl 2): 97S–104S.

Povel, C. M. et al. (2011). Genetic variants and the metabolic syndrome: a systematic review. *Obesity Reviews* **12**: 952–967.

Pratley, R. E. et al. (1997). Plasma leptin responses to fasting in Pima Indians. *American Journal of Physiology* **273**(3 pt 1): E644–649.

Price, R. A. et al. (1993). Obesity in Pima Indians: large increases among post-World War II birth cohorts. *Am J Phys Anthropol* **92**: 473–479.

Qi, Q. et al. (2012). Sugar-sweetened beverages and genetic risk of obesity. *New England Journal of Medicine* **367**(15): 1387–1396.

Rankinen, T. and C. Bouchard (2008). Genetics of physical activity. *In* Obesity: Genomics and Postgenomics. K. Clement and T. I. A. Sorensen, eds. pp. 277–286. New York: Informa Healthcare.

Rapp, K. et al. (2005). Obesity and incidence of cancer: a large cohort study of over 145,000 adults in Austria. *British Journal of Cancer* **93**: 1062–1067.

Ravussin, E. and J. F. Gautier (2002). Determinants and control of energy expenditure. *Annales d'Endocrinologie* **63**(2): 96–105.

Ravussin, E. et al. (1988). Reduced rate of energy expenditure as a risk factor for body-weight gain. *New England Journal of Medicine* **318**: 467–472.

Ravussin, E. et al. (1997). Relatively low plasma leptin concentrations precede weight gain in Pima Indians. *Nature Medicine* **3**(2): 238–240.

Ravussin, E. et al. (1994). Effects of a traditional lifestyle on obesity in Pima Indians. *Diabetes Care* **17**(9): 1067–1074.

Roessner, S. (2002). Obesity: the disease of the twenty-first century. *International Journal of Obesity* **26**(Suppl 4): S2–S4.

Roessner, S. and A. Oehlin (1995). Pregnancy as a risk factor for obesity: lessons from the Stockholm Pregnancy and Weight Development Study. *Obesity Research* **3**(Suppl 2): 267S–275S.

Rolls, E. T. (2007). Understanding the mechanisms of food intake and obesity. *Obesity Reviews* **8**(Suppl 1): 67–72.

Rosenbaum, M. et al. (2008). Long-term persistence of adaptive thermogenesis in subjects who have maintained a reduced body weight. *American Journal of Clinical Nutrition* **88**(4): 906–912.

Rosenbaum, M. and R. L. Leibel (2014). The role of leptin in energy homeostasis in humans. *Journal of Endocrinology* **223**(1): T83–T96.

Rosenbaum, M., R. L. Leibel, and J. Hirsch (1997). Obesity. *New England Journal of Medicine* **337**(6): 396–407.

Ryan, K. K. and R. J. Seeley (2013). Food as hormone. *Science* **339**: 918–919.

Sabogal, J. C. and L. Munoz (2001). Leptin in obstetrics and gynecology: a review. *Obstetrical and Gynecological Survey* **56**(4): 225–230.

Salbe, A. D. and E. Ravussin (2000). The determinants of obesity. *In* Physical Activity and Obesity. C. Bouchard, ed. pp. 69–102. Champaign, IL: Human Kinetics.

Schmidt, F. M. et al. (2015). Inflammatory cytokines in general and central obesity and modulating effects of physical activity. *PLoS One* **10**(3): e0121971.

Schwartz, M. W. and G. J. Morton (2002). Keeping hunger at bay. *Nature* **418**: 595–597.

Schwartz, M. W. and D. Porte (2005). Diabetes, obesity, and the brain. *Science* **307**: 375–379.

Scuteri, A. et al. (2007). Genome-wide association scan shows genetic variants in the FTO gene are associated with obesity-related traits. *PLoS Genetics* **3**(7): 1200–1210.

Shungin, D. et al. (2015). New genetic loci link adipose and insulin biology to body fat distribution. *Nature* **518**: 187–209.

Silva, M. C. P. et al. (2006). Adult obesity and number of years lived with and without cardiovascular disease. *Obesity* **14**: 1264–1273.

Simonds, S. E. et al. (2014). Leptin mediates the increase in blood pressure associated with obesity. *Cell* **159**: 1404–1416.

Simonen, R. L. et al. (2003). Genome-wide linkage scan for physical activity levels in the Quebec Family Study. *Medicine & Science in Sports & Exercise* **35**(8): 1355–1359.

Smemo, S., J. J. Tena, and K-H. Kim (2014). Obesity-associated variants within *FTO* form long-range functional connections with *IRX3*. *Nature* **507**: 371–375.

Stafford, L. D. and A. Whittle (2015). Obese individuals have higher preference and sensitivity to odor of chocolate. *Chemical Senses* **40**: 279–284.

Stone, S. et al. (2006). TBC1D1 is a candidate for a severe obesity gene and evidence for a gene/gene interaction in obesity predisposition. *Human Molecular Genetics* **15**(18): 2709–2720.

Stunkard, A. J. et al. (1990). The body-mass index of twins who have been reared apart. *New England Journal of Medicine* **322**(21): 1483–1487.

Stunkard, A. J., T. I. Sorensen, and C. Hanis (1986). An adoption study of human obesity. *New England Journal of Medicine* **314**: 193–198.

Stutzmann, C. S. et al. (2009). Combined effects of MC4R and FTO common genetic variants on obesity in European general populations. *Journal of Molecular Medicine* **87**(5): 537–546.

Sutherly, B. (2007). Where does our food come from? Often from a processing plant here in Ohio. Dayton Daily News, 1/22/07.

Taubes, G. (2012). Unraveling the obesity-cancer connection. *Science* **335**: 28–32.

Thompson, A. M. et al. (2002). Secular trend in the development of fatness during childhood and adolescence. *American Journal of Human Biology* **14**: 669–679.

Trivedi, B. P. (2014). Dissecting appetite. *Nature* **508**: 564–565.

Ulijaszek, S. J. (2000). Work and energetics. *In* Human Biology. S. Stinson, B. Bogin, R. Huss-Ashmore, and D. O'Rourke, eds. pp. 345–376. New York: Wiley.

Ulijaszek, S. J., F. E. Johnston, and M. A. Preece (1998). The Cambridge Encyclopedia of Human Growth and Development. Cambridge: Cambridge University Press.

Ulijaszek, S. J. and H. Lofink (2006). Obesity in biocultural perspective. *Annual Review of Anthropology* **35**: 337–360.

van de Woestijne, A. P. et al. (2011). Adipose tissue dysfunction and hypertriglyceridemia: mechanisms and management. *Obesity Reviews* **12**(10): 829–840.

Van Gaal, L. F., I. L. Mertens, and C. E. De Block (2006). Mechanisms linking obesity with cardiovascular disease. *Nature* **444**: 875–880.

Velloso, L. A., W. Savino, and E. Mansour (2009). Leptin action in the thymus. *Annals of the New York Academy of Sciences* **1153**: 29–34.

Virtue, S. and A. Vidal-Puig (2008). It's not how fat you are, it's what you do with it that counts. *PLoS Biology* **6**(9): 1819–1823.

Wearing, S. C., E. M. Henning, and N. M. Byrne (2006). Musculoskeletal disorders associated with obesity: a biomechanical perspective. *Obesity Reviews* **7**(3): 239–250.

Webber, J. (2003). Energy balance in obesity. *Proceedings of the Nutrition Society* **62**(2): 539–543.

Wells, J. C. K. (2013). Commentary: the thrifty phenotype and the hierarchical preservation of tissues under stress. *International Journal of Epidemiology* **42**: 1223–1227.

Wijers, S. L. J., W. H. M. Saris, and W. D. M. Lichtenbelt (2009). Recent advances in adaptive thermogenesis: potential implications for the treatment of obesity. *Obesity Reviews* **10**: 218–226.

Williams, G. and G. Fruehbeck (2009). Obesity: Science to Practice. West Sussex, UK: John Wiley & Sons.

Wisse, B. E., F. Kim, and M. W. Schwartz (2007). An integrative view of obesity. *Science* **318**: 928–929.

Wolanski, N. (1998). Comparison of growth patterns of subcutaneous fat tissue in Mexican and Polish with US and Peruvian populations. *Annals of Human Biology* **25**(5): 467–477.

Wolfrum, C. et al. (2004). Foxa2 regulates lipid metabolism and ketogenesis in the liver during fasting and in diabetes. *Nature* **432**: 1027–1031.

Woods, S. C. et al. (2000). Food intake and the regulation of body weight. *Annual Review of Psychology* **51**: 255–277.

Woods, S. C. and R. J. Seeley (2002). Understanding the physiology of obesity: review of recent developments in obesity research. *International Journal of Obesity* **26**(Suppl 4): S8–S10.

Woods, S. C. et al. (1998). Signals that regulate food intake and energy homeostasis. *Science* **280**: 1378–1383.

Yang, W., T. Kelly, and J. He (2007). Genetic epidemiology of obesity. *Epidemiologic Reviews* **29**: 49–61.

Yehuda-Shnaidman, E. and B. Schwartz (2012). Mechanisms linking obesity, inflammation and altered metabolism to colon carcinogenesis. *Obesity Reviews* **13**: 1083–1095.

Yen, S. S. C., R. B. Jaffe, and R. L. Barbieri (1999). Reproductive Endocrinology: Physiology, Pathophysiology, and Clinical Management. Philadelphia: W.B. Saunders Company.

Young, T. K. (1993). Diabetes mellitus among Native Americans in Canada and the United States: an epidemiological review. *Am J Hum Biol* **5**: 399–413.

Zhang, Y. et al. (1994). Positional cloning of the mouse *obese* gene and its human homologue. *Nature* **372**: 425–432.

Zhu, S. et al. (2003). Percentage body fat ranges associated with metabolic syndrome risk: results based on the third National Health and Nutrition Examination Survey (1988–1994). *American Journal of Clinical Nutrition* **78**: 228–235.

4

THE TOXIC ENVIRONMENT

Introduction

Compared to other populations, why do so many Americans have obesity? Genes and physiology have not changed in the few decades since the obesity epidemic trended upward, and it now seems that all human populations possess the powerful biological imperative for efficient energy storage. But the environmental context within which human biology functions actually has changed a great deal. The genes that influence energy metabolism are expressed differently by exposure to various environmental factors, from nutrients in foods, gut bacteria, chemical pollutants in soil, air and water, and metabolic products of physical activity and stress. Other environmental cues affect behavior related to energy intake and expenditure. The obesogenic environment of the US plays a powerful role in the obesity epidemic in a number of ways.

Humans can alter the conditions of their existence and have done so for more than 2.5 million years. Their steadfast goal has always been to increase the quantity and improve the quality of available energy sources to enhance survival under challenging conditions. These efforts ultimately created extreme energy abundance in industrialized countries, and today starvation and extinction are no longer threats there. The environment created during the last century promotes greater energy intake than is needed and much less energy expenditure than was required in the past. Energy balance has tipped to the positive side. *Environment* refers to the many aspects of the external physical, social, economic, political, and cultural context of human behavior and health.

The health of recent immigrants, the fastest-growing segment of the U.S. population, testifies to the obesogenic power of the American environment. Without biological alterations, their obesity rates more than doubled on average after only 15 years in the country (Goel et al. 2004). Asian-American and Hispanic adolescents born in the US are more than twice as likely to have obesity as first-generation residents (Popkin and Udry 1998).

Many dieters make firm plans to eat fewer calories and to exercise more. Clearly they know what to do, but have difficulty carrying out their plans. It may well be that some lack the willpower to persist, but at least a good part of the inability to meet their goals is that the American way of life is simply not conducive to implementing sensible lifestyle changes. Enormous personal effort is needed to change consumption and activity patterns under the many conditions that actively promote energy accumulation and conservation. Very few are able to resist such environmental pressures (Cohen and Babey 2012).

The situation has been likened to a runaway "weight gain" train equipped with powerful accelerators but with very weak brakes (Swinburn and Egger 2004). The obesogenic environment has caused the train to take off from the station in the direction of overweight and obesity. Its braking system consists mostly of social pressures to avoid the appearance of sloth and gluttony, the personal embarrassment and physical discomfort of being fat, and frequent medical advice to lose weight for the sake of good health. But the braking system has been more than overcome by the accelerators, which consist of powerful external inducements to consume and conserve energy that interact with internal energy-conserving biological mechanisms.

More than 30 years ago, Albert Stunkard (Stunkard 1975) pointed out that most medical guidelines for weight loss are directed solely toward changing individual behaviors. They paid little attention to the environment that in many cases successfully negated individual efforts to control energy intake and increase expenditure. Stunkard identified a long list of items in the obesogenic environment that played such a role. His recommendations for change were largely ignored by policy makers, and obesity rates continued to climb.

Obesity prevalence in America is the cumulative effect of not one but a multitude of varying external factors working in combination with diverse biological predispositions. Unfortunately, the current state of science is much more familiar with individual biological traits related to obesity than with the complex environmental influences that interact with them. Based on the best evidence currently available, medical professionals still recommend personal lifestyle changes, tackling the obesity epidemic one patient at a time, without much success. Research to identify contextual forces that encourage overindulgence and inactivity are still relatively rare. And of the external factors that have been considered to date, a great deal more is known about the nutritional environment than about factors related to physical activity and energy expenditure. Efforts to understand and implement changes in the conditions of daily life are more difficult to observe and measure, and possibly also more resistant to change. Nevertheless, some obesity researchers are aware of their significance and are calling attention to conditions external to the individual that impact obesity.

The nations of North America and Europe have created a standard of living like none other in the world. It is the pride of those who are privileged to enjoy it, and the goal of those who aspire to it. It only takes a brief visit to any less developed country to become aware of what is taken for granted in the US, a lifestyle of ease and convenience, abundance and plenty, and countless choices for physically effortless work and leisure pursuits. Jobs in heavy industry have virtually disappeared, and more and more workers spend entire days in sedentary, knowledge-based occupations that actually induce higher spontaneous energy intake than even simple rest in a sitting position (Chaput and Tremblay 2007). Figure 4.1 shows that American occupations requiring moderate activity have decreased from 50 percent to 20 percent since 1960, while sedentary occupations have climbed. Building a major highway without the use of heavy construction machinery, as personally observed in China along the main road from Beijing to the Great Wall, is unheard of in the US. This huge project involved arduous manual labor to smash rocks and remove baskets-full on human shoulders. Bulldozers and trucks could have done this work much faster, with less labor and fewer workers.

The American standard of living is probably unmatched in the post-industrial world. But there is a price to pay for this life of relative luxury, not only in the environmental degradation related to industrial and agricultural mass production, but also in the deterioration of health associated with excessive consumption and inactivity.

What has happened gradually to the general U.S. population is now also well underway in less developed countries, where at first small groups of wealthy elites and now ever larger segments of society are reaping the benefits and ills of industrialization and westernization. But it is not necessary to look beyond the national borders to find dramatic examples of the impact of modernization on small societies. What has happened to bring about the obesity epidemic in the US in the last two decades has also affected this country's indigenous peoples.

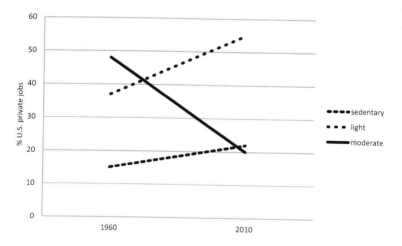

FIGURE 4.1 U.S. trends in occupations requiring moderate, light, and sedentary activity. Adapted from Church et al. (2011).

A CASE STUDY: THE PIMA

The desert southwest of the United States is an unlikely place to make a living by farming, but for over 2,000 years several Native American societies inhabiting this region had successfully practiced desert agriculture in that forbidding environment, long before Europeans arrived in the New World (Castetter and Bell 1942; Sturtevant 2004). The Hohokam, who at one time inhabited the entire region from what is today northern Mexico to Arizona and New Mexico, were the only group of ancient desert farmers to use irrigation. Their direct descendants are the Akimel O'Odham (River People) of Arizona and Mexico also known as the Pima, who still live there today, but in communities separated by the border between the US and Mexico. Remnants of the elaborate canal networks that diverted water from the Gila River to the Arizona Pima fields of native corn, beans, squash, pumpkin, and cotton can still be seen today. With simple hand tools and human labor, the Pima mobilized entire communities to dig miles of canals as much as three meters (10 feet) deep. They maintained their canals, built and rebuilt the dams that diverted Gila River waters, and planted, cultivated, weeded, harvested, processed, and stored their crops by hand.

In spite of periodic droughts and famines during which the Pima made greater use of wild plants like mesquite beans and cactus fruits, and in spite of spring floods that periodically washed out their newly planted fields, the Pima clung to their land and its uncertainties. By rotating their fields, they were able to farm without fertilizer. They planted salt-tolerant crops in areas that were not flushed regularly by floodwaters, and they hunted wild game in the surrounding hills to supplement their harvests. Thus they enjoyed a varied diet of plant and animal products that filled all their nutritional requirements. Nevertheless, their storage bins were empty for at least one month of each year, the Hunger-Hurting Moon, when the previous year's harvest had been consumed and new crops and wild plant foods were not yet mature. Not until Spanish explorers and missionaries, greatly impressed with the agricultural skill and ingenuity of the Pima, introduced wheat that ripened during the season when indigenous foods became scarce could Pima farmers count on steady sources of food the entire year round.

In the 18th century, the Pima abandoned some of their land and their pueblos and formed a confederation with other farming tribes for protection against nomadic Apache raiders who stole crops and destroyed villages. In addition to laboring in their fields, they now had to defend their lands and homes from the raiders as well. They probably would have continued even this tenuous existence but for the sale of their territories by Mexico to the US. The flood of new Anglo settlers ended their traditional lifestyle and subsistence forever, for the settlers took over the hunting grounds and diverted upstream waters of the Gila River to their own fields, depriving the Pima of their most

(continued)

(continued)

essential natural resources. By the end of the 19th century, the Pima were forced to abandon their farming and supplemental foraging traditions, as well as their healthy diets, and turn to cattle herding, food purchases, and government handouts for the greater part of their livelihood (Castetter and Bell 1942).

Desperately poor, many Arizona Pima families moved to cities to find work in factories. During World War II, men were drafted to serve in the U.S. armed forces. With increased cash incomes and integration into Anglo society, their lifestyles and diets rapidly became westernized, and within a single generation the Pima became the most obese population in the US (Gladwell 2000). Meanwhile, their Mexican relatives from whom they had been separated for nearly 1000 years continued to live much as they had for centuries (Ravussin, et al. 1994). The Mexican Pima still cultivate their traditional crops of corn, beans, potatoes, and peaches, along with garden produce of vegetables and chilies. Their daily diet includes corn tortillas and beans, eggs and potatoes, and rare servings of meat and chicken. Income from labor in livestock breeding, wood milling, road construction, and mining supplements their basic resources.

Today, the Arizona Pima eat twice as much food and consume 50 percent more calories from fat than their Mexican relatives (Ravussin et al. 1994). Their diet is now essentially the same as the typical diet of most other Americans (Yracheta et al. 2015). They weigh an average of 26 kilograms (57 pounds) more, and their average BMI is 38 compared to the Mexican Pima average of 25. Arizona Pima perform less than one-tenth the hours of vigorous physical work done by Mexican Pima subsistence farmers and homemakers (Kriska et al. 1993). And their diabetes rates are among the highest in the world, eight times the U.S. national average.

Why did the Pima become so fat? Their thrifty (energy-conserving) genes and their physiology, which had evolved over millennia to protect them from periodic starvation, suddenly became liabilities in the modern American high-energy/low-activity environment. The Pima are quite aware of the causes of their extraordinary obesity and illness rates. After all, for decades the entire Pima Indian community has participated in a longitudinal study of obesity and diabetes conducted by U.S. National Institutes of Health scientists (DeMouy et al. 1995). And yet they seem unable to stop the progression of the epidemic, which has now spread to their children.

What happened to the Pima is not unlike the story of the transition to high rates of obesity in the general U.S. population during the last three decades. The main difference is one of timing. Having lived for years under conditions of near-starvation after loss of their land and water, but unable to participate in U.S. economic development until World War II, the Pima very rapidly modified their diet and lifestyle to conform to the typical U.S. pattern. Other Americans had begun the process of change much earlier, during the Industrial

Revolution of the late 19th century, and therefore saw a more gradual change in lifestyle and obesity levels. Of course, the possibility also exists that the Pima, like many non-European peoples who have faced periodic food shortages for many generations, have a stronger genetic predisposition for obesity and are more physiologically sensitive to dietary modifications and changes in physical activity (Lee et al. 2005; Ma et al. 2004).

Like the Pima, Americans of European, Asian and African ancestry are biologically designed to withstand food scarcity and energy-draining physical activity. And, as in the case of the Pima, the societal changes that have led to the obesity epidemic originated in forces beyond individual control and action. Large social, cultural, economic, and political developments affecting the entire country interacted with deeply ingrained food habits and activity patterns to increase energy intake and reduce energy expenditure. The Pima were particularly vulnerable to these forces in their need to participate in the U.S. economy and gain acceptance in American society. Their old ways became unsustainable, so they had to adopt new ones in their efforts to survive in an alien, dominant culture. Yet even other Americans, whose survival had not been threatened, have gradually but inexorably replaced the more rigorous but healthful lifestyles of the past with new patterns of consumption and behavior in the name of progress and modernization, unaware of the deleterious consequences to health and wellbeing.

It appears that what many consider to be the world's highest standard of living actually threatens the health and wellbeing of most Americans. So, what forces shape energy consumption and physical activity in the US? What are the pathways from environmental conditions to individual behaviors and from these to disruptions of energy-balancing mechanisms and the development of obesity?

The microenvironment

Among the external factors that influence human obesity are some that are actually internal, in the human intestinal tract, particularly the colon. Humans, like many other animals, harbor trillions of beneficial intestinal bacteria and other organisms, collectively known as the *microbiota*. As many as 1,000 different microbial species may inhabit the human gut, the most common of them members of the Bacteroidetes, Firmicutes, Actinobacteria, and Proteobacteria phyla. The collective genome of all gut microbes is known as the *microbiome*, which is unique to each individual person. Genetic analysis has shown that human gut microbiota underwent rapid evolutionary changes (Moeller 2014), reflecting the shift from a largely plant-based to animal-based diet during human evolution. Together with the co-evolved human genome, the microbiome has important roles in metabolism and immunity (Tsai 2009).

Gut microbes perform an array of useful functions. One of them is the breakdown and fermentation of indigestible, complex plant fibers in fruits, vegetables, and grains. Each bacterial strain is highly specialized to degrade a specific group of fiber components. The bacteria produce vitamins and short-chain fatty acids that can be readily absorbed through the intestinal wall. This process harvests as much as 10–15 percent of the energy required by the human body, an important adaptation for humans and other animals living in energy-scarce environments (Fukuda and Ohno 2014; Inman 2011; Natarajan and Pluznick 2014; Tsai and Coyle 2009; Turnbaugh et al. 2006). Other mechanisms thought to be involved in the development of obesity as a function of microbiota include regulating host genes for fat deposition, stimulating neural effects on hunger, and even modifying physical activity levels (Tsai and Coyle 2009).

The composition of gut microbiota is influenced by diet (Yatsunenko et al. 2012). Populations whose diet is rich in proteins (such as Americans) have different gut microbe combinations than those consuming mostly plant-based diets (such as African and South American Indian populations) (David et al. 2014; Foerster et al. 2014). Individuals with obesity tend to have a larger proportion of Firmicutes bacteria, and lean individuals have more of the Bacteroidetes, which suggests that Firmicutes may be more efficient at extracting energy from food and contribute more to fat stores, or that Bacteroidetes may help prevent fat accumulation. When individuals with obesity lose weight, the ratio of these two types changes to approximate that of lean persons (Jumpertz et al. 2011; Turnbaugh et al. 2009). Studies in mice and humans show that host genes also influence microbial diversity, possibly in interaction with dietary variations (Holscher et al. 2015; O'Connor et al. 2014; Turnbaugh et al. 2009).

An experiment exposing germ-free lab mice to gut bacteria from lean humans and those with obesity found that lean-derived bacteria induced mice to become lean, and obese-derived bacteria induced obesity (Walker and Parkhill 2013). Obese mice slimmed down when exposed to lean-derived microbes and fed a low-fat, high-fiber diet. In another trial, mice fed a high-fat diet not unexpectedly became obese. But when given the bacterium *Akkermansia muciniphila* (more common in healthy-weight humans than individuals with obesity) along with the high-fat diet, obesity did not develop (Deweerdt 2014). These findings suggest a possible new method for treating obesity in humans.

Research on the role of gut microbiota in human obesity is still in its initial stages, and it is not yet known whether exposure to microbial strains (and which ones) has the same effect on humans as lab mice. It is also not yet conclusively known just how microbial composition and function are linked to obesity (Goel et al. 2014) and some obesity-related diseases such as cancer (Ohland and Jobin 2014; Ohtani et al. 2014; Rogers et al. 2014) and liver disease (Ferolla et al. 2014), although one pathway may be through activation of metabolic and inflammatory disorders (Ferreira et al. 2014).

Infants begin to develop their gut microbiota at birth and usually achieve stable microbial populations by the age of two to three years (Voreades et al. 2014).

Infant microbiota composition is influenced by maternal obesity, type of birth (vaginal or cesarean), diet (breast milk or formula, types of solid foods, especially dietary fat) (Salonen and de Vos 2014), antibiotic treatment in infancy (Bailey et al. 2014), and even mothers' use of artificial sweeteners and antibiotic treatment during pregnancy (Araujo et al. 2014; Mueller et al. 2014). Failure to establish mature gut microbiota composition and function (due to malnutrition, for example) is thought to affect immune function and the regulation of genes involved in fat and carbohydrate metabolism throughout life (Canani et al. 2011). In both adults and children, exposure to antibiotics alters microbiota composition in favor of obesogenic microbes (Azad et al. 2014; Murphy et al. 2014). Antibiotic prescription for a variety of conditions is very common in the US, and overuse, especially in children, has become a matter of concern (Dooling et al. 2014).

There is some evidence that increased sugar consumption during recent decades may have changed the microbiotic balance in the U.S. population and contributed to the obesity trend (Payne et al. 2012). Imbalance of the gut microbiota (*dysbiosis*) can also result from disruption of circadian rhythm. Work shift changes and travel across time zones leading to jet lag have resulted in microbiota alterations that promote glucose intolerance and obesity (Thaiss et al. 2014). Diets high in saturated fat (from animals, tropical oils) increase microbes that secrete inflammatory products causing intestinal and systemic inflammation and leading to insulin resistance (Shen et al. 2014). Dysbiosis is associated with a variety of disease conditions, including inflammatory bowel disease, colon cancer, allergies, diabetes, fatty liver disease, heart disease, and obesity (Fukuda and Ohno 2014).

The recent findings about the importance of gut microbiota in obesity and related diseases have stimulated investigation of gut microbe manipulation as a treatment strategy for these conditions. Ingestion of probiotics (live beneficial bacteria), supplementation with dietary fiber, and fecal microbiota transplantation are among techniques being studied in the effort to achieve a healthy microbial profile (Borody et al. 2014; Chen et al. 2014; Holscher et al. 2015; Walsh et al. 2014).

Energy intake and the environment

Energy from food and drink is either used or stored, depending on an individual's nutritional state and metabolism. Dietary fats and carbohydrates are converted into adipose tissue, and both activate energy-conserving genes that contribute to obesity (Poirier and Eckel 2000). During the last 30 to 40 years, the US has seen a large increase in food availability, and, despite a small recent decline, American adults have increased their daily average energy intake by 240 calories during those decades (Ford and Dietz 2013). Food is available everywhere, cheap and readily obtained, prompting Americans to consume at any time of day or night. In fact, modern industrial societies simply continue a food production and consumption trend begun millions of years ago. Just as Paleolithic hunters increased their energy resources by exploiting greater amounts of nutrient-rich animal flesh and fat, modern food producers have found ways to promote consumption of a great variety of fatty, sugary, tasty, energy-dense foods and snacks. And just as Neolithic farmers improved the reliability of their food supply and enhanced its energy content by producing storable, high-carbohydrate grains and fatty animal products, modern industry has developed new ways to create and market inexpensive, abundant, high-carbohydrate, high-fat food products for consumers.

Adult Americans require an average of at least 2,000 calories of energy per day (USDHHS 2005). Caloric requirements are higher for men than for women (2,200–3,000 vs 1,800–2,200) and vary by body weight and activity level for both sexes. A moderately active healthy man between the ages of 19 and 30 years needs 2,600–2,800 calories each day to maintain body weight, while a sedentary woman of the same age needs only 2,000 cal. Since 1970, the total U.S. annual food supply (some of which is wasted) has increased from an average of 3,300 to 3,800 calories per capita per day, nearly double the average daily requirement for women (Briefel and Johnson 2004). During the last century, consumption of dietary fat doubled, from an annual average of 14.5 kilograms (32 pounds) to 29 kilograms (63 pounds) per person. Although Americans recently responded very positively to public health messages to reduce dietary fat intake, they compensated by consuming more refined carbohydrates that were ultimately stored as body fat and continued to gain weight (Block 2004). A four-fold increase of inexpensive, corn-based fructose usage to sweeten most processed foods and beverages and a doubling of soft drink consumption among children and adolescents also coincided with the increase in obesity rates. Milk consumption declined in the last 30 years, but an increase in cheese consumption (think pizza) more than made up for the decrease in milk fat consumed. Sweets, soft drinks, alcohol, salty snacks, and fruit-flavored drinks are high-calorie, nutrient-poor items making up one-third of the total energy sources for Americans today. Even though the consumption of fresh fruits and vegetables also increased by 24 percent, and many supermarkets now carry nearly 20 percent more fresh produce items than in the 1970s, Americans still do not consume enough to meet recommended intake levels (CDC 2010). In the land of plenty, many Americans are basically malnourished, lacking adequate amounts of dietary fiber and plant-based vitamins and minerals (Liebman 2013; USDHHS 2005).

It is much easier to make resolutions to eat less than to actually do so. New food items are constantly being developed, manufactured, and aggressively advertised and marketed by food producers. Supermarkets offer an immense array of edible products in various stages of preparation, from entirely raw and unprocessed to fully cooked meals. Refrigerated trucks carry fresh produce and meats from one end of the country to the other. Foods from every corner of the Earth can be purchased at affordable prices. Items that were once available only in season are stocked all year round. The choices of ways to spend food dollars appear to be endless.

But are they really? The wild animal and vegetable foods collected by foraging ancestors were much more nutritious and varied than domesticated ones produced by giant agri-businesses today (Cordain et al. 2002). Even the fruits, vegetables, eggs, cheese, and meat hand-produced 100 years ago on American farms were of higher nutritional quality than the mass-produced selections in the supermarkets of today. Meat from domestic cattle contains much lower levels of the healthy long-chain polyunsaturated fats than wild game. The pasture-fed cattle of the early 20th century yielded meat with low levels of saturated fats much like wild game, while meat from today's grain-fed, feed-lot-fattened animals contains two to three times more saturated fat. The modern weight-loss Paleolithic Diet (Imamura et al. 2015; Zhang et al. 2015), which promotes consumption of lean meats and non-starchy vegetables while avoiding dairy products, grains, and legumes, is based on just these considerations, but it is difficult to see how the ancient diet can be replicated with today's mass-produced supermarket items.

Today most high-quality items are usually found only in the organic section of some supermarkets or in seasonal farmers' markets. They cost more than mass-produced items and are not available at all to large segments of the U.S. population. While supermarkets appear to offer greater selections in every area, today's foods are of much poorer quality (lacking in fiber, for example) and lower in essential nutrients, although certainly not in quantity and variety of form (Hardman et al. 2015). And to make these apparently ever-increasing options more competitive in the food market, they are loaded with preservatives to increase their shelf-life. They also contain added salt, sugar, and saturated fat, and are much higher in caloric value than minimally or non-processed foods to make them tastier and more appetizing (Moss 2013; Weaver et al. 2014). They are processed, refined, and offered in various shapes and styles to make them especially attractive and desirable to customers.

This kind of dietary variety is one of many suspected causes of the obesity epidemic. Research shows that variety in color, flavor, and texture of fatty or sweetened foods encourages greater consumption, possibly because humans appreciate novelty in tastes and mouth-feel of different foods. In one study, participants given four courses of different foods (bread and butter, sausage, chocolate, bananas) consumed 44 percent more food and 60 percent more calories than when they were served any one of these foods alone in separate, sequential courses. Greater dietary variety was also associated with greater body weight and more body fat in this study (Raynor and Epstein 2001; Raynor et al. 2005). Although there is now growing concern about obesity in European countries, personal observation of food markets in Germany suggests that Europeans do not have such a wide array of choices, and that the quality of meats, eggs, and produce is better than in large U.S. supermarkets. Virtually every city has open-air farmers' markets that offer fresh produce, cheese, eggs, meats, and fish all year round. European cattle are not fed hormones to hasten their maturation and fatten their meat. Free-ranging chickens produce more flavorful meat and more nutritious eggs. Tree-ripened fruits and fresh vegetables from several Mediterranean countries are available even in the wintertime. An Oxfam report ranked the US 21st on a list of countries in which to find a balanced, nutritious diet including fresh produce, nutritious proteins, and clean water. Western European countries make up most of the top 20 ranks (www.oxfam.org).

Because of the bountiful food supply, Americans can afford to waste edible items. The Garbage Project, initiated by University of Arizona archaeologists in

1973, discovered that Americans throw away 10–15 percent of the food they buy, and that produce is the largest food waste item (35–40 percent) (Rathje and Murphy 2001). In studies comparing participants' dietary self-reports with analysis of their garbage and trash (participants being fully aware of the comparison), the archaeologists found that people tended to under-report snacks and over-report fresh produce consumption. A group of mothers in Tucson reported making from scratch all baby foods, but a check of their household garbage showed that they tossed out just as many empty baby food jars as households that reportedly purchased prepared baby foods. The sizable discrepancy between self-reports (perceptions of behavior) with garbage analysis (actual dietary behavior) suggests that people are aware of healthy dietary practices and know what they should be eating, but that their actual behavior is quite at odds with those ideals.

It has become abundantly clear that Americans consume too much energy-dense food (fatty, sugary, starchy, highly processed items), but too little nutritious food (high-fiber micronutrient fruits and vegetables) (Rolls 2009). Only one-quarter of Americans eat recommended amounts of vegetables and only one-third eat recommended amounts of fruit per day (CDC 2010). Fruit and vegetable consumption among high school students is extremely low, with a median of only one fruit or vegetable per day. One-fourth of students in a recent study consumed less than one fruit per day, and one-third ate vegetables less than once a day (Kim et al. 2012). Why would rational human beings concerned about their health and physical appearance over-consume non-nutritious food and avoid healthful foods? Many don't overindulge, of course, but enough do to encourage the food industry to produce and distribute even more high-energy, low-nutrient items and to minimize the promotion of fresh produce, low-fat dairy products, and other nutritious items.

Food pervades daily lives, and Americans eat incessantly in homes, schools, churches, places of work, even in their cars, which now come equipped with mini-refrigerators and large cup holders. They are surrounded by snack foods that are used as enticements for all sorts of events the year round, from country fairs to city celebrations. Eating is a part of every social occasion, athletic event, religious ritual, and leisure activity, especially television and movie viewing, which is now done in large, soft, reclining chairs and sofas also equipped with cup- and bottle-holders for maximum viewing pleasure. Schools and workplaces have vending machines that dispense empty calories, and co-workers bring goodies to share on any number of occasions. More often than not, eating is not a response to actual hunger or energy depletion, but rather many other cues that have to do with socializing, recreation, or pleasure-seeking. Brian Wansink (Wansink 2011) describes these consumption patterns as "mindless eating," making automatic, unconscious eating decisions in response to a variety of external cues to eat, including those from watching others consume. Even the atmosphere in restaurants (lighting, music) is designed to affect eating behavior (Wansink and van Ittersum 2012) and is exploited to boost consumption.

Americans spend a smaller proportion of income on food than people in any other country, where the higher cost of food discourages excessive purchase, consumption, and wastage. Government policies have kept food prices low in the US. In the 1970s, new subsidies to American farmers led to a corn glut and the development of many new corn-based food products, among them inexpensive high-fructose corn syrup (Tillotson 2004). Consumption of a multitude of sweeteners has risen by about 26 percent since then, with the most dramatic rise in fructose consumption (Cullen and Zakeri 2004; Popkin and Nielsen 2003) (Figure 4.2). At the same time the prevalence of overweight and obesity began to climb. Concurrently, the prevalence of Type 2 diabetes more than doubled and for the first time reached alarming levels among children and adolescents.

Although it is certainly not the only cause of obesity, the ubiquity of fructose in foods is strongly correlated with obesity. A personal, non-scientific survey of food labels in a large, local chain supermarket showed that fructose is listed as one of the top five ingredients in applesauce, canned tomato soup, fruit juices, power drinks, sodas, fruit yogurts, syrups, salad dressings, catsups, marshmallows, some cereals, breads and bagels, and wieners and sausages. It is a minor ingredient in some chips, cookies, graham crackers, canned spaghetti and meatballs, other cereals, and boxed prepared foods such as scalloped potatoes and hamburger dinners. A study of sugar-sweetened beverages and fruit juice drinks found that many made with high-fructose corn syrup actually contain more fructose than indicated on their labels (Walker et al. 2014). Sugars, including fructose, hidden in ordinarily non-sweet foods enhance their taste and stimulate greater food intake (Johnson et al. 2007; Moss 2013). In the US, sugar alone adds an average of 600 calories per person per day to the foods available for consumption (Lustig et al. 2012). A study

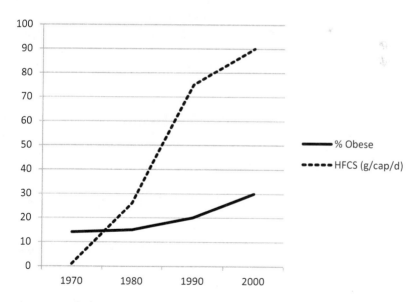

FIGURE 4.2 High-fructose corn syrup (HFCS) availability and obesity.
Adapted from Bray et al. (2004b).

of fructose consumption in the US showed that infants and young children fed a typical diet ingest 10 times the amount of naturally occurring fructose consumed by adults in fruit because it is added to many of the foods and drinks prepared especially for them, such as sweetened fruit juices (Bray et al. 2004a). High-fructose consumption by mothers during fetal development of fetus and exposure of infants during introduction of new foods can actually alter normal neuroendocrine function and lead to adult obesity (Goran et al. 2013).

The metabolic effects of fructose appear to differ significantly from those of glucose, the primary sweetener used in the past (Elliott et al. 2002; Ludwig 2013; Lustig 2012; Lustig et al. 2012; Page et al. 2013; Saris 2003; Stanhope and Havel 2010; Walker et al. 2014). Fructose is processed in the liver, which converts it to fat, while glucose serves as fuel for the body. Unlike glucose, fructose does not stimulate insulin secretion by the pancreas, nor does it stimulate the *LEP* gene in adipose tissue to produce leptin. Normally both insulin and leptin signal brain centers to regulate energy metabolism and to reduce energy intake. Furthermore, fructose does not suppress the appetite-stimulating hormone ghrelin as glucose does. Consumers of fructose sweeteners therefore cannot sense that a high-calorie meal has been ingested and subsequently do not compensate by reducing further energy intake. Indeed, they exhibit increased rates of lipogenesis, up to twice the rate relative to consumers of glucose. Fructose is therefore a major contributor to increased adiposity and obesity in the US. Fructose also promotes insulin resistance and glucose intolerance and raises total cholesterol, low-density lipoprotein (LDL)-cholesterol, and blood pressure in susceptible individuals.

Actually, Americans have increased their consumption of all sweetened foods and drinks during recent decades, in concert with the rise in obesity (Bleich et al. 2009; Olsen and Heitman 2009). Nearly 75 percent of all packaged foods and beverages consumed in the US between 2005 and 2009 contained some type of caloric sweetener (Ng et al. 2012). Since 1988, daily consumption of sweetened drinks increased by six ounces per person, with greater consumption among young adults compared to elderly, and among young blacks in comparison to whites and Mexican-American adults. In 2010 more than half of all high school students drank a daily serving of sugar-sweetened beverage (regular soda or pop, sports drink) (Brener et al. 2011). Even individuals intending to lose weight consumed sweetened drinks averaging 278 calories per day. Many elementary schools still serve sweetened, high-calorie drinks with lunch or from vending machines, despite dietary guidelines limiting drinks to 1 percent or nonfat milk, water, or 100 percent juice (Turner and Chaloupka 2011). Numerous studies have directly linked intake of sugar-sweetened beverages with weight gain in adults and children, and there is strong evidence that lowering their consumption reduces the prevalence of obesity and related diseases (de Ruyter et al. 2012; Ebbeling et al. 2012; Malik and Hu 2011; Malik et al. 2006; Te Morenga et al. 2012).

Artificial sweeteners have not stemmed the obesity epidemic. Since 1987, the number of Americans who consume products with sugar-free sweeteners has more than doubled, yet the prevalence of obesity increased from 15 percent to 30 percent of the population during that time (Hampton 2008). Low-calorie sweeteners may actually stimulate the appetite for sweet foods and promote overeating and obesity by blunting the body's energy-expenditure mechanism (Bellisle and Drewnowski 2007) and the brain's satiety response (Frank et al. 2008).

Alcoholic beverage commercials vigorously promote consumption in the US, and some Americans are heavy drinkers. Potential intoxication and alcoholism are the obvious risks, but little attention has been paid to the connection between alcohol consumption and obesity (Block 2004; Kerr and Greenfield 2003) or to the caloric content of alcoholic beverages; depending on brand, a 12-ounce can of beer contains up to 330 calories (popsugar.com). When consumed before meals, alcohol stimulates appetite, limits satiety, and weakens the ability to compensate with smaller meals after a large one, so it both directly and indirectly contributes to increased energy intake (Mattes 2006). Large prospective studies of British men and women have shown that heavy drinking contributes to weight gain, especially among younger women (Wannamethee et al. 2004; Wannamethee and Shaper 2003). A study following more than 120,000 Americans for more than 20 years (Mozaffarian et al. 2011) showed that weight gain in adults was linked to consumption of alcohol, potato chips, potatoes, sugar-sweetened beverages, unprocessed red meats, processed meats, and smoking cessation, television watching, and insufficient or excessive sleep, while consumption of vegetables, whole grains, fruits, nuts, and yogurt, plus physical activity, had the opposite effect.

Eating out

Perhaps because of hectic work schedules, ever-increasing demand for individual productivity, and generally stressful living, Americans devote a sizable portion of their income to leisure pursuits (TVs, movies, vacations, sports and leisure equipment, RVs) due to the high value they place on limited free time. But because of the constant rush and pressure, they often skip meals and over-eat later. They depend heavily on convenience foods and quick-cooking devices such as microwave ovens. Today half of all food dollars are spent on meals prepared away from home and sold in restaurants, vending machines, and carry-outs (McCrory et al. 1999). The number of meals served in fast-food restaurants has tripled in the last three decades. Fast-food outlets are everywhere, even in schools and children's hospitals, where they function as an important revenue source for these institutions (McDonald et al. 2006). What makes them so attractive is the low price of menu items and the high levels of fat, sugar, and salt that are standard components of fast food, specifically designed to appeal to human taste buds (Moss 2013; Smith 2002). Fast food promotes increased consumption of saturated fat, sodium, and energy (Schmidt et al. 2005). The proximity of fast-food restaurants to schools influences obesity – ninth graders whose school is located within one-tenth of a mile from a fast-food restaurant have higher obesity rates than those who have less easy access (Currie et al. 2009).

With both parents working outside the home in many American families, it is not surprising that on any given day nearly half of all U.S. adults patronize a restaurant. The frequency of eating out is positively associated with increased energy intake and body fatness in all segments of society. The restaurant industry is one of the largest businesses in the US and the second-largest employer (only the government has more). While the number of grocery stores in the US has declined in recent years, ready-to-eat outlets have actually more than doubled in number. The American family has outsourced its meal preparation. Many parents do not know how to cook because they did not have an opportunity to learn, and consequently depend on packaged, frozen, fully prepared meals. Their children have had little experience with home-cooked meals and their preparation or taste (Lichtenstein and Ludwig 2010). Participants in *The Biggest Loser* television program, who live for months on the ranch where taping takes place, must cook their own meals. Many contestants had lost or never had the ability to cook because they always "ate out" and must now learn to prepare their own meals, an activity meant to help them appreciate the nutrient and energy content of home-cooked food compared to restaurant offerings (Moskin 2009).

Restaurant and convenience meals are generally higher in energy content and lower in fiber than those prepared at home. The restaurant industry, like other food industries, exploits the natural human preference for salt, sugar, and fat, boosting these ingredients to enhance the taste of purchased meals and to encourage return for more. Part of the enormous increase in consumption of sweeteners is via restaurant meals and fast-food servings and snacks, especially in sweetened fruit beverages and soft drinks. Even fast-food salads, usually thought to be more healthful than burgers and fries, are often served with high-fat dressings. They also usually cost more than a standard hamburger. The local McDonald's offers salads with grilled chicken (220–320 calories, according to Nutrition Facts posted on the back of placemats) for $4.69. Hamburgers or cheeseburgers (250–350 calories) are just $.89 and $1.19, respectively, while the Quarter Pounder Meal, which includes a sandwich, medium drink and medium French fries (up to 950 calories), costs $4.99. Incidentally, fructose is a prominent ingredient in McDonald's buns, ketchup, barbecue, mustard, and sweet 'n' sour sauces, birthday cakes, low-fat chocolate milk, sodas, and power drinks.

Not only do Americans consume more high-energy frozen, packaged, and restaurant foods today, but meal portions have ballooned since the 1970s (Diliberti et al. 2004; Kral et al. 2004; Nielsen and Popkin 2003; Young and Nestle 2002). Restaurants serve food on larger plates than in the past, and snacks are sold in much larger packages. Many ready-to-eat foods and beverage servings have more than doubled in volume and weight. Today's typical serving of cooked pasta, for example, is at least five times larger than the U.S. Department of Agriculture (USDA) standard and fills an entire extra-large dinner plate. A regular serving of soda is now more than three times the original size; single servings of Coke have increased from 6.5 ounces in 1916 to 10–12 ounces in the 1950s and to 20 ounces in the 1990s. Even the small, elegant, single-serving, glass Coke bottle has increased in girth, so that auto manufacturers have had to install larger drink holders in recent model cars. The very best New York bagels are today more than twice the size of traditional ones, victims of competition for greater profits in the bagel business. Even frozen diet dinners have become supersized. A local restaurant memorializing the late race car driver Dale Earnhardt, Sr. served a hamburger the size of a large dinner plate named the "Intimidator." The local university meal service offered a Finals Week Refill Special – free refills of fountain beverages (sodas and sweetened fruit drinks) when students used the 24-ounce promotional cup. A student taking advantage of this generous offer therefore consumed 48 ounces of a fountain drink to get through final exams. At a time when Wendy's and McDonald's were making a point of advertising low-calorie items on their menus, Hardee's promoted the Monster Thickburger, a truly super-super-sized meal of a 2/3 pound of beef containing 1,420 calories and 1,079 grams of fat. Needless to say, the media uproar, including exposure on the *David Letterman Show*, had the desired result, and Monster Thickburger sales took off.

Consumers generally consider current portion sizes typical and normal because they are unaware of food portion standards and gradual portion size increases. In a recent feeding experiment, when foods were served in large bowls or from bowls that were automatically refilled, study participants consumed more food than when served from smaller bowls or bowls that were not refilled (Wansink and Cheney 2005; Wansink et al. 2005). Even those who do recognize that serving portions are larger than recommended view them as irresistible "bargains" and subsequently consume larger amounts and much more energy than they would have in the past. Who can resist a McDonald's Quarter Pounder with Cheese Extra Value Meal, including *large* fries and a *large* drink (1,390 calories) (nutrition.mcdonalds. com), costing less per ounce than the separately purchased Quarter Pounder with cheese, *small* fries, and a *small* drink (980 calories)? This deal conforms perfectly to the ancient human drive to obtain as much energy as possible at the smallest possible cost. And who can buy only one bag of chips if this week's supermarket special is two for the price of one? That deal appeals to the American sense of thrift. The trouble is that the two bags are consumed about as quickly as a single one. And individuals consume the same amount of food, whether meals consist of high-calorie foods or bulky, low-calorie ones (Ello-Martin et al. 2005; Kral et al. 2004). Those who eat super-size meals for as many as 11 days do not compensate by reducing energy intake during subsequent meals (Rolls et al. 2007). Thus children and adults significantly increase their energy intake when served larger food portions during meals and snacks (Ebbeling et al. 2004; Fisher et al. 2003; Raynor and Wing 2007). Clearly, external cues influence eating behavior by overriding internal hunger indicators.

Children and food

Parents determine what children eat, right? Not always. Parents' food purchases are strongly influenced by their children's advertisement-driven demands. Food marketing to children was deregulated in 1984. Susan Linn (Linn 2004), author of *Consuming Kids*, considers today's food ads to be as life-threatening as TV depictions of violence. Her study of food advertisers revealed their cynical goal of convincing children to demand forbidden foods and undermine parental authority over family meals, which Linn sees as dangerous exploitation of children's vulnerabilities. Children with obesity are particularly susceptible to the emotional message conveyed by food commercials – that food is happiness and power.

Their choices ultimately impact the nutritional status of entire families, since children are largely dependent on adults to provide their meals, and parental eating behavior is largely imitated by young children (Johannsen et al. 2006). Parents with obesity are more likely to have children with obesity, not only because family members share obesity genes but also because they share food and eating patterns and develop similar food tastes and habits (Birch 1999; Farshchi et al. 2005a; Farshchi et al. 2005b). Contrary to common belief, children do not instinctively select well-balanced diets if they are constantly confronted with attractive inducements to eat sweet, salty, and fatty foods in the absence of whole grains, fruits, and vegetables (Faith et al. 2004). From early infancy, children learn to prefer certain foods through a combination of genetic predispositions, eating experiences, and social influences. If other family members reject nutritious foods in favor of non-nutritious ones, children are likely to do the same. Furthermore, parents who restrict children's eating are more likely to have adolescent children with obesity (Loth et al. 2013).

Breakfast is becoming obsolete in the US for children and adults. Only half of Americans under the age of 54 years report eating breakfast regularly – and the foods eaten range from cold pizza to cold cereal – while senior citizens with presumably more time to prepare meals are much more likely to eat a traditional warm breakfast (Langer 2005). In a breakfast consumption experiment, daily energy intake was significantly lower and insulin sensitivity was significantly higher when participants ate breakfast than during the breakfast-omitted portion of the trial (Farshchi et al. 2005b). Regularly skipping breakfast could well result in weight gain if it leads to higher energy intake later in the day. This may be one reason for the supposed Freshman 15 (actually, an average of 7.5 lb) gained by two-thirds of first-year college students (Vadeboncoer et al. 2015). Dramatic life changes, unlimited food choices, time constraints and sleep deprivation, stress, and the novelty of personal autonomy probably all combine to develop poor eating and exercise habits for some college freshmen (Wray 2005).

Many young and old Americans eat irregularly throughout the day, consume a heavy evening meal, and raid the fridge at night. Regular family meals are becoming rarer, another contributor to metabolic changes leading to obesity. A carefully designed study to find out if regular meal consumption affects energy metabolism showed that individuals who eat irregularly tend to consume more food energy, have higher levels of LDL-cholesterol and lower insulin sensitivity, and use less energy to digest their food (the Thermic Effect of Food (TEF)) (Farshchi et al. 2005b). Since TEF levels function as satiety signals to the brain's appetite control center, these individuals tend to consume more energy at each meal.

Even the earliest eating experience, milk consumption by a newborn infant, can influence later food preferences. Mother's milk, but not infant formula, is flavored by the foods the mother has eaten and exposes her baby to the tastes preferred by the family (Forestell and Mennella 2007). *Breastfeeding* not only guides the developing infant toward specific food preferences learned through early contact with their tastes in a warm and comforting setting, but may also influence weight control (Singhal and Lanigan 2007; von Kries et al. 1999). Breastfed children exhibit a pattern of growth that differs from the pattern seen in formula-fed children (Dewey 1998). Breast milk promotes slower growth and less weight gain in the early years, while formula feeding is more often associated with rapid growth and childhood overweight and obesity (Arenz et al. 2004; Gillman et al. 2001; Grummer-Strawn and Mei 2004). Breastfed children are also better at self-regulating caloric intake and adapting to new foods such as vegetables. Since overweight youngsters are more likely than children of healthy weight to become obese in adulthood (Guo 1994), early feeding patterns can have a life-long impact. Exclusive breastfeeding of newborn infants has more than doubled in the US since the 1970s, but nearly one-third of new mothers never attempt it. There is considerable diversity in breastfeeding initiation and duration rates among segments of the American population; Hispanic and black mothers and women in southern states are less likely to breastfeed than white women from the northeastern and western states (Ryan et al. 2002). These breastfeeding patterns almost exactly coincide with U.S. obesity patterns. Although a recent global review of its effects (Horta and Victora 2013) shows that at best breastfeeding is related to no more than a 24 percent reduction in obesity in high, middle, and low-income countries, this is one of many ways to prevent obesity and improve child nutritional health and immunity to disease.

Mothers in developing countries usually have no other option but to breastfeed their babies because of the high cost of formula. Mothers in industrialized countries are more likely to purchase infant formulas, or are offered free formula in feeding programs for low-income families. Formula producers encourage this by advertising their products as healthy alternatives to breastfeeding, by giving rebates to feeding programs such as Women, Infants, and Children (WIC) that distribute free formula, and by promoting sales through samples and coupons given to new mothers in hospitals. Educational efforts to inform mothers about the health risks of formula feeding have been swamped by the industry's promotional efforts, so most mothers are unaware of the link between formula feeding and infant infection rates, developmental problems, and childhood obesity (AAP 2005).

Nutrition education

Efforts to educate the U.S. public about good nutrition and the dangers of having obesity have been singularly unsuccessful in modifying behavior and changing body weight, but it must also be said that such educational efforts are quite limited. Nutrition education, formerly part of the public school home economics and health curricula, has largely disappeared and has been replaced by emphasis on academic subjects. While some public schools do incorporate nutrition education into teaching materials such as mathematics lessons that calculate caloric values of foods and the like, these rather subtle messages are contradicted by the very obvious presence of high-calorie foods in school cafeterias and vending machines. A pizza lunch with teacher is used as an incentive and reward for academic performance. Educational Channel One is viewed on school TV, but along with the academic programs students see numerous food advertisements and other commercial entice-ments. Selling candy is a common school fundraising project. Instead of nutritional integrity and a strong unified message about healthy food habits, children are confronted daily in school by conflicting messages about consumption.

Another school feature that counters efforts to instill good nutrition is purely structural. Largely because of crowded conditions, many schools have to schedule multiple short lunch periods. Some begin as early as 10:30 a.m. and others not until after 1:30 p.m., leaving students hungry in the afternoon or late morning respectively. Lunch periods of less than 30 minutes force students to eat hurriedly, unable to enjoy food and respond appropriately to satiety signals (hhdev.psu.edu) (Nakazawa 2005).

Food education efforts have been successful in encouraging consumers to read food labels and increase their consumption of low-fat, high-fiber foods. But there is no evidence of a reduction in overall energy content of consumed food, perhaps in part because the "calories per serving" listed on the labels do not correspond to the actual serving size as typically consumed.

Energy expenditure and the environment

Energy expenditure, mainly in the form of physical activity, is at least as impor-tant, and possibly more so, than reduced energy intake in helping to control body weight. Energy expenditure is the somewhat neglected child of obesity research because it is more difficult to measure and assess than energy intake, but its impor-tance is finally beginning to be more widely appreciated (Wendel-Vos et al. 2007). Participants in the National Weight Control Registry have made rigorous daily exercise a regular part of their successful maintenance regimen, strong proof of its value in controlling obesity (Phelan et al. 2003). A one-year study of participants with extreme obesity clearly demonstrated that physical activity contributed signif-icantly to weight loss and improvement of cardiac health (Goodpaster et al. 2010).

Obesity develops when energy output is less than intake. The relationship between energy intake and expenditure is determined to a great degree by the genetic and physiological mechanisms described in Chapter 3. Increased fat storage can occur even without excess food intake as a result of metabolic disequilibrium, such as leptin or insulin resistance, or due to physical inactivity and reduced energy utilization, as in prolonged bed rest. Physical activity is largely under conscious control and only partly influenced by genes or metabolism, so the external envi-ronment is the primary influence on individual physical exertion (Brownson et al. 2005; Poirier and Eckel 2000; Salbe and Ravussin 2000). Not only do Americans enjoy many technological improvements that have reduced occupational work-loads and household labor, but access to many new forms of sedentary leisure pastimes has increased as well in the form of televisions, videos, and computers, multiple examples of which are now in virtually every home.

Of the more than 3,000 counties in the United States, McIntosh County, North Dakota has the most residents over 85 years of age (Kilborn 2003). The tiny county seat of Ashley is populated by retired wheat farmers and ranchers, largely of German ancestry, many of them in their 80s and 90s and a few even 100 years old. In spite of their regular diet of sausages, strudel, dumplings, and ice cream laced with chocolate sauce, most of these elders live long and healthy lives and remain active far beyond their retirement years. Although townspeople cite plenty of fresh air, neighborliness, and the absence of stress and poverty as contributing factors, Ashley's only physician attributes their longevity to many years of very hard work. Most of the elderly retirees ended their education in elementary school because they were needed to assist on family farms. They spent many decades doing rigorous manual farm labor and housework, and even in old age continue to help out their sons and daughters with their farm work.

Human beings expend energy in maintaining bodily functions, reproducing (the energy costs borne by women in pregnancy, lactation, and infant care), growth and development, digesting, metabolizing and storing food, and physical work (Ulijaszek 2000). For most non-pregnant, healthy adults, daily energy requirements are largely determined by individual body weight and physical activity levels, which can vary greatly from individual to individual and even in the same individual over time. When food is scarce, people scale down their physical activities to conserve energy, a survival strategy used even today by undernourished populations throughout the world. Heavy labor without adequate energy support leads to weight loss. But the US faces the opposite situation – reduced physical activity with increased calorie consumption resulting in storage of excess energy as fat and additional body weight. This must be what Paleolithic ancestors dreamed of – more food, less work, and a sizable store of body fat. Modern Americans have achieved that dream and then some.

Over the last century everyday lives have gradually become more convenient and easy. The technologically sophisticated environment created in the US demands little effort or energy expenditure. Before the development of industrial technology, virtually all the tasks of daily living required considerable labor. Most work was done by hand and often required cooperation and collaboration for the most demanding tasks. Today's occupations and leisure pursuits depend heavily on mechanized transportation and labor-saving devices.

Physically demanding manufacturing jobs declined from 30 percent of all private sector occupations in the 1960s to only 12 percent in 2008, and service occupations climbed to an all-time high (Church et al. 2011). Agricultural occupations declined by two-thirds and manufacturing jobs by half in recent decades (Tillotson 2004). Sedentary service occupations, on the other hand, have increased, as for example the 26 percent rise in jobs in the financial sector. Even the most strenuous occupations such as in construction or agriculture have become more computerized, mechanized, and much less labor-intensive than in the past. Estimated mean daily work-related energy expenditure has dropped by about 100 calories since the 1960s, helping to account for an average of about 13 kilograms (29 pounds) of increased body weight for both men and women.

At best some Americans manage to fit regular exercise into their daily lives, but most cannot even approach the routine level of energy output required just a few generations ago. Throughout most of human history and prehistory life demanded daily physical effort, but now physical inactivity has become the order of the day for young and old, making it easy to become overweight or obese.

There is, however, one group of Americans whose lifestyle still resembles the pre-industrial condition. Members of the *Old Order Amish*, an American religious sect, maintain strict separation from the "outside world" by refusing to use automobiles, electricity, or telephones, by dressing in distinctive clothing fastened with hooks and eyes instead of zippers, and by using only horses for transportation and farm work, which is their preferred occupation. Their low-tech "simple life," deliberately chosen because it keeps them "close to the land," necessarily entails much manual labor on the part of every member of the community.

A study of one Old Order Amish community in Ontario found that adults engaged in very high levels of daily physical activity (Bassett et al. 2004). Pedometers, used to count the number of steps taken each day, recorded daily averages of more than 18,000 steps by men and 14,000 steps by women; even on Sunday, the traditional day of rest, both men and women recorded 10,000 steps on average. For comparison, Americans today are encouraged to gradually increase their daily number of steps to 10,000 by America on the Move, an organization that promotes physical activity for health. Rates of overweight (22 percent) and obesity (4 percent) in the Ontario Amish community are much lower than for the general U.S. population (67 percent). The Amish are known for working hard and eating accordingly, consuming meat, potatoes, gravy, eggs, bread, pies, and cakes with abandon – in short, a high-calorie diet that makes nutritionists shudder. Their overweight and obesity prevalence is therefore attributable not to modest energy intake, but rather to extreme energy output in the physical work of daily living. Amish children, who are generally expected to finish their formal education by the eighth grade, join the workforce in their early teens, so all community members are engaged in high energy expenditure during most of their lives.

The health benefits of physical activity are obvious (Wilkinson and Blair 2003). Muscular activity uses the energy stored in adipose tissue to build more muscle tissue, which in turn uses more stored energy. Because of individual metabolic variations and because of the difficulty of measuring the energy expenditure associated with various activities, developing standardized physical activity recommendations for individuals is still a scientific challenge. Pedometers count the number of steps taken each day and are quite appropriate for measuring activity in the generally sedentary U.S. population. But step-counting alone could not capture all of the energy output involved in Old Order Amish life. Lifting and tossing hay bales, carrying infants and baskets of wet laundry, climbing ladders and stairs, chasing cows and chickens, pushing and pulling all sorts of heavy loads, kneading bread dough, digging soil, weeding, hoeing, and cultivating gardens, shoveling manure, harvesting garden and farm produce, dragging logs and chopping wood, constructing houses and barns by hand – all of these are rigorous activities that cannot be measured with pedometers, yet contribute to the impressive energy output of Amish workers.

Despite their strong commitment to tradition, Old Order Amish lives are slowly changing. Farming can no longer financially sustain all Amish communities, and many members are forced to work in the "outside world," where they have to use modern technology. It remains to be seen whether their inexorable transition to modernity and less physically demanding occupations will lead to higher rates of overweight and obesity.

Americans believe in the value of "hard work," but the nature of work has changed drastically. Human labor has been replaced by machines: the automatic alarm clock and the smell of coffee brewing in an automatic coffee maker programmed before bedtime; the electric toothbrush to keep teeth sparkling; electric hair dryers and razors for presentable appearance; remote controls for TV, garage doors, fireplaces, and window blinds; toasters to heat pre-sliced bread to go with orange juice that has been chilled in the electric refrigerator for breakfast; newspapers delivered by car (no longer by the paper boy on foot or bicycle) or on the internet; cars equipped with automatic locks, windows, and transmissions; escalators or elevators for convenient transportation to shop or office; computers, telephones, faxes, copying machines, and intercoms for "work"; automatic toilet flushing mechanisms, faucets, and towel dispensers; drive-in banks to deposit paychecks (or automatic deposit); drive-in restaurants for fully prepared take-home dinners, complete with drinks and dessert; encyclopedia programs, word processors, and spreadsheets on the computer; television sets in kitchens, living rooms, and bedrooms. Automatic sprinklers, dishwashers, washers and dryers, cordless phones, riding mowers, power tools, golf carts, and countless other machines have eased work and even reduced the energy requirements of leisure activity. Gadgets and labor-saving devices save much time and effort, but at the same time consume huge quantities of fossil fuels, not to mention sizeable portions of incomes. Sales of the Roomba, a robotic vacuum cleaner that sweeps floors by remote control, are high. One of the more expensive new items is the Segway Human Transporter, designed to run on city sidewalks and to reduce the need to walk. It is a popular "pedestrian" tourist activity in Washington DC, to maneuver to various sites near the National Mall.

Biological anthropologist Stanley Ulijazek calls obesity a "disorder of convenience" (Ulijaszek 2006). Altogether, countless small activity-sparing devices have an enormous impact. For example, the regular use of automatic dishwashers and power vacuum cleaners (instead of washing dishes and sweeping floors by hand) alone conserves an average of 111 cal per day per person (Lanningham-Foster et al. 2003).

Recent national surveys determined that only one-half to two-thirds of American adults meet public health recommended levels of physical activity (CDC 2008a; CDC 2009; Ulijaszek 1999). Among children, moderate to vigorous physical activity declines from childhood to adolescence, with corresponding increases in computer use (Nader et al. 2008; Nelson et al. 2006). One-fourth of all U.S. public school students receive no physical education, and more schools support interscholastic contests for small groups of elite athletes than promote intramural sports for the entire student body (Gordon-Larsen et al. 2000). More than one-fourth of all Americans report that they do not participate in any recreational activity (CDC 2008b; CDC 2009). According to the Nationwide Personal Transportation Study, biking and walking trips have declined from 9 percent to 5 percent since 1977, while trips by automobile (including RVs and trucks) increased from 84 percent to 89 percent during the same period (FHA 1997). It is no coincidence that a greater proportion of individuals who use car transport are overweight than those who walk or bicycle to work and school (Gordon-Larsen et al. 2005).

Television watching has become the focus of considerable obesity-related study, and for very good reason (Kaiser Foundation 2004; Klesges et al. 1993; Tucker and Bagwell 1991). Virtually all American homes have several TV sets, and most adults, one-third of whom report no physical activity during their leisure time, watch TV as their primary form of recreation. Videos and computer games also offer many hours of sedentary entertainment. Children's increasing screen media habits happen to parallel increases in obesity. Every hour spent watching TV is one hour less of vigorous social interaction and physical activity. Even infants and toddlers are accustomed to many hours of passive, mesmerizing, metabolism-reducing, energy-conserving TV-watching. Each year new programs and channels targeting very young children are developed and marketed to parents as early educational experiences.

Snacking is inevitably linked with TV viewing by adults and children alike, and is one of the reasons for concern about the many hours children spend watching TV (Gortmaker et al. 1996; Klesges et al. 1993; Matheson et al. 2004). Children who watch the most hours of TV are also the most likely to have obesity, a relationship first observed by Bill Dietz 25 years ago (Dietz and Gortmaker 1985), and confirmed again and again by other scientists (Falbe et al. 2013). There is a clear link between TV-watching, increased consumption of advertised, non-nutritious foods, and decreased intake of fruits and vegetables by adults and children alike (Giammattei et al. 2003). Not only does TV actively promote the purchase of high-calorie food through advertising, it also directly influences its consumption during hours of passive entertainment. Gary Ruskin, executive director of Commercial Alert in Portland, Oregon, calls the television set an "obesity machine" (commercialalert.org).

Even though TV-hours and obesity levels are linked, it is not always clear whether increased TV-watching is a cause or a consequence of increased obesity. On the one hand, extended hours of passivity and snacking tend to increase body weight; on the other hand, persons with obesity may consider the discomfort of physical activity something to be avoided and therefore prefer to quietly watch TV. What is certain is that inactivity and overweight and obesity are closely related, and these in turn are linked to obesity-related conditions such as diabetes, cardiovascular disease, and all-cause mortality (Grontved and Hu 2011).

Nearly all participants in the National Weight Control Registry who have successfully maintained their large weight losses engage in heavy doses of physical activity (Wing and Phelan 2005) and spend a minimal amount of time watching TV – most watch 10 hours or less per week (Raynor et al. 2006). Most Americans know that regular exercise reduces the risk of obesity and its associated ills, especially diabetes, high blood pressure, heart disease, and certain forms of cancer. So why do so many Americans avoid physical activity? It could be assumed that inactive people are lazy, willfully ignorant, irresponsible, and otherwise unreasonable in the face of overwhelming evidence for the benefits of physical activity. But like food consumption, individual decisions about physical activity are heavily influenced by forces beyond personal control whose primary concern is not the health and fitness of American citizens and whose power is difficult to resist on an individual basis.

Promoting inactivity

U.S. obesity rates have increased in spite of the fitness industry's explosive growth, ubiquitous sporting goods stores, increased sales of exercise programs and equipment, and construction of more fitness facilities. The pressure is on individuals to become more active, and the focus is on exercise – special outfits, equipment, and activities conducted during special times of the day or week – rather than on routine physical activity as part of daily life. They purchase spa and fitness club memberships, treadmills and weight-lifting equipment, expensive athletic shoes and special clothing, while they also rush to acquire the latest in modern gadgets and labor-saving devices – weed whackers, automatic coffee grinders, electric cork screws and pencil sharpeners, remote-controlled TVs, VCRs, and air conditioners. Both the health and fitness industry and the home appliance industry benefit, but health suffers. True, no one is forced to purchase these items; they choose to spend their hard-earned income in this way. But as with food, they are strongly influenced, often very subtly, by industry marketing, peer pressure, and the need to adhere to a certain standard of living that conforms to deeply held notions of "the good life."

Until recently, very little was known about the reasons for avoiding physical activity, but the growing obesity epidemic has encouraged scientists to investigate the problem. Large-scale surveys had previously explored individual perceptions of environmental facilitators and barriers to leisure-time physical activity. As might be expected, opportunity for activity and accessibility of safe places to engage in activity turned out to be very important incentives (Lumeng et al. 2006). But of surprising importance, even greater than weather and safety issues, was the aesthetic nature of the outdoor environment. Attractive scenery with hills and trees and friendly neighbors were seen as important stimulants for recreational activity (Owen et al. 2004). A study conducted in six European countries found that what mattered most in motivating people to become physically active was not only specific knowledge about facilities and options for activity and sport but also social support from family, friends, school, and the workplace (Stahl et al. 2001). Much as development of obesity can be traced through a social network, social contagion can promote physical activity through interpersonal cues that activity is considered normal and socially acceptable behavior.

A nationwide study using census and survey data demonstrated the relationship between community design, leisure activity, obesity, and health (Ewing et al. 2003). More than 500 U.S. counties and metropolitan areas were assigned urban sprawl indices based on their residential density and other carefully selected factors. Large cities such as San Francisco and New York were the most densely populated communities with the lowest sprawl indices included in this study. At the higher end of the sprawl scale were suburban counties of the American Southeast and Midwest where residential populations were least compact. The study confirmed the researchers' expectations. Residents of sprawling communities were less likely to walk during their leisure hours and were more likely to be overweight and have hypertension, diabetes, and heart disease than those living in compact residential areas. This study, which assessed not just personal perceptions but the actual nature of the *built environment*, is one of the first to demonstrate clearly the importance of community design in promoting physical activity and human health.

Outside large urban centers where public transportation is available and residents must walk at least as far as the nearest taxi, bus, or subway stop, modern U.S. communities are designed primarily to accommodate private vehicle traffic (Figure 4.3). The first suburbs appeared in the late 19th century, and were linked to cities by streetcars that transported residents to their places of work, but it was

FIGURE 4.3 Suburban design. Courtesy of Trekandshoot via Shutterstock.com.

shortly after World War II that suburban development grew rapidly, stimulated by returning military personnel who needed homes (Thomas 1998). The US was the only country involved in the war that did not experience large-scale destruction and therefore did not have to invest in rebuilding the country's infrastructure. This advantage contributed to increased post-war affluence and gave Americans the ability to purchase private homes and automobiles. The Federal-Aid Highway Act of 1956 called for the construction of a national network of superhighways and drastically reduced support for public transportation. Middle-class white families were able to escape the unhealthy, crowded environment of inner cities, leaving ethnic minorities and the poor concentrated in the urban areas.

In contrast to urban centers, residential suburbs (particularly the newer developments) usually have winding streets, many of which are not connected, lead nowhere, and lack sidewalks and bike lanes. Community and commercial centers, strictly segregated from homes, can be reached only by automobile. Children are transported to schools, families ride to churches and shopping malls even if these are not far away, and going to work means commuting in one of the family cars. In fast-growing communities where construction of new roads, schools, and shopping centers disrupts traffic patterns, drivers can spend hours in their cars crawling through heavy traffic to and from work (Lyman 2005). Driving is the most common mode of travel; in the US today 91 percent of all person-miles are traveled by auto, while only 1 percent are walked (FHA 1997; Owen et al. 2004). Even very short trips are made by automobile; only 16 percent of trips of less than one mile are walked and less than 1 percent of all trips under five miles are biked instead of driven. Although Great Britain and Canada come close, this is the highest rate of passive travel in the world. Europeans drive half as much and walk or bike twice as much as Americans. Germany, for example, has developed subsidized *auto-freie* communities, where residents walk or ride bikes to nearby shops, schools, and recreation facilities, but may temporarily rent from a car pool for extended trips outside the community. In the US the automobile rules – the most heavily advertised American product is the private car, which costs less to own, license, park, and fill with gas than in any other country in the world.

Visiting another country makes one quite aware of Americans' extreme inactivity. Walking and bicycling are important modes of transportation, even in the highly developed countries of Europe. German and Dutch citizens make one-third to one-half of all urban trips on foot or by bike (Pucher and Dijkstra 2003). Admittedly it is much more expensive to own and operate an automobile in Europe, and walking and bicycling are more dangerous in the US because of the general lack of bike lanes and sidewalks where auto traffic is heavy. But it is noteworthy that in contrast to the US, walking and bicycling increases with age in Germany and the Netherlands. In both countries elderly persons over the age of 75 years use these modes of transportation more than younger individuals and nearly 10 times as often as American elderly of a similar age. A study of American adults who moved to a higher-walkability environment found that they did more transport walking – for example, to school or work – and experienced a reduction in BMI (Hirsch 2014). Walking even as little as one hour per week significantly reduces the risk of cardiovascular disease (Owen et al. 2004).

Like sprawling suburbia, some building interiors also present barriers to physical activity. Commercial and industrial establishments have attractively designed elevators and shiny escalators located in prominent places. Staircases, on the other hand, are often difficult to find and unpleasant or even hazardous to use. The more recent trend to design buildings with attractive, open staircases that promote walking will hopefully continue.

Physical activity has also declined in American schools. Children have fewer opportunities to engage in physical activity during school hours than in the past. The frequency and duration of physical education classes have been reduced or even eliminated in many areas of the US, in part as a result of budget cuts that also affected art and music education. The reduction in physical education has had a deleterious effect on just those students most at risk for overweight. Black and Hispanic adolescent girls who attend poorer, racially segregated schools are less physically active than white girls in schools with predominantly white student bodies (Richmond et al. 2006).

Today fewer physical education classes are taught by trained teachers, and fewer schools require regular physical activity. Fewer than 15 percent of American children and adolescents walk or bicycle to school today, compared to half of all school children and 87 percent of children living within one mile of school in 1969 (CDC 2005a). Distance to school and traffic-related danger are reported by parents to be the primary barriers to children's active transport. Because the number of U.S. schools has decreased by more than 1,000 since 1969, the distance to school has increased for many students. So children are bussed or driven to school by parents, sometimes in long commutes, and are discouraged from carrying book bags for fear of straining their backs. They are dismissed from school early in the afternoon and return home to the passive entertainment of their TVs, VCRs, and computers. Except for elite athletes, few school children are encouraged to develop a life-long appreciation of physical activity or taught how to incorporate it into their daily lives. Nearly half of all American youth aged 12 to 21 years are not vigorously active on a regular basis. Adolescence seems to be the crucial time for declining physical activity, especially among girls (Gordon-Larsen et al. 2000; Nelson et al. 2006).

The importance of school-related physical activity has been documented by the National Longitudinal Study of Adolescent Health, a survey of more than 17,000 students aged 11 to 21 years from all regions of the US (Gordon-Larsen et al. 2000). Results of the survey demonstrated that students who participated in school physical education programs were more physically active in their daily lives. A Pennsylvania Department of Health study comparing middle school students in 30-minute daily physical education classes with controls in schools without daily physical education found significant health and behavior benefits from physical activity (Erfle 2014). Physical education offerings in schools, along with crime-free neighborhoods and the presence of community recreation facilities, are important environmental factors that promote activity among adolescents, whose rising obesity rates are becoming a major public health issue in the US.

Muscle action requires energy, most of which comes from fat molecules stored in adipose tissue. Physical activity is a potent stimulator of lipolysis, the breakdown and release of stored fatty acids (Oguman and Shinoda-Tagawa 2004). Physical activity also lowers blood concentrations of insulin, the hormone that promotes fat storage (Hu 2008). Through regular physical activity lipolytic efficiency and insulin response are improved, resulting in loss of excess body fat. Exercise opposes the normally strong energy-sparing metabolic response of individuals who previously had obesity and the blunted lipolytic action of persons with advanced age. Since physical activity selectively reduces fat, significant health benefits can be expected from exercise (Irwin et al. 2003; Janssen et al. 2004). Physical activity alone has been shown to be at least as effective as dieting in promoting loss of body fat, although the combination of exercise and calorie restriction is even more effective than either one alone (Ross et al. 2000).

Physical activity also appears to offer some protection against chronic disease and early death, even in individuals with obesity. The risk for all-cause and cardio-vascular mortality is lower in individuals with good aerobic fitness, in spite of high BMI values, than in those with normal BMI and poor fitness. Nevertheless, high BMI, even in fit individuals, increases the risk of Type 2 diabetes and the prevalence of cardiovascular and diabetes risk factors (Fogelholm 2010). The Surgeon General of the United States reported that significant health benefits can be achieved with only moderate amounts of daily physical activity, such as a daily 30-minute brisk walk, 30 minutes of lawn-mowing and leaf-raking, a 15-minute run, or a 45-minute volleyball game (CDC 1996). But these benefits are lost within several months after ceasing regular activity, which must be continued for its beneficial effects. While even higher levels of physical activity, such as daily 60-minute brisk walks, provide even more protection, virtually everyone benefits from moderate exercise – smokers and non-smokers, normal weight and obese, healthy and unhealthy, hypertensive and normotensive, those with elevated cholesterol or triglycerides, and those with normal values.

Even seemingly trivial body movements can help prevent weight gain and obesity. Non-exercise thermogenesis activity (NEAT), spontaneous movement of the body such as fidgeting or jiggling a leg, can burn as much as 700 cal above and beyond daily energy expenditure for body maintenance (Levine et al. 2005). Individuals with obesity tend to sit still for two and a half hours more daily than lean individuals, who, although also in sedentary occupations, expend 350 cal more each day through NEAT (Levine et al. 2006).

Decreased time spent in physical activity is a global phenomenon (Ng and Popkin 2012). All over the world technology has reduced the need for physical activity in occupational work, domestic tasks, active leisure, and travel, and even greater declines in coming years are predicted. In China physical activity by adults, measured in metabolic equivalents of task (MET)-hours per week, has declined from 399 MET-hours per week in 1991 to 213 in 2009, most of it in occupational physical activity. The US saw a decline from 235 to 160 MET-hours per week from 1965 to 2009, also largely in the area of occupational activity. At the same time sedentary time increased in both countries, from 15 to 20 hours per week in China and from 25 to 40 hours per week in the US, much of it related to TV viewing. In a large U.S. study of healthy adults, sitting time was associated with all-cause mortality, and more than seven hours per day of TV viewing doubled the risk of cardiovascular disease compared to watching TV an average of only one hour per day (Matthews 2012).

Sleep deprivation and obesity

Inadequate sleep has consistently been shown to be directly related to obesity (Cizza et al. 2005). Many Americans are sleep-deprived due to their hectic daily schedules. Because of staff reductions to cut costs, shift workers in many retail, restaurant, and other businesses are forced to "clopen," both close and open the company doors with only a few hours of rest between shifts (Greenhouse 2015). Current scientific evidence suggests that there is a link between sleep deprivation, appetite, and metabolism, influenced to some degree by genes involved in circadian rhythms and dietary fat and protein intake (Dashti et al. 2015). Disruption of the normal 24-hour *circadian system*, controlled by the "master clock" in the hypothalamus as well as by biological clocks in other tissues, alters insulin, leptin, melatonin, and adiponectin levels and raises the risk of obesity and diabetes (Broussard et al. 2012; Buxton et al. 2012; Cipolla-Neto et al. 2014; Gangwisch 2009; Johnston et al. 2009). More than 1,000 participants in the Wisconsin Sleep Cohort Study, a longitudinal study of sleep habits and disorders, provided blood samples for hormonal assays that showed that their leptin and ghrelin hormonal profiles and BMI levels differed from those who had adequate sleep (Spiegel et al. 1999). Chronic sleep debt is also associated with increased glucose intolerance and insulin resistance as well as higher levels of the stress hormone cortisol, all of which are known to contribute to obesity (Hanlong and Van Cauter 2011; Taheri et al. 2004a; Taheri et al. 2004b). Furthermore, humans burn more fat during the fasting hours of sleep than during waking and feeding hours, when more glucose is oxidized as an efficient source of immediate energy while fat is stored rather than used.

Sleep loss activates appetite-related areas of the hypothalamus (Hanlong and Van Cauter 2011; Magee et al. 2010; St-Onge et al. 2012), stimulates appetite and hunger, and causes individuals to consume more calories than can be expended during extra waking hours (Chaput et al. 2006; Chaput et al. 2007; Knutson and Van Cauter 2008; Schecter et al. 2014; Spiegel et al. 2004; St-Onge et al. 2011). Data from the Nurses' Health Study (1986–2002) indicated that the women who slept five hours or less per night gained more weight during the 16 years of the study than the women who slept seven to nine hours (Patel 2009). Infants, children, and adolescents exhibit the same effect of short sleep duration on BMI (Bell and Zimmerman 2010; Chaput et al. 2006; Chaput et al. 2007; Lumeng et al. 2007; Mitchell et al. 2013; Taveras et al. 2008). Children and adolescents sleeping for short durations have twice the risk of overweight or obesity, compared with those with long-duration sleep (Fatima et al. 2015). As a result of poor or inadequate sleep, daytime fatigue probably also lowers physical activity and energy expenditure.

Average American sleep time has dropped from nine hours per night in 1910 to seven and a half hours today (CDC 2005b; Cizza et al. 2005). Successive National Health and Nutrition Examination Surveys (NHANES) documented the trend in sleep deprivation. Between 1985 and 2004, the proportion of American adults who reported sleeping six hours or less increased from 20 percent to 25 percent; the most sleep-deprived groups are men and women between the ages of 30 and 64 (CDC 2005b). Changes in U.S. sleep patterns have been attributed to the Edison Effect, the increased use of artificial light that disrupts normal circadian rhythm and shortens sleep duration (Media 2011). But longer and non-standard working hours by families where both parents are responsible for income, housework, and childcare, and the attractions of late-night television and other entertainments, also play important roles (Magee et al. 2010; Mozaffarian et al. 2011; Nedeltcheva et al. 2009). It remains to be seen if improved sleep duration can help individuals with obesity to control their weight (Lamberg 2006; Patel 2009; Pearson 2006).

The obesogen hypothesis

Obesogens are synthetic chemicals and naturally occurring, estrogen-like molecules belonging to a class of endocrine-disrupting compounds that have wide-ranging hormonal-like effects, including increased fat accumulation and obesity (Gruen 2010; Janesick and Blumberg 2012; Shug et al. 2011). Obesogens are widely dispersed and pervasive, especially in industrialized nations such as the US. Their contribution to obesity rates in the US has only recently come to be appreciated. It is likely that the age, sex, and population differences in obesity levels and associated diseases are at least in part due to variations in exposure to environmental chemicals (Bouchard et al. 2010; Campion et al. 2009; Demerath 2010; Gallou-Kabani et al. 2008; Gluckman et al. 2008; Junien and Nathanielsz 2007).

Obesogens activate or suppress the normal function of hormone receptors, increase adipocyte cell number and fat mass, promote inflammation, and lower thyroid action and basal metabolic rate (Gruen and Blumberg 2009; Le Corre et al. 2015; Major et al. 2007a). They disrupt the normal expression of genes regulating energy metabolism and induce individuals to become permanently obese, regardless of diet or physical activity.

Obesogens include such chemicals as PCB (polychlorinated biphenyl) used as lubricants and coolants in electrical appliances, banned in the 1970s but still persisting in the environment; DDE, a metabolite of the insecticide DDT; phthalates used as plasticizers and stabilizers in many consumer products; and numerous other chemicals in furniture, foods, jet fuel, and cosmetics and shampoos. Phthalates are ingested with food and water, inhaled in polluted air, and absorbed through the skin (Hatch et al. 2008). Among their effects is an increase in average BMI and waist circumference in both men and women. Exposure to PCB has a greater effect on obesity development in girls and women than in boys and men (Pereira-Fernandes et al. 2014; Tang-Peronard et al. 2011). International monitoring of environmental PCB distribution using starling eggs revealed that the US has the highest mean concentrations when compared with Australia, New Zealand, and European countries (Eens et al. 2013).

Tributyltin (TBT) is a biocide in paint applied to ship bottoms to protect against attachment of marine organisms (Rantakokko et al. 2014). It is released into sea water and consumed by fish and other marine organisms, causing abnormalities in their reproductive systems (Sousa et al. 2014). Humans consume contaminated fish and are also exposed by direct contact with TBT-treated products and inhalation of dust (Sousa et al. 2014). TBT disrupts energy balance by activating the protein PPAR gamma, which stimulates lipid uptake and adipogenesis. It is known to be involved in development of obesity, diabetes, atherosclerosis, and cancer (Gruen 2014; Janesick and Blumberg 2011; Janesick and Blumberg 2012; Pereira-Fernandes et al. 2013b).

Natural estrogenic compounds such as genistein found in soy-based products and some pharmaceutical items function as obesogens (Newbold et al. 2009). Bisphenol A (BPA) also has estrogenic properties and is an ingredient of polycarbonate plastics and epoxy resins in many consumer products (Vandenberg 2011). It is found in baby bottles, reusable water bottles, sports equipment, eyeglasses, CDs, medical devices, coatings of food and beverage cans, water pipes, dental sealants, paints, papers, cardboards, cigarette filters, and American banknotes, as well as in the environment in air, dust, sewage, and water and leaches out of products under normal use. Levels of BPA known to permanently harm animals have been found in urine samples of people from Asia, the European Union, Canada, and the US (Vandenberg 2011), with children and adolescents manifesting the highest levels. BPA and many other endocrine disrupters were found in sewage effluents in Australia, Canada, Germany, Italy, Spain, Korea, Japan, China, the UK, and the US (Sun et al. 2014). Even though Canadian and U.S. citizens did not differ in BPA exposure until 1994, the U.S. population now has concentrations that are twice as high as Canadians, perhaps due to differences in packaging practices, production levels, or other (unknown) factors. Even low exposure to BPA can affect development of reproductive organs, timing of puberty, and regulation of body mass and metabolism (Le Corre et al. 2015). BPA also activates PPAR gamma that induces adipogenesis (Janesick and Blumberg 2011; Pereira-Fernandes et al. 2013a).

Obesogens such as BPA and tributyltin alter the expression of genes that direct hormonal messages related to energy metabolism. They either silence or upregulate gene expression by attaching chemical structures called *methyl groups* to the cytosine nucleotides of DNA molecules (Diamanti-Kandarakis et al. 2009; Tang-Peronard et al. 2011). The DNA molecules themselves are left unaltered and, with methyl tags still attached, may even be passed on to succeeding generations. An example of such an *epigenetic* process contributing to obesity is the silencing of the *LPL* gene coding for the enzyme lipoprotein lipase that breaks down triglycerides. Blocking the function of this gene prevents release of fatty acids from their storage in the adipocytes (Campion et al. 2009).

Many obesogenic chemicals are lipid-soluble and accumulate in adipose tissue. Individuals with greater fat mass exhibit higher concentrations of pesticide organo-chlorines than lean individuals (Pelletier et al. 2002). Plasma organochlorine concentrations actually increase in individuals undergoing a weight-loss program and in athletes whose lipid stores are mobilized during training. Reduction in fat mass releases the chemicals sequestered in adipose tissue and thus increases exposure, lowering thyroid action and basal metabolic rate (Major et al. 2007b). The effects of multiple classes of such chemicals may be additive and synergistic (Diamanti-Kandarakis et al. 2009).

Conclusion

It cannot be a coincidence that so many environmental changes parallel the growing prevalence of obesity in the US. Increased use of certain medications and industrial chemicals, food and drink sweeteners, labor-saving technology, television viewing, restaurant and processed industrial foods, diet programs, auto transport, as well as declines in nutrient-dense foods, active transport, manual labor, and physical education have had enormous cumulative effects. Individualized efforts to end the obesity epidemic, such as nutrition education, behavioral counseling, and phar-maceutical treatments, have had only very limited success in the context of the

FIGURE 4.4 *Schlaraffenland* by Pieter Bruegel the Elder. Courtesy of Art Resource, NY.

modern obesogenic environment. Extreme personal effort is needed to overcome the ubiquitous temptations of consumption and inactivity in the US, and individuals have little direct control over the toxic environment that alters metabolic processes and encourages excessive energy intake, poor nutrition, and physical inactivity. The American obesogenic environment is a powerful barrier to individual efforts at weight control.

In 18th-century Germany the Brothers Grimm collected many folktales that had been told to European children for centuries, and their publications became the famous fairytales. A favorite of poor German peasants whose lives were ruled by deprivation and hardship, wars, starvation, and oppression was the fairytale of *Schlaraffenland* (Figure 4.4), the land flowing with milk and honey, with houses made of pancakes and fences of sausages, trees hung with sweet pastries, roasted fish and fowl floating through the air for easy picking, and endless ease and leisure (hence, the land's name referring to lazy oafs) (weihnachtsseiten.de/weihnachtsmaerchen/schlaraffenland/schlaraffenland.html). The modern obesogenic environment with its comfortable standard of living is truly Schlaraffenland, but it comes with unexpected threats to health and quality of life.

References

AAP (2005). American Association of Pediatrics policy statement: breastfeeding and the use of human milk. *Pediatrics* **115**(2): 496–506.

Araujo, J. R., F. Martel, and E. Keating (2014). Exposure to non-nutritive sweeteners during pregnancy and lactation: impact in programming of metabolic diseases in the progeny in later life. *Reproductive Toxicology* **49**: 196–201.

Arenz, S. et al. (2004). Breast-feeding and childhood obesity – a systematic review. *International Journal of Obesity* **28**: 1247–1256.

Azad, M. B. et al. (2014). Infant antibiotic exposure and the development of childhood overweight and central adiposity. *International Journal of Obesity* **38**(10): 1290–1298.

Bailey, L. C. et al. (2014). Association of antibiotics in infancy with early childhood obesity. *Journal of American Medical Association Pediatrics* **168**(11): 1063–1069.

Bassett, D. R., Jr., P. L. Schneider, and G. E. Huntington (2004). Physical activity in an Old Order Amish community. *Medicine & Science in Sports & Exercise* **36**(1): 79–85.

Bell, J. F. and F.J. Zimmerman (2010). Shortened nighttime sleep duration in early life and subsequent childhood obesity. *Archives of Pediatric & Adolescent Medicine* **164**(9): 840–845.

Bellisle, F. and A. Drewnowski (2007). Intense sweeteners, energy intake and the control of body weight. *European Journal of Clinical Nutrition* **61**: 691–670.

Birch, L. L. (1999). Development of food preferences. *Ann Rev Nutr* **19**: 41–62.

Bleich, S. N., Y. C. Wang, and S. L. Gortmaker (2009). Increasing consumption of sugar-sweetened beverages among US adults: 1988–1994 and 1999–2004. *American Journal of Clinical Nutrition* **89**: 372–381.

Block, G. (2004). Foods contributing to energy intakes in the US: data from NHANES III and NHANES 1999–2000. *Journal of Food Composition and Analysis* **17**: 439–447.

Borody, T. J., L. J. Brandt, and S. Paramsothy (2014). Therapeutic faecal microbiota transplantation: current status and future developments. *Current Opinion in Gastroenterology* **30**(1): 97–105.

Bouchard, L. et al. (2010). Differential epigenomic and transcriptomic responses in subcutaneous adipose tissue between low and high responders to caloric restriction. *American Journal of Clinical Nutrition* **91**: 309–320.

Bray, G. A., S. J. Nielsen, and B. M. Popkin (2004a). Consumption of high-fructose corn syrup in beverages may play a role in the epidemic of obesity. *American Journal of Clinical Nutrition* **79**: 537–543.

Bray, G. A., S. J. Nielsen, and B. M. Popkin (2004b). Letters to the editor: Reply to MF Jacobson, Erratum. *American Journal of Clinical Nutrition* **80**(4): 1090.

Brener, N. D. et al. (2011). Beverage consumption among high school students - United States, 2010. *Journal of the American Medical Association* **306**(4): 369–371.

Briefel, R. R., and C. L. Johnson (2004). Secular trends in dietary intake in the United States. *Ann Rev Nutr* **24**: 401–431.

Broussard, J. L. et al. (2012). Impaired insulin signaling in human adipocytes after experimental sleep restriction; a randomized, crossover study. *Annals of Internal Medicine* **157**(8): 549–557.

Brownson, R. C., T. K. Boehmer, and D. A. Luke (2005). Declining rates of physical activity in the United States: what are the contributors? *Annual Review of Public Health* **26**: 421–443.

Buxton, O. M. et al. (2012). Adverse metabolic consequences in humans of prolonged sleep restriction combined with circadian disruption. *Science Translational Medicine* **4**(129): 1–10.

Campion, J., F. I. Milagro, and J. A. Martinez (2009). Individuality and epigenetics in obesity. *Obesity Reviews* **10**(4): 383–392.

Canani, R. B., M. Di Costanzo, and L. Leon (2011). Epigenetic mechanisms elicited by nutrition in early life. *Nutrition Research Reviews* **24**: 198–205.

Castetter, E. F. and W. H. Bell (1942). Pima and Papago Indian Agriculture. Albuquerque: University of New Mexico Press.

CDC (1996). Physical Activity and Health: A Report of the Surgeon General. Centers for Disease Control and Prevention.

CDC (2005a). Barriers to children walking to or from school – United States, 2004. *JAMA* **294**(17): 2160–2161.

CDC (2005b). QuickStats: percentage of adults who reported an average of <6 hours of sleep per 24 – hour period, by sex and age group – United States, 1985 and 2004. *JAMA* **294**(21): 2692.

CDC (2008a). Prevalence of regular physical activity among adults – United States, 2001 and 2005. *JAMA* **299**(1): 30–32.

CDC (2008b). Prevalence of regular physical activity among adults – United States, 2001 and 2005. *JAMA* **299**(1): 30–32.

CDC (2009). Prevalence of self-reported physically active adults – United States, 2007. *JAMA* **301**(9): 926–927.

CDC (2010). State-specific trends in fruit and vegetable consumption among adults – United States, 2000–2009. *Morbidity and Mortality Weekly* **59**(35): 1125–1130.

Chaput, J-P. M. Brunet, and A. Tremblay (2006). Relationship between short sleeping hours and childhood overweight/obesity: results from the 'Quebec en Forme' Project. *International Journal of Obesity* **30**(7): 1080–1085.

Chaput, J-P. et al. (2007). Short sleep duration is associated with reduced leptin levels and increased adiposity: results from the Quebec Family Study. *Obesity* **15**: 253–261.

Chaput, J-P. and A. Tremblay (2007). Acute effects of knowledge-based work on feeding behavior and energy intake. *Physiology & Behavior* **90**: 66–72.

Chen, J., X. Z. He, and J. H. Huang (2014). Diet effects in gut microbiome and obesity. *Journal of Food Science* **79**(4): R442–R451.

Church, T. S. et al. (2011). Trends over 5 decades in U.S. occupation-related physical activity and their associations with obesity. *PLoS ONE* **6**(5): e19654.

Cipolla-Neto, J. et al. (2014). Melatonin, energy metabolism, and obesity: a review. *Journal of Pineal Research* **56**(4): 371–381.

Cizza, G., M. Skarulis, and E. Mignot (2005). A link between short sleep and obesity: building the evidence for causation. *Sleep* **28**(10): 1217–1220.

Cohen, D. A. and S. H. Babey (2012). Contextual influences on eating behaviours: heuristic processing and dietary choices. *Obesity Reviews* **13**: 766–779.

Cordain, L. et al. (2002). Fatty acid analysis of wild ruminant tissues: evolutionary implications for reducing diet-related chronic disease. *European Journal of Clinical Nutrition* **56**: 181–191.

Cullen, K. W. and I. Zakeri (2004). Fruits, vegetables, milk, and sweetened beverages consumption and access to a la carte/snack bar meals at school. *American Journal of Public Health* **94**(3): 463–467.

Currie, J. et al. (2009). The Effect of Fast Food Restaurants on Obesity. Cambridge, MA: *National Bureau of Economic Research.*

Dashti, H. S. et al. (2015). Habitual sleep duration is associated with BMI and macronutrient intake and may be modified by *CLOCK* genetic variants. *American Journal of Clinical Nutrition* **101**: 135–143.

David, L. A. et al. (2014). Diet rapidly and reproducibly alters the human gut microbiome. *Nature* **505**: 559–563.

Demerath, E. W. (2010). Causes and consequences of human variation in visceral adiposity. *American Journal of Clinical Nutrition* **91**: 1–2.

DeMouy, J. et al. (1995). The Pima Indians: Pathfinders for Health. NIH pub 95–3821. Washington: National Institute of Diabetes and Digestive and Kidney Diseases, Dept Health and Human Services, Public Health Service.

de Ruyter, J. C. et al. (2012). A trial of sugar-free or sugar-sweetened beverages and body weight in children. *New England Journal of Medicine* **367**: 1397–1406.

Deweerdt, S. (2014). Microbiome: a complicated relationship status. *Nature* **508**: S61–S63.

Dewey, K. G. (1998). Growth characteristics of breast-fed compared to formula-fed infants. *Biol Neonate* **74**: 94–105.

Diamanti-Kandarakis, E. et al. (2009). Endocrine-disrupting chemicals: an Endocrine Society scientific statement. *Endocrine Reviews* **30**(4): 293–342.

Dietz, W. H. and S. L. Gortmaker (1985). Do we fatten our children at the TV set? Obesity and television viewing in children and adolescents. *Pediatrics* **75**: 807–812.

Diliberti, N. et al. (2004). Increased portion size leads to increased energy intake in a restaurant meal. *Obesity Research* **12**: 562–568.

Dooling, K. L. et al. (2014). Overprescribing and inappropriate antibiotic selection for children with pharyngitis in the United States, 1997–2010. *Journal of American Medical Association Pediatrics* **168**(11): 1073–1074.

Ebbeling, C. B. et al. (2004). Compensation for energy intake from fast food among overweight and lean adolescents. *Journal of American Medical Association* **291**: 2828–2833.

Ebbeling, C. B. et al. (2012). A randomized trial of sugar-sweetened beverages and adolescent body weight. *New England Journal of Medicine* **367**: 1407–1416.

Eens, M. et al. (2013). Can starling eggs be useful as a biomonitoring tool to study organohalogenated contaminants on a worldwide scale? *Environmental International* **51**: 141–149.

Elliott, S. S. et al. (2002). Fructose, weight gain, and the insulin resistance syndrome. *American Journal of Clinical Nutrition* **76**: 911–922.

Ello-Martin, J. A., J. E. Ledikwe, and B. J. Rolls (2005). The influence of food portion size and energy density on energy intake: implications for weight management. *American Journal of Clinical Nutrition* **82**(1): 236S–241S.

Erfle, S. (2014). Analyzing the effects of daily physical education in middle schools on obesity: evidence from Pennsylvania's Active Schools Program. *In* Handbook of Physical Education Research: Role of School Programs, Children's Attitudes and Health Implications. R. Todaro, ed. pp. 91–108. New York: Nova Science Publishers, Inc.

Ewing, R. et al. (2003). Relationship between urban sprawl and physical activity, obesity, and morbidity. *Am J Health Promot* **18**(1): 47–57.

Faith, M. S. et al. (2004). Parent-child feeding strategies and their relationships to child eating and weight status. *Obesity Research* **12**: 1711–1722.

Falbe, J. et al. (2013). Adiposity and different types of screen time. *Pediatrics* **132**(6): e1497–e1505.

Farshchi, H. R., M. A Taylor, and I. A. Macdonald (2005a). Deleterious effects of omitting breakfast on insulin sensitivity and fasting lipid profiles in healthy lean women. *American Journal of Clinical Nutrition* **81**(2): 388–396.

Farshchi, H. R., M. A. Taylor, and I. A. Macdonald (2005b). Beneficial metabolic effects of regular meal frequency on dietary thermogenesis, insulin sensitivity, and fasting lipid profiles in healthy obese women. *American Journal of Clinical Nutrition* **81**: 16–24.

Fatima, Y., S. A. R. Doi, and A. A. Mamun (2015). Longitudinal impact of sleep on over-weight and obesity in children and adolescents: a systematic review and bias-adjusted meta-analysis. *Obesity Reviews* **16**(2): 137–149.

Ferolla, S. M. et al. (2014). The role of intestinal bacteria overgrowth in obesity-related nonalcoholic fatty liver disease. *Nutrients* **6**(12): 5583–5599.

Ferreira, C. M. et al. (2014). The central role of the gut microbiota in chronic inflammatory disease. *Journal of Immunology Research* doi 10.1155/2014/689492.

FHA (1997). Nationwide Personal Transportation Survey. U.S. Department of Transportation, Research and Technical Support Center, Federal Highway Administration.

Fisher, J. O., B. J. Rolls, and L. L. Birch (2003). Children's bite size and intake of an entree are greater with large portions than with age-appropriate or self-selected portions. *American Journal of Clinical Nutrition* **77**: 1164–1170.

Foerster, J. et al. (2014). The influence of whole grain products and red meat on intestinal microbiota composition in normal weight adults: a randomized crossover intervention. *PLoS One* doi 10.1371/journal.pone.0109606.

Fogelholm, M. (2010). Physical activity, fitness and fatness: relations to mortality, morbidity and disease risk factors. A systematic review. *Obesity Reviews* **11**: 202–221.

Ford, E. S. and W. H. Dietz (2013). Trends in energy intake among adults in the United States: findings from HHANES. *American Journal of Clinical Nutrition* **97**(4): 848–853.

Forestell, C. A. and J. A. Mennella (2007). Early determinants of fruit and vegetable acceptance. *Pediatrics* **120**(6): 1247–1254.

Frank, G. K. W., T. A. Oberndorfer, and A. N. Simmons (2008). Sucrose activates human taste pathways differently from artificial sweetener. *Neuroimage* **39**(4): 1559–1569.

Fukuda, S. and H. Ohno (2014). Gut microbiota and metabolic diseases. *Seminars in Immunopathology* **36**: 103–114.

Gallou-Kabani, C. et al. (2008). Implications for obesity and common diseases. *In* Obesity: Genomics and Postgenomics. K. Clement and T. I. Sorensen, eds. pp. 365–405. New York: Informa Healthcare.

Gangwisch, J. E. (2009). Epidemiological evidence for the links between sleep, circadian rhythms and metabolism. *Obesity Reviews* **10**(Suppl 2): 37–45.

Giammattei, J. et al. (2003). Television watching and soft drink consumption. *Archives of Pediatrics & Adolescent Medicine* **157**: 882–886.

Gillman, M. W. et al. (2001). Risk of overweight among adolescents who were breastfed as infants. *Journal of American Medical Association* **285**(19): 2461–2467.

Gladwell, M. (2000). The Pima paradox. *In* Nutritional Anthropology: Biocultural Perspectives on Food and Nutrition. A. H. Goodman, D. L. Dufour, and G. H. Pelto, eds. pp. 358–368. Mountain View, CA: Mayfield Publishing Company.

Gluckman, P. D. et al. (2008). Effect of in utero and early-life conditions on adult health and disease. *NEJM* **359**(1): 61–73.

Goel, A., M. Gupta, and R. Aggarwal (2014). Gut microbiota and liver disease. *Journal of Gastroenterology and Hepatology* **29**(6): 1139–1148.

Goel, M. S. et al. (2004). Obesity among US immigrant subgroups by duration of residence. *JAMA* **292**(23): 2860–2867.

Goodpaster, B. H. et al. (2010). Effects of diet and physical activity interventions on weight loss and cardiometabolic risk factors in severely obese adults. *JAMA* **304**(16): 1795–1802.

Goran, M. I. et al. (2013). The obesogenic effect of high fructose exposure during early development. *Nature Reviews Endocrinology* **9**(8): 494–500.

Gordon-Larsen, P., R. G. McMurray, and B. M. Popkin (2000). Determinants of adolescent physical activity and inactivity patterns. *Pediatrics* **105**(6): e83–391.

Gordon-Larsen, P., M. C. Nelson, and K. Beam (2005). Associations among active transportation, physical activity, and weight status in young adults. *Obesity Research* **13**(5): 868–875.

Gortmaker, S. L. et al. (1996). Television viewing as a cause of increasing obesity among children in the United States, 1986–1990. *Arch Pediatr Adolesc Med* **150**: 356–362.

Greenhouse, S. (2015). In service sector, no rest for the working. New York Times, 02/22/15.

Grontved, A. and F. B. Hu (2011). Television viewing and risk of type 2 diabetes, cardiovascular disease, and all-cause mortality: a meta-analysis. *JAMA* **305**(23): 2448–2455.

Gruen, F. (2010). Obesogens. *Current Opinion in Endocrinology, Diabetes and Obesity* **17**(5): 453–459.

Gruen, F. (2014). The obesogen tributyltin. *In* Endocrine Disrupters. G. Litwak, ed. pp. 277–325, Vol. 94. San Diego: Academic Press.

Gruen, F. and B. Blumberg (2009). Endocrine disrupters as obesogens. *Molecular and Cellular Endocrinology* **304**: 19–29.

Grummer-Strawn, L. M. and Z. Mei (2004). Does breastfeeding protect against pediatric overweight? Analysis of longitudinal data from the Centers for Disease Control and Prevention Pediatric Nutrition Surveillance System. *Pediatrics* **113**(2): e81–e86.

Guo, S. S. (1994). The predictive value of childhood body mass index values for overweight at age 35 y. *Am J Clin Nutr* **59**(4): 810–819.

Hampton, T. (2008). Sugar substitutes linked to weight gain. *JAMA* **299**(18): 2137–2138.

Hanlong, E. C. and E. Van Cauter (2011). Quantification of sleep behavior and of its impact on the cross-talk between the brain and peripheral metabolism. *Proceedings of the National Academy of Sciences* **108**(Suppl 3): 15609–15616.

Hardman, C. A. et al. (2015). So many brands and varieties to choose from: does this compromise the control of food intake in humans? *PLoS One* doi 10.1371/journal. pone.0125869.

Hatch, E. E. et al. (2008). Association of urinary phthalate metabolite concentrations with body mass index and waist circumference: a cross-sectional study of NHANES data, 1999–2002. *Environmental Health* **7**: 27–42.

Hirsch, J. A. (2014). Change in the Built Environment and Its Association with Change in Walking and Obesity in Middle Age and Older Adults doctoral dissertation, Epidemiological Science, University of Michigan.

Holscher, H. D. et al. (2015). Fiber supplementation influences phylogenetic structure and functional capacity of the human intestinal microbiome: follow-up of a randomized controlled trial. *American Journal of Clinical Nutrition* **101**: 55–64.

Horta, B. L. and C. G. Victora (2013). Long-term effects of breastfeeding: a systematic review. Geneva: World Health Organization.

Hu, F. B. (2008). Obesity Epidemiology. New York: Oxford University Press.

Imamura, F. et al. (2015). Dietary quality among men and women in 187 countries in 1990 and 2010. *The Lancet Global Health* **3**: e132–e142.

Inman, M. (2011). How bacteria turn fiber into food. *PLoS Biology* **9**(12): e100127.

Irwin, M. L. et al. (2003). Effect of exercise on total and intra-abdominal body fat in postmenopausal women. *JAMA* **289**(3): 323–330.

Janesick, A. S. and B. Blumberg (2011). Minireview: PPAR gama as the target of obesogens. *Journal of Steroid Biochemistry and Molecular Biology* **127**: 4–8.

Janesick, A. S. and B. Blumberg (2012). Obesogens, stem cells and the developmental programming of obesity. *International Journal of Andrology* **35**(3): 437–448.

Janssen, I., P. T. Katzmarzyk, and R. Ross (2004). Fitness alters the associations of BMI and waist circumference with total and abdominal fat. *Obesity Research* **12**: 525–537.

Johannsen, D. L., N. M. Johannsen, and B. L. Specker (2006). Influence of parents' eating behaviors and child feeding practices on children's weight status. *Obesity Research* **14**: 431–439.

Johnson, R. J. et al. (2007). Potential role of sugar (fructose) in the epidemic of hypertension, obesity and the metabolic syndrome, diabetes, kidney disease, and cardiovascular disease. *American Journal of Clinical Nutrition* **86**: 899–906.

Johnston, J. D., G. Frost, and D. T. Otway (2009). Adipose tissue, adipocytes and the circadian timing system. *Obesity Reviews* **10**(Suppl 2): 52–60.

Jumpertz, R. et al. (2011). Energy-balance studies reveal associations between gut microbes, caloric load, and nutrient absorption in humans. *American Journal of Clinical Nutrition* **94**: 58–65.

Junien, C. and P. Nathanielsz (2007). Report on the IASO Stock Conference 2006: early and lifelong environmental epigenomic programming of metabolic syndrome, obesity and type II diabetes. *Obesity Reviews* **8**: 487–502.

Kaiser Foundation (2004). Issue Brief: The Role of Media in Childhood Obesity. Menlo Park, CA: Henry J. Kaiser Foundation.

Kerr, W. C. and T. K. Greenfield (2003). The average ethanol content of beer in the U.S. and individual states: estimates for use in aggregate consumption statistics. *Journal of Studies on Alcohol* **64**(3): 439–440.

Kilborn, P. T. (2003). North Dakota town's payoff for hard lives is long life. New York Times, 07/31/03.

Kim, S. A. et al. (2012). Fruit and vegetable consumption among high school students – United States, 2010. *JAMA* **307**(2): 135–137.

Klesges, R. C., M. L. Shelton, and L. M. Klesges (1993). Effects of television on metabolic rate: potential implications for childhood obesity. *Pediatrics* **91**(2): 281–286.

Knutson, K. L. and E. Van Cauter (2008). Associations between sleep loss and increased risk of obesity and diabetes. *Annals of the New York Academy of Sciences* **1129**(Suppl 1): 287–304.

Kral, T. V. E., L. S. Roe, and B. J. Rolls (2004). Combined effects of energy density and portion size on energy intake in women. *American Journal of Clinical Nutrition* **79**: 962–968.

Kriska, A. M. et al. (1993). The association of physical activity with obesity, fat distribution and glucose intolerance in Pima Indians. *Diabetologia* **36**: 863–869.

Lamberg, L. (2006). Rx for obesity: eat less, exercise more, and – maybe – get more sleep. *JAMA* **295**(20): 2341–2344.

Langer, G. (2005). Poll: what Americans eat for breakfast. ABC News, 6/1/05.

Lanningham-Foster, L., L. J. Nysse, and J. A. Levine (2003). Labor saved, calories lost: the energetic impact of domestic labor-saving devices. *Obesity Research* **11**(10): 1178–1181.

Le Corre, L., P. Besnard, and M-C. Chagnon (2015). BPA, an energy balance disrupter. *Critical Reviews in Food Science and Nutrition* **55**(6): 769–777.

Lee, Y. H. et al. (2005). Microarray profiling of isolated abdominal subcutaneous adipocytes from obese vs. non-obese Pima Indians: increased expression of inflammation-related genes. *Diabetologia* **48**: 1776–1783.

Levine, J. A. et al. (2005). Interindividual variation in posture allocation: possible role in human obesity. *Science* **307**: 584–586.

Levine, J. A. et al. (2006). Non-exercise activity thermogenesis: the crouching tiger hidden dragon of societal weight gain. *Arteriosclerosis, Thrombosis and Vascular Biology* **26**(4): 729–736.

Lichtenstein, A. H. and D. S. Ludwig (2010). Bring back home economics education. *JAMA* **303**(18): 1857–1858.

Liebman, B. (2013). The changing American diet: a report card. *Nutrition Action Healthletter.* 11.

Linn, S. (2004). Consuming Kids: The Hostile Takeover of Childhood. New York: The New Press.

Loth, K. A. et al. (2013). Food-related parenting practices and adolescent weight status: a population-based study. *Pediatrics* **131**(5): e1443–e1450.

Ludwig, D. S. (2013). Examining the health effects of fructose. *JAMA* **310**(1): 33–34.

Lumeng, J. C. et al. (2006). Neighborhood safety and overweight status in children. *Arch Pediatr Adolesc Med* **160**: 25–31.

Lumeng, J. C. et al. (2007). Shorter sleep duration is associated with increased risk for being overweight at ages 9 to 12 years. *Pediatrics* **120**(5): 1020–1029.

Lustig, R. H. (2012). Fat Chance: Beating the Odds Against Sugar, Processed Food, Obesity, and Disease. New York: Hudson Street.

Lustig, R. H., L. A. Schmidt, and C. D. Brindis (2012). The toxic truth about sugar. *Nature* **482**: 27–29.

Lyman, R. (2005). In exurbs, life framed by hours spent in the car. New York Times, 12/18/05.

Ma, L. et al. (2004). Melanocortin 4 receptor gene variation is associated with severe obesity in Pima Indians. *Diabetes* **53**: 2696–2699.

Magee, C. A. et al. (2010). Examining the pathways linking chronic sleep restriction to obesity. *Journal of Obesity* doi 10.1155/2010/821710.

Major, G. C., E. Doucet, and P. Trayhurn (2007a). Clinical significance of adaptive thermogenesis. *International Journal of Obesity* **31**: 204–212.

Major, G. C. et al. (2007b). Clinical significance of adaptive thermogenesis. *International Journal of Obesity* **31**: 204–212.

Malik, V. S. and F. B. Hu (2011). Sugar-sweetened beverages and health: where does the evidence stand? *American Journal of Clinical Nutrition* **94**(5): 1161–1162.

Malik, V. S., M. B. Schulze, and F. B. Hu (2006). Intake of sugar-sweetened beverages and weight gain: a systematic review. *American Journal of Clinical Nutrition* **84**: 274–288.

Matheson, D. M. et al. (2004). Children's food consumption during television viewing. *American Journal of Clinical Nutrition* **79**(6): 1088–1094.

Mattes, R. D. (2006). Fluid energy – where's the problem? *Journal of the American Dietetic Association* **106**(12): 1956–1961.

Matthews, C. E. (2012). Amount of time spent in sedentary behaviors and cause-specific mortality in US adults. *The American Journal of Clinical Nutrition* **95**(2): 437–445.

McCrory, M. A. et al. (1999). Overeating in America: association between restaurant food consumption and body fatness in healthy adult men and women ages 19 to 80. *Obesity Research* **7**(6): 564–571.

McDonald, C. M. et al. (2006). Nutrition and exercise environment available to outpatients, visitors, and staff in children's hospitals in Canada and the United States. *Arch Pediatr Adolesc Med* **160**: 900–905.

Media, Council on Communications and the (2011). Children, adolescents, obesity, and the media. *Pediatrics* **128**: 201–208.

Mitchell, J. A. et al. (2013). Sleep duration and adolescent obesity. *Pediatrics* **131**(5): e1428–e1434.

Moskin, J. (2009). In kitchen, 'losers' start from scratch. New York Times, 2/4/09.

Moss, M. (2013). Salt Sugar Fat: How the Food Giants Hooked Us. New York: Random House.

Mozaffarian, D. et al. (2011). Changes in diet and lifestyle and long-term weight gain in women and men. *New England Journal of Medicine* **364**(25): 2392–2404.

Mueller, N. T. et al. (2014). Prenatal exposure to antibiotics, cesarean section and risk of childhood obesity. *International Journal of Obesity* **39**: 665–670.

Murphy, R. et al. (2014). Antibiotic treatment during infancy and increased body mass index in boys: an international cross-sectional study. *International Journal of Obesity* **38**(8): 1115–1119.

Nader, P. R. et al. (2008). Moderate-to-vigorous physical activity from ages 9 to 15 years. *JAMA* **300**(3): 295–305.

Nakazawa, L. (2005). In crowded schools, lunch feels the pinch. Christian Science Monitor, 5/31/05.

Natarajan, N. and J. L. Pluznick (2014). From microbe to man: the role of microbial short chain fatty acid metabolites in host cell physiology. *American Journal of Physiology – Cell Physiology* **307**(11): C979–C985.

Nedeltcheva, A. V. et al. (2009). Sleep curtailment is accompanied by increased intake of calories from snacks. *American Journal of Clinical Nutrition* **89**(1): 126–133.

Nelson, M. C. et al. (2006). Longitudinal and secular trends in physical activity and sedentary behavior during adolescence. *Pediatrics* **118**(6): e1627–e1634.

Newbold, R. R., E. Padilla-Banks, and W. N. Jefferson (2009). Environmental estrogens and obesity. *Molecular and Cellular Endocrinology* **304**: 84–89.

Ng, S. W. and B. M. Popkin (2012). Time use and physical activity: a shift away from movement across the globe. *Obesity Reviews* **13**: 659–680.

Ng, S. W., M. M. Slining, and B. M. Popkin (2012). Use of caloric and noncaloric sweeteners in US consumer packaged foods, 2005–2009. *Journal of the Academy of Nutrition and Dietetics* **112**: 1828–1834.

Nielsen, S. J. and B. M. Popkin (2003). Patterns and trends in food portion sizes, 1977–1998. *JAMA* **289**(4): 450–453.

O'Connor, A. et al. (2014). Responsiveness of cardiometabolic-related microbiota to diet is influenced by host genetics. *Mammalian Genome* **25**: 583–599.

Oguman, Y. and T. Shinoda-Tagawa (2004). Physical activity decreases cardiovascular disease risk in women: review and meta-analysis. *American Journal of Preventive Medicine* **26**(5): 407–418.

Ohland, C. L. and C. Jobin (2014). Bugs and food: a recipe for cancer? *Cell Metabolism* **20**(6): 937–938.

Ohtani, N., S. Yoshimoto, and E. Hara (2014). Obesity and cancer: a gut microbial connection. *Cancer Research* **74**(7): 1885–1889.

Olsen, N. J. and B. L. Heitman (2009). Intake of calorically sweetened beverages and obesity. *Obesity Reviews* **10**: 68–75.

Owen, N. et al. (2004). Understanding environmental influences on walking: review and research agenda. *Am J Prev Med* **27**(1): 67–76.

Page, K. A. et al. (2013). Effects of fructose vs glucose on regional cerebral blood flow in brain regions involved with appetite and reward pathways. *JAMA* **309**(1): 63–69.

Patel, S. R. (2009). Reduced sleep as an obesity risk factor. *Obesity Reviews* **10**(Suppl 2): 61–68.

Payne, A. N., C. Chassard, and C. Lacroix (2012). Gut microbial adaptation to dietary consumption of fructose, artificial sweeteners and sugar alcohols: implications for host-microbe interactions contributing to obesity. *Obesity Reviews* **13**(9): 799–809.

Pearson, H. (2006). Sleep it off. *Nature* **443**: 261–263.

Pelletier, C., J-P. Despres, and A. Tremblay (2002). Plasma organochlorine concentrations in endurance athletes and obese individuals. *Medicine and Science in Sports and Exercise* **34**(12): 1971–1975.

Pereira-Fernandes, A. et al. (2013a). Evaluation of a screening system for obesogenic compounds: screening of endocrine disrupting compounds and evaluation of the PPAR dependency of the effect. *PLoS One* doi 10.1371/journal.pone.0077481.

Pereira-Fernandes, A. et al. (2013b). Unraveling the mode of action of an obesogen: mechanistic analysis of the model obesogen tributyltin the 3T3–L1 cell line. *Molecular and Cellular Endocrinology* **370**(1–2): 52–64.

Pereira-Fernandes, A. et al. (2014). Expression of obesity markers and persistent organic pollutants levels in adipose tissue of obese patients: reinforcing the obesogen hypothesis? *PLoS One* **9**(1): e84816.

Phelan, S. et al. (2003). Recovery from relapse among successful weight maintainers. *Am J Clin Nutr* **78**: 1079–1084.

Poirier, P. and R. H. Eckel (2000). Adipose tissue metabolism and obesity. *In* Physical Activity and Obesity. C. Bouchard, ed. pp. 181–200. Champaign, IL: Human Kinetics.

Popkin, B. M. and S. J. Nielsen (2003). The sweetening of the world's diet. *Obesity Research* **11**(11): 1325–1332.

Popkin, B. M. and J. R. Udry (1998). Adolescent obesity increases significantly in second and third generation U.S. immigrants: the National Longitudinal Study of Adolescent Health. *Journal of Nutrition* **128**: 701–706.

Pucher, J. and L. Dijkstra (2003). Promote safe walking and cycling to improve public health: lessons from the Netherlands and Germany. *American Journal of Public Health* **93**(9): 1509–1516.

Rantakokko, P. et al. (2014). Association of placenta organotin concentrations with growth and ponderal index in 110 newborn boys from Finland during the first 18 months of life: a cohort. *Environmental Health* **13**(1): 1–20.

Rathje, W. and C. Murphy (2001). Rubbish! The Archaeology of Garbage. Tucson, AZ: University of Arizona Press.

Ravussin, E. et al. (1994). Effects of a traditional lifestyle on obesity in Pima Indians. *Diabetes Care* **17**(9): 1067–1074.

Raynor, D. A. et al. (2006). Television viewing and long-term weight maintenance: results from the National Weight Control Registry. *Obesity* **14**: 1816–1824.

Raynor, D. A. and R. R. Wing (2007). Package unit size and amount of food: do both influence intake? *Obesity* **15**: 2311–2319.

Raynor, H. A. and L. H. Epstein (2001). Dietary variety, energy regulation, and obesity. *Psychological Bulletin* **127**: 325–341.

Raynor, H. A. et al. (2005). Amount of food group variety consumed in the diet and long-term weight loss maintenance. *Obesity Research* **13**(5): 883–890.

Richmond, T. K. et al. (2006). Can school income and racial/ethnic composition explain the racial/ethnic disparity of adolescent physical activity participation? *Pediatrics* **117**(6): 2158–2166.

Rogers, C. J., K. S. Prabhu, and M. Vijay-Kuman (2014). The microbiome and obesity – an established risk for certain types of cancer. *Cancer Journal* **20**(3): 176–180.

Rolls, B. J. (2009). The relationship between dietary energy density and energy intake. *Physiology & Behavior* **97**: 609–615.

Rolls, B. J., L. S. Roe, and J. S. Meengs (2007). The effect of large portion sizes on energy intake is sustained for 11 days. *Obesity* **15**: 1535–1543.

Ross, R. et al. (2000). Reduction in obesity and related comorbid conditions after diet-induced weight loss or exercise-induced weight loss in men. *Annals of Internal Medicine* **133**: 92–103.

Ryan, A. S., Z. Wenjun, and A. Acosta (2002). Breastfeeding continues to increase into the new millennium. *Pediatrics* **110**(6): 1103–1109.

Salbe, A. D. and E. Ravussin (2000). The determinants of obesity. *In* Physical Activity and Obesity. C. Bouchard, ed. pp. 69–102. Champaign, IL: Human Kinetics.

Salonen, A. and W. M. de Vos (2014). Impact of diet on human intestinal microbiota and health. *Annual Review of Food Science and Technology* **5**: 239–262.

Saris, W. H. M. (2003). Sugars, energy metabolism, and body weight control. *American Journal of Clinical Nutrition* **78S**: 850S–857S.

Schecter, A., M. A. Grandner, and M-P. St-Onge (2014). The role of sleep in the control of food intake. *American Journal of Lifestyle Medicine* **8**(6): 371–374.

Schmidt, M. et al. (2005). Fast-food intake and diet quality in Black and White girls. *Archives of Pediatrics & Adolescent Medicine* **159**: 626–631.

Shen, W., H. R. Gaskins, and M. K. McIntosh (2014). Influence of dietary fat on intestinal microbes, inflammation, barrier function and metabolic outcomes. *Journal of Nutritional Biochemistry* **25**: 270–280.

Shug, T. T. et al. (2011). Endocrine disrupting chemicals and disease susceptibility. *Journal of Steroid Biochemistry and Molecular Biology* **127**(3–5 SI): 204–215.

Singhal, A. and J. Lanigan (2007). Breastfeeding, early growth and later obesity. *Obesity Reviews* **8**(Suppl 1): 51–554.

Smith, E. O. (2002). When Culture and Biology Collide: Why We Are Stressed, Depressed, and Self-Obsessed. New Brunswick, NJ: Rutgers University Press.

Sousa, A. C. A. et al. (2014). History of organotin compounds, from snails to humans. *Environmental Chemistry Letters* **12**(1): 117–137.

Spiegel, K., R. Leproult, and E. Van Cauter (1999). Impact of sleep debt on metabolic and endocrine function. *Lancet* **354**: 1435–1439.

Spiegel, K. et al. (2004). Sleep curtailment in healthy men is associated with decreased leptin levels, elevated ghrelin levels, and increased hunger and appetite. *Annals of Internal Medicine* **141**: 846–850.

St-Onge, M-P. et al. (2011). Short sleep duration increases energy intakes but does not change energy expenditure in normal-weight individuals. *American Journal of Clinical Nutrition* **94**(2): 410–416.

St-Onge, M.-P. et al. (2012). Sleep restriction leads to increased activation of brain regions sensitive to food stimuli. *American Journal of Clinical Nutrition* **95**: 818–824.

Stahl, T. et al. (2001). The importance of the social environment for physically active lifestyle – results from an international study. *Social Science & Medicine* **52**: 1–10.

Stanhope, K. L. and P. J. Havel (2010). Fructose consumption: recent results and their potential implications. *Annals of the New York Academy of Sciences* **1190**: 15–24.

Stunkard, A. J. (1975). Obesity and the social environment. *In* Recent Advances in Obesity Research: I, Proceedings of the 1st International Congress on Obesity. pp. 178–190. London: Newman.

Sturtevant, W. C. (2004). Handbook of North American Indians. Volume 10. Southwest. Washington DC: Smithsonian Institution.

Sun, Y. et al. (2014). Occurrence of estrogenic endocrine disrupting chemicals concern in sewage plant effluent. *Frontiers of Environmental Science & Engineering* **8**(1): 18–26.

Swinburn, B. and G. Egger (2004). The runaway weight gain train: too many accelerators, not enough brakes. *BMJ* **329**: 736–739.

Taheri, S. et al. (2004a). Short sleep duration is associated with reduced leptin, elevated ghrelin, and increased body mass index. *PLoS Med* **1**: 210–217.

Taheri, S. et al. (2004b). Sleep duration affects appetite-regulating hormones. *PLoS Med* **1**(3): e68.

Tang-Peronard, J. L. et al. (2011). Endocrine-disrupting chemicals and obesity development in humans: a review. *Obesity Reviews* **12**(8): 622–636.

Taveras, E. M., S. L. Rifas-Shiman, and E. Oken (2008). Short sleep duration in infancy and risk of childhood overweight. *Archives of Pediatric & Adolescent Medicine* **162**(4): 305–311.

Te Morenga, L., S. Mallard, and J. Mann (2012). Dietary sugars and body weight. Systematic review and meta-analyses of randomised controlled trials and cohort studies. *British Medical Journal* **345**: e7492.

Thaiss, C. A. et al. (2014). Transkingdom control of microbiota diurnal oscillations promotes metabolic homeostasis. *Cell* **159**: 514–529.

Thomas, G. S. (1998). The United States of Suburbia: How the Suburbs Took Control of America and What They Plan to Do With It. New York: Prometheus Books.

Tillotson, J. E. (2004). America's obesity: conflicting public policies, industrial economic development, and unintended human consequences. *Ann Rev Nutr* **24**: 617–643.

Tsai, F. and W. J. Coyle (2009). The microbiome and obesity: is obesity linked to our gut flora? *Current Gastroenterology Reports* **11**: 307–313.

Tucker, L. A. and M. Bagwell (1991). Television viewing and obesity in adult females. *Am J Public Health* **81**(7): 908–911.

Turnbaugh, P. J. et al. (2009). A core gut microbiome in obese and lean twins. *Nature* **457**(22): 480–485.

Turnbaugh, P. J., R. E. Ley, and M. A. Mahowald (2006). An obesity-associated gut microbiome with increased capacity for energy harvest. *Nature* **444**: 1027–1031.

Turner, L. and F. J. Chaloupka (2011). Wide availability of high-calorie beverages in US elementary schools. *Archives of Pediatric & Adolescent Medicine* **165**: 223–228.

Ulijaszek, S. J. (1999). Physical activity, lifestyle and health of urban populations. *In* Urbanism, Health and Human Biology in Industrialised Countries. L. M. Schell and S. J. Ulijaszek, eds. pp. 250–279. New York: Cambridge University Press.

Ulijaszek, S. J. (2000). Work and energetics. *In* Human Biology: An Evolutionary and Biocultural Perspective. S. Stinson, B. Bogin, R. Huss-Ashmore, and D. O'Rourke, eds. pp. 345–376. New York: Wiley-Liss.

Ulijaszek, S. J. (2006). Obesity: a disorder of convenience. *Obesity Reviews* **8**(Suppl 1): 183–187.

United States Department of Health and Human Services (USDHHS) (2005). Dietary guidelines for Americans 2005. Washington DC: USDHHS.

Vadeboncoer, C., N. Townsend, and C. Foster (2015). A meta-analysis of weight gain in first year university students: is freshman 15 a myth? *BMC Obesity* **2**: 22.

Vandenberg, L. N. (2011). Exposure to bisphenol A in Canada: invoking the precautionary principle. *Canadian Medical Association Journal* **183**(11): 1265–1269.

von Kries, R. et al. (1999). Breast feeding and obesity: cross sectional study. *BMJ* **319**: 147–150.

Voreades, N., A. Kozil, and T. L. Weir (2014). Diet and the development of the human intestinal microbiome. *Frontiers in Microbiology* **5**: 1–9.

Walker, A. and J. Parkhill (2013). Fighting obesity with bacteria. *Science* **341**: 1069–1070.

Walker, R. W., K. A. Dumke, and M. I. Goran (2014). Fructose content in popular beverages made with and without high-fructose corn syrup. *Nutrition* **30**(7–8): 928–935.

Walsh, C. J. et al. (2014). Beneficial modulation of the gut microbiota. *FEBS Letters* **588**(22): 4120–4130.

Wannamethee, S. G. et al. (2004). Alcohol intake and 8-year weight gain in women: a prospective study. *Obesity Research* **12**: 1386–1396.

Wannamethee, S. G. and G. A. Shaper (2003). Alcohol, body weight, and weight gain in middle-aged men. *American Journal of Clinical Nutrition* **77**(5): 1312–1317.

Wansink, B. (2011). Mindless eating: environmental contributors to obesity. *In* The Oxford Handbook of the Social Science of Obesity. J. Cawley, ed. pp. 385–414. New York: Oxford University Press.

Wansink, B. and M. M. Cheney (2005). Super bowls: serving bowl size and food consumption. *JAMA* **293**(14): 1727–1728.

Wansink, B., J. E. Painter, and J. North (2005). Bottomless bowls: why visual cues of portion size may influence intake. *Obesity Research* **13**: 93–100.

Wansink, B. and K. van Ittersum (2012). Fast food restaurant lighting and music can reduce calorie intake and increase satisfaction. *Psychology Reports: Human Resources & Marketing* **111**(1): 228–232.

Weaver, C. M. et al. (2014). Processed foods: contributions to nutrition. *American Journal of Clinical Nutrition* **99**: 1525–1542.

Wendel-Vos, W. et al. (2007). Potential environmental determinants of physical activity in adults: a systematic review. *Obesity Reviews* **8**: 425–440.

Wilkinson, W. J. and S. N. Blair (2003). Exercise. *In* Obesity: Mechanisms and Clinical Management. R. H. Eckel, ed. pp. 476–502. Philadelphia: Lippincott Williams & Wilkins.

Wing, R. R. and S. Phelan (2005). Long-term weight loss maintenance. *American Journal of Clinical Nutrition* **82**(Suppl): 222S–225S.

Wray, A. (2005). Battling the bulge: new students weigh-in on problems with added inches. The Guardian, 9/14/05: 13.

Yatsunenko, T., F. E. Rey, and M. J. Manary (2012). Human gut microbiome viewed across age and geography. *Nature* **486**: 222–227.

Young, L. R. and M. Nestle (2002). The contribution of expanding portion sizes to the US obesity-epidemic. *American Journal of Public Health* **92**(2): 246–248.

Yracheta, J. M. et al. (2015). Diabetes and kidney disease in American Indians: potential role of sugar-sweetened beverages. *Mayo Clinic Proceedings* **90**(6): 813–823.

Zhang, L. et al. (2015). Dermal adipocytes protect against invasive *Staphylococcus aureus* skin infections. *Science* **357**(6217): 67.

5

OBESITY IN AMERICAN SOCIETY

Introduction

Why do so many Americans have obesity? Yet another answer lies in several characteristics of U.S. society. Over the past 25 to 30 years obesity rates increased along the lines of a social pattern, with the highest obesity rates manifesting among certain social groups – women, ethnic minorities, and low-income Americans – the most disadvantaged and vulnerable segments of U.S. society.

In nearly all societies, women are more likely than men to become obese (see Chapters 1 and 2). Females are biologically more predisposed to acquire and accumulate body fat than males after childhood. While both boys and girls respond to negative life events in childhood with greater risk of obesity at age 15 (Lumeng et al. 2013), girls are even more susceptible to poor environmental conditions than boys (Singh et al. 2010); five-year-old girls but not boys who experience high levels of social adversity such as financial stress, family violence, maternal depression, substance abuse, and paternal incarceration are more likely to have obesity than girls without these social risk factors or boys faced with the same stresses (Suglia et al. 2012; Hernandez and Pressler 2015). The relationship between socioeconomic disadvantage and Body Mass Index (BMI) is stronger in women than in men in both directions (Hediger et al. 2001); that is, socioeconomic stress is more strongly related to a higher risk of obesity in women, and obesity impedes women's socioeconomic efforts more than men's.

Members of some ethnic minority groups are also more prone to obesity than others. Although the majority of Americans who have obesity are not minorities, the proportion of people within minority groups who have obesity is relatively high compared to whites. Hispanics and blacks are the largest U.S. minority populations and have the highest adult obesity rates, while Hispanic children have the highest rates of childhood overweight and obesity (Murguia 2010). As minorities they face more discrimination and isolation, both known to be associated with high levels of social stress. Residential and occupational segregation, rotating night and day shift work, and sleep deprivation (Carnethon et al. 2011) are more often experienced by these minority groups. Overeating is a common coping strategy for stress.

Economic status is another important social factor contributing to obesity rates. The global distribution of obesity reflects socioeconomic disparities, but with a distinct difference between high-income societies and the rest. In lower-income nations such as India, well-off citizens have higher rates of obesity than the poor (Friel et al. 2007; Neuman et al. 2011; Dinsa et al. 2012). Beginning in the 1950s, refined foods, high-fat meat and dairy products, supermarkets, fast-food outlets, modern entertainment venues, and mechanized transportation became available all over the globe. But in the poorest, least-developed countries the more affluent were much more likely to afford this abundance of food and energy-sparing technology and enjoy the pleasures of the modern obesogenic environment. For the poor in these countries, such relatively new developments were desirable but largely unattainable. Today they still face more food shortages, scarcity, and energy-depleting manual labor than those in more well-off social strata.

In the high-income countries of Europe and North America, however, the relationship between socioeconomic class and obesity is reversed, with poorer individuals, especially women and ethnic minority groups, manifesting the highest obesity rates (Caballero 2005). Educational level, used in many research projects as a proxy for economic class, exemplifies the relationship between social status and obesity in countries of low- and high-income economies; in the poorest countries, women with the highest educational attainment have more than two times the obesity rate of women with the lowest educational level, but in high-income economies highly educated women have only half the obesity rate of the least-educated women (Monteiro et al. 2004).

In the US the relationship between social disparities and obesity rates is complex (Clarke et al. 2009). It is actually very difficult to disentangle the separate influences of sex, ethnicity, and economic class because these interact with each other. Poverty disproportionately affects women and ethnic minorities in the US. They are more likely to have low levels of education, income, personal resources, and high rates of obesity than men and American whites.

Compared to U.S. men, whose obesity rates vary little by ethnic affiliation, ranging from 36 percent to 39 percent, obesity rates among American women differ dramatically. In 2009–10, the prevalence of obesity among white women was 32 percent, Hispanic women 41 percent, and black women 59 percent (Figure 5.1). Thus variation by sex was much greater in black than white populations. These relationships are complicated by income disparity. Among men, low-income whites and blacks have the highest obesity rates compared to middle- and high-income men. But black middle- and high-income women have significantly higher obesity rates than low-income black women (Ogden et al. 2010).

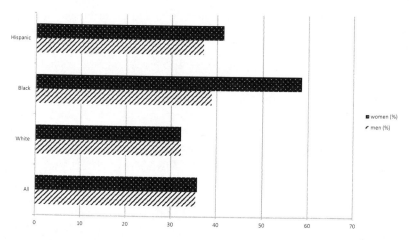

FIGURE 5.1 Obesity prevalence among U.S. adults aged ≥20 years by sex and ethnicity, 2009–10.

Adapted from CDC (2012).

Poverty and obesity in the United States

When asked why he insisted upon emigrating to the United States, an acquaintance of Dinesh D'Souza replied that he very much wanted to live in a country where poor people are fat (D'Souza 2003). For a person from India the fact that poor people could be anything but thin and hungry was remarkable. In his country fatness was an indication of wealth and plenty that was entirely out of the realm of possibility for most Indians. So a land where even the poor can become fat must be a wonderful place indeed.

Since 2008, the U.S. poverty rate has risen every year (census.gov), and real median income has declined by 8 percent (DeNaras-Walt et al. 2012). The Census Bureau's Supplemental Poverty Measure (SPM), based on current criteria that differ considerably from the original measure developed in the 1960s, considers housing and transportation costs in addition to the traditional food costs. By these new standards, 16 percent of Americans (nearly 50 million) are now living in poverty. The poorest Americans are blacks (26 percent) and Hispanics (28 percent), in comparison to whites (11 percent) and Asian-Americans (17 percent). Two-thirds of all black children live in neighborhoods with significant poverty, compared to one-sixteenth of white children (Roy 2008). For the first time in at least 50 years, the majority (51 percent) of students attending U.S. public schools come from low-income families (Brewis 2011).

With few exceptions, individuals in the lowest economic ranks have the highest obesity rates (Johnston and Gordon-Larsen 1999; Drewnowski and Darmon 2005). Among women with less than a high school education and incomes below the poverty threshold, whose ability to purchase food is limited, obesity is twice as common as among women with the highest income and education levels, who can afford to buy all the food they need or want (Zhang and Wang 2004). There is now a growing understanding of this paradox. It is becoming obvious that the obesogenic environment in which America's poor live and work often overwhelms human physiology and individual effort to maintain healthy weights. Inadequate nutrition and lack of physical activity, manifested to some degree in all segments of U.S. society, are exacerbated by the living conditions of America's poor, who have little personal control over many aspects of their lives (Figure 5.2).

Before Hurricane Katrina, poor people were essentially invisible to most middle- and upper-class Americans. The natural disaster that struck New Orleans and the southern coast of the US revealed just how desperately poor some Americans are, so poor that they lacked the transportation or funds to escape the coming flood. America's poor live, work, attend church and school, and shop in neighborhoods not frequented by wealthier citizens. More fortunate Americans are largely unaware of the challenges they face every day (Ehrenreich 2001; Shipler 2004). Because many have paying jobs, it is not always obvious that they are poor and quite often hungry. Most Americans are only dimly aware of food banks, soup kitchens, the *Supplemental Nutrition Assistance Program* (SNAP – the federal food stamp program), and the people who have to use them.

While waiting in line at the supermarket checkout one might experience "food stamp resentment." A shopper is using food stamps "unwisely" to purchase luxury items such as steak and chocolate. This shopper and her children obviously have obesity but are also obviously poor – the *poverty paradox*. At first glance, the apparent misuse of taxpayer-provided food aid is very disturbing. But to accurately

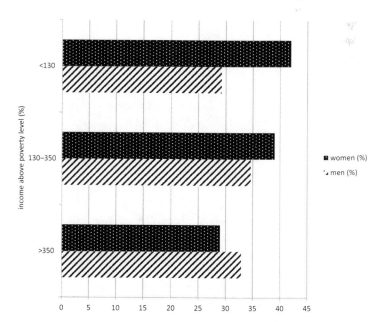

FIGURE 5.2 Obesity, income, and sex among U.S. adults ≥20 years, 2005–8.

Adapted from Ogden et al. (2010).

judge the scene at the checkout counter, more information about the lifestyles of America's poor citizens is required.

Welfare reform in the 1990s forced many poor Americans into low-wage jobs without ensuring that they have adequate housing, child care, health care, and food. As a result, according to the Economic Policy Institute, the US has the highest incidence of low-paying work among OECD high-income countries (epi.org). Today one-quarter of American workers are juggling two or more low-paying jobs but cannot earn enough to keep a family above the poverty line (bls.gov). Some are spending more than half of their income on housing, which has become much more expensive. Even though the federal minimum hourly wage was raised recently, it is still below the inflation-adjusted minimum wage of 1960. A full-time minimum wage ($7.25/h) employee earns an annual income of only $15,080 (LLC 2009).

Poverty is closely associated with poor health all over the world (MacIntyre 1998; Wilkinson 1998; Pena and Bacallao 2002; Eibner and Evans 2004). The most extreme demographic disparities in health and disease are in the developing world, but the pattern is also evident in the US (Woolf and Braveman 2011). Infant mortality rates are higher and lifespans are shorter among the poor than for people in higher income levels. Poor children and adults suffer more disease and illness during their lifetime (Crooks 1995; Isaacs and Schroeder 2004; Marmot 2004). Hypertension, strokes, heart disease, diabetes, kidney disease, and certain cancers are more prevalent among the poor, who are more likely to lack adequate health care and live in more deprived, polluted, and dangerous neighborhoods. Even though overall mortality rates declined in all U.S. ethnic groups between 1960 and 1980, socioeconomic disparities in death rates actually increased. The *Place Matters* report on Orleans Parish (JCPES 2012) documented the health gap in post-Katrina New Orleans. Average life expectancy in the poorest zip code in the city is 54.5 years compared to 80 years in the wealthiest zip code, a 25.5-year disparity.

An obesity gap also exists in the US. More than 30 years ago, Albert Stunkard found a strong association between socioeconomic status and obesity rates, particularly among women (Stunkard 1975). Citing the 1962 Mid-Town Manhattan Study of economic status and mental illness, Stunkard noted that 30 percent of women in the lowest social class had obesity compared to only 16 percent of middle- and 5 percent of high-status women. The relationship between social class and obesity persisted over several generations, with downwardly mobile individuals having more obesity than upwardly mobile persons. In 1962 there was no obvious explanation for the paradoxical association of low income and obesity. But today the picture is somewhat clearer because of growing understanding of the role of *food insecurity* in the development of obesity among the poor. Food insecurity, which rose dramatically with the recession in 2008, is defined as the lack of access to enough food to fully meet basic needs at all times due to a lack of financial resources (FRAC 2009). The proportion of the U.S. population that is food-insecure (16 percent) is greater than the global average of 13 percent (Pray et al. 2012) and includes a significant proportion of military veterans returning from Iraq and Afghanistan (marketwatch.com). According to the U.S. Department of Agriculture, food-insecure households spend 24 percent less on food, even with SNAP support, than households with adequate income (Coleman-Jensen et al. 2012). Dr. Deborah Frank of the Whittier Street Health Center in a poverty-stricken neighborhood of Roxbury, Massachusetts has had to hospitalize babies for severe malnutrition and iron deficiency, and the number of such hospitalizations has tripled since 1999 (Smith 2004). When told that their children should eat at least three times a day, the mothers of her small patients burst into tears because they simply could not meet this recommendation.

An article in the *Corvallis Gazette-Times* reported that a farm worker in California's Central Valley, source of much of the nation's fresh fruits and vegetables, cannot afford to purchase enough food for her family and herself and is often hungry (Barbassa 2004). Iris Caballero is overweight and has diabetes. The mini-mart in her neighborhood offers a large selection of processed and snack foods rich in satisfying salt, sugar, and fat, but its fresh produce offerings are virtually nonexistent or prohibitively expensive. Ironically, Iris, who picks fruits and vegetables all day, cannot afford to buy the $2 head of lettuce her husband would like for a salad. Her children attend an elementary school where every single student qualifies for free lunches, and where teachers recently held an emergency workshop on how to deal with blood sugar fluctuations in their many students with diabetes.

Food insecurity and poor nutrition lower disease resistance, impair cognitive function, and affect height and weight growth (FRAC 2009). Food insecurity is also related to overweight, most notably in Hispanic, black, and Native American children, and to a lesser degree in poor whites (Pan et al. 2012; Pan et al. 2013). Poverty-stricken populations may therefore include both undernourished and children and adults with obesity (Crooks 2001). Obesity is clearly not a good indicator of sufficient food and adequate nutrition; among the nation's poor, obesity is more likely a sign of food insecurity and malnutrition.

Food is generally inexpensive in the US (Drewnowski and Darmon 2005; Drewnowski 2010). On average, Americans spend 9 percent of their disposable income on food, less than anywhere else in the world (Pray et al. 2012). Virtually all Americans can buy some food, and starvation is really not a national issue. But family income determines the type and quality of food purchased and consumed (Rehm et al. 2011). High-fiber, low-calorie fresh produce and good-quality protein items are relatively expensive. According to the Institute of Medicine's TV report, "The Weight of the Nation," the cost of fresh fruits and vegetables has more than doubled in recent years, while the cost of sweetened soda has increased by only 20 percent. Food insecurity means that nutrient intake is lower because of the high cost of fresh produce, that cheap cuts of fatty meats and poultry are more likely to be consumed, and that families who have lived for several generations under impoverished conditions may have lost the knowledge and skills to prepare more nutritious, lower-fat meals (Mello et al. 2010). Critics of dietary behavior among low-income Americans fail to consider that lack of food preparation knowledge and habits ingrained by generations of poverty also affect nutritional decisions. Families accustomed to drinking sugary soda with meals will not easily switch to calorie-free water, nor will diners prompted to eat everything on their plates toss the fatty skin of a roasted chicken into the garbage.

Compared to high-income Americans, poor people are squeezed by living costs (GlobalMacroMonitor 2011). While wealthier Americans spend only 7 percent of their income on food and gasoline, the poor must spend nearly half of their limited income on these two items. A study of poor urban teenagers found that, contrary to expectations, the girls consumed adequate amounts of important nutrients such as calcium, iron, zinc, and folate, but they achieved this by eating excessive amounts of low-cost, low-quality food (Johnston and Gordon-Larsen 1999). Foods that are available and affordable for the poor generally have higher energy content and lower nutritional value than the fresh produce, whole grains, and sources of lean protein purchased by those with higher incomes. Low-cost foods are also easier and less time-consuming to prepare and provide more immediate satisfaction to hungry family members because of their generally high fat, sugar, and salt content.

While treating a poor mother and her young daughter for complications of obesity, William Dietz (Dietz 1995) became aware of a link between poverty and obesity he had not considered before. His patients suffered regular food scarcity and relied on low-cost, high-fat foods to stave off *hunger* during the days before the monthly welfare check arrived. Episodic food shortages, Dietz postulated, had altered the eating behavior of his patients, and triggered an adaptive, energy-conserving physiological response to food insufficiency. Dietz had noted as well that women who were cyclic dieters tended to have more body fat and less fat-free muscle than those who did not diet repeatedly. Binge eaters who restrained their eating between binges weighed more than binge eaters who did not consciously control food intake. Dietz called for large studies to explore this link between obesity and temporary food insufficiency. He also suggested that one way to prevent obesity in the first place is to ensure continuous adequate food supplies for low-income and impoverished populations, rather than to promote food restriction and dieting to treat obesity among the poor.

One of the few large-scale studies that addressed Dietz's concern confirmed the direct link between poverty and obesity. The California Women's Health Study (Adams et al. 2003) found that obesity was prevalent in twice as many of the women categorized as food-insecure as those with adequate nutrition, regardless of ethnic background. But the risk was greatest in women of color. Obesity levels increased from food-secure groups, to groups that were food-insecure without hunger, to groups that were food-insecure and suffered periodic hunger.

Several possible explanations were offered for these counter-intuitive but consistent results. Poor people may consume excessive high-energy foods because these are inexpensive, satisfy hunger, and are easy to prepare. The memory of past hunger and food deprivation may encourage subsequent over-consumption as a psychological defense or even as a cultural marker of adequacy and normalcy. Episodic hunger may stimulate physiological satiety and adiposity mechanisms to compensate for earlier "fasting" with excessive energy intake and storage during "feasting."

Native Americans living on reservations in the US are among the poorest of Americans today (NA 2009; Gordon and Oddo 2012). Their mean and median incomes are far below those of other Americans; college graduation rates are less than half, and unemployment, poverty, and food insecurity are more than twice as great. The prevalence of obesity and diabetes among some Native Americans exceeds that of all other Americans of any age, sex, or ethnic group. Dietary factors play an important role. Many native peoples have abandoned their low-calorie, fiber-rich traditional foods, in large part because they no longer have access to them. They have adopted a modern diet which, combined with a possibly exceptionally strong genetic predisposition to store and conserve energy as a result of their long history of periodic food shortages (Szathmary 1994), accounts for much of their increase in obesity. But poverty is also an important factor in Native American obesity, for precisely the same reasons that high rates of obesity are found among other American poor. Nutritious modern foods are beyond the reach of their family budgets.

Today food insecurity in the US is at its highest since 1995, and more than 14 percent of American households struggled against hunger in 2013 (usda.gov), one of the worst hunger problems in the developed world (pewresearch.org). Food insecurity is most prevalent in single-mother households with children, among black and Hispanic minorities, and in families with incomes below the poverty line (Coleman-Jensen et al. 2012). Hispanic children (those with the highest obesity rates among minority children) are the largest group with food insecurity. Members of nearly 7 million households suffer very low food security. In 2005, more than one-third (12.4 million) of all food-insecure people in the US were children under the age of 18 years (Cook and Frank 2008). Today only 20 percent of American children aged two to six years consume what is considered to be a nutritionally adequate diet. With rising costs of higher education, food insecurity has even appeared on college campuses (FRAC 2014). For the first time many have opened food pantries for students and staff who cannot afford to purchase healthy food (diamondbackonline.com/news).

Appalachia is a generally underdeveloped region of the southeastern US and is characterized by low incomes, low levels of urbanization, unmet educational needs, and a lower standard of living than the rest of the nation. West Virginia is the only state designated by the Appalachian Regional Commission (ARC) as entirely within Appalachia. Of the 55 counties in West Virginia, 26 are considered "distressed" by the ARC, with high unemployment and poverty. The economic plight of West Virginia is clearly reflected in the health of its residents. West Virginia has one of the highest rates of hypertension and obesity in the nation, and the age-adjusted rate of death due to heart disease is 21 percent higher than the national average.

The Coronary Artery Risk Detection in Appalachian Communities program is a school-based cardiovascular health program that covers all public school fifth-graders in West Virginia. The program estimates the prevalence of childhood obesity and identifies children in need of clinical testing, medical intervention, and health education to reduce obesity (Muratova et al. 2001; Demerath et al. 2003). West Virginia children are among the most obese pediatric populations in the nation, similar to the high prevalence observed among poor Native Americans and Mexican-Americans. Their obesity rate was associated with five times the risk of having low levels of high-density lipoprotein (HDL) (good) cholesterol, and three times the risk of high blood pressure. Cardiovascular disease risk factors tended to cluster in those with obesity, such that 70 percent of boys and 65 percent of girls with obesity had one or more cardiovascular disease risk factors. Obesity is just as likely to precipitate heart disease and diabetes in children as in adults. Surprisingly, only a small number of the overweight and children with obesity or their parents had received any information concerning weight management or guidance regarding diet and exercise.

Female-headed households are nearly five times more likely to be poor than those where fathers are present. In California, the 1994–6 Continuing Survey of Food Intakes by individuals revealed that overweight and obesity increased with food insecurity among women but not men. Mildly food-insecure women were 30 percent more likely to be overweight or have obesity than those who were food-secure, and moderate food insecurity was associated with a 50 percent greater risk of overweight or obesity (Townsend et al. 2001). Food-insecure women aged 19–55 years in the 1988–94 National Health and Nutrition Examination Survey (NHANES III) were more likely to be overweight than those who had sufficient food. Their daily diet was also of poorer quality and contained more calories, fewer fruits and vegetables, less milk and less food variety (Basiotis and Lino 2002). Food assistance programs for children such as food stamps and school breakfast and lunch programs moderate the effects of family food insecurity and seem to protect girls but not boys from developing overweight (Jones et al. 2003). Girls between the ages of five and 12 years who were from food-insecure families and participated in these programs had a 68 percent lower risk of becoming overweight than those who did not participate.

On a map of the United States, poverty, food insecurity, and obesity overlap. Obesity rates are highest in southern states, which also rank highest for poverty (Figure 5.3). Many of the states with the lowest poverty rates also have the lowest obesity rates.

Managing food insecurity

To the unaware, low-income individuals seem to make irrational decisions about nutrition and physical activity, choosing a poor diet and little exercise. But scarcity has a profound effect on decision-making (Shah et al. 2012; Zwane 2012).

Resource scarcity creates its own mindset, changing how people look at problems. Low-income families are often information-poor as well as resource-poor. Both restrictions tend to limit their choices so that quality decisions are difficult or impossible to make. When the primary goal is obtaining enough to feed the family, good nutrition and exercise have lower priority.

Food insecurity means that families often do not know where their next meal will come from. A 2011 nationwide Harris poll commissioned by Generations United discovered that one in 10 adults went without a basic need such as food or medicine to ensure that another family member could eat (Peterson and Heiges 2012). Since

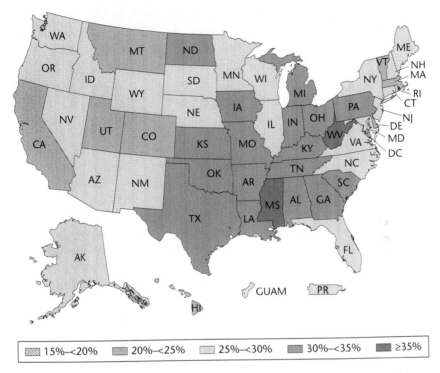

FIGURE 5.3   Adult obesity rates in the United States, 2013; no state had a prevalence of obesity below 20 percent; the South had the highest prevalence of obesity (30.2 percent), followed by the Midwest (30.1 percent), the Northeast (26.5 percent), and the West (24.9 percent).

Source: Centers for Disease Control and Prevention (cdc.gov/obesity/data/prevalence-maps.html).

mothers are held responsible for feeding their children, it is women with children who usually skip meals or eat less than men or child-free women, and who consequently have higher rates of nutrient deficiencies and obesity (Martin and Lippert 2012). When eating frequencies of black and white girls aged 9–20 years were compared, black girls – who ate less often than white girls – developed greater increases in BMI over a 10-year span (Ritchie 2011). Food insecurity means that mothers water down infant formula to keep their babies fed, a practice in 27 percent of food-insecure families receiving Women, Infants, and Children (WIC) supplements (newswise. com 1/23/2012). Food insecurity means that food dollars and food stamps must be stretched very thin to cover family needs until more resources become available. Food insecurity means that families live literally from hand to mouth and hope that no emergency arises to divert food dollars to unexpected medical bills or car repairs. Housing costs also impact food security; children in poor families without housing subsidies are more than twice as likely to be undernourished as children in subsidized families (Meyers et al. 2005). Poor families are forced to reduce food expenditures during winter months (when wealthier families spend more on food) because the cost of heating fuel consumes more of their income (Bhattacharya et al. 2003).

Poor families economize to make the most of their limited income, but they have few options. Unlike middle- and upper-class families, they are often forced to balance their tight budgets by simply doing without. Since the rent and utilities have to be paid, the only choice is to cut down on food purchases and to omit some foods altogether when there is a temporary cost spike or cash shortage. This involves maximizing intake and satiety while minimizing cost; in other words, to get more food energy for less money.

A study of food purchasing behavior (Blisard et al. 2004) showed that low-income buyers face overall higher food prices but spend less on food than middle- and high-income buyers. They manage by purchasing more discounted products, generic brands, less expensive and lower-quality products, and, when possible, larger-volume packages. Participants in the SNAP program spend more time in grocery shopping and meal preparation than higher-income individuals, presumably because they eat more of their meals at home and cook from scratch, although they also spend less time eating than high-income individuals (Leibtag and Kaufman 2003; Hamrick et al. 2011). The working poor, especially those who hold multiple jobs, must also balance food costs with time. They may opt for time-saving convenience and therefore frequently spend precious food dollars on fast-food restaurant meals and more costly prepared foods even though these contain fewer important nutrients and more calories than home-made meals.

Interviews with New Jersey nutrition educators revealed many other sometimes unusual techniques that are used by their food-insecure clients to manage limited resources (Kempson et al. 2002). In addition to preparing meals with inexpensive foods such as generic brands, spoiled foods were "amended" and eaten: slime was washed off lunchmeats, mold was cut from cheeses and breads, insects were removed from cereals, rotten parts of fruits and vegetables were cut out and discarded, and stews, soups, juices, and milk were diluted. Household members were allocated "food quotas," their portions labeled with their names. Food was hidden or locked up to prevent unauthorized consumption. Whenever possible, leftover food from churches, senior-dining sites, and nutrition education classes was taken home for later family consumption. Parents and teenagers went without meals to provide for younger children. To avoid questioning, they explained that they were fasting. Family members ate only once each day to stretch food supplies. And in the most extreme cases, paper, pet foods, and road kill were consumed. To save on food costs the rural poor attended "food auctions" where outdated food items were sold. Urban hunters provided freshly killed squirrels, rabbits, and raccoons. Not only did these practices contribute to malnutrition, but they also endangered health by potential infection and food poisoning.

Hospitality and sharing are important survival strategies for many poor families, especially among ethnic minorities (Fitchen 2000). Barbara Ehrenreich (Ehrenreich 2011), author of the best-selling *Nickle and Dimed: On (Not) Getting By in America*, recounted that the most common coping strategy by the poor is for families to double up in dwellings, sometimes renting couch sleeping space to non-family members. Food is shared with temporary guests, who are expected to reciprocate in the future. Even children are expected to share whatever they have with others. But the additional mouths force families to stretch the food supply even further, leaving some undernourished. Invariably it is the wife or mother who sacrifices her meal so that guests and other family members can eat the scarce meat and vegetables, leaving only the more plentiful starchy foods for her. The typical female social role interacts with family poverty to increase mothers' susceptibility to obesity.

Food-insecure individuals develop food anxieties and preoccupations that can last throughout their lives and even persist into the succeeding generations that have escaped poverty (Fitchen 2000). So they binge when food is temporarily plentiful, or they snack constantly throughout the day, even when they are not in danger of going hungry. Mothers respond too readily to their children's food demands and do not set limits on snacking. The ability to provide food, regardless of nutritional value, is a matter of pride for poor, food-insecure parents, who, like other Americans, want to exercise their right to choose what to eat for themselves and their children.

As Dietz has already noted, the food purchasing habits and consumption practices of poor, food-insecure individuals are now known to activate the human metabolic system in favor of energy conservation. Alternating between hunger and over-consumption of poorly balanced nutrients in cycles of plenty and scarcity mobilize physiological processes to accumulate and store energy as fat. Excessive dietary sugar and fat, not balanced by adequate proteins, vitamins, minerals, and fiber, also activate metabolic pathways for increased energy efficiency. Poor Americans are confronted with both the feast-and-famine cycles of Paleolithic foraging ancestors and the poor-quality diets of Neolithic farming forebears.

Most Americans, rich or poor, generally consume less than the recommended amounts of fruits and vegetables each day (Blisard et al. 2004; Guthrie et al. 2005). There are numerous reasons for this, among them lack of education about adequate nutrition and lack of experience preparing and eating nutritious and fresh foods, sometimes carried over many generations of deprivation, especially in poor families. Fresh foods require adequate storage facilities and time-consuming preparation, both of which may be lacking in many poor households. A national survey of eating choices (Mancino et al. 2004) found that more overweight women than women of healthy weight shopped for food only once a month or less and chose food items on the basis of storability and taste rather than nutritional value.

But even with education, experience, and financial support, the poor lack the ability to make real choices because of the limitations of their physical environment. Upper- and middle-income suburban families have easy access to modern, well-stocked full-service grocery stores with a vast range of available food items, but America's poor live in what Marion Nestle calls "food deserts" (Nestle 2002), neighborhoods where such stores are few and far between and farmers' markets are nonexistent. A study of food outlets in Mississippi, North Carolina, Maryland, and Minnesota revealed that, although population density was higher in poorer neighborhoods, there were only one-third as many supermarkets as in wealthier neighborhoods (Morland et al. 2002). In predominantly white neighborhoods the ratio of supermarkets to residents was one per 3,816 residents versus one per 23,582 in predominantly black areas. Combined with lack of mobility, food shopping becomes a serious challenge. Poor shoppers must resort to public transportation, which limits how much they can carry home. They must depend on friends and relatives with cars to reach distant supermarkets, or they have to use expensive taxi or delivery services (Clifton 2004). Small convenience stores with very limited selections of nutritious foods and higher prices for all items, as well as fast-food restaurants, bars, and taverns, are more common in poorer and ethnically mixed neighborhoods (Fleischhacker and Evenson 2011). Poor neighborhoods are also targets for food marketing schemes that promote inexpensive, high-calorie foods to specific ethnic groups (fried chicken and pork rinds, for example). Ramona Gardens, a Hispanic neighborhood in L.A., isolated from commercial areas by surrounding freeways, train tracks, and industrial warehouses, has no supermarket or even fast-food outlets (del Barco 2011). The only place to purchase food is one local convenience store, where products are often out of date, spoiled, and much more costly than in a large supermarket. A street vendor who comes when many residents are usually at work is the only source of fresh fruits and vegetables. The nearest market is three miles away, necessitating a bus ride and limiting the number of grocery bags that can be carried home.

Even food programs for the poor may contribute to the problem. A study of the New York City *Special Supplemental Nutrition Program for Women, Infants, and Children (WIC)* population found that 40 percent of the two to four-year-old children in the program were overweight or at risk for overweight (Nelson et al. 2004). Government commodity programs have a dual and often contradictory purpose – to distribute food to the poor but also to provide markets for surplus agricultural produce. Although these programs were originally established to combat undernutrition among the poor, particularly children, the nutritional quality of the foods distributed is not a high priority. As a result, food handouts consist mostly of high-calorie, low-fiber foods, such as peanut butter, cheese, cereals, whole milk, and items prepared with corn-based sweeteners, without assuring that adequate amounts of vitamin-, mineral-, and fiber-rich fruits and vegetables are also provided. Some stores established specifically for clients of the WIC program charge more for WIC-approved items than typical supermarkets, so that poor consumers actually get less for their food coupons (Pear 2004).

WIC distributes free infant formula to mothers of newborn infants. Although WIC distribution centers are mandated to promote breastfeeding, which provides better infant nutrition and helps to prevent obesity in both mothers and children (Owen et al. 2005), poor mothers face obstacles to breastfeeding, as many other working mothers do. In fact, the working environments of poor women are even less likely to accommodate breastfeeding mothers, who need to have their infants nearby, to take breaks from work for feeding sessions, and to have access to clean and comfortable locations for infant feeding or for pumping and storing breast milk. Breastfeeding rates are lower among poor, urban black mothers than among any other group (AAP 2005).

Private food banks and emergency food providers depend heavily on donations for supplies distributed to the poor. They often cannot stock fresh produce and other nutritious items, and, because of cuts in government programs, have had increasing difficulty in meeting emergency food needs in recent years. Especially during cold weather shocks in winter, when poor families must make "heat or eat"decisions (Bhattacharya et al. 2003), they are severely challenged to meet the demand. Under such conditions they must trade off quality for quantity of food.

Physical activity in social groups

America's poor also have limited opportunities to engage in health-promoting physical activity. At first this may seem contrary to logic. After all, poor people are less likely to have access to private transportation, so adults would have to walk to their jobs, stores, churches, and other venues, and children would walk to schools instead of being driven in the family car. Low-income blue-collar workers usually hold jobs involving more manual labor than white-collar or professional employees. Many working poor parents are engaged in multiple tedious jobs (cleaning women, migrant farm workers, store sales clerks). But leisure-time physical activity is lowest among low-income workers, among individuals with less education, and especially among ethnic minorities and women (Crespo and Andersen 2004). Workers belonging to ethnic minority groups usually live in segregated neighborhoods and spend long hours commuting to work (Brownson et al. 2005). They are simply too exhausted or too pressed for time to see to it that they and their children engage in exercise programs or recreation.

Of the only 26 percent of American adults who engage in recommended levels of leisure physical activity, the least active are members of ethnic minorities, individuals with lower levels of education, and residents of southern states (Crespo and Andersen 2004; Brownson et al. 2005). Patterns of leisure-time inactivity, poverty, and obesity are closely matched in these groups. Black women who are homemakers are twice as likely as white women homemakers to be inactive. They are also more likely to have obesity.

Kaboom, a national organization promoting childhood play, notes that today's youngsters suffer from a play deficit, with reduced school recess time, increased screen media usage, lack of conveniently located playgrounds, and poor understanding by adults of the importance of play for child development (kaboom.org 12/11/12). Most healthy children are by nature active, but physical activity declines sharply during adolescence. A national survey found that only 50 percent of boys and 24 percent of girls in grades nine to 12 participate in vigorous physical activity three or more times a week, with black and Hispanic adolescents reporting much lower rates than whites (Malina 1998). Adolescent girls manifest dramatic declines in physical activity, especially if their parents have little education or if they live in single-parent homes. Physical activity among black girls declines at twice the rate of white girls during adolescence (Kimm et al. 2002).

Only one-third of all nine to 13-year-olds in the US participate in organized physical activity outside school, and over one-quarter of all children in this age group do not participate in any physical activity at all during their free time. Not surprisingly, black and Hispanic children and children from lower-income families are less likely to be involved in organized activities than white children from wealthier families (NA 2009). Black children are less likely to play outdoors and therefore spend more time watching TV and engaging in other sedentary activities than white children (Crespo and Andersen 2004). Poor and black women also watch TV longer than women with higher incomes (Mancino et al. 2004).

The environments surrounding America's poor discourage physical activity and are associated with increased odds of obesity among children (Singh et al. 2010). Poor neighborhoods are more likely to lack recreational facilities and transportation to such places (Gordon-Larsen et al. 2006). Schools in poverty-stricken neighborhoods are rarely able to provide opportunities for physical education and activity, not to mention adequate health and nutrition education. Poverty-stricken neighborhoods lack lighting and sidewalks, parks, malls, and other spaces for safe playing and walking. Pedestrian fatalities are more frequent in poor neighborhoods (Frumkin 2002). Many are so downright unattractive, crime-ridden, and dangerous that mothers do not dare let their children play outside, forcing children to stay inside, watching TV in relative safety. The finding that girls living in such neighborhoods were two to four times more likely to be overweight or have obesity than boys (Singh et al. 2010) indicates that the need for protection from risky conditions limits their opportunities for physical activity and health. Segregation and unsafe neighborhoods promote social isolation, another barrier to physical activity. Being part of a community group such as a church or club and knowing other individuals who exercise help to break down these barriers. Women who have such social contacts are more likely to be physically active (Eyler et al. 2003).

Children's involvement in organized sports depends mainly on parental economic resources (Malina 1998). In addition to club membership fees, there are special clothing and shoes, protective gear, and equipment to pay for, and these items must be age-appropriate and need to be replaced regularly. Poor families simply cannot afford such luxuries. There is no "soccer mom" in a poor family – she does not have a car and cannot chauffer her children to sports practices and events.

As children increase in age, organized sports activities become more specialized and selective, with the most rigorous training and participation reserved for the talented elite. Participation becomes progressively and systematically more exclusive. So while many white children from higher-income families are guided toward life-long athletics and sports activities during their childhood, most poor children have few options after leaving school. Lower participation in physical activity by blacks and Hispanics represents to some extent their relative lack of access and financial resources, and possibly also exclusion due to racism.

Poverty and social stress

Even though Americans enjoy high personal income and standard of living, income disparity between rich and poor is the greatest in the industrial world and growing (census.gov) (CBO 2011). This gap is partly due to the loss of industrial jobs and the growth of low-wage service occupations, and partly because of federal government policies that have cut social programs and redistributed wealth to the rich. The top 1 percent of households gained 275 percent in income between 1979 and 2007, while the middle class gained only 40 percent, and the bottom fifth grew by only 18 percent. Real wages for workers in lower- and middle-income brackets actually declined, and job quality and living standards deteriorated, but the share of total after-tax income of the top 1 percent doubled. According to economist Timothy Smeeding (Smeeding 2005), Americans have experienced the greatest increase in income inequality in the past 20–30 years, the decades that happen to coincide with the dramatic increase in obesity prevalence in the US.

According to British physician Michael Marmot (Marmot 2004), the primary source of social stress is not absolute low income or poverty, but rather social and economic inequality, relatively low status and discrimination, social isolation and exclusion, and uncertainty and lack of control over life circumstances. It is not the disparity *between* societies that is stressful, but rather the gap *within* each one. Compared to poor people in less developed countries such as India, America's poor have relatively high incomes. But within the US their economic status is very low indeed, and they are acutely aware of the socioeconomic distance between themselves and middle- and upper-class groups.

During the 1960s the Pennsylvania town of Roseto caught the attention of epidemiologists because of its surprisingly low rate of heart-disease-related deaths compared to surrounding towns (Marmot 2004). After examining all the usual factors that contribute to good health, the scientists concluded that the very close-knit and egalitarian nature of this Italian-American community accounted for its health advantage. Conspicuous consumption and excessive pursuit of wealth were socially unacceptable, so that rich and poor members of the community could not be distinguished by dress, speech, or behavior. Strong family ties formed safeguards against disaster, and neighborly concern provided protection and security. As the epidemiologists predicted, when the social values of this community changed in succeeding generations, the health of the community deteriorated. Family and neighborhood support networks were weakened, and social cohesion was replaced by economic competition and social tension.

Social tensions are particularly conspicuous in urban areas where rich and poor neighborhoods are in close proximity but strictly segregated. Income disparity creates a social gulf and becomes a source of anger, frustration, and stress for the poor which middle- and upper-income Americans seldom experience. American society identifies individual members by occupation and income and ranks them accordingly. Marmot's study of British civil servants showed clearly that those in high-status positions, many with heavy responsibilities but also a great deal of control over their working conditions, were happier and healthier than those in demanding lower-status jobs who had little control over decisions related to their duties and were less satisfied in their occupations (Marmot 2004). It was not the normal stress of work demands but rather the stress of relatively low job positions that was associated with poor health and depression. And today long-term unemployment and cuts in retirement pensions can be added to the stress and obesity levels experienced by American workers (gallup.com).

Parental stress affects children, who tend to consume more fast foods than children in families not under stress (Parks et al. 2012). Even young children are affected by the stress of inequality. In a Canadian study, six- to 10-year-olds from lower socioeconomic classes had higher salivary cortisol levels than children from wealthier families (Lupien et al. 2001). Psychosocial stressors associated with financial hardship in low-income families have been shown again and again to relate to childhood obesity and health (Kubzansky et al. 2001; Eisenmann et al. 2011; Gundersen et al. 2011). Often parents under stress are unable to create a secure environment for their children, who then form insecure attachments known to be related to unhealthy responses and the development of obesity (Anderson and Whitaker 2011). Childhood abuse and adverse experiences (not limited to low-income families) have also been linked to adult obesity (Lumeng et al. 2006; Lumeng et al. 2013; Wells 2013; Solis et al. 2015).

For poor people in the US, longer and more complex daily commutes to work (Khattak et al. 2000), anxiety about material resources and family relationships, lack of control over one's life, and the effects of social inequality, discrimination, and absence of fairness are among the many sources of chronic stress. The psychological consequences of poverty, even more than its material deprivations, may be the basis for the human "socioeconomic-health gradient," found even among the monkeys psychologist Robert Sapolsky studied for many years (Sapolsky 2004). Top-ranking alpha male baboons show signs of psychological distress when challenged by upstart lower-ranking males, but these signs are dispelled when social stability is once again achieved. It is the subordinate males generally at the mercy of the alphas who develop the symptoms of chronic stress – higher cortisol levels, lower HDL-cholesterol, higher triglycerides, higher fasting glucose, and abdominal obesity. Humans, of course, are even more likely to be acutely conscious of and anxious about the significance of social divisions and subject to the consequences of social stress than monkeys.

One-third of U.S. workers feel that they are chronically overworked, and more than half feel overwhelmed (Galinsky et al. 2005). More than one-third (37 percent) do not plan to take all the vacation days they are entitled to because of the pressure to make up work afterwards for the time away from the job. A Harris poll found that more than half of working Americans did not use all of their allotted time off in 2011 (Tucker 2012). This contrasts with employees in European countries who receive longer vacations and use them fully. The working poor in America, who often juggle two or more jobs at once, are likely to receive little or no vacation time at all while being constantly subjected to performance pressures. They are more prone to sleep deprivation, which is also associated with elevated cortisol levels and obesity (Van Cauter and Spiegel 1999). It is no wonder that fast-food outlets serving satisfying, high-calorie, low-cost meals have become so popular and essential to overworked Americans, and particularly to Americans on very tight budgets. The current economic crisis marked by job losses and home foreclosures is a major source of chronic stress for Americans today, a burden that is only magnified by denials that a class structure exists in the US, and increased by warnings that acknowledging socioeconomic differences and disadvantages would initiate a "class war."

Low-income working individuals have described themselves as helpless, hopeless, powerless, defenseless, and "sucked down." Not unlike Sapolsky's baboons, stress and low social status are both strongly associated with high cortisol levels and visceral obesity in humans (Bjorntorp and Rosmond 2000). Cortisol, a hormone secreted by the adrenal glands in greater amounts under acute conditions, helps to convert fat to energy in the liver. But when stress is prolonged, continuously high cortisol levels elevate blood pressure and pulse rate and lead to insulin resistance and subsequent rise of blood sugar levels. Cortisol is strongly related to increased food intake (Dallman et al. 2003; Adam and Epel 2007) and to the accumulation of visceral adipose tissue (VAT), possibly due to disruption of the appetite and adiposity hormonal system in the brain (Bjorntorp 2001). Although not everyone is a "stress-eater," and, in fact, some individuals lose both appetite and weight during stressful periods (Epel et al. 2004), those who do overeat seem to prefer energy-dense foods with high sugar and fat content. The modern world, and especially the current U.S. economic crisis, offer numerous sources of stress at work and school, in segregated neighborhoods, and in abusive relationships (Thompson 2002; Chang 2006; Mamun et al. 2007; Noll et al. 2007; Fowler-Brown et al. 2009).

Blacks and Hispanics face the additional stress of racism. Residential isolation and racial discrimination are associated with greater odds of being overweight and other health problems such as lower birth weight, higher infant mortality, lower life expectancy, elevated blood pressure, higher rates of depression, and higher BMI (Gravlee 2009). Epidemiologist Nancy Krieger (Krieger 2005) refers to these conditions as the "embodiment of inequality." Tragically, individuals who experienced the trauma of physical or sexual abuse and peer bullying in childhood and adolescence are also more likely to be plagued by eating problems and obesity in adulthood than other adults (Taylor 2010; Midei and Matthews 2011; Lumeng et al. 2013). *Binging* is a common coping mechanism because it numbs negative feelings of anxiety and loneliness (Thompson 2002). Eating problems among black and Hispanic women are often dismissed because of stereotypical assumptions that women's obesity is more socially acceptable among these ethnic groups. They are less likely to receive treatment for either their eating and obesity issues or the effects of abuse.

In a study of stress and eating behavior (Klein et al. 2004), participants were first subjected to excessive noise and a stressful, unsolvable puzzle exercise and then were offered a variety of snack foods. A subset of participants was given control over the noise level but did not attempt to adjust it during the test. The women but not the men who had no perceived control over noise levels had the highest stress levels as indicated by increases in blood pressure and heart rate after the exercises ended. They selected and consumed more food and more fatty snacks than study participants who did not register high stress. Even women who performed well under these trying circumstances showed evidence of high stress levels and apparently found relief in comfort food. High-calorie foods, often consumed compulsively, help some depressed or stressed individuals to feel better, possibly by signaling brain centers to inhibit cortisol-stimulating hormones and thereby reducing stress responses (Dallman et al. 2003). Indeed, a study of well-educated middle-class women showed that those who were more fatigued, stressed, and anxious during their otherwise normal pregnancies consumed more food energy (carbohydrates and fats) but fewer essential micronutrients (folate, Vitamin C) than those women who felt less stressed (Hurley et al. 2005).

Life for poor families in disadvantaged, disrupted neighborhoods is very stressful. Combined with financial worries and food insecurity, this environment helps to account for the high rates of anxiety and depression among the poor, especially single mothers who bear the sole responsibility for supporting their children. The effects of maternal depression and stress are transmitted to their children, who respond by spending many more hours watching TV than children with healthy mothers (Burdette et al. 2003) and by consuming more fast food (Parks et al. 2012). Even among wealthy mothers, depression is known to result in inattention to hunger and nutrition, lack of systematic meal times, and frustration and abuse during meals. Poor mothers function in survival mode much of the time, overwhelmed by many concerns, of which feeding their families is just one.

Poverty and environmental pollution

Poor and minority neighborhoods are disproportionately exposed to environmental toxins and pollutants (Powell and Stewart 2001). Minority populations inhabit 75 percent of the communities with hazardous waste facilities, and Superfund sites are more often located in poor and minority communities than in more affluent and white neighborhoods. Poor children are particularly at risk for contact with toxic substances such as lead paint in old houses, industrial wastes, pesticides, and air pollutants. Residents of low-income communities are more likely to consume fish obtained from local ponds and streams, even though fishing may have been banned in such places. Adults are more likely to be exposed to environmental toxins and endocrine-disrupting chemicals than wealthier citizens, both on the job and in the neighborhoods where they live (Schell and Czerwinski 1998). Among these chemicals are the obesogens described in Chapter 4, chemicals that disrupt metabolic processes involved in energy regulation during fetal development and in adults as well. Environmental pollution is a significant factor in the development of obesity and related diseases among America's poor and minority populations (Hicken et al. 2011).

Developmental origins of obesity

Scientific ethics prohibit potentially harmful experiments with human subjects, but occasionally a historical event provides a "natural experiment" and new insights into the obesity epidemic. During the Dutch Hunger Winter of 1944–5, the Nazi army occupying the Netherlands severely rationed the food supply of Dutch citizens. Years after the end of the war, the daughters of Dutch women who were pregnant during the famine were discovered to have higher levels of adiposity, cholesterol, and triglycerides than daughters whose mothers had not suffered hunger (Stein et al. 2007; Lumey et al. 2009). Women who were exposed to famine during early gestation had higher overall adult cardiovascular and cancer mortality risk than women not exposed, while men exposed to famine during gestation showed no such effects (van Abeelen et al. 2011). Similarly, Hmong refugees who were born in the war zones of Laos during the Second Indochina War and later settled in the energy-rich environment of the US developed higher adiposity and visceral obesity than those who resettled in French Guiana (Clarkin 2008). These examples suggest that obesity is not only the outcome of adult behavior and lifestyle, but may also be established biologically in the developing fetal metabolic system during times of early nutritional stress.

A predisposition to obesity originates in early fetal development when organs and organ systems are biologically programmed for survival in stressful environments. Maternal nutritional stress favors accumulation of visceral fat over muscle development in the fetus, enhancing susceptibility to excess adiposity in later life, even before the external environment has a direct effect on the developing individual (Gluckman et al. 2008). The fetus receives chemical signals from its mother about her supply of nutrients and energy and, in the case of nutritional insufficiency, translates these signals into changes in metabolism, hormone production, and tissue sensitivity for fat storage. These regulatory changes are adaptive under conditions of nutritional stress and ensure the survival of the fetus and the rapidly growing body and brain of the newborn infant. But in an obesogenic environment, the infant is thus pre-programmed to become obese.

Both maternal undernutrition and maternal overnutrition are related to increased vulnerability to obesity in offspring. Pima mothers with diabetes gave birth to large babies with high fat mass and a greater predisposition to accumulate fat, but infants born to the same mothers before they had developed diabetes lacked these adverse traits (Adair 2008). In gestational diabetes, the fetus receives high concentrations of glucose, lipids, and amino acids via the placenta, leading to high birth weight and increased fat mass in the neonate and a tendency for increased obesity in later life. In a study of women who had bariatric surgery, offspring of mothers with extreme obesity had 50 percent higher obesity rates than children who were born after the mothers had surgery and lost weight (Kral et al. 2006). Poor and minority mothers, who tend to have high rates of obesity, are also more likely to give birth to infants programmed for later obesity.

The postnatal period is also critical. Infants of mothers under nutritional stress, such as those surviving the Dutch famine, often exhibited rapid catch-up growth when adequate nutrition was reestablished and were more likely to become obese adults. Today it is well known that rapid growth from birth to age two years is linked to a two to three times greater likelihood for obesity in childhood, adolescence, and adulthood (Ong and Loos 2006).

Over-feeding during early infancy boosts the chances for developing obesity that may persist through life (Adair 2008; Gillman 2008). Although the evidence is mixed (Hediger et al. 2001), formula feeding of newborn infants appears to promote rapid weight gain, which increases the risk of developing abdominal obesity, diabetes, high cholesterol, and elevated blood pressure in later life. On the other hand, breastfeeding, which provides infants not only with high-quality nutrition but also with the hormone leptin proportional to maternal levels, is associated with slower weight gain during the first year of life and appears to somewhat mitigate obesity risks in children and adults (Dewey 1998; Hediger et al. 2001; Moschos et al. 2002; Arenz et al. 2004; Grummer-Strawn and Mei 2004). In the case of overnutrition, the young infant's developing metabolic system is influenced by the excess energy in its chemical environment. Since poor and ethnic minority mothers are more likely to be obese and diabetic during pregnancy and less likely to breastfeed their infants after birth (Hediger et al. 2001; Nommsen-Rivers et al. 2010), their children are at higher risk for developing obesity.

A relatively new research field, *Developmental Origins of Health and Disease (DOHD)*, now focuses on the effects of these early developmental influences on adult adiposity, reproduction, immune function, and stress physiology to better understand population variation in biological susceptibility to obesity and chronic diseases (Gluckman and Hanson 2006; Kuzawa and Quinn 2009). This work began with the discovery and identification of "thrifty phenotypes" (Barker 1996) and helped to explain why individuals with below normal birth weight and subsequent rapid catch-up growth during early infancy were predisposed to later overweight, obesity, and coronary heart disease.

Maternal nutritional stress during pregnancy evokes a fetal adaptive response which slows prenatal growth and disrupts normal development, impairing pancreatic insulin production, inducing insulin and leptin resistance, and compromising the functioning of other digestive tract components. Abnormal functioning of these tissues in early life disturbs the development of normal energy regulation and predisposes the growing child and later the adult to obesity (Barker 2002; Rich-Edwards et al. 2005; Shonkoff et al. 2009). Also, because of especially rapid structural and functional developments during human fetal and early postnatal life, this is a particularly critical period of susceptibility to the adverse effects of endocrine-disrupting chemicals in the environment (Diamanti-Kandarakis et al. 2009; Newbold et al. 2009).

While the mechanisms of developmental programming are not yet fully understood, it is now clear that early fetal exposure to chemical messages via the placenta and from the neonate's nutritional environment can influence the early developmental stages of the energy regulatory system and disrupt its function in later life. Low birth weight is particularly prominent among infants born to poor mothers, and its rates have been increasing with growing poverty in recent years (NA 2009). Racial segregation, adding another level of maternal stress, is also linked to low birth weight (Grady 2006). Infants of black mothers are twice as likely to be born below normal weight as white infants (Crooks 1995), and adult complications of low birth weight are more common in individuals of low social position (Barker et al. 2005). The effects of maternal stress are thus transmitted to succeeding generations, a chain of events that can only be broken with adequate maternal nutrition and health care which benefits the mother as well as her children and even grandchildren.

Social and economic consequences of obesity

While economic disadvantage contributes to obesity, obesity also affects economic status. A seven-year study following groups of young people with a variety of chronic conditions found that the only group that was economically affected was the one with obesity (Gortmaker et al. 1993). In comparison to women of normal weight, the women in this group with obesity completed fewer years of education, earned an average of $6,710 less in annual income, had higher poverty levels, and were less likely to be married. The latter outcome is the only one the young women with obesity shared with the men with obesity in the study, whose education and income did not differ from men of normal weight. Results of a British study were similar – women's persistent obesity lowered the chance of gainful employment and of having a partner, but had no effect on men who had obesity (Viner and Cole 2005).

White women with obesity are less likely to hold managerial or professional positions and are more likely to have low-paying jobs. Even if they hold the same job as women of normal weight, they earn less (Averett and Korenman 1999; Finkelstein et al. 2005). They are also more than twice as likely to be subject to long-term unemployment. Women with obesity report more illness conditions that limit their work and quality of life when compared with normal-weight working women (Muenning et al. 2006; Tunceli et al. 2006).

Limited personal wealth is associated with obesity. Since 1979 the National Longitudinal Survey of Youth has followed the socioeconomic development of young people born between 1957 and 1964 (Zagorsky 2005). The survey found that among white Americans the net worth of men and women with obesity is $20,000 to $40,000 less than the net worth of those with normal BMI. Women who lost or gained large amounts of weight during the time of the survey saw the greatest gains or losses in their net worth.

Girls and women with obesity suffer more severe social consequences than boys and men, and the stress of *stigmatization* adds to their direct health burden (Kim and Kawachi 2008). Women with obesity in ethnic minority groups are in double jeopardy and carry the heaviest social and economic burdens. There have even been cases of children with obesity being removed from family custody at the request of physicians and Children's Services agencies who held their mothers solely responsible for the children's condition (Belkin 2001; Sheeran 2011).

Girls with obesity are less likely to enter college, a phenomenon that has been attributed to discrimination by college admission personnel and procedures (Crosnoe 2007). A less direct cause has also been identified; adolescent girls in the Add Health study avoided college attendance to escape further rejection. Already stigmatized because of obesity throughout their earlier school years in ways that boys were not, girls' educational and economic opportunities were thus more restricted. As a young woman interviewed on "The Weight of the Nation" put it, "Being fat holds you back – it builds walls because of appearance."

The negative cycle of obesity, stigmatization, and economic disadvantage has prompted a new social movement in America. The rise of the *size-acceptance movement* is a collective reaction to *fatism*, the victimization of and discrimination against fat individuals (Puhl and Brownell 2006). Founded in 1969, the National Association to Advance Fat Acceptance (NAAFA) is a nonprofit civil rights organization dedicated to ending size discrimination in all of its forms (naafa.org). Organizations like NAAFA aim to educate the public about the complex origins of obesity, the futility of dieting, and the pain of discrimination. They promote the idea of a society that accepts a range of size variation, especially for women, instead of the narrowly defined body image achievable by only a few.

The special case of immigrants

One of every five American children is a child of immigrants, who are among the poorest residents of this country (Hernandez 2004). Immigrants share many economic disadvantages with native-born low-income Americans, but also face some unique challenges. They are generally under-employed or employed in very low-paying jobs and live in extremely poverty-stricken neighborhoods. Lack of education and language skills limit their job prospects and leave them under-insured and without other benefits. Most immigrants are people of color and experience segregation and discrimination. Furthermore, some immigrants are undocumented and subject to arrest and expulsion (Coll and Szalacha 2004). Official (that is, conservative) poverty rates for children of immigrants are substantially higher than for children of native-born families; when poverty measures based on the current cost of living are used, the poverty rate of immigrants is double that of native-born Americans (Hernandez 2004).

Nevertheless, some immigrants display remarkable advantages over other Americans of the same socioeconomic level. They are more likely to live in large, intact, extended families where other adults besides working parents can provide child care and support (Shields and Behrman 2004; Lara et al. 2005). Immigrant children and adults are generally as healthy as or even healthier than their native-born counterparts. This observation is termed the "healthy immigrant effect," or, because it is more pronounced in Hispanic immigrants, the *Hispanic paradox* (Flores and Brotanek 2005). Despite their many risk factors for poor health, immigrants and their children have higher rates of immunization and breastfeeding, and lower rates of smoking, alcohol, and drug abuse, teen sexual activity, asthma and other allergic conditions, as well as lower rates of infant mortality and low birth weight (Harris 1999).

Many foreign-born immigrants also have lower rates of obesity than would be expected in a low-income population (Harris 1999; Goel et al. 2004). This is not surprising, considering that many have arrived from countries where wars, extreme poverty, malnutrition, and infectious diseases are common. But many adult immigrants maintain healthy body weights for years after immigrating to the US, and even some first-generation adolescents born and raised in America to immigrant parents have lower obesity rates than native-born white Americans. For instance, although a larger proportion of white immigrants (25 percent) earns only $20,000 or less in annual wages than native-born whites (17 percent), fewer white immigrants (15 percent) have obesity, in comparison to native-borns (21 percent); 33 percent of Hispanic immigrants are poor (versus 26 percent of American-born Hispanics), but only 20 percent have obesity (versus 31 percent of American-born Hispanics) (Flores and Brotanek 2005).

It is not until after adult immigrants have lived in the US for at least 10 to 15 years, or after the third generation is born in this country, that obesity rates rise among immigrant populations. But they still remain lower than those of native U.S. groups. The difference reflects immigrants' level of *acculturation*, the adoption of cultural elements of the dominant American society (Lara et al. 2005). The longer the duration of residence in the US, the greater the assimilation into American cultural, dietary, and activity patterns (Goel et al. 2004; Himmelgreen et al. 2004). Unacculturated Mexican immigrants in Washington State consumed more servings of fruits and vegetables than non-Hispanic white residents, but with increasing acculturation their fat intake increased when they began to add butter and margarine to bread and potatoes (Neuhouser et al. 2004). Foreign-born Mexicans and Cubans ate more low-fat, high-fiber fruits, beans, tortillas, and rice, and spent much less time watching TV and playing computer games than their U.S.-born counterparts (Gordon-Larsen et al. 2003; Lara et al. 2005). Slow or limited acculturation appears to protect against the negative effects of poverty on obesity and health in the US (Mazur et al. 2003). The nutrition and activity environment and behavior of recent immigrants may offer some clues to help all Americans avoid obesity.

But some immigrant groups rapidly adopt American customs, habits, and obesity levels. Biological anthropologist Barry Bogin and his colleagues (Bogin 1999; Smith et al. 2003) have conducted long-term studies of the growth and health of Maya children whose families fled their homeland in Guatemala during the civil war of the 1980s and settled in Florida and California. Although the children's general health improved rapidly in the US, these benefits were accompanied by a dramatic increase in obesity. In part, this rapid change fits the Developmental Origin hypothesis, for it is known that Guatemalan mothers were nutritionally deprived during early pregnancy, altering fetal metabolism to favor carbohydrate oxidation and increased accumulation and storage of body fat. Within 20 years of leaving their original homes in Guatemala, the "Maya in Disneyland" became taller and fatter than their Guatemalan relatives. While the Guatemalan Maya children continued to work with their parents in the fields, to care for their younger siblings, and to carry wood and water to their homes, the American Maya children quickly adopted the language, dress, food choices, and screen media behavior typical of American culture. They attended school, played video and computer games, and watched TV for many hours each week (Tuller 2002). And 46 percent became overweight or obese, compared to only 4 percent in Guatemala (Smith et al. 2003).

The interaction of culture change and human biology to promote the relatively sudden development of obesity among Mayan immigrants raises new questions. Why is acculturation associated with increased obesity? What cultural aspects contribute to America's obesity rates?

Conclusion

The risk of developing obesity is not equally distributed in the United States. According to the concept of risk focusing (Schell 1992), economically disadvantaged social groups are at greater risk for poor health and obesity, which in turn lower their economic opportunities even further. In developing countries, relatively rapid globalization and economic modernization have helped to create new disparities in socioeconomic status and obesity in many populations. Americans have experienced more gradual changes, but nearly the entire population still fails to meet federal dietary guidelines, and the discrepancy between high- and low-income families has actually widened (Pelto and Pelto 2000). Declining nutritional quality and rising obesity rates reflect growing economic inequality and stress among U.S. women, minority groups, and low-income families. Black and Hispanic households are the hardest hit, with 26 percent and 24 percent, respectively, suffering from food insecurity (frac.org).

The use of food stamps by American households has more than doubled since 2000. One in five U.S. children (16 million) now rely on food stamps (census.gov) compared to one in nine (9.5 million) before the great recession. Yet Congress passed and the President signed into law the Agriculture Act of 2014 (the Farm Bill), which includes $8.6 billion in cuts to SNAP (frac.org). It can be expected then that the nutritional effects of poverty will increase and obesity rates will remain high and may even increase in the near future.

A startling trend has emerged among high-income Americans. Since the 1970s, obesity rates rose steadily in all ethnic and socioeconomic groups, but the most dramatic increases occurred recently in the highest-income segments of the population. Using BMI statistics from the NHANES series, two research groups, one using annual income and the other educational levels as markers of socioeconomic status, reached the same conclusion. Among the wealthiest Americans obesity increased at twice the rate of the lower-income groups (Maheshwari et al. 2005; Singh et al. 2011). The obesity gap between Americans with high and low educational levels still exists but is shrinking (Zhang and Wang 2004), and Americans of all socioeconomic levels are now at risk for obesity and its associated diseases.

The rapidly closing obesity gap has no known genetic basis. A population's genes and physiological functions simply do not change so quickly. Only a transformation in the environment that affects metabolic processes to promote energy conservation and weight gain can explain the sudden increase in obesity rates. The environment of high-income groups may differ considerably from that of low-income Americans and yet contribute to obesity. Living the American Dream envisioned by immigrants and the poor of America can endanger health and wellbeing of the well-to-do, just as frustrated aspiration does for low-income groups. What are the common cultural features shared by all social strata that contribute to American obesity? Chapter 6 will explore some answers to this crucial question.

References

AAP (2005). American Academy of Pediatrics Policy Statement: breastfeeding and the use of human milk. *Pediatrics* **115**(2): 496–506.

Adair, L. S. (2008). Child and adolescent obesity: epidemiology and developmental perspectives. *Physiology & Behavior* **94**: 8–16.

Adam, T. C. and E. S. Epel (2007). Stress, eating and the reward system. *Physiology & Behavior* **91**(4): 449–458.

Adams, E. J., L. M. Grummer-Strawn, et al. (2003). Food insecurity is associated with increased risk of obesity in California women. *Journal of Nutrition* **133**: 1070–1074.

Anderson, S. E. and R. C. Whitaker (2011). Attachment security and obesity in US pre-school-aged children. *Archives of Pediatric & Adolescent Medicine* **165**(3): 235–242.

Arenz, S., R. Ruerkerl, et al. (2004). Breast-feeding and childhood obesity – a systematic review. *International Journal of Obesity* **28**: 1247–1256.

Averett, S. and S. Korenman (1999). Black-white differences in social and economic consequences of obesity. *International Journal of Obesity* **23**: 166–173.

Barbassa, J. (2004). The paradox of obesity. Corvallis Gazette-Times.

Barker, D. J. P. (1996). The origins of coronary heart disease in early life. Long-term Consequences of Early Environment: Growth, Development, and the Lifespan Development Perspective. C. J. K. Henry and S. J. Ulijaszek. New York, Cambridge University Press: 155–162.

Barker, D. J. P. (2002). Fetal origins of adult disease: strength of effects and biological basis. *International Journal of Epidemiology* **31**: 1235–1239.

Barker, D. J. P., T. Forsen, et al. (2005). Size at birth and resilience to effects of poor living conditions in adult life: longitudinal study. *British Medical Journal* **323**: 1–5.

Basiotis, P. P. and M. Lino (2002). Food insufficiency and prevalence of overweight among adult women. Alexandria, VA, USDA Center for Nutrition Policy and Promotion: 1–2.

Belkin, L. (2001). Watching her weight. New York Times. New York.

Bhattacharya, J., T. DeLeire, et al. (2003). Heat or eat? Cold-weather shocks and nutrition in poor American families. *American Journal of Public Health* **93**(7): 1149–1154.

Bjorntorp, P. (2001). Thrifty genes and human obesity. Are we chasing ghosts? *The Lancet* **358**: 1006.

Bjorntorp, P. and R. Rosmond (2000). Obesity and cortisol. *Nutrition* **16**: 924–936.

Blisard, N., H. Stewart, et al. (2004). Low-income households' expenditures on fruits and vegetables. Agricultural Economic Report #833. Washington DC, USDA Economic Research Service.

Bogin, B. (1999). Patterns of Human Growth. Cambridge, Cambridge University Press.

Brewis, A. A. (2011). Obesity: Cultural and Biocultural Perspectives. New Brunswick, NJ, Rutgers University Press.

Brownson, R. C., T. K. Boehmer, et al. (2005). Declining rates of physical activity in the United States: what are the contributors? *Annual Review of Public Health* **26**: 421–443.

Burdette, H. L., R. C. Whitaker, et al. (2003). Association of maternal obesity and depressive symptoms with television-viewing time in low-income preschool children. *Archives of Pediatric & Adolescent Medicine* **157**: 894–899.

Caballero, B. (2005). A nutrition paradox – underweight and obesity in developing countries. *New England Journal of Medicine* **352**: 1514–1516.

Carnethon, M. R., K. Knutson, et al. (2011). Contributions of cardiovascular disease risk factors to racial/ethnic differences in sleep duration: Chicago Area Sleep Study. *Association of Professional Sleep Societies*. Boston, Circulation. **124**: Abstract 16363.

CBO (2011). A CBO study: trends in the distribution of household income between 1979 and 2007. Washington DC, The Congress of the United States, Congressional Budget Office.

CDC (2012). Morbidity and Mortality Weekly Report – Quick Stats: prevalence of obesity among adults aged >20 years, by race/ethnicity and sex – National Health and Nutrition Examination Survey, United States, 2009–2010. U.S. Department of Health and Human Services, Centers for Disease Control and Prevention

Chang, V. W. (2006). Racial residential segregation and weight status among US adults. *Social Science & Medicine* **63**: 1289–1303.

Clarke, P., P. M. O'Malley, et al. (2009). Social disparities in BMI trajectories across adulthood by gender, race/ethnicity and lifetime socio-economic position: 1986–2004. *International Journal of Epidemiology* **38**(2): 499–509.

Clarkin, P. E. (2008). Adiposity and height of adult Hmong refugees: relationship with war-related early malnutrition and later migration. *American Journal of Human Biology* **20**: 174–184.

Clifton, K. J. (2004). Mobility strategies and food shopping for low-income families. *Journal of Planning Education and Research* **23**: 402–413.

Coleman-Jensen, A., M. Nord, et al. (2012). ERS Report Summary: household food security in the United States in 2011. Washington, DC, Economic Research Service, U.S. Department of Agriculture: 1–2.

Coll, C. G. and L. A. Szalacha (2004). The multiple contexts of middle childhood. *The Future of Children* **14**(2): 81–104.

Cook, J. T. and D. A. Frank (2008). Food security, poverty, and human development in the United States. *Annals of the New York Academy of Sciences* **1136**: 193–209.

Crespo, C. J. and R. E. Andersen (2004). Physical activity in Black America. Praeger Handbook of Black American Health. I. L. Livingston. Westport, CN, Praeger: 427–450.

Crooks, D. L. (1995). American children at risk: poverty and its consequences for children's health, growth and school achievement. *Yearbook of Physical Anthropology* **38**: 57–86.

Crooks, D. L. (2001). Poverty and nutrition in eastern Kentucky: the political economy of childhood growth. Building a New Biocultural Synthesis: Political-Economic Perspectives on Human Biology. A. H. Goodman and T. L. Leatherman. Ann Arbor, University of Michigan Press: 339–358.

Crosnoe, R. (2007). Gender, obesity, and education. *Sociology of Education* **80**: 241–260.

D'Souza, D. (2003). What's so great about America? Christian Science Monitor.

Dallman, M. F., N. Pecoraro, et al. (2003). Chronic stress and obesity: a new view of comfort food. *Proceedings of the National Academy of Science* **100**(20): 11696–11701.

del Barco, M. (2011). L.A. community starved for healthful food options. National Public Radio. Washington, DC.

Demerath, E., V. Muratova, et al. (2003). School-based screening in rural Appalachia. *Preventive Medicine* **37**: 553–560.

DeNaras-Walt, C., B. D. Proctor, et al. (2012). Income, poverty, and health insurance coverage in the United States, 2011. Washington DC, US Census Bureau.

Dewey, K. G. (1998). Growth characteristics of breast-fed compared to formula-fed infants. *Biology of the Neonate* **74**: 94–105.

Diamanti-Kandarakis, E., J.-P. Bourguignon, et al. (2009). Endocrine-disrupting chemicals: an Endocrine Society scientific statement. *Endocrine Reviews* **30**(4): 293–342.

Dietz, W. H. (1995). Does hunger cause obesity? *Pediatrics* **95**(5): 766–767.

Dinsa, G. D., Y. Goryakin, et al. (2012). Obesity and socioeconomic status in developing countries: a systematic review. *Obesity Reviews* **13**(11): 1067–1079.

Drewnowski, A. (2010). The cost of US foods as related to their nutritive value. *American Journal of Clinical Nutrition* **92**: 1181–1188.

Drewnowski, A. and N. Darmon (2005). The economics of obesity: dietary energy and energy cost. *American Journal of Clinical Nutrition* **82**(Suppl) 265S–273S.

Ehrenreich, B. (2001). Nickled and Dimed: On (Not) Getting by in America. New York, Metropolitan Books.

Ehrenreich, B. (2011). Barbara Ehrenreich: on turning poverty into an American crime, Truthout.org.

Eibner, C. E. and W. N. Evans (2004). The income–health relationship and the role of relative deprivation. Social Inequality. K. M. Neckerman. New York, Russell Sage Foundation: 545–568.

Eisenmann, J. C., C. Gundersen, et al. (2011). Is food insecurity related to overweight and obesity in children and adolescents? A summary of studies, 1995–2009. *Obesity Reviews* **12**: e73–e83.

Epel, E., S. Jiminez, et al. (2004). Are stress eaters at risk for the metabolic syndrome? *Annals of the New York Academy of Sciences* **1032**: 208–210.

Eyler, A. A., D. Matson-Koffman, et al. (2003). Quantitative study of correlates of physical activity in women from diverse racial/ethnic groups: the Women's Cardiovascular Health Network Project summary and conclusions. *American Journal of Preventive Medicine* **25**(3): 93–103.

Finkelstein, E. A., C. J. Ruhm, et al. (2005). Economic causes and consequences of obesity. *Annual Review of Public Health* **26**: 239–257.

Fitchen, J. M. (2000). Hunger, malnutrition, and poverty in the contemporary United States: some observations on their social and cultural context. Nutritional Anthropology: Biocultural Perspectives on Food and Nutrition. A. H. Goodman, D. L. Dufour and G. H. Pelto. Mountain View, CA, Mayfield: 335–347.

Fleischhacker, S. E. and D. A. Evenson (2011). A systematic review of fast food access studies. *Obesity Reviews* **12**(5): e460–e471.

Flores, G. and J. Brotanek (2005). The healthy immigrant effect: a greater understanding might help us improve the health of all children. *Archives of Pediatric & Adolescent Medicine* **159**: 295–297.

Fowler-Brown, A. G., G. G. Bennett, et al. (2009). Psychosocial stress and 13-year BMI change among blacks: The Pitt County Study. *Obesity* **17**(11): 2106–2109.

FRAC (2009). Hunger in the U.S. Washington, DC, Food Research & Action Center.

FRAC (2014). Food insecurity in the U.S.: new research. Washington DC, Food Research & Action Center.

Friel, S., M. Chopra, et al. (2007). Unequal weight: equity oriented policy responses to the global obesity epidemic. *British Medical Journal* **335**: 1241–1243.

Frumkin, H. (2002). Urban sprawl and public health. *Public Health Reports* **117**: 201–217.

Galinsky, E., J. T. Bond, et al. (2005). Overwork in America: when the way we work becomes too much. New York, Families and Work Institute.

Gillman, M. W. (2008). The first months of life: a critical period for development of obesity. *American Journal of Clinical Nutrition* **87**: 1587–1589.

GlobalMacroMonitor (2011). How U.S. income groups get squeezed by food prices. http://macromon.wordpress.com/2011/02/02.

Gluckman, P. D. and M. A. Hanson (2006). Developmental Origins of Health and Disease. New York, Cambridge University Press.

Gluckman, P. D., M. A. Hanson, et al. (2008). Effect of in utero and early-life conditions on adult health and disease. *New England Journal of Medicine* **359**(1): 61–73.

Goel, M. S., E. P. McCarthy, et al. (2004). Obesity among US immigrant subgroups by duration of residence. *JAMA* **292**(3): 2860–2867.

Gordon-Larsen, P., K. M. Harris, et al. (2003). Acculturation and overweight-related behaviors among Hispanic immigrants to the US: the National Longitudinal Study of Adolescent Health. *Social Science & Medicine* **57**: 2023–2034.

Gordon-Larsen, P., M. C. Nelson, et al. (2006). Inequality in the built environment underlies key health disparities in physical activity and obesity. *Pediatrics* **117**: 417–424.

Gordon, A. and V. Oddo (2012). Addressing child hunger and obesity in Indian country: report to Congress. Alexandria, VA, USDA, Food and Nutrition Service, Office of Research and Analysis.

Gortmaker, S. L., A. Must, et al. (1993). Social and economic consequences of overweight in adolescence and young adulthood. *New England Journal of Medicine* **329**: 1008–1012.

Grady, S. C. (2006). Racial disparities in low birthweight and the contribution of residential segregation: a multivariate analysis. *Social Science & Medicine* **63**(12): 3013–3029.

Gravlee, C. (2009). How race becomes biology: embodiment of social inequality. *American Journal of Physical Anthropology* **139**: 47–57.

Grummer-Strawn, L. M. and Z. Mei (2004). Does breastfeeding protect against pediatric overweight? Analysis of longitudinal data from the Centers for Disease Control and Prevention Pediatric Nutrition Surveillance System. *Pediatrics* **113**(2): e81–e86.

Gundersen, C., D. Mahatmya, et al. (2011). Linking psychosocial stressors and childhood obesity. *Obesity Reviews* **12**(5): e54–e63.

Guthrie, J. F., B.-H. Lin, et al. (2005). Understanding economic and behavioral influences on fruit and vegetable choices. Washington DC, Amber Waves: USDA Economic Research Service.

Hamrick, K. S., M. Andrews, et al. (2011). ERS Report Summary: How much time do Americans spend on food? Washington DC, Economic Research Service, U.S. Department of Agriculture: 1–2.

Harris, K. M. (1999). The health status and risk behaviors of adolescents in immigrant families. Children of Immigrants. D. J. Hernandez. Washington DC, National Academy Press: 286–347.

Hediger, M. L., M. D. Overpeck, et al. (2001). Association between infant breastfeeding and overweight in young children. *JAMA* **285**(19): 2453–2460.

Hernandez, D. C. and E. Pressler (2015). Gender disparities among the association between cumulative family-level stress & adolescent weight status. *Preventive Medicine* **73**: 60–66.

Hernandez, D. J. (2004). Demographic change and the life circumstances of immigrant families. *The Future of Children* **14**(2): 17–48.

Hicken, M., R. Gragg, et al. (2011). How cumulative risks warrant a shift in our approach to racial health disparities: the case of lead, stress, and hypertension. *Health Affairs* **30**(10): 1895–1901.

Himmelgreen, D. A., R. Perez-Escamilla, et al. (2004). The longer you stay, the bigger you get: length of time and language use in the U.S. are associated with obesity in Puerto Rican women. *American Journal of Physical Anthropology* **125**: 90–96.

Hurley, K., L. E. Caulfield, et al. (2005). Psychosocial influences in dietary patterns during pregnancy. *Journal of the American Dietetic Association* **105**: 963–966.

Isaacs, S. L. and S. A. Schroeder (2004). Class – the ignored determinant of the nation's health. *New England Journal of Medicine* **351**: 1137–1142.

JCPES (2012). Place matters for health in Orleans Parish: ensuring opportunities for good health for all, a report on health inequities in Orleans Parish, Louisiana. Washington DC, Joint Center for Political and Economic Studies, Health Policy Institute.

Johnston, F. E. and P. Gordon-Larsen (1999). Poverty, nutrition and obesity in the USA. Urbanism, Health and Human Biology in Industrialised Countries. L. M. Schell and S. J. Ulijaszek. New York, Cambridge University Press: 192–209.

Jones, S. J., L. Jahns, et al. (2003). Lower risk of overweight in school-aged food insecure girls who participate in food assistance. *Archives of Pediatric & Adolescent Medicine* **157**: 780–784.

Kempson, K. M., D. P. Keenan, et al. (2002). Food management practices used by people with limited resources to maintain food sufficiency as reported by nutrition educators. *Journal of the American Dietetic Association* **102**: 1795–1799.

Khattak, A. J., V. Amerlynck, et al. (2000). Are travel times and distances to work greater for residents of poor urban neighborhoods? Washington DC: Transportation Research Board Annual Meeting.

Kim, D. and I. Kawachi (2008). Obesity and health-related quality of life. Obesity Epidemiology. F. B. Hu. New York, Oxford University Press: 234–260.

Kimm, S. Y. S., N. W. Glynn, et al. (2002). Decline in physical activity in black girls and white girls during adolescents. *New England Journal of Medicine* **347**(10): 709–715.

Klein, L. C., M. M. Faraday, et al. (2004). Gender differences in biobehavioral aftereffects of stress on eating, frustration, and cardiovascular responses. *Journal of Applied Social Psychology* **34**(3): 538–562.

Kral, J. G., S. Biron, et al. (2006). Large maternal weight loss from obesity surgery prevents transmission of obesity to children who were followed for 2 to 18 years. *Pediatrics* **118**(6): e1644–e1649.

Krieger, N. (2005). Embodiment: a conceptual glossary for epidemiology. *Journal of Epidemiology and Community Health* **59**: 350–355.

Kubzansky, L. D., N. Krieger, et al. (2001). United States: social inequality and the burden of poor health. Challenging Inequities in Health. T. Evans, M. Whitehead and F. Diderichsen. Oxford, Oxford University Press: 106–121.

Kuzawa, C. W. and E. A. Quinn (2009). Developmental origins of adult function and health: evolutionary hypotheses. *Annual Review of Anthropology* **38**: 131–147.

Lara, M., C. Gamboa, et al. (2005). Acculturation and Latino health in the United States: a review of the literature and its sociopolitical context. *Annual Review of Public Health* **26**: 367–397.

Leibtag, E. S. and P. R. Kaufman (2003). Current issues in economics of food markets: exploring food purchase behavior of low-income households: how do they economize? Washington, DC, US Dept Agriculture: 1–7.

LLC (2009). State minimum wage rates, www.laborlawcenter.com.

Lumeng, J. C., D. Appugliese, et al. (2006). Neighborhood safety and overweight status in children. *Archives of Pediatrics and Adolescent Medicine* **160**: 25–31.

Lumeng, J. C., K. Wendorf, et al. (2013). Overweight adolescents and life events in childhood. *Pediatrics* **132**(6): e1506–e1512.

Lumey, L. H., A. D. Stein, et al. (2009). Lipid profiles in middle-aged men and women after famine exposure during gestation: the Dutch Hunger Winter Families Study. *American Journal of Clinical Nutrition* **89**: 1737–1743.

Lupien, S. J., S. King, et al. (2001). Can poverty get under your skin? Basal cortisol levels and cognitive function in children from low and high socioeconomic status. *Development and Psychopathology* **13**(3): 653–676.

MacIntyre, S. (1998). Social inequalities and health in the contemporary world: comparative overview. Human Biology and Social Inequality. S. S. Strickland and P. S. Shetty. Cambridge, UK, Cambridge University Press: 20–35.

Maheshwari, N., J. G. Robinson, et al. (2005). Obesity prevalence increasing three times faster in high than low income groups – the National Health and Nutrition Examination Surveys 1971 to 2002. *Circulation* **111**(14): E254.

Malina, R. M. (1998). Physical activity, sport, social status and Darwinian fitness. Human Biology and Social Inequality. S. S. Strickland and P. S. Shetty. Cambridge, Cambridge University Press. 39th symposium: 165–192.

Mamun, A. A., D. A. Lawlor, et al. (2007). Does childhood sexual abuse predict young adult's BMI? A birth cohort study. *Obesity* **15**: 2103–2110.

Mancino, L., B.-H. Lin, et al. (2004). The Role of Economics in Eating Choices and Weight Outcomes. Agriculture Information Bulletin #791. Washington DC, USDA Economic Research Service.

Marmot, M. (2004). The Status Syndrome: How Social Standing Affects Our Health and Longevity. New York, Times Books.

Martin, M. A. and A. M. Lippert (2012). Feeding her children, but risking her health: the intersection of gender, household food insecurity and obesity. *Social Science & Medicine* **74**: 1754–1764.

Mazur, R. E., G. S. Marquis, et al. (2003). Diet and food insufficiency among Hispanic youths: acculturation and socioeconomic factors in the third National Health and Nutrition Examination Survey. *American Journal of Clinical Nutrition* **78**: 1120–1127.

Mello, J. A., K. M. Gans, et al. (2010). How is food insecurity associated with dietary behaviors? An analysis with low-income, ethnically diverse participants in a nutrition intervention study. *Journal of the American Dietetic Association* **110**(12): 1906–1911.

Meyers, A., D. Cutts, et al. (2005). Subsidized housing and children's nutritional status: data from a multisite surveillance study. *Archives of Pediatric & Adolescent Medicine* **159**(6): 551–556.

Midei, A. J. and K. A. Matthews (2011). Interpersonal violence in childhood as a risk factor for obesity: a systematic review of the literature and proposed pathways. *Obesity Reviews* **12**(5): e159–e172.

Monteiro, C. A., E. C. Moura, et al. (2004). Socioeconomic status and obesity in adult populations of developing countries: a review. *Bulletin of the World Health Organization* **82**(12): 940–946.

Morland, K., S. Wing, et al. (2002). Neighborhood characteristics associated with the location of food stores and food service places. *American Journal of Preventive Medicine* **22**(1): 23–29.

Moschos, S., J. L. Chan, et al. (2002). Leptin and reproduction: a review. *Fertility and Sterility* **77**(3): 433–444.

Muenning, P., E. Lubetkin, et al. (2006). Gender and the burden of disease attributable to obesity. *American Journal of Public Health* **96**(9): 1662–1668.

Muratova, V., S. Islam, et al. (2001). Cholesterol screening among children and their parents. *Prev Med* **33**: 1–6.

Murguia, J. (2010). Solutions to the Latino child nutrition crisis in the U.S. www.huffingtonpost.com/janet-murguia.

NA (2009). Kids count data book. Baltimore, Annie E. Casey Foundation.

Nelson, J. A., M. A. Chiasson, et al. (2004). Childhood overweight in a New York City WIC population. *American Journal of Public Health* **94**(3): 458–462.

Nestle, M. (2002). Hunger in the United States: policy implications. Food in the USA: A Reader. C. M. Counihan. New York, Routledge: 385–400.

Neuhouser, M. L., B. Thompson, et al. (2004). Current research; higher fat intake and lower fruit and vegetables intakes are associated with greater acculturation among Mexicans living in Washington state. *Journal of the American Dietetic Association* **104**: 51–57.

Neuman, M., J. E. Finlay, et al. (2011). The poor stay thinner: stable socioeconomic gradients in BMI among women in lower- and middle-income countries. *The American Journal of Clinical Nutrition* **94**(5): 1348–1357.

Newbold, R. R., E. Padilla-Banks, et al. (2009). Environmental estrogens and obesity. *Molecular and Cellular Endocrinology* **304**: 84–89.

Noll, J., M. H. Zeller, et al. (2007). Obesity risk for female victims of childhood sexual abuse: a prospective study. *Pediatrics* **120**(1): e61–e67.

Nommsen-Rivers, L. A., C. J. Chantry, et al. (2010). Delayed onset of lactogenesis among first-time mothers is related to maternal obesity and factors associated with ineffective breastfeeding. *American Journal of Clinical Nutrition* **92**: 574–584.

Ogden, C. L., M. M. Lamb, et al. (2010). NCHS Data Brief No. 50: Obesity and socio-economic status in adults: United States 1988–1994 and 2005–2008. Hyattsville, MD, U.S. Department of Health and Human Services, Centers for Disease Control and Prevention, National Center for Health Statistics: 1–7.

Ong, K. K. and R. J. F. Loos (2006). Rapid infancy weight gain and subsequent obesity; systematic reviews and hopeful suggestions. *Acta Pediatrica* **95**: 904–908.

Owen, C. G., R. M. Martin, et al. (2005). Effect of infant feeding on the risk of obesity across the life course: a quantitative review of published evidence. *Pediatrics* **115**(5): 1367–1377.

Pan, L., H. M. Blanck, et al. (2012). Trends in the prevalence of extreme obesity among US preschool-aged children living in low-income families, 1999–2010. *Journal of the American Medical Association* **308**(24): 2563–2565.

Pan, L., A. L. May, et al. (2013). Incidence of obesity among young US children living in low-income families, 2008–2011. *Pediatrics* **132**(6): 1006–1013.

Parks, E. P., S. Kumanyika, et al. (2012). Influence of stress in parents on child obesity and related behaviors. *Pediatrics* **130**(5): e1096–e1104.

Pear, R. (2004). Selling to poor, stores bill U.S. for top prices. New York Times. New York.

Pelto, G. H. and P. J. Pelto (2000). Diet and delocalization: dietary changes since 1750. Nutritional Anthropology: Biocultural Perspectives on Food and Nutrition. A. H. Goodman, D. L. Dufour and G. H. Pelto. Mountain View, CA, Mayfield Publishing Company: 269–278.

Pena, M. and J. Bacallao (2002). Malnutrition and poverty. *Annual Review of Nutrition* **22**: 241–253.

Peterson, J. and W. Heiges (2012). Hunger and nutrition: what's at stake for children, families & older adults. Washington DC, Generation United.

Powell, D. L. and V. Stewart (2001). Children: the unwitting target of environmental injustices. *Pediatric Clinics of North America* **48**(5): 1291–1305.

Pray, L., L. Pillsbury, et al. (2012). Exploring health and environmental costs of food: workshop summary. Washington DC: Institute of Medicine.

Puhl, R. and K. D. Brownell (2006). Confronting and coping with weight stigma: an investigation of overweight and obese adults. *Obesity* **14**(10): 1802–1815.

Rehm, C. D., P. Monsivais, et al. (2011). The quality and monetary value of diets consumed by adults in the United States. *American Journal of Clinical Nutrition* **94**: 1333–1339.

Rich-Edwards, J. W., K. Kleinman, et al. (2005). Longitudinal study of birth weight and adult body mass index in predicting risk of coronary heart disease and stroke in women. *British Medical Journal* doi 10.1136/bmj.38434.629630.EO (published 27 April 2005).

Ritchie, L. D. (2011). Less frequent eating predicts greater BMI and waist circumference in female adolescents. *American Journal of Clinical Nutrition* **95**(2): 290–296.

Roy, J. (2008). Most Black children grow up in neighborhoods with significant poverty. Washington DC: Economic Policy Institute.

Sapolsky, R. M. (2004). Social status and health in humans and other animals. *Annual Review of Anthropology* **33**: 393–418.

Schell, L. M. (1992). Risk focusing: an example of biocultural interaction. Health and Lifestyle Change. R. Huss-Ashmore, J. Schall and M. Hediger. Philadelphia, University of Pennsylvania Press: 137–144.

Schell, L. M. and S. Czerwinski (1998). Environmental health, social inequality and biological differences. Human Biology and Social Inequality. S. S. Strickland and P. S. Shetty. Cambridge, UK, Cambridge University Press: 114–131.

Shah, A. K., S. Mullainathan, et al. (2012). Some consequences of having too little. *Science* **338**: 682–685.

Sheeran, T. J. (2011). Ohio officials take 200-pound boy from mother. Dayton Daily News. Dayton.

Shields, M. K. and R. E. Behrman (2004). Children of immigrant families: analysis and recommendations. *The Future of Children* **14**(2): 4–16.

Shipler, D. K. (2004). The Working Poor: Invisible in America. New York, Knopf.

Shonkoff, J. P., W. T. Boyce, et al. (2009). Neuroscience, molecular biology, and the childhood roots of health disparities. *Journal of American Medical Association* **301**(21): 2252–2259.

Singh, G. K., M. Siahpush, et al. (2011). Dramatic increases in obesity and overweight prevalence and body mass index among ethnic-immigrant and social class groups in the United States, 1976–2008. *Journal of Community Health* **36**: 94–110.

Singh, G. K., M. Siahpush, et al. (2010). Neighborhood socioeconomic conditions, built environments, and childhood obesity. *Health Affairs* **29**(3): 503–512.

Smeeding, T. (2005). Public policy, economic inequality, and poverty: the United States in comparative perspective. *Social Science Quarterly* **86**(Suppl): 956–983.

Smith, P. K., B. Bogin, et al. (2003). Economic and anthropological assessments of the health of children in Maya immigrant families in the US. *Economics and Human Biology* **1**: 145–160.

Smith, S. (2004). The cost of good nutrition: why the poor eat so poorly. The Boston Globe. Boston.

Solis, C. B., M. Kelly-Irving, et al. (2015). Adverse childhood experiences and physiological wear-and-tear in midlife: findings from the 1958 British birth cohort. *Proceeding of the National Academy of Science* doi: 10.1073/pnas1417325112.

Stein, A. D., H. S. Kahn, et al. (2007). Anthropometric measures in middle age after exposure to famine during gestation: evidence from the Dutch famine. *American Journal of Clinical Nutrition* **85**(3): 869–876.

Stunkard, A. J. (1975). Socioeconomic status and obesity. Recent Advances in Obesity Research: I Proceedings of the First International Congress on Obesity. A. Howard. London, Newman: 178–191.

Suglia, S. F., C. S. Duarte, et al. (2012). Cumulative social risk and obesity in early childhood. *Pediatrics* **129**(5): 1173–1179.

Szathmary, E. J. E. (1994). Non-insulin dependent diabetes mellitus among aboriginal North Americans. *Annual Review of Anthropology* **23**: 457–482.

Taylor, S. E. (2010). Mechanisms linking early life stress to adult health outcomes. *Proceedings of the National Academy of Sciences* **107**(19): 8507–8512.

Thompson, B. W. (2002). A way outa no way: eating problems among African-American, Latina, and White women. Food in the USA: A Reader. C. Counihan. New York, Routledge: 219–230.

Townsend, M. S., J. Peerson, et al. (2001). Food insecurity is positively related to overweight in women. *Journal of Nutrition* **131**: 1738–1745.

Tucker, R. (2012). More Ohioans aren't using vacation time. Dayton Daily News. Dayton.

Tuller, D. (2002). Maya children face serious weight problems. New York Times. New York.

Tunceli, K., K. Li, et al. (2006). Long-term effects of obesity on employment and work limitations among U.S. adults, 1986 to 1999. *Obesity* **14**(9): 1637–16446.

van Abeelen, A. F. M., M. V. E. Veenendaal, et al. (2011). Survival effects of prenatal famine exposure. *The American Journal of Clinical Nutrition* **95**(1): 179–183.

Van Cauter, E. and K. Spiegel (1999). Sleep as a mediator for the relationship between socioeconomic status and health: a hypothesis. *Annals of the New York Academy of Sciences* **896**: 254–261.

Viner, R. M. and T. J. Cole (2005). Adult socioeconomic, educational, social, and psychological outcomes of childhood obesity: a national birth cohort study. *British Medical Journal* doi 10.1136/bmj.38453.422049.E0.

Wells, J. C. K. (2013). Commentary: the thrifty penotype and the hierarchical preservation of tissues under stress. *International Journal of Epidemiology* **42**: 1223–1227.

Wilkinson, R. G. (1998). Equity, social cohesion and health. Human Biology and Social Inequality. S. S. Strickland and P. S. Shetty. Cambridge, UK, Cambridge University Press.

Woolf, S. H. and P. Braveman (2011). Where health disparities begin: the role of social and economic determinants – and why current policies may make matters worse. *Health Affairs* **30**(10): 1852–1859.

Zagorsky, J. L. (2005). Health and wealth: the late-20th century obesity epidemic in the U.S. *Economics and Human Biology* **3**: 296–313.

Zhang, Q. and Y. Wang (2004). Trends in the association between obesity and socioeconomic status in U.S. adults: 1971–2000. *Obesity Research* **12**(10): 1622–1632.

Zwane, A. P. (2012). Implications of scarcity. *Science* **338**: 617–618.

6

THE OBESITY EPIDEMIC AND AMERICAN CULTURE

Introduction

Why do so many Americans have obesity? Certain distinctive American cultural features may also provide answers to this key question. Newcomers to the US are confronted with an unfamiliar language, novel foods, a different lifestyle, new ideas and rules for behavior – in short, a new *culture*. Although it may borrow cultural features from others, each society is distinguished by a unique constellation of cultural elements including social structures, institutions, technology, environmental adaptations, and a particular worldview (Farb and Armelagos 1983). A society's culture determines what is considered normal, ethical, and acceptable. Despite ethnic variations on the main theme, the American cultural environment consists largely of a shared pattern of ideas and beliefs, symbols and meanings, and values and norms (Bryant et al. 2003) that characterize much of life in the US. Several cultural values are particularly relevant to our understanding of the American obesity epidemic. They are related to ideas about ideal body size and weight norms and acceptable consumption of both food and material goods, which will be examined briefly in this chapter. During the last two centuries dramatic cultural changes associated with industrialization and modernization have shaped both of these viewpoints.

Culture and body size

The world's remarkable variety of cultural traditions and customs reflects the unique histories and environments of its many societies. What is considered right, morally correct, and beautiful in one society may be considered wrong, unacceptable, and ugly in another. Members of some societies view a large body as a positive attribute, representing prosperity and fertility, while others view it negatively, symbolizing poverty and illness (Kulick and Meneley 2005). Where food shortages are common, and hard manual labor is a daily requirement, generous amounts of body fat and heavy weight are usually symbols of health and beauty (Brown and Bentley-Condit 1998). For example, a woman with massive obesity in the Azawagh Arab region of Niger is considered to be very attractive and sexually desirable (Popenoe 2004). In Nigeria, young Anang women used to be kept in fattening rooms and required to consume rich food and drink to achieve a body size that signaled to potential bridegrooms her family's wealth and her fecundity (Brink 1995). A number of South Pacific societies also valued obesity in women and men (Bindon 1995; Pollock 1995); the large size of Hawaiian and Tahitian chiefs and nobles was legendary. In the tiny island nation of Nauru, women were fattened like Anang girls. In recent years, phosphate mining brought prosperity to this little population, allowing the now affluent Nauruans to import plenty of food and achieve the large body size they prize as a symbol of wellbeing and generosity.

The Japanese Sumo wrestler is a male version of ideal large body size. His BMI is in the extremely obese category, but he also has a high proportion of muscle mass compared to the untrained, healthy Japanese man (Hattori et al. 1999). And yet Japanese society applies great pressure to individuals to be slim, and the government mandates waist circumference limits (Nakamura 2009). In the US professional football players are noted for their size and strength, which encourages some high school athletes to emulate them by putting on excessive body weight (Laurson and Eisenmann 2007). A number of male hip-hop stars and stand-up comedians embrace obesity as marks of their successful careers (Gross 2005). The Florida Marlins baseball franchise hired a new group of cheerleaders, the Manatees, to perform and reverse dwindling attendance at their games (Goddard 2008). As their name suggests, the 14 Manatees are 300 to 400-pound guys selected specifically for their "big bellies with the biggest jiggles" to strut around, strike poses, and belly-bump into each other to entertain the crowds.

But more commonly, and paradoxically, in the US where food is abundant and much "labor" is automated and mechanized, the opposite ideal body image prevails – it is thinness that symbolizes health and beauty, high economic status, and moral rectitude, especially among women. U.S. views of body fatness changed from healthy and attractive to unhealthy and ugly between the 1880s and 1920s and continued to change as women's roles shifted from primarily mothers and wives to labor market employees with careers (Bonafini and Pozzilli 2011). Plumpness was no longer a positive sign of prestige and prosperity, but rather a negative attribute. Today's American cultural heroes and heroines are the slim, attractive movie stars and the well-muscled and extremely active sports figures who bear little physical resemblance to the majority of the population. In the 1950s when rich food was less abundant, the ideal female body was ample and curvaceous, but today a large body is associated with low socioeconomic status, moral failure, laziness, and gluttony. It is often the basis for social ostracism and stigmatization (Wilson 2005).

In the US great emphasis is placed on physical appearance. Stringent standards of beauty for women (but less so for men) are broadly disseminated by various media – TV, movies, women's magazines, newspapers, and billboards (Nichter 2000; SEF 2015). Body weight is therefore a powerful criterion of self-worth for American women. A slender woman embodies a cultural image of self-discipline to control her appetite and to exercise regularly, to sacrifice and deny gratification in the context of vast energy abundance and leisure (Brown and Konner 1998). White teenage girls and women are greatly influenced by this cultural ideal and often become preoccupied with body weight and shape. In scientific studies using self-reports of height and weight, American overweight adolescent girls have been shown to significantly underestimate their weight (which compromises the accuracy of many study findings based on self-reports) (Sherry et al. 2007). Studies of weight misperception among American adolescents found that an average of three out of 10 overweight adolescent girls and boys actually did not consider themselves overweight or obese (Edwards et al. 2010; Sarafrazi et al. 2014).

Fat is an important topic of daily conversation and the focus of competition in which girls who are judged to be too thin or too fat are excluded from certain social groups or even bullied. Over half of the teenagers participating in the Teen Lifestyle Project conducted by anthropologist Mimi Nichter (Nichter 2000) reported that they were dieting, with varying degrees of success. They attempted to lose weight primarily to improve their appearance and reduce social exclusion and stigmatization. Fat bias is common in the US and growing (naafa. org), even among persons with obesity (Latner et al. 2005; Schwartz et al. 2006; Puhl and Heuer 2009), and highly educated individuals (insiderhighered.com), including health care providers (Khandalavala et al. 2014; Phelan et al. 2015). According to some scholars, fat bias is even stronger than racism, ageism, and sexism and is meant to shame and motivate persons with obesity to lose weight (Moskovich et al. 2011). A recent Pew survey found that Americans view obesity as a national problem, but not so much among their friends and themselves as among others (Taylor 2006). Although only a few respondents admitted to being discriminated against or mistreated because of their weight, many women who participated in the survey underreported their body weight while men tended to exaggerate theirs.

Fat bias, discrimination, and stigmatization of people with obesity actually have the opposite of the desired and expected effect. Instead of motivating individuals to lose weight, negative attitudes and judgments by health care professionals often lead to mistrust and avoidance of medical care, and ultimately poorer health (Brewis 2014; Phelan et al. 2015). White women with obesity are less likely than women of normal weight to undergo medical screening procedures, possibly because of judgment by medical professionals and embarrassment (Maruthur et al. 2012). Stigmatization is stressful for those individuals who perceive themselves to be heavy, raising cortisol levels and stimulating eating and abdominal obesity (Himmelstein et al. 2015). Thus prejudice against individuals with obesity actually increases their potential to gain weight and promotes obesity (Jackson et al. 2015).

In response to fat bias and the pressures to conform to an ideal body image, many women with obesity attempt extreme diets which almost invariably fail. Eventually the lost weight is regained, and even more pounds are added (Field et al. 2007), a predictable result of increased metabolic efficiency.

In response to anti-fat bias, the current fat pride movement is gaining popularity in television shows and plays such as "Huge," "Girls," "The Mindy Project," and "Fat Pig." The fashion and clothing industry has discovered that the sale of large-sized clothing is very profitable; plus-size clothing fashions were featured in the New York Fashion Week for the very first time in 2013 (america.aljazeera.com). Pointing out that bias creates psychological and medical problems for its victims, the fat acceptance movement resists and rejects the narrow culturally and medically determined body size ideal for women, the prevailing fat phobia and repugnance for individuals with obesity, and the meaning of obesity as self-induced, voluntary, and individually controllable. However, obesity-related health risks are overlooked and even denied in the "fatosphere" with its justifiable emphasis on tolerance for body size variation (Rabin 2008).

Black women are reported to be less susceptible than white women to the dominant body size ideal (Faith et al. 1998; Fitzgibbon et al. 2000; SEF 2015) and more tolerant of individuals with obesity (Latner et al. 2005). Their criterion for evaluating others is not so much physical appearance as strong personality (Nichter 2000). While white girls talk endlessly about their body weight and even state that they would rather be divorced or die one year earlier than to be obese, most black girls are less anxious about being overweight and instead admire personality characteristics such as self-reliance and resourcefulness. Despite being on average heavier than white girls, they seem to have greater body satisfaction and higher self-esteem. They are also less likely to underreport their energy intake in daily food records than white girls (Kimm et al. 2006). Thinness is not always considered an attractive trait among many black women whose definition of beauty is based on internal characteristics such as personal style and positive attitude. It is the woman "who's got it going on" – the woman who has put her personal resources and attributes together in her own distinctive way – who is considered attractive. Dieting may be appropriate for someone who has extreme obesity but not for persons who are simply overweight, and many black girls consider it harmful to their health. Thinness is also associated among blacks with illnesses such as tuberculosis or AIDS (Kumanyika 2002) and is therefore to be avoided. Nevertheless, there is increasing variation in body satisfaction among black teenaged girls who live in middle-class neighborhoods and attend more affluent schools, where they participate in sports and other physical activities in part to achieve lean bodies (Muoio and Newgard 2014). The gradually emerging trend among some black women toward the dominant American ideal of slimness appears to have less connection to concerns about health risks than to the desire to be accepted in mainstream society (Franko et al. 2005). Still, in contrast to the inverse relationship between socioeconomic status and body size among white women, black women whose economic status improved over the life-course experienced greater weight gain than the less advantaged (Bennett et al. 2007).

Culture and food

Culture is actually a prescription for living that influences human thinking and behavior (Kottack 2007). Each society's dominant cultural program is instilled in its new members – children and immigrants – by social institutions that thoroughly train them in the language, customs, and traditions of the majority. Not wanting to be labeled deviant and risk marginalization, most Americans voice mainstream beliefs and values, even when their behaviors do not always conform to them. In each society culture channels the vast store of potential ideas and actions into narrower repertoires of acceptable ones. Americans have access to many edible items, for example, but culture determines what is suitable for eating and when and how to eat.

Food has many important meanings. In the US beef is symbolic of the strength and virility of Texas cowboys, and a sirloin steak dinner is the epitome of a prestigious meal, especially for men. For Hindus in India, on the other hand, cattle are sacred and not meant for human consumption. Americans do not eat the flesh of dogs and horses, but it is routinely consumed in a number of Asian and Eastern European countries. In the US, certain foods identify the cultures of various regions – Boston baked beans, southern soul food, TexMex burritos, mid-western corn flakes, and California avocados. For Native Americans foods have important social and spiritual significance. Elderly Pima and Papago women consider the loss of knowledge about wild desert foods and medicinal plants among their young people as an abandonment of their very cultural heritage (Nabhan 2002). Anthropologist Sidney Mintz (Mintz 1996) asserts that the ability to consume prestige foods once reserved for elites symbolizes a degree of power and freedom for the man on the street, a particularly strong cultural principle in a democratic society.

Humans everywhere have the natural urge to maximize benefits with minimal effort, but culture provides the sanctioned means and also the limits for doing so in each society. Just as brain structure and physiology direct the body's metabolic processes, so do the shared cultural maps stored in human minds guide consumption and activity behaviors and ultimately body weight and health. A consideration of the food-related cultural beliefs and practices of China helps to show by example how shared ideas influence humans everywhere.

The traditional greeting in southern China is, "Have you eaten yet?" (Sun 2005). It is an ancient greeting still used today, which literally means, "Have you eaten enough to be full and satisfied?" Adequate food is of great concern for the peoples of China, and their greatest cultural preoccupation is with the amount of available food. Agriculture has been the foundation of the Chinese economy for thousands of years, and even today the majority of Chinese are rural farmers. The collective memory of droughts, crop failures, and periods of widespread famines is vivid, starvation never having stopped being a dominant concern. An old Chinese saying asserts that "a farmer's life depends on God," signifying human inability to control the supply of food and life itself.

The Chinese have developed sophisticated regional *cuisines* based on cereal grains – rice mostly in the south and wheat in the north (Du et al. 2002). The visual impact of the foods served, harmonious flavors, and a yin-yang balanced diet (Jing 2000) are emphasized, but the balance is not derived from the macro- and micronutrients familiar to westerners, but rather from the hot, cold, temperate, or cool nature of individual foods (cultural designations that have nothing to do with temperature) and their salty, sour, sweet, bitter, or acrid flavors. Traditional Chinese cuisines consist largely of grains and vegetables, with sugar, meat, or fat usually served only on festive occasions. The typical Chinese diet is low in energy density and high in complex carbohydrates and dietary fiber, which is considered by nutrition scientists to be a healthy diet. What is offered as Chinese food in the US is actually rich, luxury food once reserved for Chinese elites. General Tso's Chicken, honoring an important historical military leader, was eaten only by emperors of the Qing Dynasty. Ice cream, in its original form of frozen rice pudding, was prepared exclusively for consumption by the empress and carried to the palace in blocks of ice.

Food beliefs are deep-seated and influence human perceptions and behaviors. Certain foods, preparation techniques, and taste preferences shared by a group of people constitute their cuisine (Bryant et al. 2003). The Chinese staple rice is a very demanding crop, requiring just the right amount of irrigation water for ample yields. When a rice crop fails, fallback foods such as sweet potatoes are consumed, either alone or mixed with small amounts of rice. But although they also provide plenty of energy and important micronutrients, a Chinese diner believes that such foods do not "last" and are not satisfying. Without rice at meals, one is still hungry no matter how much other food has been consumed.

Unlike most other societies whose distinctive food prohibitions and preferences mark their *ethnic identity* that sets them apart from other groups, the US (arguably) lacks a single national cuisine (Pillsbury 1998; Counihan 2002; Gabaccia 2002; Mintz 2002a; Bryant et al. 2003; Baker and Friel 2014). Hui Chinese and Orthodox Jews abstain from pork; Hopi Indians consume maize in a specified harmonious and balanced way because of its social and spiritual value representing purity and strength. Nearly every society reserves certain foods for special or ritual occasions. But the American cuisine is not marked by any single food or food-related practice. Regional specialties are available all over the country, fresh fruits and vegetables are available no matter the season, luxury foods once reserved for elites and special occasions are served daily everywhere, and most foods are assimilated Americanized versions of items originating elsewhere in the world. Food innovations, blending of foods of distinctly different ethnic origins, continually changing food trends, and conflicting dietary recommendations prevail. If anything characterizes the American menu, it appears to be mass-produced foods, value meals, and convenience items offering economic advantages and time savings. Thus, without cultural constraints Americans consume whatever individual tastes dictate in any combination and order. Without apparent cultural or social brakes, despite the emphasis on slimness, the evolutionary imperative to consume the fats, sugars, and salts that humans are predisposed to prefer drives American appetites. Instead of a common traditional cuisine, Americans emphasize individualized tastes and preferences, even when sharing a common meal within the family setting.

The Thanksgiving feast comes closest to a distinctive American meal, but of course its components are of various national origins. Coca-Cola may be the only distinctively American drink product and common American consumer experience. During World War II, this entirely non-nutritious, high-calorie beverage symbolized America and was distributed freely to GIs to boost their morale and energy (Weiner 2002). Zahi Khouri, a Palestinian-American, established a Coca-Cola franchise in the West Bank and Gaza, not only as a business venture but also as "a miniature ambassador from America" (Khouri 2006). Coca-Cola's major competitor, Pepsi, increased its sales volume through a large marketing effort targeting blacks to convince them that Pepsi was the more ethnically appropriate beverage (Capparell 2007). The company opened integrated military canteens that served Pepsi in competition with the segregated Army's service of Coke, thus echoing the trend in American civil rights.

The proper response to the traditional Chinese greeting is "Yes, I'm doing fine." Occasionally the reluctant response is, "No, I'm hungry," and then the greeter is obligated to provide food. However, Chinese people are very reluctant to admit that they are hungry, for hunger signals poverty and failure, as does thinness. Plump women with round hips are much admired, since they symbolize family wealth and leisure, while poor farmers' wives, who labor long hours in homes and fields, do not have the luxury of storing excess calories and becoming noticeably plump. Thus, in China as everywhere else in the world, food not only nourishes the body but also serves as a powerful cultural symbol. The various combinations of food, particularly rice and wheat, the foods produced from them, and the foods that accompany them are closely linked with specific Chinese ethnic groups. The quality of food is indicative of social class, with the wealthiest Chinese having access to the richest and rarest items and the greatest quantity of food, symbolizing triumph over the forces of nature, agricultural success, and a man's ability to provide for his family.

Hui Chinese, the Muslims of the ancient city of Xi'an, are forbidden to eat pork or lard, and do not eat foods prepared by ethnic majority Han Chinese because these are thought to have been exposed to pork products (Gillette 2005). The pork taboo is a well-known Islamic tradition everywhere, but for the Muslims of Xi'an this tradition is also an important marker of ethnic distinction. Sharing food is a ubiquitous hospitable act in China, but Hui Chinese practice it only among themselves and not with their Han neighbors. Even a Han Chinese offer of a cup of tea is refused because it is thought that no amount of dishwashing can remove the traces of pork the cup has contacted in the past.

Not all cultural beliefs and practices are adaptive; they may have been imposed by powerful authorities. Traditional values and behaviors that were once beneficial may have acquired negative consequences in a new setting. Even within cultures there are inconsistencies. Quite often values and beliefs contradict one another and do not fit neatly into a coherent system. Although Americans admire individuals who control their food intake, exercise vigorously, and remain slim, excessive consumption is promoted (Guthman 2011) and recreational eating is an important function at many public events (Samavati 2004). Competitive eating is the "fastest growing sport" in the US (Fagone 2006). The mother of all events, Nathan's Famous Fourth of July International Hot Dog Eating Contest, is sponsored by the International Federation of Competitive Eating, whose motto is *in voro veritas* ("in gorging, truth"). Until recently, the world champion gurgitator was Japanese Takeru Kobayashi, who consumed 54 hot dogs in 12 minutes in the 2006 contest at Nathan's Hot Dog Stand in Coney Island (Figure 6.1). He was defeated in 2007 by American Joey Chestnut, who ate 66 hot dogs in 12 minutes, while Kobayashi downed only 63 and then regurgitated (McShane 2007). Chestnut has been a regular winner of the $40,000 prize since then (nathansfamous.com).

Competitive eating has grown since its 1916 origin at Nathan's to hundreds of contests all over the country, some of which are broadcast live on ESPN and

FIGURE 6.1 Nathan's July 4th hot dog eating contest. Courtesy of dj0ser via Flickr (CC BY 2.0).

CNN. College student Kate Stelnick, who weighs only 100 pounds, met the challenge of Denny's Beer Barrel Pub by consuming a 6-pound hamburger with 5 pounds of fixings (onion, tomato, cheese, ketchup, mayonnaise, buns) in 2 hours and 54 minutes (AP 2005). The World Grilled Cheese Eating Championship in Venice Beach, Florida is a tribute to the Virgin Mary, who appeared on a grilled-cheese sandwich. Female Nathan's hot dog eating champion (40 hot dogs and buns in 2011), "Black Widow" Sonya Thomas, at five foot five inches and 103 pounds, put away 25 grilled-cheese sandwiches in 10 minutes, to defeat such competitors as 400-pound Ed "Cookie" Jarvis and 420-pound Eric "Badlands" Booker and win the prize of $3,500. The contest announcer referred to competitive eating as "the battleground upon which God and Lucifer battle for men's souls." Here is a clear example of a cultural contradiction – veneration of obesity and gluttony in the name of competitive sport versus religious asceticism, which usually values abstention and self-sacrifice.

Immigrants and dietary change

Imagine a recent immigrant from China confronted with the great abundance of inexpensive, tasty, high-energy foods available in America, including the prestige foods reserved in China for elites. Starvation is a distant memory here, and work usually requires much less physical effort. There is plenty of time for relaxation and social gatherings, and wives and daughters can finally acquire the highly preferred rounded look. Many immigrants come to the US from regions of the world that have experienced chronic food shortages, periodic droughts, severe famines, and unequal distribution of food supplies. Unlike Europeans and their descendants who faced only brief and rare food insufficiencies throughout most of their history – albeit some serious ones like the Irish potato famine – the populations of the developing world suffered many occasions of hunger and continue to do so today (Diamond 1997). Under such precarious conditions, they were partially protected from starvation by the evolution of their especially thrifty metabolic systems. With astonishing rapidity, sometimes within just one or two generations, some immigrant groups experience dramatic increases in obesity levels in the US, where food is always readily available, where manual labor and other forms of physical exertion are generally disparaged and often actually unnecessary, and where they are subjected to the psychological stresses of acculturation and assimilation. Their biological heritage and the modern American cultural environment combine to produce obesity, cardiovascular disease, and diabetes.

Immigrants come to the US to make a better life for themselves and their families, to escape wars, oppression, hunger, poverty, and exhausting labor, to find peace and opportunity, and to improve their standard of living – in short, to seek the American Dream. Although cultural traditions and symbols are deeply ingrained, and most immigrants try to maintain familiar habits and customs, they eventually adopt the patterns of work, education, land and home ownership, and other forms of consumption that characterize American culture. At first they cling to their traditional lifestyles and food ways as symbols of ethnic identity and the collective memory of the homeland. But they eventually become Americanized, as did the Hispanic immigrants in Brownsville, Texas, who were accustomed to walking to stores, but had to start driving to their destinations when they felt conspicuous and worried about being perceived as illegal aliens (Tavernise 2013). Meat consumption was and still is one important way immigrants can distance themselves from the poverty and hunger they escaped when they came to America (Sheumaker and Wajda 2008). Coming from regions of the world where meat was a rare treat or even completely absent from the daily diet, its ready availability in the US is a distinct improvement in living standards.

Traditional cuisines, the results of many generations' efforts to provide a variety of nutritional foods in environments of scarcity, sooner or later break down in the US due to the inability to obtain original ingredients, use traditional cooking techniques, and celebrate original customs and occasions marked by special foods. Immigrants are generally eager to become *bona fide* citizens of their adopted country. Foreign-born immigrants do consume more fruits and vegetables and have a lower risk of becoming obese than their U.S.-born offspring and grandchildren (Bennett et al. 2007; Stimpson and Urrutia-Rojas 2007). However, study after study has shown that second and third American-born generations invariably fully adopt local consumption and activity patterns, and just as invariably achieve local rates of obesity (Goel et al. 2004).

Second-generation Asian-American and Latino adolescents are more than twice as likely as their first-generation parents to become obese (Popkin and Udry 1998; Samavati 2004). They are more acculturated than their parents, speaking English as their first language and readily adopting American lifestyles as their own. According to the third comprehensive National Health and Nutrition Examination Survey (NHANES III), Mexican-Americans born in the US had larger waist circumferences than Mexican-Americans who had been born in Mexico (Sundquist and Winkleby 2000). The more acculturated, English-speaking adults consumed more dietary fat, had greater abdominal obesity (U.S.-born women had an average waist circumference more than 6 cm greater than Mexican-born women), and were at greater risk for heart disease, diabetes and other obesity-related conditions. Mexican-American mothers born in the US were twice as likely to have overweight children compared with Mexican-American women born in Mexico (Hernandez-Valero et al. 2007). Mexican-American children have some of the highest childhood obesity levels in the US and are particularly likely to develop diabetes (Weil 2005). Latino cultural values include protectiveness toward female children, so girls spend much time in sedentary, indoor activities. A belief that overweight is healthy is also prominent among Latinos (Diaz et al. 2007). A recent study (Olvera et al. 2005) found that, although 34 percent of acculturated Latino girls were at risk for overweight, mothers viewed their daughters' body size as ideal. Mexican-American parents may have escaped the poverty and hunger of their home country, but the memory of those deprivations often prompts them to over-compensate their children with rich food and other indulgences.

While culture change coincides with increased obesity in the immigrant population, in an odd twist it also coincides with changed perceptions of body image and definitions of obesity (Himes and Thompson 2007). More acculturated Latino children identify thinner figures as more attractive than their less acculturated counterparts.

Culture change and obesity

Obesity was once thought to be a *culture-bound syndrome* limited to wealthy industrialized countries, particularly the US (Ritenbaugh 1982; Brown and Bentley-Condit 1998). But the epidemic has now gone global, appearing even in the poorer, less developed countries of the world (Drewnowski and Popkin 1997; James 2002; Popkin 2002; Popkin and Gordon-Larsen 2004; Mendez et al. 2005; Popkin 2006) where hunger and under-nutrition predominated only a generation ago. Today more of the world's people are overweight or have obesity (1.3 billion) than are underweight (800 million) (Popkin 2007), and obesity is everywhere associated with the same health risks as in developed nations – diabetes, cardiovascular disease, cancers, osteoarthritis, and more. The prevalence of Type 2 diabetes has tripled in developing nations undergoing rapid modernization and subsequent increases in obesity rates (Hossain et al. 2007). Nearly one-third of all Chinese suffer from hypertension, and one-seventh of all Mexicans have diabetes (Popkin 2007). American-Indians, Pacific Islanders, Australian Aborigines, migrant Asian-Indians, and Mexican-Americans are especially severely affected (Zimmet et al. 1997).

Economic globalization has brought great cultural changes to the many indigenous societies that adopt western cultural features to claim their place in the modern world. The introduction of western material goods, entertainment media, foods, and lifestyles into developing countries has been called the "coca-colonization" of the world (Zimmet and Alberti 2006) (Figure 6.2). It has caused a dramatic convergence of the world's dietary patterns, with the loss of much richly varied uniqueness and distinctiveness, not to mention local agricultural traditions and indigenous crops (Shiva 2001), fostering dependence on imported, mass-produced, western foods. Accompanying the imported material goods are the ideas and values of the west, distributed through media and high-tech information transmission, commerce, markets and advertising, cultural and student exchanges, and tourism and international travel.

The American drive for affluence and innovation is shared by much of the world, and one consequence is a global *nutrition transition*. Everywhere rural life and traditional agricultural pursuits were abandoned for more rewarding work in urban centers and for direct participation in cash economies, necessitating the purchase of imported, industrialized, processed foods. While consumption of healthy foods improved somewhat across the globe, unhealthy food consumption and diet quality worsened as well in both middle- and low-income countries (Baker and Friel 2014; Mayen et al. 2014; Imamura et al. 2015). High-income countries experienced the greatest extremes in these developments, having the most healthy

FIGURE 6.2 Coca-colonization. Courtesy of the author (taken in UAE, 1991).

(fiber, complex carbohydrates, fruits and vegetables) but also the most unhealthy (high-calorie, sugar, fat) dietary consumption. Before World War II, few of the 17,000 citizens of the Micronesian state of Pohnpei had obesity and none had diabetes (Ward 2005). But in the few decades after the war, rates of obesity, high blood pressure, cardiovascular disease, and diabetes shot up. Pohnpei was under U.S. military occupation and had imported American foods and other products. The Nauruans (see Chapter 1) became wealthy from the export of phosphate fertilizer extracted from bird droppings that virtually covered the island, enabling them to import western foods and technology. While tourists to Middle Eastern countries seek out restaurants serving the famous traditional Mediterranean diet, Lebanese, Greeks, Spaniards, and Italians prefer richer fare and abandon the once iconic healthy diet because it is associated with post-war poverty (Alexandratos 2006; Ciezadlo 2011; de Lago 2011). An American in Beijing offers very popular cooking and baking classes to Chinese women, who are learning to make novel dishes such as pizza and cheesecake from American ingredients offered in stores that carry imported products (Vasquez 2007). Excessive energy consumption and physical inactivity are no longer confined to North America and Europe.

Adult obesity rates have more than doubled in China since 1991 (Reynolds et al. 2007), especially among high-income, urban adults. Nearly 22 percent of Chinese are overweight or have obesity, with concomitant increases in hypertension, cardiovascular disease, and diabetes (Wang et al. 2007). More than 240 million Chinese (9.7 percent of the population) have diabetes or pre-diabetes (Yang et al. 2010). Increased family income has enabled many Chinese to afford high-fat, sweetened foods and to eat out in restaurants more often. Young Chinese are eager to assume their roles as consumers in the emerging modern economy of China. For the first time, Chinese children have pocket money for their own independent purchases, which the western and western-style Chinese restaurants exploit through advertisements targeting children. Hundreds of McDonalds and KFCs have sprung up in Beijing and other large Chinese cities since the 1980s (Watson 2002). They are considered very fashionable, expensive public symbols of consumerism and attract a large clientele. Although fast food and soft drinks are still a very small proportion of children's diets in China compared to the US, where fast food provides about 20 percent of food energy, children's eating patterns in many developing countries including China are beginning to resemble those of American children (Adair and Popkin 2005).

In the 1990s the Chinese nutrition transition from diets dominated by grains and vegetables high in fiber to more westernized ones including large amounts of protein, fats, and simple carbohydrates accompanied the country's rapid development and increased personal incomes (Du et al. 2002). Chinese versions of American processed foods are available in the new large urban supermarkets (Santora 2006) and are adopted by Chinese consumers. Eighty-eight percent of Chinese now own TVs; vigorous physical activity has declined for all but rural populations still involved in manual labor and for those who ride bicycles or walk for transportation in urban areas. From 1980 to 2003 the number of cars sold to mostly urban Chinese customers quadrupled.

Overweight and obesity among school children have risen from 2 percent to 17 percent and 10 percent in boys and girls respectively. Obesity-related diseases are now more common than under-nutrition and starvation. Urban mortality rates related to diabetes have increased five-fold since 1972. Weight loss clinics have sprung up in city after city, and children are sent to summer boot camps to work off their excess weight (Rosenthal 1999; Johnson 2002; Rosenthal 2002). For the first time, dieting is a common practice among Chinese women, and thinness has become a (westernized) female beauty ideal, ironically at the very time that Americans seem to have increased their weight norms and lowered social pressures to lose weight (Burke and Heiland 2007). A national survey found that the average desired weight for an American woman shifted upwards from 132 pounds in 1994 to 135 pounds in 2002, while the average actual weight had increased from 147 to 153 pounds. Another survey noted that the majority of American men and women, including nearly half of those whom had obesity, believed that their body weights were socially acceptable (Rand and Resnick 2000).

The global economy has also had a dramatic effect on the dietary practices of the Muslim Hui of Xi'an (Gillette 2005). "Foreign" foods such as packaged snacks, candy, and Coca-Cola, at first imported but now produced locally in Chinese factories, are widely available in the markets of Xi'an. Children clamor for them, and grandparents purchase them as treats for the little ones. Since these mass-produced items are not made by human hands, the Hui see them as "clean" and "pure" and therefore not on the list of forbidden foods. Their elders consider them to have a strange taste and tend to avoid them, but children consume most of these treats, with predictable consequences. The good news is that these ritually neutral foods have enabled Hui and Han to overcome a few social barriers and eat together.

Unlike China, where obesity rates increased rapidly with globalization and higher personal incomes, rising obesity rates actually followed increasing poverty among Native Americans. Not only did they lose their lands to European settlers, but they were encouraged by Christian missionaries and Anglo educators to abandon their "primitive" food systems based on farming and foraging and to reject their "pagan" rituals and cultural patterns associated with food production. The religions of farming groups such as the Pima of Arizona had focused on the annual agricultural cycle and the need for rain to support their crops (Gladwell 2000). Their traditional foods had great social and spiritual value, and their annual round of ceremonies had served as their cultural identity, distinguishing them from tribes such as the nearby Apache whose subsistence was based largely on hunting. Nutritional experiments among the Pima comparing the health effects of traditional dietary items with those of western foods (Nabhan 2002; Nabhan 2008) leave little doubt that despite their genetic predisposition to diabetes, these indigenous peoples were protected from the disease by the mesquite cakes, corn hominy, and acorn and venison stews of their ancient but now mostly lost food traditions. Today their diabetes rates top those of all other Native Americans. Many wild desert foods contain large amounts of soluble fibers and polysaccharide gums that slow the digestion and absorption of nutrients and prevent the glucose spikes associated with western energy-rich, fiber-poor foods. The potatoes, bread, and processed cereals of their acculturated diets produced insulin insensitivity. It is not only the caloric value of food that has changed with acculturation but also, and perhaps more importantly, the composition of the foods that once protected against *diseases of civilization.*

Today few Native Americans can recall their tribes' ancient food habits, and even fewer still know where to find and how to grow, harvest, and prepare the traditional food items. Recognizing that these foods not only promote health but also symbolize the richness of their ancient heritage and adaptive traditions, some tribes are working to make them part of the everyday life of their people again. The Tohono O'odham Community Action (TOCA), a Papago grassroots organization which "strives to create effective, culturally based responses to the problems of our community," (Lopez et al. 2002) has initiated a program of desert farming and foraging that calls upon the elders to share their knowledge and skills to revive ancient food systems, develop ways to produce and distribute traditional foods throughout the community, and restore some aspects of their ancient culture.

However, traditional foods do not always promote nutritional health. Fry-bread made of flour, sugar, and lard and deep-fried in fat is considered to be the pan-Indian "traditional" food, but is actually a historic remnant of the days when U.S.

government commodities were distributed to impoverished native communities. Its nutritional value is a far cry from Hopi piki, Muscogee sofkee, cornbread and tamales, and other corn-based breads of long ago (Harjo 2005). Like fry-bread, "soul food" is of great ethnic importance to black people in the US (Hughes 1997). A black woman's role as nurturer is of central significance in her family, and her ability to prepare traditional dishes ensures her reputation in a society that values the sharing of food. On the other hand, black leaders, anxious to prevent obesity in school children, urge the substitution of baked chicken and steamed broccoli for southern fried chicken, fried chitterlings, corn pone, and collards cooked in lard, all very heavily salted according to southern tastes. But these foods represent historic survival for one of the poorest regions in the US. And significantly, they are symbolic of the dietary distinctions between southern slaves and their white owners and oppressors who consumed "plantation foods," the very types of foods now promoted by public health professionals. Efforts to change these traditional menus have met with considerable resistance (Jonsson 2006).

It is no small irony that the spread of western economic culture and activities has also led to the increased popularity of the western ideal of slimness for female beauty (Brewis et al. 2011). Mauritanian women, traditionally force-fed in childhood to become plump brides and advertise their family's affluence, are now resisting this practice which causes serious health problems later in life. For the first time young women are watching their weight and even dieting to avoid becoming fat (Soares 2006). High school girls in Fiji, a nation known to appreciate large meals and large bodies, now want to look thin like American TV stars (Becker et al. 2005). Curves, the popular American women's fitness establishment, has opened outlets in Ecuador (Phillips 2006). Greek women no longer aspire to the Aphrodite image and are dieting to achieve the look of the "next supermodel" (Davenport 2002). Rwandan beauty queens are tall and slim (Moore 2008), but the 1994 genocide has made Rwandans rethink their European-based standards of female beauty and consider a possible return to the more traditional African woman's body shape as their ideal.

Human genetics and physiology have not changed during the last 100 years, but recent cultural changes around the globe have created novel environments which impact, among other things, nutrition and physical activity, and contribute to the rise in obesity rates. These modern ideas, which contrast rather sharply with local traditions, are easy to spot in developing countries undergoing rapid modernization. But in the US, where modernization and the nutrition transition began many decades ago and proceeded more gradually, they are less obvious. It is necessary to take a closer look at fundamental American cultural values, which, combined with the enormous social and technological changes of the last century, have contributed to the recent upsurge in obesity in the US and have been exported to the rest of the world. Interacting with universal human biology geared to conserving and storing energy, unique American cultural features have driven obesity rates to unusually high levels. Three closely linked core cultural values – *corporatism, consumerism*, and *individualism* – influence American society and help to account for the magnitude of the U.S. obesity epidemic. These values are the foundation of individual and social choices and political-economic forces that promote excessive energy consumption and deficient energy expenditure among citizens of the US.

Corporatism: the priority of profits

With the rise of capitalism and the commercial middle class in Renaissance Europe, western political history took a dramatic turn. The growing wealth of entrepreneurs and merchants undermined the power of monarchs and aristo-crats and nourished notions of freedom and democracy. Eventually members of European commercial classes broke free of monarchical control, overcame the old political limits on their growth and power, and established themselves as equals and even superiors to the nobility. These great economic and political changes spilled over into the American colonies, which firmly rejected rule by monarchy and rebelled against colonial domination of their governments and economies. Democracy and freedom from colonial rule were closely linked to independent economic development and industrialism in the US (Bodley 2005). The delicate balance between capitalism's primary emphasis on profits and the general welfare of a democratic society gradually and inexorably tipped in favor of America's large corporations and businesses, which now have great influence over government policies, including those designed to safeguard the health and welfare of American citizens (Reich 2007).

The sugar industry was one of the earliest to develop under the capitalist system (Mintz 1993). Sugar, imported from Caribbean islands, once served as a medicine and spice, a luxury fit only for the wealthy in England and France. Elaborate crys-talline desserts made of sugar were served at royal feasts. With the development of the African slave trade and Caribbean plantations (Williams 1961), the cost of sugar production declined. It was sold widely throughout European countries to sweeten the bitter tea, coffee, and chocolate that were also produced on tropical planta-tions by slaves and introduced into the general European market. Sugar production spurred spin-off industries such as the building of casks to transport raw sugar to English refineries, and mining of coal to fuel their furnaces, thus stimulating fur-ther industrial development in England. Sugar became an inexpensive commodity and a high-energy dietary staple for poor European industrial workers to fuel their heavy industrial labor. It also became a democratic symbol for the general public's improved standard of living by emulating elite lifestyles.

In recent years, when international public health officials expressed concern about the health effects of increasing consumption of sugared products around the globe, sugar producers and governments of sugar-exporting countries voiced strong opposi-tion to any effort that would limit their profit margins. Consumption in the form of sweetened beverages such as sodas and fruit drinks continued to increase among all U.S. age groups surveyed in two successive NHANES studies (Figure 6.3).

Large political contributions by the sugar industry were rewarded with subsidies that increased industry profits (Ford 2004). During a recent reconsideration of

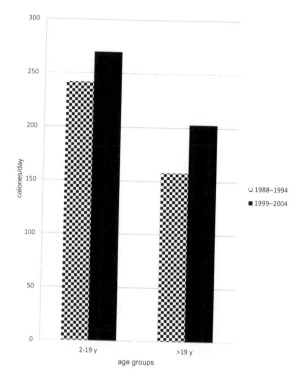

FIGURE 6.3 Sugar-sweetened beverage consumption in the US.

Adapted from Bleich et al. (2009); Wang et al. (2008).

the farm subsidy bill by the U.S. Congress, the sugar industry lobby made nearly 1,000 separate contributions totaling more than $1 million to political candidates, parties, and funds (Morgan 2007). Despite numerous public health concerns about sugar in breakfast cereals and many other foods consumed by American children, the powerful sugar lobby has been able to prevent the development of guidelines and limitations on sugar content by government agencies such as the Federal Trade Commission (Bittman 2011a; Moss 2013). Even nonprofit organizations such as the respected Save the Children, which had been a leader in soda tax campaigns in several U.S. states and cities, abandoned the efforts to discourage excessive sweetened soda consumption when it applied for a large grant from Coca-Cola (Neuman 2010). It had already received funding from the Pepsico Foundation before beginning the soda tax campaign.

The American obesity epidemic is a byproduct of corporate profit-making. Corporations and businesses involved in the production and distribution of food, labor-saving technology, and entertainment – all products that help to promote obesity – are among the largest industries in the US. The powerful, multi-billion dollar *productionist food system* (Lapp and Hansen 2007) emphasizes industrial production of generally inexpensive, low-quality foods in copious quantities, primarily for the purpose of mass distribution and large profits. While the profit margins of farmers who grow corn are relatively low, for example, the combined earnings of the productionist food system, which includes companies that design, process, package, and market the many food items made from corn, are quite substantial.

Since 1940, American consumption of protein, fats, carbohydrates, and calories has increased by 16 percent; sugar and corn syrup consumption has increased by 40 percent. The annual per capita intake of food has increased by 140 pounds (Bryant et al. 2003). Since 1970 increased consumption of soft drinks alone raised the intake of sweeteners by 30 percent, and total calories by 500 per day (Johnson et al. 2007). Today Americans have available an additional 275 pounds of food per person annually compared to 1970 (Farah and Buzby 2008). Attractive packaging, large plates, and generous portions promote "mindless eating" and excessive consumption above and beyond what is actually needed for survival (Wansink 2006).

In a market that is already thoroughly saturated, food producers and distributors compete fiercely for consumer dollars, aggressively marketing their products to convince consumers that they need and want high-calorie, low-nutrient items (Brownell and Horgen 2004; Nestle 2006) by constantly developing new food products in attractive packaging, keeping prices low, and placing products and advertisements where potential consumers can easily see them (Zimmerman 2011). The goal of these profitable marketing strategies such as large, open candy displays at checkout counters where customers wait for service exploit human impulses to consume (Cohen and Babey 2012).

Food engineering to develop the variety of items attractive to consumers removes many important nutrients (fiber, vitamins, minerals) and adds salt, sugar, and fat to improve their taste and mouth-feel (Moss 2013). American food producers capitalize on the deep-seated human preference for these high-calorie nutrients, creating cravings for more. After careful experimental research to identify the "bliss point"– the exact amount of caloric sweetener that gives a product the most attractive taste – sugar is added to many items, even to foods that are not sweet. The pleasing crunch of breakfast cereals is due to added sugar, even to those that are not actually listed as sweetened. Many sweetened breakfast cereals marketed especially to children are promoted very much like desserts; some, such as Rice Krispies Treats, are even converted from breakfast cereal to snack. Salt and fat give potato chips the irresistible flavor that makes it impossible to "eat just one." The exact balance between familiar and novel tastes of citrus, brown spices, and other secret ingredients plus the tingle of carbon dioxide gas gives Coca-Cola its unique flavor. Virtually all processed foods contain many non-nutritious ingredients, added for the sole purpose of increasing sales and consumption. Ingredients are manipulated to make the products addictive and obesogenic (Volkow et al. 2013). Macronutrients in some processed foods are deliberately skewed to constitute a low protein-to-carbohydrate ratio. The aim is to encourage greater consumption to obtain adequate protein, with the effect of promoting excessive intake of fattening items (Simpson and Raubenheimer 2014).

Not only do food corporations promote non-nutritious foods as sources of pleasure and enjoyment, they also do a very brisk business in *functional foods* such as sports drinks, energy bars, and juice drinks that claim to be heart-healthy, low-carb, or vitamin-fortified (de Jong et al. 2007). They profit greatly from ever-changing diet fads by designing new food products that boost levels of "scientifically-proven, health-promoting, obesity-preventing" nutrients – everything from high-fiber and high-protein to low-fat and low-carb items (Pollan 2008). High-fructose corn syrup, the inexpensive sugar substitute whose ubiquitous presence has contributed to the obesity epidemic, is manufactured from corn. So is Z Trim, a new product touted to help reduce obesity (ztrim.com) as a high-fiber food supplement or as a fat substitute in recipes. Although it is "U.S. Department of Agriculture (USDA) developed" and promises to be the "first and only all natural solution to weight management that does not require dieting, exercising or giving up delicious foods to achieve success," its advertisement does not explain how the effects of Z Trim differ from those of previously marketed low-fat or fat-free ineffective diet products so popular with American consumers. Food producers claim to be meeting consumer demand, but their marketing techniques are actually designed to create a demand and to persuade the public that their products meet the desire to improve their standard of living – "Live Life Better," as Z Trim advertising asserts (Z TRIM Holdings 2007).

The productionist food system does not promote fresh produce and other foods that require little or no modification to add economic value. The "produce food system" does not engage in mass marketing of fresh fruits and vegetables or organically grown foods. Neither does it enjoy substantial government subsidies and USDA underwriting. The USDA spends only $1.51 per person to promote fruits and vegetables, while the food productionist system spends 50 times as much to advertise obesogenic food products (Zimmerman 2011). It is a testimony to the great power of corporate advertising and marketing that many consumers show little interest in nutritious fresh produce which lacks the commercial sponsorship, promotions, and exposure in TV ads that make processed foods so attractive to consumers.

Because it supports a large workforce and provides a strong tax base, the U.S. productionist food system enjoys the support of the U.S. government (Sutherly 2007), which allowed it to prioritize corporate profits over public health. Government health officials have called for regulation of food advertising and changes in agricultural policies, but with little success (PCP 2007). Producers are permitted to include questionable health claims on food packaging and take legal action against smaller companies attempting to produce healthier products (Nestle 2006). Efforts of some branches of the federal government to promote scientifically based nutrition education in their development of nutritional guidelines (see MyPlate, Figure 6.4) and to preserve food freshness and safety have been compromised by political pressures from government agencies and food producers like the dairy and red-meat industries (Nestle 2002; Nestle 2003; Pollan 2008).

Although current nutrition science promotes awareness of the health risks associated with overconsumption of red meats, saturated animal fats, sugars, and

FIGURE 6.4   MyPlate. Courtesy of Basheera Designs via Shutterstock.com.

other simple carbohydrates, governmental dietary advice strongly emphasizes individual responsibility for good nutrition and exercise (Simon 2006). Thus it diverts attention from the significant role of the food industry and sidesteps the need for serious changes in food production and marketing policies to improve public health.

The federal government has a paradoxical relationship with its citizens. Increasing obesity rates are a sign of its half-hearted willingness to protect the public from the negative effects of unbridled corporatism and commodification of energy-dense food products. The USDA actually implements conflicting policies; on one hand it supports the agriculture industry and its profits, while on the other it attempts to encourage and educate the public about good nutrition. While the U.S. Centers for Disease Control and Prevention warn that only one of seven Americans eats enough fruits and vegetables and exercises enough for good health (Kruger et al. 2007; Cawley and Kirwan 2011), federal agricultural subsidies favor wheat, rice, corn, and sugar producers over fruit and vegetable growers. Fresh produce has to be imported from South American and Asian countries to meet the local demand, while a high-saturated-fat, high-sugar, low-fiber, industrialized diet is backed by government (Birnbaum 2007; Pollan 2008; Bittman 2011b). State legislatures also support the productionist food industry with laws preventing local governments from restricting toy giveaways with children's fast-food meals (Arizona) and limiting local controls over restaurant calorie and fat content labeling (Ohio). These legislatures were pressured by restaurant associations to include the prohibitions in budget bills and other broad state laws (Strom 2011).

Commercial interests even exploit American humanitarian impulses to promote the sale of cookies and candy bars by children for scouting, school projects, and athletic programs, an irresistible marketing strategy guaranteed to increase profit margins. Food industries collaborate with others to integrate snack food sales into a large variety of other businesses. High-calorie foods are available throughout the entire day, present at sporting events, in churches, schools, and workplaces. Large malls combine shopping with convenient eating and entertainment venues only a short distance from parking facilities to minimize the need for walking (Gottdiener 2001). Discount stores, book stores, hobby shops, drug stores, gas stations, fabric stores, and many, many others offer an array of candy and other snack items, often in strategic locations near checkout counters to tempt waiting customers. The ubiquity of food appeals to those who are food insecure and promotes a perception of affluence in a nation that still remembers food scarcity during times of slavery, war, and economic disaster. Starvation is forever abolished in the United States of America, but malnutrition still threatens American public health.

It is fair to say that the American food environment is shaped by the productionist food system, the second-largest advertiser after the U.S. auto industry and the source of half of all TV ads (Vandewater and Wartella 2011). To satisfy the American love of bargains, stores offer "family-size" deals. Less nutritious food items are deliberately priced low to sell in large amounts. Sweetened soft drinks, heavily advertised in the media, have become the most popular beverage in the US (Wolf et al. 2007). To counter a recent small decline in soda consumption, Coca-Cola and Pepsi introduced vitamin- and mineral-fortified colas, promoted as healthy sparkling beverages (Martin 2007a). When its profits and stock values declined several years ago, McDonald's introduced the Dollar Menu of very inexpensive cheeseburgers – much cheaper than McDonald's salad and fruit offerings whose sales subsequently dropped (Warner 2006). The Dollar Menu attracted young customers, especially blacks and Latinos, and revived McDonald's revenue stream.

Marketing to children is especially effective (McDermott et al. 2005; Connor 2006), and children have become the primary targets of food and beverage marketing in the US (IOM 2006). Advertisers spend $10 billion annually on commercials for sugared cereal, soft drinks, candy, salty snacks, and other items (Gantz et al. 2007; Powell et al. 2007; Vandewater and Wartella 2011), using familiar cartoon characters and brand mascots to influence children's food preferences (Kraak and Story 2015). Many fast-food restaurants also use marketing specifically directed to children by displaying kids' meals and toys in their ads (Ohri-Vachaspati et al. 2015). American children influence more than $200 billion in spending annually, so selling food products to them is big business. Using themes of fun and fantasy, TV food advertisements have been enormously successful in guiding children's requests for and beliefs about foods. Some children's advertising even advocates defiance of parental authority; for instance, cartoon and hero figures associated with sweetened cereals ridicule adult food choices (Green 2007). Children who watch these advertisements pressure their parents to purchase the desired items and successfully undermine parental advice regarding nutrition and health.

American children now view TV for a daily average of three sedentary hours and 19 minutes (Powell et al. 2007), a time when they are not only absorbing food marketing messages, but also consuming the advertised snack foods themselves (Giammattei et al. 2003). Calorie intake is known to increase in direct proportion to the number of hours children watch TV (Wiecha et al. 2006), and TV exposure correlates with adiposity in 2–18-year-olds (Figure 6.5). Minority children are especially at risk. Black children watch about one-third more hours of TV than white children, and cable TV programs targeting blacks include more food and beverage commercials than are shown on channels popular with white Americans (Outley and Taddese 2006). Two recent studies have shown that reducing TV watching in school-aged children lowers obesity rates (Reilly 2005). The internet and other media forms can be expected to exert even more influence on children's consumption patterns.

Although 11 big food companies recently agreed to stop advertising foods that do not meet U.S. dietary guidelines on programs for children under age 12, to limit the use of licensed cartoon characters in their commercials, and to reduce the amount of sugar in cereals, they still run ads on family shows and advertise high-calorie foods that fall just below the recommended dietary cutoffs (Barnes 2007). Skeptical experts view these developments more as the industry's attempt to avoid bad publicity and lawsuits than to reform children's food choices, but others consider them to be the first small steps in curtailing advertisements to children.

Half of all U.S. food dollars are spent on eating away from home. Restaurants of all types encourage overindulgence in numerous ways – by serving excessively large

FIGURE 6.5 Toddler watching TV. Courtesy of Greenland via Shutterstock.com.

portions at bargain prices, offering a large variety of food choices, and promoting eating for pleasure, fantasy, and entertainment outside the limits of ordinary, everyday life (Figure 6.6). Although *super-sizing* came into disfavor in recent years, it is again on the rise. McDonald's is test-marketing the Hugo, a 42-ounce, 410-calorie drink costing only 89 cents (Martin 2007b). Burger King offers the quadruple-patty BK Stacker sandwich, and Hardees has introduced the huge Charcoal Broiled Angus Thickburger. Coca-Cola encouraged restaurants to stop offering tap water to customers and to push their bottled water and revenue-generating beverages instead (huffingtonpost.com).

The demand for increased profits by the fast-food industry is unending, and companies compete by offering not better but more food for the buck. Fast-food restaurants compete with school lunch rooms by forming clusters of three or four establishments near schools to entice students away from the cafeteria (Austin et al. 2005). Their presence in many children's hospitals accounts for increased purchases of fast foods by patients and their families (Sahud et al. 2006).

Home food preparation is becoming a lost art. Many Americans feel they have little time for food planning, shopping, and preparation. Inexpensive processed, designed, and prepared foods, even ready-made entire meals, are easily available at competitive prices. Children have learned to expect and enjoy less nutritious, industrialized foods, and harried parents turn to them for convenience. New food products include Super Suppers and Dream Dinners (Severson and Moskin 2006), as well as a large range of quick "home-made" meals. Individualized portions of many purchased meals (costing more than bulk amounts) allow for serving just what is needed without the inconvenience of dealing with leftovers. Compared to the decline of sit-down restaurant meals during the Great Recession of 2007–9, fast-food purchases remained stable and even rose among employed single parents, who were the most likely to feel time pressures (ers.usda.gov).

FIGURE 6.6 Fast food. Courtesy of Africa Studio via Shutterstock.com.

The rich prestige foods that were once available exclusively to the elite now appear on the menus of nearly everyone. Just as sugar, originally consumed only by the rich and royal, became a general commodity and has been increasingly consumed throughout the world (40 percent increase in US since WWII), former special treats such as steak and other red meats, ice cream, apple pie, and French fries have become everyday foods. In fact, French fries are now the most popular "vegetable" consumed in America. Even ritual foods once consumed only on sacred occasions have morphed into secularized snack items (Sarna forthcoming). Matzah, the round unleavened bread originally prepared under very strict kosher guidelines in synagogues specifically for the Jewish Passover, came to be mass-produced in square form in American factories for the celebration, and are now consumed as a snack by Americans of various religious persuasions. Although matzah blessed by the rabbi is still shared in communal Jewish rituals, most mass-produced matzah, which is much less expensive than the hand-made version, is individually consumed entirely outside the religious context. On the other hand, some snack foods once forbidden to Orthodox Jews are now produced under rabbinic supervision and have received kosher status. These cross-over foods help Orthodox Jews to blend into the American cultural mainstream, and, like factory foods purchased by the Hui of Xi'an, allow for neighborly food-sharing with members of other social groups.

The diet industry

It is definitely not for lack of trying that so many Americans have been unable to lose excess weight. The problem is that human energy-sparing physiology which evolved over millions of years is vigorously opposed to voluntary restriction of energy intake. It shifts into over-drive to preserve energy stores and increase the appetite for high-energy foods. The diet industry has become a booming, highly profitable business because many Americans are "on a diet." Millions of dieters have lost literally tons of weight at a cost of billions of dollars – $60.5 billion in 2013 alone (marketdataenterprises.com/studies/#FS45). Yet obesity rates have continued to rise, and, in fact, there is a direct connection between constant efforts to lose weight and increasing obesity (Farley and Cohen 2001; Pietilainen et al. 2012; Macpherson-Sanchez 2015). That dieting may actually promote obesity is not as paradoxical as it may seem, since the human body counters any type of energy deprivation, be it via famine or dieting, with metabolic adaptation, the "starvation response" of increased energy efficiency inherited from Paleolithic ancestors. With each bout of food restriction, the metabolic system reduces energy requirements by lowering basal metabolic rate and physical activity. Carbohydrate oxidation increases to provide warmth and quick energy while fat oxidation decreases, shifting more fat to storage in adipose tissue. After the diet has ended, appetite and food intake increase to compensate for the loss and to maintain the stable energy state. In fact, after repeated dieting, food preferences change to sweeter and fattier items such as ice cream (Drewnowski and Holden-Wiltse 1992). Even though the effort to lose weight may be temporarily successful, maintaining the lower weight is compromised by persistent hormonal changes that raise levels of appetite-stimulating ghrelin and lower levels of satiety-promoting leptin (Sumithran et al. 2011). The diet industry is so very profitable not only because more and more individuals with obesity are trying to lose weight, but also because they repeat the effort several times in "yo-yo" dieting. In 2007 alone Americans spent $55 billion on weight loss programs (Downs and Lowenstein 2011).

None of the recent diet fads – oat-bran, eDiet, Ornish low-fat, low-glycemic, Atkins low-carb, Weight Watcher low-calorie, or Paleolithic – have a solid track record for long-term effective and sustained weight loss. The meager evidence for dieting success shows that no matter which diet is used – commercial, medical, or self-regulated – dieters with obesity lose on average only 1–2 percent of their weight, are unable to persist on their diets, and regain much of their lost weight within a few years (Dansinger et al. 2005; Tsai and Wadden 2005). Diet programs come and go quickly because they fail to provide desired long-term results.

Little is known about the safety of any of the popular diets. There has simply not been adequate scientific investigation of the long-term consequences of avoiding one or more of the essential macronutrients which are part of a well-balanced nutritional program. Low-carbohydrate, high-fat diets, for instance, may cause accumulation of ketones from the breakdown of fat, and can result in liver and kidney malfunction and salt and water depletion that leads to fatigue, constipation, and low blood pressure (Bravata et al. 2003). Although low-carb diets do not seem to increase triglycerides and low-density lipoprotein in the short term, excessive consumption of animal proteins and fats over a long period may raise cholesterol to dangerous levels in some individuals. Neither low-carb nor low-fat dieters have been systematically followed long enough to be certain that these diets are safe for human health.

Promoting rapid weight loss, as in the very popular *The Biggest Loser* TV reality show, suggests that anyone can lose weight, even though it is well known that shedding pounds in such a drastic way is very risky and unlikely to have permanent beneficial effects. Only half of the show's contestants, who were enticed to participate by enormous cash prizes, have been able to maintain most of their weight loss. The first season's winner regained nearly all of the 122 pounds he lost using methods that left him dehydrated and urinating blood. Other contestants had to be hospitalized during a one-mile race (Wyatt 2009). And, even though the contest's rigorous exercise program helped to preserve participants' muscle mass, their metabolic adaptation was greater than that of bariatric surgery patients who lost similar amounts of weight (Knuth et al. 2014). The show and its merchandising business, estimated to be worth $100 million (biggestloserclub.com), are a form of corporate exploitation of people with obesity and have little entertainment value.

Weight gain is actually more pronounced in persons who have previously lost weight. A study of 692 adolescent girls followed for four years showed that those who dieted during the study had regained more weight at the end of the study period than non-dieters (Field et al. 2003). A group of bariatric surgery candidates with obesity had dieted an average of five times and lost an average of 4.5 kilograms (10 pounds) each time, yet their average body weight had increased from 90 kilograms (200 pounds) at the time of their first diet to 144.5 kilograms (308 pounds) at the time of evaluation for surgery (Gibbons et al. 2006). In addition to dieting-induced metabolic changes, weight regain is a typical response to restrictive diets that cannot be continued over long periods of time. Dieters often compensate by overeating and binging between diets because their appetite is intensified, especially for sugary and fatty foods.

Only a minority of dieters can maintain lower weight levels for even one year (Wing and Klem 2002). The National Weight Control Registry at the University of Colorado tracks more than 4,000 volunteers who have successfully maintained weight losses of over 33 kg (about 70 lbs) for an average of six years (Raynor et al. 2005; Wing and Phelan 2005). These successful dieters closely monitor their daily calorie and fat intake even after weight loss, and maintain a strict regimen of high-level physical activity for about an hour each day. A recent study of 2,400 of these participants found that, although nearly all had remained well below their maximum lifetime weight, almost three-fourths had regained some weight two years after entry into the registry (Phelan et al. 2003). Most regains were modest, but those who had regained more weight were less able to reverse them.

Nevertheless, even modest weight loss improves health, so more realistic diets are now recommended for some individuals with obesity (Wadden et al. 1999). The evidence shows that loss of 5–10 percent of body weight is relatively easy to achieve and maintain, and still pays off in health benefits. Losing large amounts of body weight to achieve some beauty ideal is not necessary for improved blood pressure, blood sugar, cholesterol and triglyceride levels, and inflammation factors. The loss of some fat seems to reduce its metabolic activity enough for major positive gains, although it is not yet known whether these benefits last or whether they can extend the lifespan of persons at risk. However, even moderate weight losers regain on average about half of the lost weight after less than two years.

In addition to books, foods, and diet programs, there is a large industry in prescription and over-the-counter diet drugs and supplements designed to reduce appetite or increase energy expenditure. The three most effective long-term prescription drugs available induce weight loss, between 3 percent and 9 percent above placebo level within one year (Yanovski and Yanovski 2014). The drugs have improved health in some, but health risks, tolerance difficulties, and weight regain affect other patients. Several drugs used in the past have been discontinued; sibutramine raises blood pressure in some patients, and ephedra-containing drugs were banned by the Food and Drug Administration (FDA) because of increased risk of heart attacks, strokes, and liver failure (Shekelle et al. 2003). Most recently a promising drug, rimonabant, used in Europe for treating obesity, failed to gain FDA approval because of association with high rates of depression and anxiety and the potential for suicide under its influence (Rumsfeld and Nallamothu 2008). But another drug, used in lower doses to treat Type 2 diabetes, has been approved by the FDA for treatment of obesity (fda.gov), and other drugs, some of which are combinations used for other purposes, are under investigation and show promise.

All of the current medications are prescribed for treatment of obesity in conjunction with behavioral interventions recommending low-calorie diets, increased physical activity, and special weight loss strategies, along with regular consultations with professionals (Anthes 2014). Among these strategies are getting adequate sleep, reducing TV watching, and eating family meals together. What has become clear now is that sustained weight loss requires continuous long-term treatment, sometimes including medications that are very expensive and generally not covered by insurance. It is no wonder that investments in companies that produce anti-obesity drugs and the new implantable device for controlling neural hunger messages to the brain have grown and become very profitable (fda.gov; etcnbc.com).

Because the metabolic pathways involved in energy regulation also have other physiological functions, all anti-obesity drugs have unavoidable and usually unpleasant side effects (Anthes 2014). The list includes diarrhea, nausea, constipation, headaches, swollen joints, flatulence, bloating, heartburn, stomach pain, sleep disturbances, and increased nervousness, which are not conducive to adherence, either in clinical trials or treatment regimens. The 1994 discovery of the hormone leptin was expected to lead to development of a new and effective pharmaceutical approach to controlling obesity. But it soon became obvious that leptin functions in other hormonal pathways besides energy regulation and cannot be used as an anti-obesity drug without serious side effects. Besides, most forms of obesity are associated with leptin resistance rather than leptin deficiency, so pharmaceutical doses of additional leptin do not have the desired effects. Most clinicians are convinced that the best anti-obesity drugs do little more than slightly improve physical appearance with little or no beneficial effect on health (Reidenberg 2000).

Humans are highly susceptible to obesity, prone to accumulate fat, and programmed to defend fat stores against loss. Obesity is the natural response to excessive energy stores and metabolic changes during subsequent efforts to reduce them. Yet one-third of Americans do seem able to adopt a typical American diet without weight gain, possibly because of genetic variations that favor adaptation to the obesogenic environment. But most Americans typically cannot avoid gaining excess fat or eliminate it once it has accumulated. Obviously, the most effective way to counter obesity is to prevent it in the first place. The challenge is to control personal eating behavior and remain physically active while surrounded by countless incentives and inducements to consume calories and engage in sedentary activities. Good nutrition and an active lifestyle are very difficult to achieve in the current cultural environment, in which persistent messages to consume are difficult to avoid and ignore.

Bariatric surgery

Surgery is currently the most effective but also the most drastic way to treat obesity, the last hope for individuals with severe obesity who have not been able to lose weight using standard methods. The demand for bariatric surgery (also called gastric surgery) has greatly increased in recent years. The number of surgeries performed annually rose from 16,000 in 2000 (Kohn et al. 2009) to 220,000 in 2008 (healthgrades. com). Membership in the American Society for Bariatric Surgery grew from 258 in 1998 to 2,500 in 2009 (Gagner et al. 2009). And although the mechanism accounting for its success is only partially understood, bariatric surgery is now also used to treat adolescents with obesity as well as adults (Inglefinger 2011; Paulus et al. 2015). Techniques are constantly improving, and laparoscopic procedures, which are less complicated than open surgery, are now the most commonly performed types in the US and Canada (Cottam et al. 2003).

Only patients with extreme obesity or those with obesity-related life-threatening conditions such as Type 2 diabetes and cardiopulmonary diseases are considered for gastric surgery. About 5 percent of the U.S. population (more than 10 million people) have extreme obesity, defined as BMI>40 or about 45 kg (100 lb) excess weight for men and 36 kg (80 lb) for women. Compared to standard weight loss programs and medical care, bariatric surgery, especially of the gastric bypass type, is very effective in lowering weight and reducing BMI for the majority of patients (Padwal et al. 2011). The surgical procedure reduces the size of the stomach, creates a bypass of the lower stomach and upper small intestine, limits food intake, and disrupts nutrient absorption in the small intestines. It also appears to disable the normal ghrelin (increasing appetite) response to weight loss. Patients who lose large amounts of body mass as a result of surgery also have improved cardiac function and blood sugar levels and long-term survival (Dixon et al. 2008; Owan et al. 2011; Schauer et al. 2012; Yracheta et al. 2015). Type 2 diabetes was completely reversed in nearly two-thirds of bypass surgery patients six years after surgery (Adams et al. 2012), possibly because of increased intestinal release of a protein which stimulates insulin secretion. Gastric banding, another form of this surgery, is less effective for weight loss, but patients also have high rates of diabetes remission and are less likely to suffer the postoperative malabsorption and nutrient deficiencies related to bypass surgery.

The usual risks of bleeding and infections associated with any operation accompany bariatric surgery (Gagner et al. 2009). Gastric bypass surgery, for instance, has a complication rate of 30 percent during the first six months after the procedure (Encinosa et al. 2011) and up to 2 percent mortality rate (Couzin 2008). Additional bariatric surgery is sometimes needed (Ikramuddin and Livingston 2013; Dayer-Jankechova et al. 2015). Adolescent patients undergoing bypass surgery have significant weight loss, but suffer high rates of serious complications (Paulus et al. 2015). Reconstructive surgery is also often needed to remove excess skin folds developing on arms, legs, and the trunk that cause infections and mechanical impediments (Ekwobi and Greenbaum 2006). Diminished drug and nutrient absorption often results (Padwal et al. 2010). For reasons not well understood, the suicide rate among bariatric surgery patients is higher than among the general population (Peterhaensel et al. 2013). Cases of complete weight regain and relapse of Type 2 diabetes have occurred (Arterburn et al. 2012). A recent review noted considerable variability in patient response to surgery (Courcoulas et al. 2013). Long-term effectiveness and safety are actually still unknown (Kyle et al. 2014; Replogle 2014; Lumeng et al. 2015). Gastric surgery is expensive, costing as much as $50,000 for the procedure and related care, which are not always covered by health insurance.

Cosmetic medicine is also a huge business. One of the latest developments is the injection of fat-dissolving drugs deep under the skin, using a procedure called lipo-dissolve (Singer 2007). The combination of drugs used and the procedure itself, which costs $2,000 per body part, have not been clinically tested or approved by the FDA. Although many lipo-dissolve consumers report desired results, others have suffered severe side effects and no change in unwanted fat deposits.

Consumerism: the desire to acquire

Ending hunger is an important aspect of the American Dream. Another is the ability to consume labor-saving technology so integral to the ease, comfort, and convenience offered by the American standard of living. Many Americans are convinced that consumer goods bring love, status, self-esteem, and happiness. Instilled by corporate advertising, they suffer from a sense of permanent discontent and dissatisfaction with their possessions. Consumer spending accounts for as much as two-thirds of the U.S. economy (Lohr 2004), the largest in the world. The US is a mass consumption society, a bargain culture, a land of perpetual sales, discounts, and buying sprees. Shopping is an important activity of everyday life, even during vacations and holidays. Thanksgiving, the American celebration of its many blessings, actually launches the Christmas holiday shopping season and is traditionally followed by Black Friday and Cyber Monday. On these shopping days stores reach their annual break-even points, and internet sellers achieve their highest sales (Barbaro 2005). American retail outlets are filled with streams of new consumer goods that offer an overwhelming number of irresistible options in brands, qualities, and prices. Total sales are continuously monitored, and reports of shopping trends and the hottest sales items dominate the local and national news. Through internet tracking, consumers' individual wants and desires are targeted by corporate advertisements.

The culture of consumerism has a long history in America. The American Revolution began as a protest against British control of colonial economic development. Later, during the 19th-century Industrial Revolution, Americans rejected traditional Protestant thrift and self-denial to create markets for the abundant goods produced in new factories. Mass production and advertising after World War I stimulated mass consumerism and the growth of the American middle class (Gottdiener 2001). Productivity was the key to prosperity, and a vast quantity of factory-produced goods, including foods and labor-saving devices, became available (Peters 2003). American consumers felt entitled to possess many of these goods, which were priced for general consumption. Soon nearly every family owned a home, a car, a refrigerator, and a washing machine. The Great Depression led to government policies that encouraged consumerism on a grand scale to aid in the nation's economic recovery and included for the first time widespread debt-financing of homes and automobiles for a large portion of the American population. Creation of wealth through mass production as well as upward social mobility through mass accumulation of material possessions became real possibilities for both native-born Americans and the thousands of immigrants who came for opportunities to improve their standard of living. The American Dream, primarily a widely shared materialistic vision of success in the US, is the search for a better, more comfortable life: the endless pursuit of more income, more possessions, more ease, and more contentment.

After a long period of scarcity during World War II, the creation of an economy of plenty was warmly welcomed by Americans. But sustaining such an economy required uninterrupted and continually increasing production and consumption of newer items and more products (Powdermaker 1997; Peters 2003), and, of course, more hours of labor by American workers (BLS 2007). Americans became the most productive workers in the world. They average 160 hours more on the job each year now than they did in 1969 (de Graaf et al. 2002), taking less than their allotted vacation time, getting too little sleep, and even taking work to their homes where they have created miniature offices.

Government, businesses, and American households all follow the precept that the U.S. economy must grow to ensure the wellbeing of all Americans, and that economic success rests on consumer demand. Material acquisition is a patriotic duty – to expand American industry and enhance America's economic standing in the world. Thus economic and political forces have joined to sell consumerism to the American people. Congress-approved tax rebates put additional dollars in the hands of American consumers to shore up the U.S. economy. President George W. Bush even recommended shopping as an antidote for the national anxiety and economic losses brought on by the 9/11 tragedy. American society has adjusted easily to that consumerist emphasis and set the tone for many other nations in the globalized economy.

Americans are devoted consumers, spending four times as many hours shopping as Europeans do. Today Americans, unable to resist a discount or bargain, consume twice as many products and services as they did during World War II. Economic globalization has increased the volume of goods available and reduced the cost of items to make spending even easier (Schor 1992). Americans shop at all hours, even at night and on Sundays (de Graaf et al. 2002), when most citizens of other industrialized nations rest or socialize with family and friends. Going to the mall is a popular form of entertainment and an effective socializing mechanism for adolescents. The emphasis is on accumulating the latest fashions and newest items, a pursuit that becomes the focus of discussion in family conversations and social gatherings.

Americans have the largest houses, and the most cars, TVs, computers, and cell phones. They purchase vast quantities of goods, many of which are non-essential (Zukin 2003). Hyper-consumerism and *conspicuous consumption* are the norm, uninhibited by lack of funds. Self-restraint is considered to be anti-capitalist, a danger to national economic growth, and downright unpatriotic. It is even contrary to some versions of Christianity. Citing Biblical verses, evangelist Oral Roberts spread the *Gospel of Prosperity* which promised God's blessings of earthly riches to the faithful. Today's TV preachers of "health and wealth theology" promise material blessing to those who make appropriate donations to their churches, even when they risk impoverishing themselves (Luo 2006; Gorski 2007).

Foreign visitors marvel at American excesses, big-box malls, McMansions (Collins 2005; Wood 2005), walk-in closets, great rooms, huge kitchens, stretch HumVees, enormous TVs, supersized restaurant portions, and supermarkets filled to the brim with wide varieties of foods and other goods requiring the use of large shopping carts. They observe with amazement multiple bathrooms, television sets, refrigerators, cars, and telephones in most homes (Winter 2002). Houses today are on average 24 percent larger than in 1985 (Gardner 2002), and so filled with possessions that some families cannot park their cars in the garage because it has become a storage space. Some families even hire personal organizers to track their belongings.

Consumption is made as easy and convenient as possible. Each day 20 million shoppers visit Walmart, the world's largest retailer and a symbol of American consumerism, and spend $256 billion a year (Greenhouse 2004). Upper and middle-class patrons mingle with lower-class shoppers at the big-box Walmart stores where everything from household goods to groceries can be purchased in one trip. Finding low-cost bargains creates a sense of equality and democracy among consumers of every social and economic class. Computers and TVs are popular shopping venues, selling products at all hours and further blurring the distinction between entertainment and consumption.

In the past, government policies helped to develop a large, freely spending middle class, but in recent years, federal tax policies favoring privileged Americans have contributed to a growing concentration of income at the top (Sherman and Aron-Dine 2007) and a widening income gap between rich and middle-class Americans. As the buying power of the wealthiest Americans continues to increase and consumer norms escalate, growing economic inequality stimulates competitive consumption by encouraging upscale emulation (Schor 2003). In a democratic society such as America's, luxury goods once consumed exclusively by elites are now demanded by middle and lower-class consumers, who purchase them on credit (Weber 2007) and assume large personal debts, the highest in the world. Sub-luxury goods, similar to expensive originals but more affordable (Steinhauer 2005), also help meet the demand. Most luxury car manufacturers now offer less expensive versions of Mercedes and BMWs. Inexpensive designer clothing and accessory knock-offs are widely available to lower-class buyers. Thus elites have relinquished monopoly over exclusive luxury goods for the sake of profit.

Although ostentation is culturally sanctioned and a respected sign of economic success, many Americans also consider extravagant consumption to be immoral, not unlike the emphasis on slimness in the context of caloric plenty. The contradiction between the gratification of desires through lavish spending and the ideals of self-control, sacrifice, and frugality is nothing new to Americans. That early indulgence of the rich – sugar – was long considered an unnecessary luxury until it was mass-produced for general consumption (Mintz 1997).

Persuaded to buy on credit and live with high levels of personal debt (Lears 2006), Americans seem unaware of the long-term costs of hyper-consumption. Consumer debt is a huge business, and brings great profits to lending institutions from the interest on large balances that consumers carry on their credit cards and loans. Bankruptcies and property foreclosures have become very common, adding to the stress of the overworked American (Dougherty 2007). Many Americans are willing to assume large debts and tolerate environmental degradation to accommodate their consumer aims, just as they disregard the dangers of excessive consumption of high-calorie foods and labor-saving devices.

In their quest for a higher standard of living, Americans have come to depend on a wide array of technologies that ease physical labor, provide convenience, and leave plenty of time for leisure pursuits. Not only do many Americans purchase much more food than they need for health and wellbeing, they also own a long list of gadgets and items guaranteed to lower physical effort and activity. American households are stocked with countless labor-saving devices which were once rare luxuries, but these technological wonders have become necessities for most families in this democratic society. Laundry machines, dishwashers, lawn mowers, vacuum cleaners (including the fully automatic Roomba), remote-controlled TVs, window blinds, garage doors, and fireplaces, electric mixers, toothbrushes, and shavers, and countless other wonderful powered items save time and (human) energy (Lanningham-Foster et al. 2003). Drive-through restaurants, pharmacies, churches, banks, and funeral homes are everywhere.

Despite a strong work ethic and social disapproval of "couch potatoes," Americans aspire to leisure and inactivity. They mourn Blue Mondays, look forward to TGIF celebrations, and spend enormous sums on leisure entertainment. Oddly, though, even when they are entitled to them, Americans are much more reluctant to take extended vacations far from their homes and workplaces than workers in other industrialized countries. So they eagerly seek out various forms of brief, fleeting entertainment provided by the highly developed and profitable American leisure industry in the form of movies, television, sports venues, computer games, and other amusements. In this Entertainment Age (Darlin 2005), the average American spends more on entertainment than on gasoline, furniture, and clothing combined, and nearly as much as on eating out. Television is the most popular leisure diversion, and, remarkably, presents programs on exercise, cooking, and home remodeling as forms of entertainment. How many viewers actually participate in the exercises, cook from scratch the healthy meals demonstrated, or do the hard work of upgrading their own homes is not known.

Since physical activity is no longer a routine part of most Americans' occupations and lives, they are forced to seek ways to increase energy expenditure in socially acceptable ways. The fitness industries profit by promoting elaborate and expensive exercise programs. Jogging and running are popular, for instance, and, like other forms of exercise, require the purchase of special shoes, apparel, accessories, and gear and gadgets such as reflective vests, headlamps, winter outfits that wick sweat, water belts, portable carbs, salt pills, bras with heart rate monitors, GPS watches, sneakers with springs, and music devices. Runner's World has 670 stores nationwide. Sales of running shoes alone amounted to $1.99 billion in 2005 (Arnoldy 2006). Then there are stationary bikes, Nordic tracks, gym equipment, and fitness club memberships, fat farms, and spas, not to mention weight loss plans, books, and videos that offer lessons in self-control and lifestyle changes.

Ease and efficiency are highly valued, while hard manual labor is most definitely not and is left to immigrant agricultural and construction workers. The highest-paid American workers are those in white-collar occupations requiring little or no physical effort. Humans are designed for sustained, energetic body movement, but daily vigorous use of the body is no longer needed, expected, or appreciated, except by sports figures who entertain thousands of sedentary viewers and fans. Inadequate government funding of American public schools has induced them to sell candy, snack foods, and sweetened drinks from vending machines to school children to support educational programs. At the same time, physical education is virtually nonexistent, and teachers struggle to provide adequate nutrition education (CPEHN and Union 2005). The eight million American sixth through 12th-graders who watch Channel One in school are influenced by its commercials to buy products including junk foods, soft drinks, video games, TV programs, and Hollywood movies, shown on these "educational" TV programs (Wuthnow 1996; Schor 2004; Austin et al. 2006). So that their schools will be supplied with "free" electronic equipment, students are expected to watch a 10-minute current events and news program with two minutes of commercials on Channel One (Giroux 1999), a surefire way to educate the young to become adult consumers. Zapme, a Silicon Valley company, provides free computers and internet access to schools, with the condition that they receive at least four hours of continuous use, so that "consumers in training" can watch a steady stream of onscreen advertising each day.

Individualism: the prominence of personal choice

Corporatism and consumerism are closely linked to individualism, the most basic of American cultural values. As pursuers of the American Dream, Americans value inter-individual competition, personal achievement, and private economic success (Whybrow 2005). Enlightenment ideals of individual rights and freedoms are embodied in the U.S. Constitution, which promises to protect the "inalienable rights to life, liberty and the pursuit of happiness," taken by many Americans to mean the right to acquire property and improve material status. Pollsters report that young people asked to define "democracy" refer to the freedom to buy and consume whatever they wish without government restrictions (Giroux 1999). Individualism is deeply embedded in the American psyche and guides cognitive processes and views of the world (Nisbett and Masuda 2003). While many nonwestern peoples traditionally emphasize social interaction and interdependence, harmonious interpersonal relationships, and a contextual, holistic worldview, Europeans and Americans are more inclined to value autonomy, independence, individual performance, and personal agency. Asians, for example, are more generally concerned with societal constraints and the wellbeing of the larger community, while westerners place greater significance on individual control and personal privileges.

Personal freedom and the right to make individual decisions regarding all aspects of life is taken for granted – decisions regarding education and careers, selection of spouses, the number of children to have, how to make money, what to consume, and the design of lifestyles. In many families, individuals watch their favorite shows on their personal TV sets, listen to music on personal smartphones, drive their individual cars, and sleep in their individual rooms and beds. Corporations and businesses are also free to make unlimited profits, as the individuals who own them have the right, indeed the obligation, to accumulate wealth and possessions.

One of the most important symbols of American freedom and independence is the personal automobile, the most advertised product in America and the consumer goal of every red-blooded American man, woman, and high school student (Tierney 2004). Owning a car is actually a necessity in the US because of the unique American-built environment and relative lack of public transportation (Kjellstrom and Hinde 2007; Norton 2008). Suburban development design and great distances to jobs and schools have made Americans absolutely dependent upon auto travel, with government support of immense highway networks for fast and convenient individualized transportation. While American consumers can choose from dozens of auto manufacturers and hundreds of car models, all the while boosting the American consumer economy, their options for other forms of transportation are severely limited. Instead of being tied to slow public transportation in which entire communities of people ride on the same schedule and to the same destinations, individually owned and operated machines of personally selected design, color, and accessories take individuals where desire dictates. For the sake of the "automobility" (Sheumaker and Wajda 2008) and the prestige of ownership, Americans are willing to pay a high price as well as the cost of environmental degradation and poor health. Public transport, in contrast to travel by private auto, is not only more fuel efficient but also requires riders to walk to bus and subway stops and transfer points for healthy physical activity.

Americans are obligated to make their own paths to success. They evaluate others on the basis of economic status, physical appearance, and other individualized traits. Combined with the emphasis on individual initiative and relatively low tolerance for variations from the norm, individuals with obesity are held personally responsible for their conditions and expected to reform themselves to achieve an acceptable appearance (Burke and Heiland 2007). Fat is stigmatized in America, and an individual with obesity (especially a woman) is the target of severe moral judgment. Many Americans also view obesity as an offense to esthetic sensibility and as a failure to manage self-representation for success. Media play an important role (Brochu et al. 2014) (http://consciencehealth. org/2015/01); the reality show *The Biggest Loser* was shown to reinforce viewers' attribution of weight control to personal responsibility and actually increase anti-fat bias among viewers (Yoo 2013).

Parenting responsibilities are also individualized (Schwartz and Puhl 2003). Rarely do communities actively participate in child-rearing and advice-giving today. In many families the entire responsibility for child care falls on a single parent, usually the mother. Many American parents, who seem to be generally unaware of their children's overweight or obese status (Maynard et al. 2003; Hospital 2007; Hager et al. 2012), resist the advice of the "food police" and refuse to accept school nurses' reports of their children's unhealthy weight (Morris 2002). Interference from external authorities is not welcomed or appreciated. In some states even well-meaning efforts to improve the nutritional quality of school lunches and to limit in-school birthday treats are undermined by parental resistance (Kershaw 2007). Professional efforts to promote healthy diets and activity levels are often considered "elitist obsessions" and violations of personal freedom (Bleich et al. 2007; Cunningham and Black 2010). Nevertheless, a large review of macronutrient consumption data over more than 40 years found that many Americans did follow government nutrition advice to reduce consumption of fat (Cohen et al. 2015). But BMI levels continued to climb because of a concurrent 12 percent increase in carbohydrate consumption.

Without shared cultural boundaries or social guidelines, Americans are held individually responsible for their eating behavior, activity patterns, and body weight (Grier and Miller 2004). Nutritionist messages to eat better, instructions to lose weight and exercise, and pharmaceutical products to combat obesity all target individual behavior, while institutions that actively promote overconsumption and inactivity avoid responsibility. Although the link between poverty and obesity has been firmly established, it is the poor individual who is held responsible for her economic condition and health status instead of the circumstances of her poverty. A news item in the *Salt Lake Tribune* (Stewart 2006) describes a cooking program sponsored by a Provo, Utah food bank. It teaches poor mothers to cook nutritious meals using items obtained with food stamps and from food banks. Elimination of widespread food insecurity among America's poor is not mentioned. Americans seem to prefer solutions involving individual deeds rather than community or government action to bring about social change.

Even though Americans value individualism and freedom of choice, they are remarkably conformist in their behavior. They respond uncritically to marketing strategies and advertising ploys to emulate the tastes and desires of their peers in their purchasing and consumption decisions and seem unaware that their freedom to choose a healthy diet and active lifestyle is actually severely restricted. No real rational independent choice is possible (Schor 1992; Fitchen 2000), because it is constrained by availability determined by personal income and by corporate pricing strategies that have helped to destroy many small independent businesses and their local options and alternatives (Darlin 2005). Popular buffet restaurants use the principle of apparent individual choice to attract customers. But customers actually have little opportunity to choose nutritional foods from the large number of options on the steam tables. Believing in the power of individual decisions, Americans generally fail to see that they are actually guided into making "choices" by external forces, that "freedom" to choose is largely illusory, and that powerful marketing pressures influence the consumer culture (Zimmerman 2011). They are also convinced that others' weaknesses and failings are the results of their individual "choices" without considering that these too are severely limited.

Independent thinking, inculcated into American children from an early age, is exploited and marketed by the food industry to American children along with attractive foods and gimmicks to promote their sale (Linn 2004; Schor 2004; Thomas 2005). Food industry advertising to children deliberately fosters independence from parental authority, but offers so many unhealthy options that a freely chosen healthy diet is a virtual impossibility. Ironically, authoritarian parents who restrict their children's food choices are more likely to have children with obesity who resist parental control by secretly consuming forbidden snacks, than parents who are more permissive or even neglectful (Fisher and Birch 2002).

In the US rich foods are often associated with family memories and nostalgia for home cooking and family gatherings:

My Mother's Pie Crust

Light as angels' breath, shatters into flakes

with each forkful, never soggy-bottomed

or scorched on top, the lattices evenly woven,

pinched crimps an inch apart. . .

The strange marriage of fat, flour, and salt

is annealed to ethereal bites. Heaven is attainable,

and the chimes of the timer bring us to the table.
(Lines of "My Mother's Pie Crust" by Barbara Crooker from
O Taste and See: Food Poems, Bottom Dog Press, 2003.
Reprinted by permission of the publisher)

The sweet memories of security within the family circle are particularly poignant today when most food purchasing, preparation, and consumption are done individually, rather than in the social context of family. Since 1970 the average size of U.S. households has declined sharply (census.gov) – today more than half are composed of only one or two persons. Many shop for groceries alone in impersonal supermarkets, cook their food alone, and often eat their meals alone as well, beyond the view of others whose very presence and participation might promote better nutrition and inhibit excessive consumption. Convenience foods make preparation quick, easy, and individualized, no longer a social activity involving collaboration and sharing (Mintz and Du Bois 2002).

Individualized food consumption is just part of the latest stage in the history of western eating styles (Farb and Armelagos 1997). Long ago everyone ate with fingers from a common dish and drank from a common goblet. The fashion of individual place settings originated among European elites and gradually trickled down to middle and lower classes. The Chinese, on the other hand, eat from small bowls filled and refilled via chopsticks with tiny portions of food from a large common serving dish in the center of the table. During a Chinese communal meal, diners remain acutely aware of the needs and desires of others and make certain that everyone receives appropriate shares of special or favorite foods. Westerners, while they do often serve themselves from common dishes, do not show that level of interest in what others at the table need or desire.

American individual identity is based primarily upon the material goods and services one can consume and display (Mintz 1997). Self-interest is an important American cultural feature, taking precedence over concerns for the general public welfare. The capitalist world economy depends on the core belief that happiness in the form of health, wealth, and freedom comes through the expression of individual choice. Yet the political and economic environment encourages consumer conformism and vigorously promotes consumption of high-calorie foods and labor-saving devices to all. Individual efforts to resist the pressures of the obesogenic environment are more often than not overwhelmed.

Conclusion

Just as shopping has become a recreational and competitive activity for many Americans, so has recreational and competitive eating and drinking at pork festivals, ice cream socials, and beer contests. And just as the purchase of the latest electronic gadget or labor-saving device brings temporary satisfaction, and having lots of stuff is the shopper's goal, feeling stuffed after a holiday meal is "good." Just as crippling debt and credit crises are the long-term consequences of hyper-consumption of goods and services, obesity is the price Americans pay for their high standard of living. Regrettably, the consequences of both deep debt and poor health have either escaped consumers' notice or are of little concern to the American public. In spite of the strong American commitment to personal rights and responsibilities, individuals – especially the poor and undereducated – have little control, few real choices, and virtually no protection. While the profit-driven food productionist system – supported by government policies – spends billions to market mass-produced food to American consumers (Simon 2006), government agencies with much smaller budgets try to inform citizens of the health-threatening consequences of excessive consumption. Individuals who try to resist have an uphill battle to defy the deeply ingrained consumer culture and the corporate and government forces that support it.

Americans are inclined to locate problems and their potential solutions in the bodies and minds of individuals. Consumer, corporate, and individual competition pits Americans against each other and leaves them unaware of the wider sociocultural causes of the obesity epidemic. Instead of developing greater concern for the nation's public health and joining forces to solve social problems, competition hardens hearts against those who are unable to achieve the American Dream and those who are powerless against the dominant trends of wasteful and unhealthy consumption. It should be noted that the anti-fatism movement is one of the few voices for society-wide change, for tolerance of persons with obesity, and most importantly, for the recognition of society's collective responsibility for the American obesity epidemic. Collective action through regulation and legislation to improve the obesogenic environment is needed to remove many of the barriers to individual efforts and personal responsibility for human health (Brownell et al. 2010).

References

Adair, L. S. and B. M. Popkin (2005). Are child eating patterns being transformed globally? *Obesity Research* **13**: 1281–1299.

Adams, T. D., L. E. Davidson et al. (2012). Health benefits of gastric bypass surgery after 6 years. *Journal of the American Medical Association* **308**(11): 1122–1131.

Alexandratos, N. (2006). The Mediterranean diet in a world context. *Public Health Nutrition* **9**(1a): 111–117.

Anthes, E. (2014). Marginal gains. *Nature* **508**: S54–S56.

AP (2005). Woman eats six-pound hamburger. New York Times. New York.

Arnoldy, B. (2006). Backstory: remember when running was simple? Christian Science Monitor.

Arterburn, D. E., A. Bogart et al. (2012). A multisite study of long-term remission and relapse of type 2 diabetes mellitus following gastric bypass. *Obesity Surgery* **23**(1): 93–102.

Austin, E. W., Y.-C. Chen et al. (2006). Benefits and costs of Channel One in a middle school setting and the role of media-literacy training. *Pediatrics* **117**: e423–e433.

Austin, S. B., S. J. Melly et al. (2005). Clustering of fast-food restaurants around schools: a novel application of spatial statistics to the study of food environments. *Am J Public Health* **95**: 1575–1581.

Baker, P. and S. Friel (2014). Processed foods and the nutrition transition: evidence from Asia. *Obesity Reviews* **15**(7): 564–577.

Barbaro, M. (2005). Ready, aim, shop. New York Times. New York.

Barnes, B. (2007). Limiting ads of junk food to children. New York Times. New York.

Becker, A. E., S. E. Gilman et al. (2005). Changes in the prevalence of overweight and in body image among Fijian women between 1989 and 1998. *Obesity Research* **13**(1): 110–117.

Bennett, G. G., K. Y. Wolin et al. (2007). Immigration and obesity among lower income blacks. *Obesity* **15**: 1391–1394.

Bindon, J. R. (1995). Polynesian responses to modernization: overweight and obesity in the South Pacific. Social Aspects of Obesity. I. de Garine and N. J. Pollock. New York, Gordon and Breach Publishers: 227–251.

Birnbaum, J. H. (2007). Fruit and vegetable growers hope to harvest more from farm bill. The Washington Post. Washington DC.

Bittman, M. (2011a). Cereal? Cookies? Oh, what's the diff? New York Times. New York.

Bittman, M. (2011b). Local food: no elitist plot. New York Times. New York.

Bleich, S., R. Belendon et al. (2007). Trust in scientific experts on obesity: implications for awareness and behavior change. *Obesity* **15**: 2145–2156.

Bleich, S. N., Y. C. Wang, and S. L. Gortmaker (2009). Increasing consumption of sugar-sweetened beverages among US adults: 1988–1994 and 1999–2004. *American Journal of Clinical Nutrition* **89**: 372–381.

BLS (2007). Annual time use statistics. Washington DC: U.S. Department of Labor, Bureau of Labor Statistics.

Bodley, J. H. (2005). Cultural Anthropology: Tribes, States, and the Global System (4th ed). Boston: McGraw-Hill.

Bonafini, B. A. and P. Pozzilli (2011). Body weight and beauty: the changing face of the ideal female body weight. *Obesity Reviews* **12**: 62–65.

Bravata, D. M., L. Sanders et al. (2003). Efficacy and safety of low-carbohydrate diets: a systematic review. *Journal of American Medical Association* **289**(14): 1837–1850.

Brewis, A. A. (2014). Stigma and the perpetuation of obesity. *Social Science & Medicine* **118**: 152–158.

Brewis, A. A., A. Wutich et al. (2011). Body norms and fat stigma in global perspective. *Current Anthropology* **52**(2): 269–276.

Brink, P. J. (1995). Fertility and fat: the Anang fattening room. Social Aspects of Obesity. I. De Garine and N. J. Pollock. London, Gordon and Breach Publishers: 71–85.

Brochu, P. M., R. L. Pearl et al. (2014). Do media portrayals of obesity influence support for weight-related medical policy? *Health Psychology* **33**(2): 197–200.

Brown, P. J. and V. K. Bentley-Condit (1998). Culture, evolution, and obesity. Handbook of Obesity. G. A. Bray, C. Bourchard and W. P. T. James. New York, Marcel Dekker, Inc.

Brown, P. J. and M. Konner (1998). An anthropological perspective on obesity. Understanding and Applying Medical Anthropology. P. J. Brown. Mountain View, CA, Mayfield: 401–413.

Brownell, K. D. and K. B. Horgen (2004). Food Fight: The Inside Story of the Food Industry, America's Obesity Crisis, and What We Can do About It. Chicago, Contemporary Books.

Brownell, K. D., R. Kersh et al. (2010). Personal responsibility and obesity: a constructive approach to a controversial issue. *Health Affairs* **29**(3): 379–387.

Bryant, C. A., K. M. DeWalt et al. (2003). The Cultural Feast: An Introduction to Food and Society. Belmont, CA, Thomson-Wadsworth.

Burke, M. and F. Heiland (2007). Social dynamics of obesity. *Economic Inquiry* **45**(3): 571–591.

Capparell, S. (2007). The Real Pepsi Challenge. New York, Wall Street Journal Books/Free Press.

Cawley, J. and B. Kirwan (2011). Agricultural policy and childhood obesity. The Oxford Handbook of the Social Science of Obesity. J. Cawley. New York, Oxford University Press: 480–491.

Ciezadlo, A. (2011). Does the Mediterranean diet even exist? New York Times. New York.

Cohen, D. A. and S. H. Babey (2012). Candy at the cash register – a risk factor for obesity and chronic disease. *New England Journal of Medicine* **367**(15): 1381–1383.

Cohen, E., M. Cragg et al. (2015). Statistical review of US macronutrient consumption data, 1965–2011: Americans have been following dietary guidelines, coincident with the rise in obesity. *Nutrition* **31**: 727–732.

Collins, C. (2005). Americans dream of ever-grander homes. Christian Science Monitor. Boston.

Connor, S. (2006). Food-related advertising on preschool television: building brand recognition in young viewers. *Pediatrics* **118**(4): 1478–1485.

Cottam, D. R., S. G. Mattar et al. (2003). Laparoscopic era of operations for morbid obesity. *Archives of Surgery* **138**: 367.

Counihan, C. M. ed. (2002). Food in the USA. New York, Routledge.

Courcoulas, A. P., N. J. Christian et al. (2013). Weight change and health outcomes at 3 years after bariatric surgery among individuals with severe obesity. *Journal of American Medical Association* **310**(22): 2416–2425.

Couzin, J. (2008). Bypassing medicine to treat diabetes. *Science* **320**: 438–440.

CPEHN and C. Union (2005). Out of balance: marketing of soda, candy, snacks and fast foods drowns out healthful messages. Oakland, CA, California Pan-Ethnic Health Network Consumers Union: 1–27.

Crooker, B. (2003). My mother's pie crust. *In* O Taste and See: Food Poems. D. L. Garrison and T. Hermsen. Huron, OH, Bottom Dog Press: 42–43.

Cunningham, B. and J. Black (2010). The new front in the culture wars: food. The Washington Post. Washington, DC.

Dansinger, M. L., J. A. Gleason et al. (2005). Comparison of the Atkins, Ornish, Weight Watchers, and Zone diets for weight loss and heart disease risk reduction. *JAMA* **293**(1): 43–53.

Darlin, D. (2005). How to tame an inflated entertainment budget. New York Times. New York.

Davenport, C. M. (2002). Greek women trade Aphrodite for gaunt model look. Christian Science Monitor. Boston.

Dayer-Jankechova, A., P. Fournier et al. (2015). Complications after laparoscopic Roux-en-Y gastric bypass in 1,573 consecutive patients: are there predictors? *Obesity Surgery* doi 10.1007/s11695-015-1752-1.

de Graaf, J., D. Wann et al. (2002). Affluenza: The All-Consuming Epidemic. San Francisco, Berrett-Koehler Publishers, Inc.

de Jong, N., O. H. Klungel et al. (2007). Functional foods: the case for closer evaluation. *BMJ* **334**: 1037–1039.

de Lago, M. (2011). Spanish move away from Mediterranean diet. *British Medical Journal* **342**: d1509.

DeMaria, E. J. (2007). Bariatric surgery for morbid obesity. *New England Journal of Medicine* **356**(21): 2176–2183.

Diamond, J. (1997). Guns, Germs, and Steel: the Fates of Human Societies. New York: Norton.

Diaz, V. A., A. G. I. Mainous et al. (2007). Cultural conflicts in the weight loss experience of overweight Latinos. *Int J Obesity* **31**: 328–333.

Dixon, J. B., P. E. O'Brien et al. (2008). Adjustable gastric banding and conventional therapy for type 2 diabetes. *Journal of American Medical Association* **299**(3): 316–323.

Dougherty, C. (2007). Dollar's retreat raises fear of collapse. International Herald Tribune. New York.

Downs, J. S. and G. Lowenstein (2011). Behavioral economics and obesity. The Oxford Handbook of the Social Science of Obesity. J. Cawley. New York, Oxford University Press: 138–157.

Drewnowski, A. and J. Holden-Wiltse (1992). Taste responses and food preferences in obese women: effects of weight cycling. *International Journal of Obesity* **16**: 639–648.

Drewnowski, A. and B. M. Popkin (1997). The nutrition transition: new trends in the global diet. *Nutrition Reviews* **55**: 31.

Du, S., B. Lu et al. (2002). The nutrition transition in China: a new stage of the Chinese diet. The Nutrition Transition: Diet and Disease in the Developing World. B. Caballero and B. M. Popkin. New York, Academic Press: 205–221.

Edwards, N. M., S. Pettingell et al. (2010). Where perception meets reality: self-perception of weight in overweight adolescents. *Pediatrics* **125**: e452–e458.

Ekwobi, C. C. and A. R. Greenbaum (2006). Letter: reconstructive surgery is often needed after obesity surgery. *British Medical Journal* **333**(7576): 1022.

Encinosa, W., D. Du et al. (2011). Anti-obesity drugs and bariatric surgery. The Oxford Handbook of the Social Science of Obesity. J. Cawley. New York, Oxford University Press: 792–807.

Fagone, J. (2006). Horsemen of the esophagus. *The Atlantic Monthly* **297**(4): 86–93.

Faith, M. S., E. Manibay et al. (1998). Relative body weight and self-esteem among African Americans in four nationally representative samples. *Obesity Research* **6**(6): 430–437.

Farah, H. and J. Buzby (2008). U.S. food consumption up 16 percent since 1970. Washington DC: USDA Economic Research Service, Amber Waves.

Farb, P. and G. Armelagos (1983). Consuming passions: the anthropology of eating. New York, Washington Square Press.

Farb, P. and G. Armelagos (1997). The patterns of eating. 75 Readings: An Anthology (6th ed). S. V. Buscemi and C. Smith. New York, McGraw-Hill: 260–265.

Farley, T. and D. Cohen (2001). Fixing a fat nation: why diets and gyms won't save us from the obesity epidemic. *The Washington Monthly* **33**(1): 23–29.

Field, A. E., P. Aneja et al. (2007). Race and gender differences in the association of dieting and gains in BMI among young adults. *Obesity* **15**: 4456–4464.

Field, A. E., S. B. Austin et al. (2003). Relation between dieting and weight change among preadolescents and adolescents. *Pediatrics* **112**(4): 900–906.

Fisher, J. O. and L. L. Birch (2002). Eating in the absence of hunger and overweight in girls from 5 to 7 y of age. *Am J Clin Nutr* **76**: 226–231.

Fitchen, J. M. (2000). Hunger, malnutrition, and poverty in the contemporary United States: some observations on their social and cultural context. Nutritional Anthropology: Biocultural Perspectives. A. H. Goodman, D. L. Dufour and G. H. Pelto. Mountain View, CA, Mayfield: 335–342.

Fitzgibbon, M. L., L. R. Blackman et al. (2000). The relationship between body image discrepancy and body mass index across ethnic groups. *Obesity Research* **8**(8): 582–589.

Ford, P. (2004). Foes of 'globesity' run afoul of sugar's friends. The Christian Science Monitor. Boston.

Franko, D. L., D. Thompson et al. (2005). Correlates of persistent thinness in black and white young women. *Obesity Research* **13**: 2006–2013.

Gabaccia, D. R. (2002). As American as Budweiser and pickles? Nation-building in American food industries. Food Nations: Selling Taste in Consumer Societies. W. Belasco and P. Scranton. New York: Routledge.

Gagner, M., L. Milone et al. (2009) Mortality after laparoscopic adjustable gastric banding: results from an anonymous questionnaire to ASBS members. *Obesity Surgery* doi PMID: 19707838.

Gantz, W., N. Schwartz et al. (2007). Food for thought: television food advertising to children in the United States. Washington DC: Kaiser Family Foundation.

Gardner, M. (2002). What's happening to the American home? Christian Science Monitor. Boston.

Giammattei, J., G. Blix et al. (2003). Television watching and soft drink consumption. *Arch Pediatr Adolesc Med* **157**: 882–886.

Gibbons, L. M., D. B. Sarwer et al. (2006). Previous weight loss experiences of bariatric surgery candidates: how much have patients dieted prior to surgery? *Obesity Research* **14**: 70S–76S.

Gillette, M. B. (2005). Children's food and Islamic dietary restrictions in Xi'an. The Cultural Politics of Food and Eating: A Reader. J. L. Watson and M. L. Caldwell, Blackwell: 106–121.

Giroux, H. A. (1999). Corporate Culture and the Attack on Higher Education and Public Schooling. Bloomington, IN, Phi Delta Kappa Educational Foundation.

Gladwell, M. (2000). The Pima paradox. Nutritional Anthropology: Biocultural Perspectives on Food and Nutrition. A. H. Goodman, D. L. Dufour and G. H. Pelto. Mountain View, CA, Mayfield Publishing Company: 358–368.

Goddard, J. (2008). All-male, plus-size cheerleading squad set to debut for Florida Marlins. Christian Science Monitor. Boston.

Goel, M. S., E. P. McCarthy et al. (2004). Obesity among US immigrant subgroups by duration of residence. *JAMA* **292**(23): 2860–2867.

Gorski, E. (2007). Gospel of Wealth Facing Scrutiny. Associated Press. New York.

Gottdiener, M. (2001). The theming of America: dreams, media fantasies, and themed environments. Boulder, CO, Westview.

Green, T. (2007). Tricksters and the marketing of breakfast cereals. *J Popular Culture* **40**(1): 49–68.

Greenhouse, S. (2004). Wal-Mart, a nation unto itself. New York Times. New York.

Grier, P. and S. B. Miller (2004). Incredible shrinking US family. Christian Science Monitor. Boston.

Gross, J. (2005). Phat. Fat: The Anthropology of an Obsession. D. Kulick and A. Meneley. New York: Jeremy Tarcher/Penguin: 63–76.

Guthman, J. (2011). Weighing In: Obesity, Food Justice, and the Limits of Capitalism. Berkeley, CA, University of California Press.

Hager, E. R., M. Candelaria et al. (2012). Maternal perceptions of toddler body size. *Archives of Pediatric & Adolescent Medicine* **166**(5): 417–422.

Harjo, S. S. (2005). My new year's resolution: no more fat 'Indian' food. Indian Country Today. Verona, NY.

Hattori, K., M. Kondo et al. (1999). Hierarchical differences in body composition of professional Sumo wrestlers. *Annals of Human Biology* **26**(2): 179–184.

Hernandez-Valero, M., A. V. Wilkinson et al. (2007). Maternal BMI and country of birth as indicators of childhood obesity in children of Mexican origin. *Obesity* **15**: 2512–2519.

Himes, S. M. and J. K. Thompson (2007). Fat stigmatization in television shows and movies: a content analysis. *Obesity* **15**: 712–718.

Himmelstein, M. S., A. C. Incollingo Belsky et al. (2015). The weight of stigma: cortisol reactivity to manipulated weight stigma. *Obesity* **23**: 368–374.

Hospital, C. M. C. S. (2007). Parental concerns about childhood obesity: time for a reality check? Ann Arbor, MI, University of Michigan.

Hossain, P., B. Kawar et al. (2007). Obesity and diabetes in the developing world – a growing challenge. *NEJM* **356**(3): 213–215.

Hughes, M. H. (1997). Soul, black women, and food. Food and Culture: A Reader. C. Counihan and P. Van Esterick. New York, Routledge.

Ikramuddin, S. and E. H. Livingston (2013). New insights on bariatric surgery outcomes. *Journal of American Medical Association* **310**(22): 2401–2402.

Imamura, F., R. Micha et al. (2015). Dietary quality among men and women in 187 countries in 1990 and 2010: a systematic assessment. *The Lancet Global Health* **3**: e132–e142.

Inglefinger, J. R. (2011). Bariatric surgery in adolescents. *New England Journal of Medicine* **365**(15): 1365–1367.

IOM (2006). Food marketing to children and youth: threat or opportunity. Washington DC: Institute of Medicine.

Jackson, S. E., R. J. Beeken et al. (2015). Perceived weight discrimination and changes in weight, waist circumference, and weight status. *Obesity* **23**: 1105–1111.

James, W. P. T. (2002). A world view of the obesity problem. Eating Disorders and Obesity: A Comprehensive Handbook. C. G. Fairburn and K. D. Brownell. New York: The Guilford Press: 411–416.

Jing, J. (2000). Feeding China's Little Emperors: Food, Children, and Social Change. Stanford, CA: Stanford University Press.

Johnson, C. L. (2002). In China, battling the girth of a nation. Christian Science Monitor. Boston.

Johnson, R. J., M. S. Segal et al. (2007). Potential role of sugar (fructose) in the epidemic of hypertension, obesity and the metabolic syndrome, diabetes, kidney disease, and cardiovascular disease. Am J Clin Nutr 86: 899–906.

Jonsson, P. (2006). Backstory: southern discomfort food. Christian Science Monitor. Boston.

Kershaw, S. (2007). Don't even think of touching that cupcake. New York Times. New York.

Khandalavala, B. N., A. Rojanala et al. (2014). Obesity bias in primary care providers. Family Medicine 46(7): 532–535.

Khouri, Z. (2006). Things go better with rights. Wall Street Journal. New York: A8.

Kimm, S. Y. S., N. W. Glynn et al. (2006). Racial differences in correlates of misreporting of energy intake in adolescent females. Obesity Research 14: 156–164.

Kjellstrom, T. and S. Hinde (2007). Car culture, transport policy, and public health. Globalization and Health. I. Kawachi and S. Wamala. Oxford, Oxford University Press: 98–121.

Knuth, N. D., D. L. Johnnsen et al. (2014). Metabolic adaptation following massive weight loss is related to the degree of energy imbalance and changes in circulating leptin. Obesity 22: 2563–2569.

Kohn, G. P., J. A. Galanko et al. (2009). Recent trends in bariatric surgery case volume in the United States. Surgery 146(2): 375–380.

Kottack, C. P. (2007). Mirror for Humanity: A Concise Introduction to Cultural Anthropology (5th ed). Boston, McGraw-Hill.

Kraak, V. I. and M. Story (2015). Influence of food companies' brand mascots and entertainment companies' cartoon media characters on children's diet and health: a systematic review and research needs. Obesity Reviews 16(2): 107–126.

Kruger, J., M. M. Yore et al. (2007). Prevalence of fruit and vegetable consumption and physical activity by race/ethnicity – United States, 2005. Morbidity & Mortality Weekly Report (MMWR) 56(13): 301–304.

Kulick, D. and A. Meneley eds. (2005). Fat: The Anthropology of an Obsession. New York: Jeremy Tarcher/Penguin.

Kumanyika, S. K. (2002). Obesity in minority populations. Eating Disorders and Obesity: A Comprehensive Handbook. C. G. Fairburn and K. D. Brownell. New York: The Guilford Press: 439–444.

Kyle, T. K., D. M. Thomas et al. (2014). Obesity is increasingly viewed as a community problem by both the public and healthcare professionals. Obesity Week Conference. Toronto.

Lanningham-Foster, L., L. J. Nysse et al. (2003). Labor saved, calories lost: the energetic impact of domestic labor-saving devices. Obesity Research 11(10): 1178–1181.

Lapp, J. and B. Hansen (2007). Who benefits from the mystery fat substitute Z Trim? Anthropology News 48(5): 6–7.

Latner, J. D., A. J. Stunkard et al. (2005). Stigmatized students: age, sex, and ethnicity effects in the stigmatization of obesity. Obesity Research 13(7): 1226–1231.

Laurson, K. R. and J. C. Eisenmann (2007). Research letter: prevalence of overweight among high school football linemen. JAMA 297(4): 363–364.

Lears, J. (2006). The American way of debt. New York Times. New York.

Linn, S. (2004). Consuming Kids: The Hostile Takeover of Childhood. New York: The New Press.

Lohr, S. (2004). Maybe it's not all your fault. New York Times. New York.

Lopez, D., T. Reader et al. (2002). Community Attitudes toward traditional Tohono O'odham foods. Sells, AZ, Tohono O'odham Community Action: 1–30.

Lumeng, J. C., N. Kaciroti et al. (2015). Changes in body mass index associated with Head Start participation. *Pediatrics* **135**(2): e449–e456.

Luo, M. (2006). Preaching a gospel of wealth in a glittery market, New York. New York Times. New York.

Macpherson-Sanchez, A. E. (2015) Integrating fundamental concepts of obesity and eating disorders: implications for the obesity epidemic. *American Journal of Public Health* **105**, e71–e85 doi 10.2105/AJPH.2014.302507.

Martin, A. (2007a). Makers of sodas try a new pitch: they're healthy. New York Times. New York.

Martin, A. (2007b). The Feed: did McDonald's give in to temptation? New York Times. New York.

Maruthur, N. M., S. Bolen et al. (2012). Body mass index and colon cancer screening: a systematic review and meta-analysis. *Cancer Epidemiology, Biomarkers & Prevention* **21**: 737–746.

Mayen, A.-L., P. Marques-Vidal et al. (2014). Socioeconomic determinants of dietary patterns in low- and middle-income countries: a systematic review. *American Journal of Clinical Nutrition* **100**(6): 1520–1531.

Maynard, L. M., D. A. Galuska et al. (2003). Maternal perceptions of weight status of children. *Pediatrics* **111**(5): 1226–1231.

McDermott, L., M. Stead et al. (2005). Does food promotion influence children's diet? A review of the evidence. Childhood Obesity: Contemporary Issues. N. Cameron, N. G. Norgan and G. T. H. Ellison. Boca Raton, FL, CRC/Taylor & Francis: 251–265.

McShane, L. (2007). American Chestnut sets record, crowned hot dog champ. The Washington Post. Washington.

Mendez, M. A., C. A. Monteiro et al. (2005). Overweight exceeds underweight among women in most developing countries. *Am J Clin Nutr* **81**: 714–721.

Mintz, S. (1997). Sugar and morality. Morality and Health. A. M. Brandt and P. Rozin. New York, Routledge: 173–183.

Mintz, S. (2002a). Eating American. Food in the U.S.A. C. M. Counihan. New York, Routledge: 23–33.

Mintz, S. W. (1993). The changing roles of food in the study of consumption. Consumption and the World of Goods. J. Brewer and R. Porter. London, Routledge: 261–273.

Mintz, S. W. (1996). Tasting Food, Tasting Freedom: Excursions into Eating, Culture, and the Past. Boston, Beacon Press.

Mintz, S. W. and C. M. Du Bois (2002). The anthropology of food and eating. *Annu Rev Anthropol* **31**: 99–119.

Moore, J. (2008). From noses to hips, Rwandans start to redefine beauty. Christian Science Monitor. Boston.

Morgan, D. (2007). Sugar industry expands influence: donations spread beyond farm areas. The Washington Post. Washington DC.

Morris, B. R. (2002). Letters on students' weight ruffle parents. New York Times. New York.

Moskovich, A., J. Hunger et al. (2011). The psychology of obesity. The Oxford Handbook of the Social Science of Obesity. J. Cawley. New York, Oxford University Press: 87–104.

Moss, M. (2013). Salt Sugar Fat: How the Food Giants Hooked Us. New York, Random House.

Muoio, D. M. and C. B. Newgard (2014). The good in fat. *Nature* **516**: 49–50.

Nabhan, G. P. (2002). Diabetes, diet and Native American foraging traditions. Food in the USA: A Reader. C. M. Counihan. New York, Routledge: 231–237.

Nabhan, G. P. (2008). Rooting out the causes of disease: why diabetes is so common among desert dwellers. Food and Culture: A Reader. C. Counihan and P. Van Esterik. New York: Routledge.

Nakamura, D. (2009). How Japan defines fat. The Washington Post. Washington DC.

Nestle, M. (2002). Food Politics: How the Food Industry Influences Nutrition and Health. Berkeley, CA: University of California Press.

Nestle, M. (2003). Safe Food: Bacteria, Biotechnology, and Bioterrorism. Berkeley, CA: University of California Press.

Nestle, M. (2006). What to Eat. New York, Farrar, Straus and Giroux.

Neuman, W. (2010). Save the children breaks with soda tax effort. New York Times. New York.

Nichter, M. (2000). Fat Talk: What Girls and Their Parents Say About Dieting. Cambridge, Harvard University Press.

Nisbett, R. E. and T. Masuda (2003). Culture and point of view. *PNAS* **100**(19): 11163–11170.

Norton, P. D. (2008). Fighting traffic: The Dawn of the Motor Age in the American city. Cambridge, MA: MIT Press.

Ohri-Vachaspati, P., Z. Isgor et al. (2015). Child-directed marketing inside and on the exterior of fast food restaurants. *American Journal of Preventive Medicine* **48**(1): 22–30.

Olvera, N., R. Suminski et al. (2005). Intergenerational perceptions of body image in Hispanics; role of BMI, gender, and acculturation. *Obesity Research* **13**: 1970–1979.

Outley, C. W. and A. Taddese (2006). A content analysis of health and physical activity messages marketed to African American children during after-school television programming. *Arch Pediat Adolesc Med* **160**: 432–435.

Owan, T., E. Avelar et al. (2011). Favorable changes in cardiac geometry and function following gastric bypass surgery: 2-year follow-up in the Utah Obesity Study. *Journal of American College of Cardiology* **57**(6): 732–739.

Padwal, R., D. Brocks et al. (2010). A systematic review of drug absorption following bariatric surgery and its theoretical implications. *Obesity Reviews* **11**(1): 41–50.

Padwal, R., S. Klarenbach et al. (2011). Bariatric surgery: a systematic review and network meta-analysis of randomized trials. *Obesity Reviews* **12**: 602–621.

Paulus, G. F., L. E. G. de Vaan et al. (2015). Bariatric surgery in morbidly obese adolescents: a systematic review and meta-analysis. *Obesity Surgery* **25**: 860–878.

PCP (2007). 2006–2007 Annual Report. Washington, DC, President's Cancer Panel.

Peterhaensel, C., D. Petroff et al. (2013). Risk of completed suicide after bariatric surgery: a systematic review. *Obesity Reviews* **14**: 369–382.

Peters, J. C. (2003). Combating obesity: challenges and choices. *Obesity Research* **11**(Suppl): 7S–11S.

Phelan, S., J. O. Hill et al. (2003). Recovery from relapse among successful weight maintainers. *Am J Clin Nutr* **78**: 1079–1084.

Phelan, S. M., D. J. Burgess et al. (2015). Impact of weight bias and stigma on quality of care and outcomes for patients with obesity. *Obesity Reviews* **16**: 319–326.

Phillips, L. (2006). Food and globalization. *Annu Rev Anthropol* **16**: 37–57.

Pietilainen, K. H., S. E. Saami et al. (2012). Does dieting make you fat? A twin study. *International Journal of Obesity* **36**(3): 456–464.

Pillsbury, R. (1998). No Foreign Food: The American Diet in Time and Place. Boulder, CO: Westview Press.

Pollan, M. (2008). In Defense of Food: An Eater's Manifesto. New York: Penguin.

Pollock, N. J. (1995). Social fattening patterns in the Pacific – the positive side of obesity. A Nauru case study. Social Aspects of Obesity. I. de Garine and N. J. Pollock. London, Gordon and Breach Publishers: 87–109.

Popenoe, R. (2004). Feeding Desire: Fatness, Beauty, and Sexuality Among a Saharan People. London: Routledge.

Popkin, B. M. (2002). The dynamics of the dietary transition in the developing world. The Nutrition Transition: Diet and Disease in the Developing World. B. Caballero and B. M. Popkin. Boston, Academic Press: 111–128.

Popkin, B. M. (2006). Global nutrition dynamics: the world is shifting rapidly toward a diet linked with noncommunicable diseases. *Am J Clin Nutr* **84**: 289–298.

Popkin, B. M. (2007). The world is fat. *Scientific American* **297**(3): 88–95.

Popkin, B. M. and P. Gordon-Larsen (2004). The nutrition transition: worldwide obesity dynamics and their determinants. *Int J Obesity* **28**: S2–S9.

Popkin, B. M. and J. R. Udry (1998). Adolescent obesity increases significantly in second and third generation U.S. immigrants: the National Longitudinal Study of Adolescent Health. *Journal of Nutrition* **128**: 701–706.

Powdermaker, H. (1997). An anthropological approach to the problem of obesity. Food and Culture: A Reader. C. Counihan and P. Van Esterik. New York, Routledge: 203–209.

Powell, L. M., G. Szczypka et al. (2007). Exposure to food advertising on television among US children. *Arch Pediatr Adolesc Med* **161**: 553–560.

Puhl, R. M. and C. A. Heuer (2009). The stigma of obesity: a review and update. *Obesity* **17**(5): 941–964.

Rabin, R. C. (2008). In the fatosphere, big is in, or at least accepted. New York Times. New York.

Rand, C. S. W. and J. L. Resnick (2000). The good enough body size as judged by people of varying age and weight. *Obesity Research* **8**(4): 309–316.

Raynor, H. A., R. W. Jeffery et al. (2005). Amount of food group variety consumed in the diet and long-term weight loss maintenance. *Obesity Research* **13**(5): 883–890.

Reich, R. (2007). Supercapitalism: The Transformation of Business, Democracy, and Everyday Life. New York: Alfred A. Knopf.

Reidenberg, M. (2000). Are we treating health or physical appearance when we prescribe drugs for obesity? *Clinical Pharmacology & Therapeutics* **67**(3): 193–194.

Reilly, J. J. (2005). Obesity prevention in childhood and adolescence. Childhood Obesity: Contemporary Issues. N. Cameron, N. G. Norgan, and G. T. H. Ellison. Boca Raton, FL, CRC/Taylor & Francis: 205–222.

Replogle, J. (2014). Mexico's soda tax is starting to change some habits, say health advocates. PRI's The World Radio Program.

Reynolds, K., D. Gu et al. (2007). Prevalence and risk factors of overweight and obesity in China. *Obesity* **15**: 10–18.

Ritenbaugh, C. (1982). Obesity as a culture-bound syndrome. *Culture, Medicine and Psychiatry* **6**: 347–361.

Rosenthal, E. (1999). China's chic waistline: convex to concave. New York Times. New York.

Rosenthal, E. (2002). Buicks, Starbucks, and fried chicken. Still China? New York Times. New York.

Rumsfeld, J. S. and B. K. Nallamothu (2008). The hope and fear of rimonabant. *Journal of American Medical Association* **299**(13): 1601.

Sahud, H. B., H. J. Binns et al. (2006). Marketing fast food; impact of fast food restaurants in children's hospitals. *Pediatrics* **118**(6): 2290–2297.

Samavati, S. (2004). Plenty of cheap eating at Greene fair. Dayton Daily News. Dayton, OH.

Santora, M. (2006). In diabetes fight, raising cash and keeping trust. New York Times. New York.

Sarafrazi, N., J. P. Hughes et al. (2014). Perception of weight status in U.S. children and adolescents aged 8–15 years, 2005–2012. NCHS Data Brief, USDHH, Centers for Disease Control and Prevention, National Center for Health Statistics.

Sarna, J. (forthcoming). How matzah became square: Manischewitz and the development of machine-made matzah in the United States.

Schauer, P. R., S. R. Kashyap et al. (2012). Bariatric surgery versus intensive medical therapy in obese patients with diabetes. *New England Journal of Medicine* **366**: 1567–1576.

Schor, J. (2003). The new politics of consumption: why Americans want so much more than they need. Gender, Race, and Class in Media: A Text-Reader (2nd ed). G. Dines and J. M. Humez. Thousand Oaks, CA, Sage: 183–195.

Schor, J. (2004). Born to Buy: The Commercialized Child and the New Consumer Culture. New York: Scribner.

Schor, J. B. (1992). The Overworked American. New York: Basic Books.

Schwartz, M. B. and R. Puhl (2003). Childhood obesity: a societal problem to solve. *Obesity Reviews* **4**: 57–71.

Schwartz, M. B., L. R. Vartanian et al. (2006). The influence of one's own body weight on implicit and explicit anti-fat bias. *Obesity Research* **14**: 440–447.

SEF (2015). Research bulletin: a new majority – low income students now a majority in the nation's public schools. Atlanta, GA: Southern Education Foundation

Severson, K. and J. Moskin (2006). Meals that moms can almost call their own. New York Times. New York.

Shekelle, P. G., L. Hardy et al. (2003). Efficacy and safety of ephedra and ephedrine for weight loss and athletic performance. *Journal of American Medical Association* **289**(12): 1537–1545.

Sherman, A. and A. Aron-Dine (2007). New CBA data show income inequality continues to widen: after-tax-income for top 1 percent rose by $146,000 in 2004. Washington, DC: Center on Budget and Policy Priorities.

Sherry, B., M. E. Jefferds et al. (2007). Accuracy of adolescent self-report of height and weight in assessing overweight status: a literature review. *Archives of Pediatric & Adolescent Medicine* **161**(12): 1154–1161.

Sheumaker, H. and S. T. Wajda eds. (2008). Material Culture in America: Understanding Everyday life. Santa Barbara, CA: ABC-CLIO, Inc.

Shiva, V. (2001). Stolen Harvest: The Hijacking of the Global Food Supply. London: Zed.

Simon, M. (2006). Appetite for Profit: How the Food Industry Undermines Our Health and How to Fight Back. New York: Nation Books.

Simpson, S. J. and D. Raubenheimer (2014). Tricks of the trade. *Nature* **508**: 566.

Singer, N. (2007). Feel pudgy? There's a shot for that. New York Times. New York.

Soares, C. (2006). Women rethink a big size that is beautiful but brutal. Christian Science Monitor. Boston.

Steinhauer, J. (2005). When the Joneses wear jeans. New York Times. New York.

Stewart, K. (2006). Class tells how to eat well on the cheap. Salt Lake Tribune. Salt Lake City.

Stimpson, J. P. and X. Urrutia-Rojas (2007). Acculturation in the United States is associated with lower serum carotenoid levels: Third National Health and Nutrition Examination Survey. *J Am Diet Assoc* **107**(7): 1218–1223.

Strom, S. (2011). Local laws fighting fat under siege. New York Times. New York.

Sumithran, P., L. A. Prendergast et al. (2011). Long-term persistence of hormonal adaptations to weight loss. *New England Journal of Medicine* **365**: 1597–1604.

Sun, S. (2005). Interview: Chinese greetings and food. A. Bellisari. Dayton, OH.

Sundquist, J. and M. Winkleby (2000). Country of birth, acculturation status and abdominal obesity in a national sample of Mexican-American women and men. *Int J Epidemiology* **29**: 470–477.

Sutherly, B. (2007). Where does our food come from? Often from a processing plant here in Ohio. Dayton Daily News. Dayton, OH.

Tavernise, S. (2013). The health toll of immigration. New York Times. New York.

Taylor, P. (2006). Americans see weight problems everywhere but in mirror. Washington DC: Pew Research Center.

Thomas, J. S., K. Harden et al. (2005). The barriers to, and the facilitators of, healthy eating among children: findings from a systematic review. Childhood Obesity: Contemporary Issues. N. Cameron, N. G. Norgan, and G. T. H. Ellison. Boca Raton: CRC/Taylor & Francis: 223–250.

Tierney, J. (2004). The autonomist manifesto (or, how I learned to stop worrying and love the road). New York Times. New York.

Tsai, A. G. and T. A. Wadden (2005). Systematic review: an evaluation of major commercial weight loss programs in the United States. *Ann Intern Med* **142**: 56–66.

Vandewater, E. A. and E. A. Wartella (2011). Food marketing, television, and video games. The Oxford Handbook of the Social Science of Obesity. J. Cawley. New York, Oxford University Press: 350–366.

Vasquez, R. (2007). In Beijing, fascination with cupcakes and cheesecake. Christian Science Monitor. Boston.

Volkow, N. D., G.-J. Wang et al. (2013). Obesity and addiction: neurobiological overlaps. *Obesity Reviews* **14**: 2–18.

Wadden, T. A., D. A. Anderson et al. (1999). Two-year changes in lipids and lipoproteins associated with maintenance of 5% to 10% reduction in initial weight: some findings and some questions. *Obesity Research* **7**(2): 170–178.

Wang, Y., J. Mi et al. (2007). Is China facing an obesity epidemic and the consequences? The trends in obesity and chronic disease in China. *Int J Obesity* **31**: 177–188.

Wang, Y. C., S. N. Bleich, and S. I. Gortmaker (2008). Increasing caloric contribution from sugar-sweetened beverages and 100% fruit juices among US children and adolescents. *Pediatrics* **121**: e1604–e1614.

Wansink, B. (2006). Mindless Eating: Why We Eat More Than We Think. New York: Bantam.

Ward, M. (2005). Nest in the wind: Adventures in anthropology on a Tropical Island. Long Grove, IL: Waveland Press, Inc.

Warner, M. (2006). Salads or no, cheap burgers revive McDonald's. New York Times. New York.

Watson, J. L. (2002). China's Big Mac attack. Food in the USA: A Reader. C. M. Counihan. New York, Routledge: 347–357.

Weber, C. (2007). The devil sells Prada. New York Times. New York.

Weil, E. (2005). Heavy questions. New York Times. New York.

Weiner, M. (2002). Consumer culture and participatory democracy: the story of Coca-Cola during World War II. Food in the USA. C. M. Counihan. New York, Routledge: 123–141.

Whybrow, P. C. (2005). American Mania: When More Is Not Enough. New York: W. W. Norton & Company.

Wiecha, J., K. E. Peterson et al. (2006). When children eat what they watch. *Arch Pediatr Adolesc Med* **160**: 436–442.

Williams, E. (1961). Capitalism and Slavery. New York: Russell & Russell.

Wilson, M. (2005). Indulgence. Fat: The Anthropology of an Obsession. D. Kulick and A. Meneley. New York, Jeremy Tarcher/Penguin: 153–168.

Wing, R. R. and M. Klem (2002). Characteristics of successful weight managers. Eating Disorders and Obesity: A Comprehensive Handbook. C. G. Fairburn and K. D. Brownell. New York, The Guilford Press: 588–592.

Wing, R. R. and S. Phelan (2005). Long-term weight loss maintenance. *American Journal of Clinical Nutrition* **82**(Suppl): 222S–225S.

Winter, G. (2002). America rubs its stomach, and says bring it on. New York Times. New York.

Wolf, A., G. A. Bray et al. (2007). A short history of beverages and how our body treats them. *Obesity Reviews* **9**: 151–164.

Wood, D. B. (2005). When big is too big, even in L.A. Christian Science Monitor. Boston.

Wuthnow, R. (1996). Poor Richard's Principle: Recovering the American Dream Through the Moral Dimension of Work, Business, and Money. Princeton, NJ, Princeton University Press.

Wyatt, E. (2009). On 'The Biggest Loser,' health can take back seat. New York Times. New York.

Yang, W., J. Lu et al. (2010). Prevalence of diabetes among men and women in China. *NEJM* **362**: 1090–1101.

Yanovski, S. Z. and J. A. Yanovski (2014). Long-term drug treatment for obesity: a systematic and clinical review. *Journal of American Medical Association* **311**(1): 74–86.

Yoo, J. H. (2013). No clear winner: effects of *The Biggest Loser* on the stigmatization of obese persons. *Health Communication* **28**(3): 294–303.

Yracheta, J. M., M. A. Lanaspa et al. (2015). Diabetes and kidney disease in American Indians: potential role of sugar-sweetened beverages. *Mayo Clinic Proceedings* **90**(6): 813–823.

Z TRIM Holdings (2007). Z Trim: live life better. Mundelein, IL: Z TRIM Holdings.

Zimmerman, F. J. (2011). Using marketing muscle to sell fat: the rise of obesity in the modern economy. *Annual Review of Public Health* **32**: 285–306.

Zimmet, P. Z. and K. G. M. M. Alberti (2006). Introduction: globalization and the non-communicable disease epidemic. *Obesity* **14**: 1–3.

Zimmet, P. Z., D. J. McCarty et al. (1997). The global epidemiology of non-insulin-dependent diabetes mellitus and the metabolic syndrome. *J Diab Comp* **11**: 60–68.

Zukin, S. (2003). We are where we shop. New York Times. New York.

7

CONCLUSION

The anthropology of obesity

Introduction

The American obesity epidemic is a serious public health crisis and a challenge that has resisted resolution so far, in spite of great effort and expense on the part of individuals to reduce excess body fat and institutions to lower the nation's obesity rate. The US still has the highest prevalence of obesity among developed, scientifically sophisticated, wealthy countries in Europe and North America, none of which have been able to reverse the epidemic. 2007–12 National Health and Nutrition Examination Survey (NHANES) data show that obesity rates have actually increased until there are now more American adults with obesity than overweight (jamainternalmedicine.com). Many children and adolescents already manifest the serious health risks of excessive adiposity – pre-diabetes, diabetes, liver disease, metabolic syndrome, and, not least, the psychological and social burdens of being fat. Unlike adults who become obese in later life, young Americans with obesity have to look forward to a very long life of pain, disability, hardship, expensive health care, and social disadvantages.

It seems that many Americans are desensitized to obesity. Even some medical professionals are unaware of the powerful human metabolic adaptations that acquire and defend stored energy, a complex biological survival system that evolved over millions of years of human prehistory; it is more powerful than any mechanism for reducing fat stores, and triggers protective metabolic responses to all forms of food restriction. Very few individuals have been able to overcome the body's natural resistance to weight loss to recover from obesity (Ochner et al. 2015).

In addition to adapting genetically and physiologically to boost energy efficiency, human ancestors devised cultural and behavioral responses to maximize energy intake with minimal energy expenditure – creating tools to acquire energy sources, foraging and hunting for meat, producing, storing, and preparing new types of foods, sharing meals in a social setting, and developing labor-saving technology. The modern obesogenic environment is the culmination of these developments, but is not compatible with human biology designed to amass and retain a large internal store of energy. The creation of continuous energy abundance and easy living realized the American Dream, but at the cost of social disparities, excessive adiposity, and chronic health risks.

One reason for the inability to stem the obesity epidemic is a narrow scientific focus on single biological variables and processes and individual behaviors, with much less consideration of their complex external causes. It is clear that both pre- and postnatal environmental influences play important roles in the development of obesity and the magnitude of the American obesity epidemic. The constellation of multiple and redundant metabolic processes, genetic diversity, environmental variations, and their many shifting interactions produces a complex pathway to obesity, one that is arguably very difficult to unravel. A much broader ecological approach is needed, one that complements the remarkable scientific discoveries made so far regarding the biology of obesity with investigations and modifications of the obesogenic environment. High rates of obesity occur only in energy-rich environments such as those of the US and other wealthy, developed countries. Fortunately, once they are identified, environmental factors can be much more readily modified to promote health than genetic inheritance or metabolic functions. In the words of anthropologist Roberto Frisancho (1993: 7):

> Adaptation to the world of today may be incompatible with survival in the world of tomorrow, unless humans learn to adjust their cultural and biological capacities.

Obesity in America

Americans have industrialized, medicalized, and individualized obesity. Industry-produced, highly processed foods are vigorously advertised, marketed, and consumed by Americans. They are relatively inexpensive compared to unadulterated fruits, vegetables, meats, and other fresh nutritious foods, making them attractive to consumers who have tight budgets and little time for food preparation. They are also energy-rich and nutrient-poor. Work, travel, and leisure time are mechanized and relatively effortless, lowering the need for physical activity and energy expenditure in daily life. The technology industries, food services, and entertainment producers enjoy large markets and offer the ease, convenience, and pleasure that are considered the benefits of America's high standard of living.

Medicalization of obesity is more beneficial for health care professionals, pharmaceutical companies, and diet industries treating obesity with a variety of drugs, weight loss programs, surgeries, and advice than for persons with obesity. They offer simple solutions, quick and easy fixes to control adiposity, but with little success. Drugs and programs are highly profitable and thus constitute vested interests in the obesity epidemic. All of them treat obesity, often repeatedly in the same individual with obesity, instead of preventing its development in the first place. Current treatment modes and advice individualize obesity, placing primary responsibility for weight control on persons with obesity and in many cases blaming them for their increasing body weight and inability to shed pounds. Individuals with obesity are urged to change their lifestyles, while powerful environmental influences upon individual decisions and behaviors are seldom addressed.

Children are especially vulnerable since they have even less control over obesogenic influences than adults, but regulation of food advertising to children has been successfully blocked by corporate political activity and lobbying (OECD 2014). To hold children responsible without changing the environment is "unfair, hypocritical, and an abrogation of adult responsibility" (Dawes 2014: 220). According to Susan Dentzer, editor-in-chief of *Health Affairs*, America is guilty of child abuse by failing to restrain economic and political forces that hinder prevention (Dentzer 2010). Individualizing obesity has led to stigmatization, discrimination, and lowered opportunities for persons with obesity, especially women. Because of the emphasis on individual faults and accountabilities, personal rights and freedoms are invoked by those rejecting public health efforts to reduce obesity rates. Many Americans undermine efforts to prevent obesity or lower obesity rates because they fear that their individual liberties are violated.

The challenges

To lower obesity prevalence in the US, it must be contextualized, politicized, and moralized. Appeals to eat better and exercise more are virtually futile in an environmental context that vigorously encourages and promotes high levels of consumption and inactivity. To adopt healthy lifestyles, individuals are forced to struggle against powerful economic, political, and sociocultural forces over which they have no control. In efforts to overcome obesity in the US, it is necessary to address the external obesogenic environment as well as individual biological traits and behaviors.

The federal government has yet to fulfill its social contract to "provide for the general welfare." Individual Americans cannot achieve public health goals without the support of government policy makers regulating food advertisement, nutritional content, and product safety, adequately funding the American education system, ensuring a level playing field of employment and income opportunities, ending conflicting messaging that confuses consumers, and balancing protection of corporate profits with promotion of public health for the entire population.

A new morality is needed to protect the civil rights of individuals with obesity by combatting discrimination and developing tolerance for victims of the obesity epidemic. Just as individual Americans are obliged to balance immediate gratification with care about their long-term, personal health, so is U.S. society, especially its political and economic sectors, obligated to balance self-interests with general wellbeing. Just as individual Americans are expected to control risky behaviors, corporations must be required to control the environmental risks they have created and balance them with concern for their consumers.

The good news

Although the number of adults and children with obesity is still very high, the prevalence of obesity among U.S. youngsters has leveled off at 17 percent; it has not increased since 2007 and has actually decreased slightly among two- to five-year-olds (Ogden et al. 2014). Extreme obesity among pre-school children in low-income families decreased significantly since 2003 in all groups except Native Americans (Pan et al. 2012), and obesity rates among New York Women, Infants, and Children (WIC) children also declined since 2009 (eurekalert.org). Several other U.S. cities that monitor students' weight and have obesity reduction policies in place have reported small declines in obesity among children (Taber et al. 2012; Tavernise 2012). Children with obesity who had participated in Head Start programs were less obese in kindergarten than children who had not been in Head Start (Lumeng et al. 2015). New policies and actions initiated in recent years help to account for these positive signs:

- WIC food packages were revised to include vouchers for fresh produce, low-fat milk, and whole-grain items. The Food Research and Action Center reported that WIC participants are satisfied with the new foods and have seen some declines in obesity rates (http://frac.org) (Andreyeva et al. 2012).
- The 2014 farm bill passed by Congress and signed by President Obama cut some subsidies for traditional commodities and increased funding for fruits, vegetables, and organic programs (Steinhauer 2014).
- The National School Lunch Program, which provides low-cost or free lunch to more than 31 million public and private school children, now follows new rules to improve their nutritional quality recommended by the Institute of Medicine and enforced by the Healthy Hunger-Free Kids Act (although there is some industry opposition) (Baidal and Taveras 2014). The program provides lunches of better quality than lunches students bring from home (Caruso and Cullen 2014). In 32 New Orleans schools, for the first time lunch offerings include salad bars. Although improved lunches cost more and some students resist the changes, in California the majority of students accept them and like the new lunch menus. West Virginia, with one of the highest rates of childhood obesity, worked with celebrity chef Jamie Oliver to develop healthy menu options that were aired on his television show. Several New York City high schools offer a Science of Food class that combines lessons on media literacy, politics, nutrition, and cooking. New York City elementary school students saw a dip in severe obesity rates attributed to healthier meals, increased physical education, and school gardens planted with edible plants. More and more schools are removing sugary snacks and drinks from vending machines and replacing them with healthy options (N.A. 2010a; Stolberg 2011;

Vanacore 2011; Wallace 2011; Gerber 2012; Kissell 2012; Nixon 2012; Turner and Chaloupka 2012; Letsch 2014).

- From 2003 to 2010 children's energy consumption from fast foods (burgers, pizza, chicken) dropped significantly, and the number of children obtaining food and beverages from pizza restaurants was reduced by half (Rehm and Drewnowski 2015).

- Despite resistance from beverage companies and failures to pass legislation in other communities, voters in Berkeley, California, approved a tax on sodas in an effort to cut consumption of added sugars (following the example set by Mexico) (kaiserhealthnews.org) (Bittman 2013). Soda taxes are considered to be one of the most effective ways to reduce sugar consumption (Replogle 2014; Thow et al. 2014).

- Los Angeles and a number of smaller cities have enacted moratoriums against the establishment of new fast-food restaurants in poorer neighborhoods, hoping that restaurants and stores offering healthier foods would open instead (Medina 2011).

- The New York City Fruit and Vegetable Prescription Program offers Health Bucks that doctors prescribe for their patients with obesity, who can exchange them for fresh produce (npr.org).

- Several communities and fast-food restaurants have ended the free toy giveaway with fast-food meals for children (npr.org), and some fast-food companies are quietly changing their menu options by lowering fat and salt content and reducing portion sizes.

- The Walt Disney Company now excludes advertisements for candy, sugared cereal, and fast food on children's Saturday cartoon shows, and ads for sweet foods targeting young children have generally declined (although fast-food ads have increased) (Barnes 2012).

- Efforts to increase access to fresh produce and other healthy food are underway and include the Healthy Corner Store programs in New Orleans, Chicago, and other cities; new supermarkets and mobile produce stands in food deserts; the Urban Food Initiative that opens nonprofit supermarkets in low-income neighborhoods; tax breaks for urban farmers in Baltimore who convert vacant land into gardens (truth-out.org); and organic farmers' cooperatives that aim to produce healthy food and provide growers with an adequate income (Hightower and de Marco 2008; Lynn 2010; Pope 2011; Bornstein 2012; Couzin-Frankel 2012; Guy 2012; Palakshappa et al. 2014).

- Increased physical activity is promoted by the Smart Growth urban planning program and the Bronx Active Design Guidelines for construction that fosters constructing attractive and accessible staircases inside subway stops. The twin cities of Minneapolis and St. Paul, Minnesota, like several other U.S. urban areas, offer a car-sharing program (hourcar.org) which leases automobiles to clients by the hour to fill temporary transportation needs, thereby encouraging walking to nearby stores, libraries, schools, and churches. Even the screen media has contributed by developing a variety of exer-games to increase energy expenditure in an enjoyable way (Bailey and McInnis 2011; Durand et al. 2011; Hughes 2011).

- A few of the poorest Americans are beginning to see improvements in income and obesity rates. For example, California Indian tribes that opened or expanded casinos have higher per capita incomes, lower poverty rates, and small declines in childhood obesity, compared to tribes that have no casinos (Jones-Smith et al. 2014).

- Native Americans are reviving traditional cuisines using indigenous foods and ingredients. The new Sioux Chef restaurant specializing in Lakota tribal cooking opened in Minneapolis in 2014 (america.aljazeera.com), and Gila River Community (Pima) members are planting traditional crops again after regaining their water rights (Archibold 2008).

- First Lady Michelle Obama is leading a nationwide childhood obesity prevention program. Her White House organic vegetable garden (Figure 7.1) and *Let's Move* program target children's individual eating and activity behaviors, but Obama's comprehensive efforts also include steps to improve the national obesogenic environment by promoting better food labeling, offering incentives to bring fresh produce to underserved, poor urban areas, planning more nutritious school lunches, and fostering children's physical activity (N.A. 2010b). Unfortunately, feeling threatened, many large interest groups, including the School Nutrition Association (Confessore 2014), fast-food industry, agribusinesses, soft-drink manufacturers, advertisers, and the automotive industry, among others, have tried to roll back parts of the program even though it only advocates for voluntary change (Ambinder 2010; Hiatt 2010). Food producers opposed to voluntary marketing guidelines by far outspent the Center for Science in the Public Interest in lobbying, until Congress blocked the effort to limit advertising for sweetened soda, snacks, sugared cereals, and fast food aimed at children (Wilson and Roberts 2012; Gold and Hennessey 2013).

- Survey responses by a representative sample of more than 40,000 U.S. adults and health care professionals showed a significant shift of perception of obesity as a personal problem of bad choices to a view of obesity as a community problem of bad food and inactivity (Kyle et al. 2014). Also, among low-income participants, community-based strategies aimed at structural change were more effective at lowering obesity than changes targeting individual behaviors (Beauchamp et al. 2014).

These positive steps are a welcome but small start. As long as adult obesity is relatively intractable, the only practical way to stem the obesity epidemic is prevention targeting young children (AAP 2003). Prevention warrants a systems approach and necessitates action on many fronts simultaneously, directed at both individuals and social, economic, and political institutions. They must address the issue of obesity on an even greater scale than the nationwide policies put in place to prevent dangers from unsafe toys, environmental pollutants, infectious diseases (vaccination), auto accident injuries (seat belts and car seats), and contaminated food and water.

FIGURE 7.1   The White House vegetable garden. Courtesy of Tim Sloan/AFP/Getty Images.

No single individual sector of society can lower U.S. obesity rates on its own; it requires collaborative, interdisciplinary effort that attends to all of the voices with a stake in personal and public health – people living with obesity, public health professionals, social scientists, economists, and others, some of whom have been muzzled by corporate and political vested interests. Already some research agendas include integrated ecological approaches to complement biological and clinical obesity studies. There is, for example, the ANGELO method used to study interconnections of physical, economic, political, and sociocultural elements in specific obesogenic environments (Egger and Swinburn 1997; Swinburn et al. 1999; Egger and Dixon 2010), which has not yet been much used in the US. The African American Collaborative Obesity Research Network (AACORN) uses an interdisciplinary and contextualized approach to design interventions (aacorn.org). The University of Washington Center for Obesity Research facilitates interdisciplinary studies addressing biomedical, social, economic, and environmental aspects of obesity (http://depts.washington.edu/uwecor). The Strategic Plan for National Institutes of Health (NIH) Obesity Research funds broad and deep investigations of the "multiplicity and complexity" of forces driving the obesity epidemic as they act on the general human background of genetic susceptibility (Spiegel and Alving 2005). Not least, medical anthropology with its feet firmly planted in both human biology and human culture is eminently qualified to analyze environmental complexities and their interactions with genes and physiology. Its trademark approaches of direct observation, on-site fieldwork, intensive interviews, cross-cultural comparisons, and multivariate analyses are an excellent fit for studying the broader picture of obesity, its constraints and possibilities, its structural causes, and its ideological dimensions. Food insecurity around the world has long been a topic of ethnographic research (Baro and Deubel 2006), and years ago cultural anthropologist Margaret Mead led the Committee on Food charged by the National Research Council with studying ways to change eating habits to improve the nutritional status of Americans during the time of war (Warner 2010).

Public health professionals have stated that they can do little to solve the U.S. obesity problem because "most potential solutions rest either on very large changes in public policy or many very small changes that individuals and families must make in their own homes" (Weil 2005). In 1848 physician-anthropologist Rudolf Virchow advocated "radical" action for solving the great Upper Silesian typhus epidemic, which he attributed to poor living conditions (Virchow 2006). His report concluded that it would take more than medical treatment focusing on individuals to end the epidemic and prevent future ones. Virchow advocated for improved agricultural techniques, public education, tax relief, separation of church and state, and equal rights for the working people who had been forced into poverty by wealthy capitalists. He urged that social changes be implemented to reduce the poverty and unsanitary living conditions responsible for transmission of the pathogen, and thereby to protect the entire public by removing institutional barriers to good health. Similarly, individual Americans cannot stop the obesity epidemic. U.S. citizens must oppose not only their individual instincts to consume and take life easy, but also the powerful political and economic forces that exploit those instincts for gain at the expense of health (Nestle and Jacobson 2000). American society has the collective responsibility to make the connections between its policies and the major environmental barriers and obstacles to healthy eating and activity. Legislative and regulatory action to control obesogenic forces should ease the way for successful individual responsible action (Brownell et al. 2010).

Most of all, stemming the obesity epidemic demands a change in attitude, which is probably the most difficult challenge of all. A recent email exchange on a local university campus is illustrative. When several students on the campus email list tried to outdo each other with complaints about the distance from the parking lots to their classrooms, one student ended the general griping by offering this insightful response: "Quit complaining and think of it as an opportunity for much needed exercise." Her viewpoint is uncommon in a society that places a high value on expediency and convenience. To make real changes in the obesogenic environment calls for balancing immediate, private concerns with a longer view of health by both individual Americans and American institutional structures. The culture of individualism and excessive consumption needs to be balanced with a culture of health for all.

Conclusion

The direct approach to combat obesity one individual at a time is necessary but not sufficient to resolve the U.S. obesity epidemic; indirect solutions to change the obesogenic environment are also needed. In the words of geneticist James Neel (Neel 1999), Americans "need cultural engineering" to reduce obesity; they must take a long, careful look at the broader context and be prepared to make some society-wide, national-level changes in the practices and beliefs regarding obesity.

At worst, the obesity epidemic is the consequence of competitive consumption by individual Americans and cynical profiteering by political powers and industries. Driven by cultural expectations, many Americans have sacrificed their health and that of generations to come without being aware of the disastrous long-term results. At best, the obesity epidemic is the unintended result of the deep desire to realize the shared American Dream, the drive to increase family prosperity and improve the standard of living. American citizens, whose enormous contributions and sacrifices have made this country one of opportunity and hope for many, deserve a strong commitment to and generous investment in their public health.

References

AAP (2003). Policy statement: Prevention of pediatric overweight and obesity. *Pediatrics* **112**(2): 424–430.

Ambinder, M. (2010). Beating obesity. *The Atlantic* **305**(4).

Andreyeva, T., J. Luedicke et al. (2012). Positive influence of the revised special supplemental nutrition program for women, infants, and children food packages on access to healthy foods. *Journal of the Academy of Nutrition and Dietetics* **112**: 850–858.

Archibold, R. C. (2008). Indians' water rights give hope for better health. New York Times. New York.

Baidal, J. A. W. and E. M. Taveras (2014). Protecting progress against childhood obesity – the National School Lunch Program. *New England Journal of Medicine* **371**(20): 1862–1865.

Bailey, B. W. and K. McInnis (2011). Energy cost of exergaming: a comparison of the energy cost of 6 forms of exergaming. *Archives of Pediatric & Adolescent Medicine* **165**(7): 597–602.

Barnes, B. (2012). Promoting nutrition, Disney to limit junk-food ads. Times Digest. New York.

Baro, M. and T. F. Deubel (2006). Persistent hunger: perspectives on vulnerability, famine, and food security in Sub-Saharan Africa. *Annual Review of Anthropology* **35**: 521–538.

Beauchamp, A., K. Backholer et al. (2014). The effect of obesity prevention interventions according to socioeconomic position: a systematic review. *Obesity Reviews* **15**(7): 541–554.

Bittman, M. (2013). !Viva Mexico! New York Times. New York.

Bornstein, D. (2012). Conquering food deserts with green carts. New York Times. New York.

Brownell, K. D., R. Kersh et al. (2010). Personal responsibility and obesity: a constructive approach to a controversial issue. *Health Affairs* **29**(3): 379–387.

Caruso, M. L. and K. W. Cullen (2014). Quality and cost of student lunches brought from home. *JAMA Pediatrics* **169**(1): 86–90.

Confessore, N. (2014). How school lunch became the latest political battleground. New York Times. New York: 1–18.

Couzin-Frankel, J. (2012). Tackling America's eating habits, one store at a time. *Science* **337**(1473–1475).

Dentzer, S. (2010). The child abuse we inflict through child obesity. *Health Affairs* **29**(3): 342.

Durand, C. P., M. Andalib et al. (2011). A systematic review of built environment factors related to physical activity and obesity risk: implications for smart growth urban planning. *Obesity Reviews* **12**(5): e173–e182.

Egger, G. and J. Dixon (2010). Inflammatory effects of nutritional stimuli: further support for the need for a big picture approach to tackling obesity and chronic disease. *Obesity Reviews* **11**: 137–149.

Egger, G. and B. Swinburn (1997). An ecological approach to the obesity pandemic. *British Medical Journal* **315**: 477–480.

Gerber, M. (2012). Most students give more healthful state school menus thumbs up. Los Angeles Times. Los Angeles.

Gold, M. and K. Hennessey (2013). Michelle Obama's nutrition campaign comes with political pitfalls. Los Angeles Times. Los Angeles.

Guy, S. (2012). More fresh produce coming to Chicago's 'food deserts'. Sun-Times. Chicago.

Hiatt, A. (2010). How did obesity become a partisan fight? The Washington Post. Washington DC.

Hightower, J. and S. de Marco (2008). Swim against the current: even a dead fish can go with the flow. Hoboken, NJ: Wiley & Sons, Inc.

Hughes, C. J. (2011). Bronx apartment building designed to combat obesity. New York Times. New York.

Jones-Smith, J. C., W. H. Dow et al. (2014). Association between casino opening or expansion and risk of childhood overweight and obesity. *Journal of American Medical Association* **311**(9): 929–936.

Kissell, M. R. (2012). Healthier lunches costing schools, some students more. Dayton Daily News. Dayton, OH.

Kyle, T. K., D. M. Thomas et al. (2014). Obesity is increasingly viewed as a community problem by both the public and healthcare professionals. Obesity Week Conference. Toronto.

Letsch, C. (2014). Obesity among students in city public schools shrinks, according to health officials. New York Daily News. New York.

Lumeng, J. C., N. Kaciroti et al. (2015). Changes in body mass index associated with Head Start participation. *Pediatrics* **135**(2): e339–e456.

Lymn, K. (2010). Minneapolis project aims to increase access to healthy foods. Minnesota Daily. Minneapolis.

Medina, J. (2011). In South Lost Angeles, new fast-food spots get a 'no, thanks'. New York Times. New York.

N.A. (2010a). USDA to assist local food program. The Herald-Dispatch. Huntington, WV.

N.A. (2010b). From Mrs. Obama's garden. New York Times. New York.

Neel, J. V. (1999). The thrifty genotype in 1998. *Nutrition Reviews* **57**: S2–S9.

Nestle, M. and M. F. Jacobson (2000). Halting the obesity epidemic: a public health policy approach. *Public Health Reports* **115**: 12–24.

Nixon, R. (2012). New rules for school meals aim at reducing obesity. New York Times. New York.

Ochner, C. N., A. G. Tsai et al. (2015). Treating obesity seriously: when recommendations for lifestyle changes confront biological adaptations. *Lancet Diabetes Endocrinology* doi 10.1016/S2213-8587(15)00009-1.

OECD (2014). Obesity update. Paris: OECD Directorate for Employment, Labour and Social Affairs.

Ogden, C. L., M. D. Caroll et al. (2014). Prevalence of childhood and adult obesity in the United States, 2011–2012. *Journal of American Medical Association* **311**(8): 806–814.

Palakshappa, D., G. Daftary et al. (2014). An ethically appropriate strategy to combat obesity and food insecurity: the Urban Food Initiative. *JAMA Pediatrics* **168**(10): 881–882.

Pan, L., H. M. Blanck et al. (2012). Trends in the prevalence of extreme obesity among US preschool-aged children living in low-income families, 1999–2010. *Journal of the American Medical Association* **308**(24): 2563–2565.

Pope, J. (2011). New Orleans neighborhoods without grocers targeted by $14 million program. The Times-Picayune. New Orleans.

Rehm, C. D. and A. Drewnowski (2015). Trends in energy intakes by type of fast food restaurant among US children from 2003 to 2010. *JAMA Pediatrics* **169**(5): 502–504.

Replogle, J. (2014) Mexico's soda tax is starting to change some habits, say health advocates. Radio broadcast 2 December 2014. National Public Radio: PRI's The World.

Spiegel, A. M. and B. M. Alving (2005). Executive summary of the Strategic Plan for National Institutes of Health obesity research. *American Journal of Clinical Nutrition* **82**(Suppl): 211S–214S.

Steinhauer, J. (2014). Farm bill reflects shifting American menu and a senator's persistent tilling. International New York Times. New York.

Stolberg, S. G. (2011). Y.M.C.A. adopting health policies for youth. New York Times. New York.

Swinburn, B., G. Egger et al. (1999). Dissecting obesogenic environments: the development and application of a framework for identifying and prioritizing environmental interventions for obesity. *Preventive Medicine* **29**: 563–570.

Taber, D. R., J. Chriqui et al. (2012). Weight status among adolescents in states that govern competitive food nutrition content. *Pediatrics* **130**(3): 437–444.

Tavernise, S. (2012). Obesity in young is seen as falling in several cities. New York Times. New York.

Thow, A. M., S. Downs et al. (2014). A systematic review of the effectiveness of food taxes and subsidies to improve diets: understanding the recent evidence. *Nutrition Reviews* **72**(9): 551–565.

Turner, L. and F. J. Chaloupka (2012). Encouraging trends in student access to competitive beverages in US public elementary schools, 2006–2007 to 2010–2011. *Archives of Pediatric & Adolescent Medicine* **166**(7): 673–675.

Vanacore, A. (2011). Salad bars coming to 32 schools in the New Orleans area. The Times-Picayune. New Orleans.

Virchow, R. C. (2006). Voices from the past: report on the typhus epidemic in Upper Silesia (original 1848). *American Journal of Public Health* **96**(12): 2102–2105.

Wallace, H. (2011). In high schools, a critical lens on food. New York Times. New York.

Warner, J. (2010). Junking junk food. New York Times. New York.

Weil, E. (2005). Heavy questions. New York Times. New York.

Wilson, D. and J. Roberts (2012). Special report: how Washington went soft on childhood obesity. Washington DC: Reuters.

GLOSSARY

Abdominal obesity: excess adiposity within the abdomen; related to amount of visceral adipose tissue (VAT) and abdominal subcutaneous adipose tissue; indicated by apple-shaped torso; associated with risk for metabolic syndrome

Acculturation: the process of learning and adopting a new culture, as immigrants adapt to American culture by learning to speak English and adopt the predominant lifestyle of the US

Adaptation: ability to maintain internal stability (especially metabolism) despite external disruptions and stressors; human adaptation has involved genetic, physiological (functional), developmental, and cultural processes to adjust to an unreliable, unsteady energy supply during most of the human evolutionary past

Adaptive thermogenesis: metabolic production of heat to release energy

Adipocyte: a cellular component of adipose tissue specialized for storage of fatty acids in a large vacuole and secretion of fatty acids and adipokines

Adipogenesis: formation of adipose tissue by proliferation and expansion of adipocytes

Adipokine: one of many chemical products of adipocytes, including leptin and adiponectin; some adipokines are anti-inflammatory, while others contribute to the chronic low-level inflammation related to disease; in obesity the normal balance between anti- and pro-inflammatory adipokines is skewed toward inflammation.

Adiponectin: an adipokine that lowers obesity; a high level of adiponectin is a marker of low obesity level

Adipose tissue: adipocytes surrounded by connective tissue and other cells; most adipose tissue is deposited under the skin of torso and limbs (subcutaneous adipose tissue) (SAT) and within the abdominal cavity surrounding visceral organs (visceral adipose tissue) (VAT)

Adiposity: body fatness; level of body fat mass relative to fat-free mass (bones, muscle)

Adiposity rebound: small increase in fatness during childhood (about age 5–6 years) after extended gradual decrease in adiposity beginning in infancy; early adiposity rebound is associated with likelihood of obesity in adulthood

Allele: one of several alternate genes at a chromosomal locus for a specific trait; the human genome includes multiple risk alleles predisposing to obesity, such as several variants of the *FTO* gene

American Dream: the U.S. cultural ideal of social equality and economic prosperity

Androgens: primary male reproductive hormones, including testosterone; also involved in development of secondary sexual characteristics such as high proportion of body musculature and low proportion of body fat compared with females

Anthropology: the scientific study of human biology and culture in the past and present; medical anthropology is the study of human health and disease everywhere in the world and in past human populations

Arcuate nucleus (ARC): region in hypothalamus which receives and transmits chemical and neurological signals related to energy metabolism

Australopithecines: a group of extinct African hominin species representing some of the earliest human ancestors; characterized by upright posture, bipedal locomotion, small, ape-like brains, and a largely plant-based diet

Bariatric surgery: gastric surgery for extremely obese individuals to reduce the size of the stomach and to limit food intake; currently the most effective method for lowering extreme obesity

Binging: uncontrolled consumption of large amounts of food in a short period of time; sometimes followed by purging

Biomedicine: medical theory and practice which emphasizes physical and biological (scientific, objective) causes of disease, usually excluding social and cultural influences

Body composition: the relative proportion of fat and fat-free mass (bone, muscle) in a human body

Body Mass Index (BMI): most widely used measure of obesity, calculated by dividing body weight (kg) by the square of body height (m^2); BMI$\geq$30 indicates obesity and is associated with elevated health risks

Breastfeeding: infant feeding with human milk produced by maternal lactation and ingested by infant suckling; breastfed infants exhibit slower early growth and have reduced risk for later obesity; nursing mothers also benefit by losing weight gained in pregnancy relatively quickly

Brown adipose tissue (BAT): adipose tissue tinted by many small blood vessels and metabolically highly active in generating heat; more common in infants, but also found in some adult individuals

Built environment: the human-made physical environment, including suburban housing developments and highway networks; certain patterns of built environment contribute to population obesity by lowering opportunities for physical activity

Cholecystokinin (CCK): hormone produced by the duodenum of the small intestine which signals satiety to the hypothalamus

Circadian system: a system of biological clocks on a 24-hour cycle; the primary clock is controlled by the hypothalamus, and other clocks control the timing of other tissue functions such as secretion of hormones; ghrelin, leptin, insulin, and cortisol levels vary on a 24-hour circadian cycle

Conspicuous consumption: acquiring material possessions far above need; often a form of competitive consumerism and public display of personal wealth

Consumerism: belief in and action to purchase goods and services, often far beyond need; the U.S. economy is based largely on consumption of goods and services

Corporatism: cultural beliefs and practices that promote the organization of a society into industrial and professional institutions; corporations have political representation and exert considerable influence on citizen actions, such as consumer behavior

Cortisol: hormone secreted by the adrenal cortex which stimulates increase in blood glucose to supply energy during times of stress; continuous high cortisol levels are associated with obesity

Cribra orbitalia: lesions in the orbits of the human skull associated with malnutrition

Cuisine: a set of foods and methods of preparation and cooking specific to a particular nationality or society; an important aspect of ethnic identity and tradition

Culture: patterns of ideas and beliefs, symbols and meanings, values and behavioral norms that characterize a specific society; a society's culture determines what is considered to be normal, ethical, and acceptable

Culture-bound syndrome: condition associated with a specific society and its cultural beliefs and practices; high obesity prevalence was once considered to be associated specifically with developed societies and the lifestyle of ease and over-nutrition, but is now present in less-developed societies as well

Developmental Origins of Health and Disease (DOHD): research program focusing on the effects of early developmental influences on adult adiposity and biological susceptibility to obesity and chronic diseases; maternal malnutrition during pregnancy and certain environmental chemicals predispose a developing human fetus for adult obesity in a nongenetic or epigenetic process

Diabesity: global increase in obesity-related cases of Type 2 diabetes

Diseases of civilization: chronic conditions that are the primary causes of death in high-income, developed countries, including heart disease, cancer, and diabetes; until the middle of the 20th century, these were largely absent in less-developed societies where bacterial, viral, and parasitic infectious diseases dominate, but are now on the increase in these societies as well

Dominance displays: vigorous behaviors such as charging, throwing stones, shaking vegetation, etc., usually by male chimpanzees and other male primates to impress other members of their society in an effort to raise their social status

Double burden: the finding that households include both obese and underweight adults and malnourished children; more common in poorer, less-developed countries; both conditions are related to increased availability and consumption of inexpensive, low-nutrient, high-calorie foods

Dysbiosis: imbalance of gut microbiota species; associated with diseases of the digestive system, obesity, and other conditions; potential treatments with pre- and pro-biotics and fecal transplants to restore balance are currently being developed

Ectopic fat: fat in internal organs such as muscle, heart, liver; excess ectopic fat is associated with organ disease such as fatty liver disease

Energetics: the relationship between energy intake and energy expenditure in humans; during the course of their evolution, human ancestors increased energy efficiency (greater intake and less expenditure), enabling them to allocate more energy to reproduction and population growth; extremely high energy efficiency in modern human populations helps to explain the high prevalence of obesity rates, especially in industrial societies

Energy balance: energy homeostasis or stability when energy intake is equal to energy expenditure; positive energy balance refers to excess energy intake relative to output leading to fat storage and obesity; negative energy balance refers to greater expenditure than intake, leading to fat loss

Epidemic: a disease introduced rapidly into a community which attacks many individuals simultaneously; the rapid increase in obesity prevalence in the US is considered to be an epidemic by some and is associated with a dramatic increase in chronic diseases, particularly Type 2 diabetes, in many countries

Epigenetic: structural changes to DNA without alteration of the nucleotide sequence as a result of exposure to environmental obesogens or to prenatal malnutrition; these changes may be transmitted to succeeding generations and influence the risk for developing obesity

Estrogens: primary female reproductive hormones, including estradiol; influence development of female fat deposition on breasts, hips, and thighs and help to prevent cardiovascular disease in premenopausal women

Ethnic identity: the cultural affinity of an individual; ethnic identity is based on national origins, primary language, and cultural traditions, including dietary and activity patterns

Evolution: changes in the genes and physical traits of populations over time in response to environmental stresses and changes; during the course of human evolution, humans adapted to energy-scarce environments in both biological and behavioral (cultural) traits

Evolutionary medicine: in anthropology, the application of evolutionary principles to issues of health and disease; from this perspective, obesity is the natural outcome of human energy-conserving genes functioning in an obesogenic environment

"Fat-but-fit" hypothesis: the proposal that some obese individuals are able to remain healthy through exercise and physical fitness, and that physical fitness opposes the negative metabolic and health consequences of obesity; a small proportion of the American population is obese but seems to have a low risk for chronic disease

Fatism: bias, prejudice, and discrimination against persons with obesity; associated with beliefs that fat people are ugly, lazy, and unable to control their appetites

Fecundity: the ability to reproduce; requires good nutrition and a critical level of stored energy

Food desert: neighborhood or region having relatively few supermarkets and stores that offer a variety of high-nutrient, low-energy foods such as fresh fruits and vegetables

Food insecurity: uncertainty of having or being able to acquire enough food to meet the needs of all household members at all times due to insufficient funds or resources; food insecurity, which had been declining in the US, rose again with the recent economic depression; food-insecure Americans have to reduce the quality or quantity of their food; very low food security refers to the situation where people are unable to provide enough food for the household, and both adults and children frequently cut back or skip meals

Free fatty acids: fat molecules produced by lipolysis of stored triglycerides that are transported to target tissues by blood circulation

Functional foods: specific food products that are claimed to provide some particular health advantage

Genome: the entire genetic endowment of an individual; the human genome includes several large-impact obesity genes and multiple low-impact genes; geneticists continue to search for more obesity genes and their functions

Gestation: pregnancy; demands a high level of energy to maintain developing fetus and prepare mother for birth and lactation

Gestational diabetes: temporary insulin insensitivity or deficiency during pregnancy that usually leads to excessive growth of the fetus

Ghrelin: hormone secreted by the empty stomach which functions as an appetite signal

Globesity: worldwide spread of obesity, particularly to countries that previously had low rates of overweight or obesity; associated with increases in chronic diseases once considered to predominate in wealthy, developed countries

Glucose: a simple sugar, primary source of energy for the human brain

Glucose intolerance: impaired glucose tolerance, often resulting from insulin resistance, and a leading cause of Type 2 diabetes

Glycerol: sweet oily fluid produced by lipolysis of triglycerides stored in adipocytes

Gospel of Prosperity: "health and wealth theology," promoted mainly on religious TV programs; promises material blessings to its members, who often pay high membership fees

Handaxe: stone tool produced by extinct human ancestors that had a distinctive, tear-drop shape, sharp edges for cutting, and a pointed tip for piercing; it may have functioned as an all-purpose tool for food acquisition and preparation

Heritability: the part of variation in a particular trait in a given population that can be explained by genetic factors; in the U.S. population heritability ranges from 65–75 percent for body fat mass and 25–90 percent for Body Mass Index (BMI)

High-density lipoprotein (HDL): transports fat molecules, removes fats including cholesterol from cells and transports to liver for excretion; forms "good cholesterol"

High-fructose corn syrup (HFCS): an artificial sweetener produced from corn; because it is less expensive than sucrose, it is commonly used to sweeten many food and beverage products in the US; scientists have found that its metabolic and neuroendocrine effects differ from those of sucrose

Hispanic paradox: the finding that poor Hispanic immigrants are healthier than American-born members of the same ethnic group; also that people of Hispanic origin, who on average have higher rates of obesity, have lower rates of diabetes, heart disease, and other obesity-related conditions than other Americans

Holistic: the typical anthropological approach of considering interactions of multiple social and cultural variables with genetic and physiological factors in the search for causes of health issues such as obesity

Homeostasis: stability of internal environment despite diverse, disruptive external environment; result of adaptation, e.g. ability to maintain adequate energy level despite food shortage

Hominin: humans, their extinct ancestors, and other closely related fossil species; characterized by skeletal traits that enable bipedal locomotion, in contrast to other primates, which are quadrupedal

Hormone: a compound produced in one organ that is transported in blood to stimulate or inhibit specific cells in another part of the body; hormones interact with receptors on cell-surfaces or cell nuclei to regulate or alter activity

Hunger: the uneasy or painful sensation caused by lack of food; in the US many children and adults do go hungry and chronic mild undernutrition does occur

Hyperlipidemia: abnormally high levels of blood lipids (total cholesterol, triglycerides, low-density lipoprotein (LDL)-cholesterol); associated with heart disease and stroke

Hypertension: high blood pressure, often related to obesity; serious risk for heart disease and stroke

Hypothalamus: neural structure located deep within the brain consisting of numerous nerve centers that regulate autonomic functions, including maintaining energy balance

Individualism: a prominent American cultural value that tends to prioritize personal freedom and individual rights and responsibilities above collective or communal values

Inflammation: immune response to an antigen; adipocytes secrete chemicals evoking immune response by macrophages and other cells, resulting in tissue damage as in osteoarthritis and atherosclerosis; obesity is a disease involving chronic, low-grade inflammation

Insulin: hormone secreted by pancreatic cells that stimulates uptake of glucose by muscle and liver cells; also signals satiety and adiposity levels to hypothalamus

Insulin resistance: the failure of cells to respond to the insulin signal due to a change in their surface receptors; cells therefore cannot absorb glucose and fatty acids, whose concentration in blood plasma is increased; eventually leads to toxic levels of glucose and fatty acids in bloodstream; may result in Type 2 diabetes

Intermuscular adipose tissue (IMAT): fat accumulation between muscle tissues and fibers

Jane Goodall: primatologist who initiated the longest study of a wild chimpanzee community in Tanzania; her observations of chimpanzee food-related and other behaviors provide important comparisons for understanding human dietary behavior and physical activity

Lactation: in mammalian females, including humans, the process of milk production by mammary glands for nourishing newborns and infants; requires energy above level of maternal body maintenance

Leptin: hormone secreted by adipocytes which signals both short-term satiety and long-term adiposity levels to the hypothalamus

Linear enamel hypoplasia: dental lesions resembling horizontal lines in tooth enamel that are associated with malnutrition during dental development

Lipid: a class of compounds which include waxes and fats (triglycerides), and which along with proteins and carbohydrates constitute living cells; lipids are structural components of cell membranes, Vitamins A, D, E, K, cholesterol, and fatty acids; lipids in the form of triglycerides are stored in adipocytes as an energy source

Lipogenesis: process of converting dietary energy to fat

Lipolysis: chemical breakdown of stored lipids into free fatty acids and glycerol

Lipoprotein lipase: enzyme that removes the fatty acids from circulation and directs their conversion to triglycerides

Lipostat: neuroendocrine system involving the hypothalamus and chemical messengers which senses and regulates adiposity level

Low-density lipoprotein (LDL): protein that transports fat molecules in blood; it is considered to be "bad" for health since high blood levels of LDL are associated with the development of atherosclerosis and cardiovascular disease

Macrophage: specialized cell that is part of the body's immune system; attacks foreign substances and cells, and destroys and digests them; in obesity, a large adipose tissue mass contains large numbers of macrophages that release excessive pro-inflammatory secretions

Magnetic resonance imaging (MRI): medical imaging technique used to visualize detailed internal body organs and tissues; used in obesity research to visualize and measure visceral adipose tissue (VAT)

Maize: corn, the primary food crop of American prehistoric populations; its high-carbohydrate content provided energy for agricultural populations but also caused dental caries and, when not balanced by adequate protein and other nutrients, contributed to malnutrition in early farming communities

Malnutrition: inadequate nutrition, nutrient deficiencies, or imbalance of macro-nutrients such as proteins and carbohydrates; obesity may be considered a form of malnutrition involving deficiency of fiber and essential vitamins and minerals and excessive fats and sugars

Medicalization: presenting a health issue or human biological variation as a medical problem requiring pharmaceutical treatment; a goal of the pharmaceutical industry is to develop an effective and profitable anti-obesity drug

Metabolic syndrome: a constellation of inter-related risk factors for cardiovascular disease, including obesity, high blood pressure, high cholesterol levels, insulin resistance, and diabetes

Metabolically Healthy Obese (MHO): a subgroup of obese individuals with high Body Mass Index (BMI) who do not manifest the typical obesity-related metabolic risks and diseases

Metabolism: chemical transformations in the cells of living organisms that sustain life, allow for growth and reproduction, and enable organisms to adapt to their environments; energy metabolism refers to the chemical changes involved in acquiring, processing, and storing energy to maintain a balance between intake and expenditure

Methyl group: a chemical group composed of one carbon atom and three hydrogen atoms which bonds with a segment of a DNA molecule to suppress gene expression

Microbiome: the collection of genes in gut microbiota, a total of about 600,000 genes; the microbiome is nearly 25 times larger than the human host genome; the combination of human genome and microbiome helps to account for the diversity in human body weight

Microbiota: the bacterial assembly that lives in human intestines; certain types of these bacteria, which are especially efficient at breaking down complex plant fibers, are associated with obesity

Micronutrient: nutrient needed in small quantities, such as vitamins and minerals

Morbidity: illness or disease state; morbidity rate is the proportion of a population that is ill during a specific time period

Mortality: death; mortality rate is the proportion of a population that died during a specific time period

National Institutes of Health (NIH): U.S. government agency concerned with research and application of scientific knowledge to public health

Neolithic: New Stone Age; period in human prehistory beginning about 12–13,000 years ago when foraging was gradually replaced by food production (agriculture) around the world; the name refers to ground stone tool use (rather than chipped or flaked stones) predominating at that time; the Neolithic Revolution was a dramatic change in human subsistence from hunting and gathering wild foods to domestication of plants and animals

Neurotransmitter: chemical that transmits signals from nerve cells (neurons) to target cells; activates or inhibits metabolic pathways

Non-exercise activity thermogenesis (NEAT): energy expenditure by apparently unnecessary body movements and gestures such as fidgeting, standing, gesturing

Nutrigenomic profiling: using an individual's specific genetic profile to develop and recommend a personalized diet

Nutrition transition: the shift from a population's traditional foods and dietary patterns to a modern diet generally higher in fat and refined carbohydrates that is associated with increasing obesity and related chronic diseases

Obesity: abnormal or excess body fat accumulation which may impair health; excess body fat secretes many hormones and other chemical substances that damage the function of organs such as the liver, pancreas, and cardiovascular system

Obesogenic environment: influences of the physical, social, and cultural setting that contribute to obesity; factors beyond personal control that promote a low physical activity lifestyle and a high-energy, low-nutrient diet

Obesogens: environmental chemicals that disrupt metabolic processes and increase adiposity by altering gene expression; the most common action of an obesogen involves attaching a methyl group to a DNA segment to silence a gene that prevents obesity

Old Order Amish: American Christian sect distinguished by an agricultural lifestyle and abstention from use of modern technology

Order Primates: group of mammals that includes monkeys, apes, and humans, which share unique physical and behavioral traits such as stereoscopic vision, grasping hands with opposable thumbs, and relatively large and complex brains

Oxidation: combining with oxygen to produce energy; oxidation of fat produces energy and prevents its storage in adipocytes

Paleoanthropologist: scientific expert on human evolution based on studies of fossil hominin remains and artifacts such as stone tools; their analysis of hominin bones, teeth, and artifacts sheds light upon the lifestyles and diets of human ancestors

Paleolithic: Old Stone Age; period in human prehistory beginning about 3–2 million years ago when human ancestors developed chipped and flaked stone tools for processing plant and animal foods obtained by foraging

Paleolithic diet: a weight loss program of diet and exercise based on information about prehistoric forager nutrition; the diet is characterized by high levels of lean red meats, fruits, vegetables, seeds, and nuts and avoidance of saturated fats, legumes, grains, salt, sweets, and dairy products

Periostosis: thickening of the outer layer of human long bones caused by infection and present more often in early farming populations than in foragers

Polyunsaturated fat: type of fat found in nuts, fish, and leafy greens that is associated with reduced risks of heart attack and certain cancers; omega-3 fatty acid is an example

Porotic hyperostosis: lesions in the bones of the skull vault associated with malnutrition

Portal vein: blood vessel that conducts blood from the gastrointestinal tract to the liver; transports nutrients from food, including fats to the liver where they are processed

Poverty: low economic status based on annual income before taxes, not including non-cash benefits; based on historical estimates of the portion of an average household's income required to purchase a minimally nutritious diet; is updated annually for inflation

Poverty paradox: relatively high rates of obesity among poor people in the US, who would be expected to be undernourished and thin, but because of limited resources, America's poor purchase inexpensive, high-calorie, low-nutrient food items that contribute to obesity

Prevalence: proportion of a population currently affected by disease or other condition

Productionist food system: industrial production, marketing, and selling of generally inexpensive, low-quality foods in quantities far exceeding what is needed for human survival, primarily for the purpose of mass distribution and profits

Resting metabolic rate (RMR): energy cost of bodily functions while at rest, including the pumping action of the heart, neural activity of the brain, and movement of the diaphragm during breathing

Risk: the likelihood that an undesirable event or effect will occur; the increased probability of contracting a disease; risk alleles are genetic variants that increase the probability of becoming obese in a specific environment

Satiety: the state of being fed to capacity; the neuroendocrine system involving the hypothalamus and chemical messengers that senses and regulates appetite

Saturated fat: type of fat found in animal-based foods such as cheese, lard, meat, and also in many prepared foods; high consumption is associated with heart disease, some cancers, low bone mineral density

Savanna: open grassland regions of eastern Africa; the shift from a tropical rainforest habitat to the savanna involved a change in diet and behavior of human ancestors who had to walk long distances for food and water, ate a large variety of plant and animal foods, and competed with predators for meat

Secular: long-term body size and weight trend over several generations in a specific population; the secular trend of increasing obesity in the US is influenced by gradual changes in nutritional and activity environments, and not by changes in the human genome

Size-acceptance movement: social movement to reject stigmatization and discrimination of individuals with obesity and to promote consideration of the role of the obesogenic environment

Skinfold: a double thickness of skin held between thumb and finger and pulled away from underlying muscle to be measured with calipers; the sum of skinfold thicknesses at specific body sites is a measure of subcutaneous body fatness; skinfolds cannot be used to measure visceral adipose tissue (VAT)

Special Supplemental Nutrition Program for Women, Infants, and Children (WIC): a federal food program that provides foods, nutrition education, and access to health care to low-income pregnant women, new mothers, and infants and children at nutritional risk. Eligibility is based on income, nutritional risk, and categorical status (pregnant women, new mothers, breastfeeding women, infants, children under age five)

Stigmatization: extreme social disapproval of a specific group or individual perceived to possess a common culturally sanctioned characteristic such as obesity; since the world's cultures have different ideal body images, obesity is stigmatized in some but not in others

Subcutaneous adipose tissue (SAT): adipose tissue layers just beneath the skin, covering most of the trunk and limbs; stored fat that is less metabolically active than visceral adipose tissue (VAT)

Super-sizing: marketing technique that offers excessively large meals and food portions at bargain prices

Supplemental Nutrition Assistance Program (SNAP): federal food assistance for eligible Americans; formerly the Food Stamp program

Sustained positive energy balance: a process of long-term energy consumption and fat accumulation exceeding fat oxidation and energy utilization leading to obesity; negative energy balance is the result of energy utilization exceeding energy consumption, leading to weight loss

Thermic Effect of Food (TEF): the energetic cost of digestion, absorption, metabolism, and storage of nutrients; TEF is lower in obese compared to non-obese individuals

Thermogenesis: production of heat by oxidation of an energy source

Thrifty genotype: hypothetical human gene thought to promote efficient uptake and storage of energy to prevent death by starvation, but contributing to obesity and diabetes in an obesogenic environment; James Neel proposed this hypothesis, which led to the search for and discovery of multiple genes associated with human obesity

Thrifty phenotype: adaptation to nutritional stress or certain other environmental exposures during fetal development, resulting in abnormal metabolic functioning of tissues and organs, and predisposing the growing child and adult to abnormal energy regulation, obesity, diabetes, and heart disease

Total Daily Energy Expenditure (TDEE): energy cost of body maintenance and activity

Triglyceride: lipid form of fat stored in adipocytes

Type 2 diabetes: deficiency of or insensitivity to insulin which causes elevated, toxic levels of blood sugar; obesity is one of the most important risk factors for developing insulin insensitivity and Type 2 diabetes

Uncoupling proteins (UCP): proteins that promote heat production in muscles and the dissipation of excess energy instead of storage in adipose tissue

Undernutrition: lack of adequate nutrition for health; involves inadequate food supplies or deficiencies of one or more macro or micronutrients such as protein or Vitamin A

Underweight: weight below the norm for an individual's age and sex; having a Body Mass Index (BMI) of less than 18.5; associated with increased risk of mortality in comparison to normal weight

Vagus nerve: nerve that transmits satiety signal to hypothalamus; also transmits signal from hypothalamus to stomach to stimulate its secretion of digestive chemicals

Visceral adipose tissue (VAT): adipose tissue surrounding internal abdominal organs; large deposits are associated with disease risks such as diabetes and heart disease

Waist circumference: measure of abdominal girth at the level of umbilicus; used to estimate adipose tissue at abdomen and associated health risks; WC = 88 cm (35 in) in women and WC = 102 cm (40 in) in men represent the lower levels of obesity

World Health Organization: a United Nations agency concerned with international public health, including non-communicable and chronic diseases; publishes the *World Health Report*

INDEX